BUILDING ACCESS

BUILDING ACCESS

Universal Design and the Politics of Disability

Aimi Hamraie

UNIVERSITY OF MINNESOTA PRESS
MINNEAPOLIS · LONDON

Chapter 3 was published in an earlier version as "Inclusive Design: Cultivating Accountability toward the Intersections of Race, Aging, and Disability," *Age Culture Humanities* no. 2 (2015): 337–46. Portions of chapter 6 were previously published as "Universal Design and the Problem of Post-Disability Ideology," *Design and Culture 8*, no. 3 (2016): 285–309.

Published by the University of Minnesota Press
111 Third Avenue South, Suite 290
Minneapolis, MN 55401-2520
http://www.upress.umn.edu

Printed in the United States of America on acid-free paper

The University of Minnesota is an equal-opportunity educator and employer.

24 23 22 21 20   10 9 8 7 6 5 4 3

Library of Congress Cataloging-in-Publication Data

Names: Hamraie, Aimi, author.
Title: Building access : universal design and the politics of disability / Aimi Hamraie.
Description: Minneapolis : University of Minnesota Press, 2017. |
Includes bibliographical references and index. |
Identifiers: LCCN 2017005479 (print) | ISBN 978-1-5179-0163-9 (hc) |
ISBN 978-1-5179-0164-6 (pb)
Subjects: LCSH: Universal design—Political aspects—United States. | People with disabilities—United States.
Classification: LCC NA2547.H36 2017 (print) | DDC 720.87—dc23
LC record available at https://lccn.loc.gov/2017005479

For the misfits

UNIVERSAL DESIGN

QUESTIONS DESIGNERS SHOULD ASK

Why design something that can't be used?

Why say something that can't be heard?

Why write something that can't be understood?

Why draw something that can't be seen?

Why build something that is inaccessible?

Why construct something that can't be climbed?

Why paint something that is invisible?

Why sculpt something that can't be felt?

Why bridge something that can't be crossed?

Who are designers designing for?

What are designers designing?

When are designers designing?

How are designers designing?

Are designers making life elegant for everyone?

How do the blind turn off the lights?

How do the deaf listen to music?

How do the mute speak?

How do the paralyzed feel?

How do the tasteless taste?

Whose standards are standard?

Whose norms are normal?

Whose solution is universal?

Whose microcosm is worldly?

Whose exclusivity is inclusive?

BUT DESIGNERS WILL—

Build the Building!

Design the Design!

Sculpt the Sculpture!

Etch the Etching!

Draw the Drawing!

Draft the Drafting!

Paint the Painting!

Detail the Details!

Communicate the Communication!

Photograph the Photograph!

Film the Film!

Plan the Plan!

Color the Color!

Structure the Structure!

Texture the Texture!

BUT DESIGNERS SHOULD ASK–

WHO IS THE DESIGN FOR?

WHAT IS THE DESIGN PROBLEM?

WHERE WILL THE DESIGN BE USED?

WHEN WILL THE DESIGN BE USED?

HOW WILL THE DESIGN BE USED?

UNIVERSAL DESIGN IS POSSIBLE IF THE ANSWERS ARE–

EVERYONE

UNIVERSALITY!

EVERYWHERE

ALWAYS!

UNIVERSALLY!

–BRUCE HANNAH, professor emeritus, Pratt Institute, School of
Art and Design. Universal Design Teach-in, Pratt Institute, January 14, 1994

Contents

Preface

Who belongs where, under what auspices or qualifications, and during what times
or through what particular thresholds?

—TANYA TITCHKOSKY, *The Question of Access*

Let's begin by traveling.

If you are sighted, if the bus will take you there, and if the altitude suits you,
you can see it from the outside. At the Blusson Spinal Cord Center in Vancouver, a
colorful ramp winds around a glass atrium to three of the upper floors (Figure P.1),
where rehabilitation professionals conduct bench science and people with spinal
cord injuries receive therapy. Some use the ramp as a training space for wheelchair
sports, ascending to increase endurance, speed, and efficiency. A statue of a wheelchair basketball player, holding arms upright as if poised to shoot, sits at the ramp's
base. Amid the statue, the ramp, spacious bathrooms with grab bars, and the elevators
with their large, wheel-in buttons, the most recognizable visual symbol of disability—
the International Symbol of Access—is nowhere to be found.

Across the continent, at the Institute for Human Centered Design in Boston, access
is everywhere, both marked and unmarked. A large silver button featuring the International Symbol of Access appears on the right side of a glass door (Figure P.2).
Whether you press, kick, or nudge the button, a door opens into an airy, bright space,
speckled with the green of plants enjoying natural light. An attractive retail area
showcasing colorful kitchen products, chic felt tote bags, and toys feeds into a wide
hardwood ramp, a library and comfortable reading space, accessible restrooms with
hands-free toilets and faucets, a demonstration kitchen, and offices. Visual and Braille
signs on three-dimensional art displays invite you to touch the work.

Just south of Austin, Texas, a crowd of children and adults gathers for admission to
Morgan's Wonderland, an accessible theme park. Through the gates and past a line of
"family" restrooms (each marked with the access symbol), a large, three-dimensional

Figure P.1. The glass and steel structure of the Blusson Spinal Cord Center in Vancouver, British Columbia, discloses a glass atrium with a winding, colorful ramp (2010). Photograph by author.

tactile map communicates the park's layout and offerings: wheelchair-accessible rides, swings, playgrounds, and a carousel; sensory activities such as fountains and xylophones; and an amphitheater for live performances. Cardboard cutouts of children dressed as superheroes—some with wheelchairs, crutches, glasses, or service animals, and others, like Morgan, an autistic girl for whom the park was named, without—double as signs directing you throughout the space. Follow the signs, feel free to play, and notice what happens when bodies that rarely access public space do so together.

◆

In a dark hotel ballroom, two screens and two American Sign Language interpreters flank a table of presenters. On one screen, a speaker shows slides, and on another, a transcriber documents their words. "Would anyone benefit from a printed copy?" the moderator asks before each talk. "I have twelve- and eighteen-point font." Many raise

Figure P.2. A view of the library and seating area at the Institute for Human Centered Design, Boston, Massachusetts (2010). Photograph by author.

hands or canes, wave, or call out. The event is a plenary session on race, disability, and literature, but across the Society for Disability Studies conference, similar affordances and very different bodies appear in nearly every room.

◆

Each of these spaces illustrates at least some elements of Universal Design, a late twentieth-century design philosophy aimed at creating built environments that are accessible for both disabled and nondisabled users. But each space also embodies a very different way of understanding the concept of disability, whether as a medical category in need of correction, a category of identity and shared experience, a consumer designation, or an inevitable aspect of human community, which societies should anticipate and value.[1] Nearly a decade ago, when I began traveling to these and other spaces, I thought that I understood Universal Design. It was common sense, really: the world should be designed with all of us in mind. But as my bodymind came to inhabit some ways of sensing, perceiving, and moving through the world that are called "disability," traveling and taking up space came to mean very different things:

not easy passage, but frictioned negotiations of access and privilege.[2] As I traveled, sensed, and inhabited these spaces, it became clear that the concept of Universal Design was not common sense at all. Rather, what designers, users, and advocates mean by this term can be as varied as their conceptions of and relations to the idea of disability. In each space, promises of Universal Design for "everyone" materialized in relation to particular types of users, and whether I (or anyone else) was part of that "everyone" depended on whether our presence had been anticipated, in what ways, and for what purposes.

Building Access explores these conditions of knowing, making, and relating. When the goal is to design for "everyone," I ask, who counts as everyone and how do designers know?

Introduction

Critical Access Studies

The difficult intersectional, interdisciplinary work to be done includes within one frame the spaces of the political economic and the ontological, the battles of the activist and the epistemologist, the tracings of the historian and the artist.

—BEATRIZ DA COSTA and KAVITA PHILLIP,
Tactical Biopolitics

ADA NOW! ADA NOW! ADA NOW!

One hundred stairs divide a gathering crowd from the U.S. Capitol Building above. Numbering in the hundreds, they chant and hold signs. A group breaks off, leaving behind wheelchairs and crutches to lay flesh on stairs and crawl to the top. Framed against the building's steps, the bodies are clearly misfits: unanticipated, noncompliant, and taking up space.[1] Walking to their offices, irritated lawmakers step over and around misfit bodies; onlookers snap photographs; news anchors interview activists as they crawl to the top. Framed by the stairs in a striking image, these public bodies communicate what signs and chants alone cannot: this building, a symbol of governance and democratic citizenship for all—an embodiment of the nation itself—was not designed with disabled people in mind.[2]

The event was the "Capitol Crawl," a disability rights protest demanding that Congress pass the Americans with Disabilities Act (ADA) of 1990, landmark antidiscrimination legislation that identified a civil right to accessible buildings, public transportation, and workplaces for disabled citizens. Widely credited as the final push that resolved congressional deadlock, the Capitol Crawl demonstrated the power of disabled people as resourceful agents whose novel tactics showed visible evidence of disability discrimination, rather than patients in need of medical cure (Figure I.1).[3] But the critical work of these visible tactics went far beyond the ADA itself. The demonstration professed a particular disability theory of architecture: that built forms convey material rhetorics, which reveal cultural assignments of knowledge and power. In the Capitol Crawl, disabled people spoke back against the steps by deploying embodied speech and lived knowledge as architectural critique.

At the twenty-fifth-anniversary celebration of the ADA in 2015, a temporary mural appeared on the steps of the Carnegie Library in Washington, D.C., bearing President George H. W. Bush's historic remarks: "With today's signing of the landmark

Figure I.1. Disability protesters at the "Capitol Crawl," leaving behind wheelchairs, power chairs, and crutches to crawl up the steps of the U.S. Capitol Building in Washington, D.C. (March 12, 1990). Photograph by Tom Olin. Courtesy of Tom Olin Photographs Collection, MSS-294, Ward M. Canaday Center for Special Collections, University of Toledo Libraries.

Americans [with] Disabilities Act, every man, woman, and child with a disability can now pass through once-closed doors into a bright new era of equality, independence, and freedom." Google's charity organization Impact Challenge commissioned the mural and others like it on staircases near the National Mall, each featuring a disability rights leader who (in the organization's words) had "asked, 'What if we could create a more inclusive world for everyone?'" For those celebrating the anniversary, the murals (and their corporate donor) signaled the secure place of disabled Americans in U.S. culture and life. Bush's words confirmed the post-ADA narrative that the time for disability rights had finally arrived. But working in concert with post-racial narratives, which insist that American racism ended along with state-sanctioned segregation, the post-ADA narrative uses the formal guarantee of disability equality to elide the existence of material inequalities.[4] By painting Bush's promise of universal access on the built form of a staircase—the same structure that was the Capitol Crawl's focal point—the murals hid in plain sight (and without a hint of irony) the persistent architectural, attitudinal, and economic barriers that disabled people continue to face in the post-ADA world.[5]

Despite the optics of disability rights, the causes of discrimination are often invisible and illegible. Disability law scholars and policymakers have documented the ADA's failures to improve access to employment, housing, and public spaces, attributing these limitations to the law's limited provisions and inability to address structural, systemic, and attitudinal discriminations that disabled people face.[6] Disabled people continue to leave evidence that the ADA has not resulted in a postdiscrimination world, emphasizing that normal, taken-for-granted aspects of built environments, such as the prevalence of stairs, work in tandem with discriminatory attitudes. Disabled painter Sunaura Taylor's *Thinking Stairs* illustrates this argument through a series of comic book–style frames, showing a grayscale sidewalk flanked with cartoonish red stairs emitting empty speech bubbles (Figure I.2). "When I go out," Taylor writes, "it's as if the stairs are all bright red. It's as if they are all talking about me. But I don't know what they are saying.... They are manifestations of something more sinister: discrimination." The landscape appears disembodied, impartial, until the final frame, in which Taylor herself appears as a black-and-white figure driving her power chair amid staring pedestrians. Wordlessly, the *stairs* communicate what the people—and their stares—appear to think: that Taylor is out of place; the world was not designed with her in mind.[7]

The post-ADA narrative thus misses a crucial point offered by disabled users, designers, and activists: that the built world is inseparable from social attitudes, discriminatory systems, and knowledge about which users designers must keep in mind. Put another way, how we structure knowledge, interact with material things, and tell stories about the users of built environments matter for belonging and justice. When these stories embrace as common sense such values as freedom, access, and "a more inclusive world for everyone," it becomes all the more important to heed the

Figure I.2. Art animates the unspoken discriminatory effects of built environments. *Thinking Stairs* suggests that buildings communicate what people do not. Courtesy of Sunaura Taylor. Previously published in *Modern Painters* (October 2014).

critical lessons of the Capitol Crawl protestors, whose embodied architectural critique raised critical, material, and epistemological questions: who *counts* as everyone and how can we *know*? These questions—how they arose and what impact they had on new approaches to environmental design since the twentieth century—are the focus of this book.

Building Access has three primary aims: first, to provide a more critical and historical account of accessibility and Universal Design than currently exists; second, to conceptualize the historical project of knowing and making access (or what I call "access-knowledge") through critical disability, race, and feminist perspectives (and to develop a Universal Design theory that is attentive to issues of power and privilege); and third, to elucidate in broad strokes how the shifting figure of the user, particularly the disabled user, has shaped justifications for and material practices of Universal Design in the present. My focus is not to evaluate specific designed products or to endorse certain principles of design. Rather, I am concerned with the implications of how we imagine the figure of the user, justify design for particular users, and tell stories about the value of such design for broader questions of difference and belonging in the contemporary United States. *Building Access*, then, offers scholars, activists, designers, and others who support the project of accessible world-building a map of our paths to the present.

In the early twenty-first century, the term "Universal Design" gained popularity as an easy reference to the idea that inclusive design benefits everyone, regardless of disability or age. Its global circulation and reach into a number of disciplines beyond architecture, however, make it easy to forget that Universal Design is a very recent discourse, and that how this phenomenon is named, defined, and justified is a product of the post-ADA era. The post-ADA narrative dictates that accessible design, like freedom, is a self-evident, commonsense good. But how the built world *materializes* is inseparable from the value-laden politics of knowing. "All too often," wrote disabled architect and accessibility expert Ronald Mace, "designers don't take the needs of disabled and elderly people into account when they are designing a building."[8] Focused on accessible design as a site of meaning-making and world-building, *Building Access* argues that since the twentieth century, the project of designing a more inclusive world for everyone has taken shape through specific arrangements of knowing and making: the phenomenon that I am calling access-knowledge.

Access-knowledge, a regime of legibility and illegibility, emerged from interdisciplinary concerns with what users need, how their bodies function, how they interact with space, and what kinds of people are likely to be in the world.[9] While twentieth-century U.S. rehabilitation experts, ergonomists, social scientists, architects, product designers, and policymakers claimed expertise about accessibility as an objective, functional practice, disabled users positioned themselves as experts credentialed by their lived experiences to remake the world. How designers negotiated the politics of knowing-making, in turn, implicated their strategies and interventions. Behind the scenes of legible public events, such as the Capitol Crawl or the passage of legislation, Universal Design proponents conducted more subtle forms of activism, using research, technical guidance, and design education as spheres in which to challenge designers' dominant conceptions of users.

At its core, this book is about the material ramifications of stories, ideas, and representations as they coalesce into broader discourses of disability, knowledge, and nation. But it is also about knowledge and ignorance as material arrangements. To offer a more critical and theoretical understanding of Universal Design than currently exists, *Building Access* investigates how access-knowledge has animated the relationships between scientific, architectural, industrial, national, and embodied ways of "knowing" disability. Drawing on an expansive archive of ephemera, oral histories, design documents, handbooks, publications, marketing materials, physical objects and spaces, and personal papers from Universal Design's founders, *Building Access* places the claim that "designers do not design with disability in mind" in historical, theoretical, and cultural perspective. The emergence of access cannot be reduced to common sense, good will, or the affordances of the state. Nor is access simply a matter of keeping disabled users "in mind." Since the mid-nineteenth century, specific relations of knowing-making—situated histories of embodiment, ideology, science, technology, and design—have shaped the possibilities for and the politics of accessible world-building.

LOCATING ACCESS-KNOWLEDGE

"Like a bean sprout that emerges only after its root is deep and strong," wrote Molly Story, James Mueller, and Ronald Mace, "universal design has its beginnings in demographic, legislative, economic, and social changes among older adults and people with disabilities throughout the twentieth century."[10] In 1985 Mace coined the term "Universal Design" to describe the idea that many people, whether disabled or nondisabled, benefit from a more accessible built environment.[11] Mace concluded that architects and product designers should make all environments accessible, rather than requiring disabled people to request "retrofits" (or alterations) after a building has already been constructed. Although these ideas had circulated for decades, Mace's term propelled the concept into the ADA era.

While Mace's term preceded the ADA by five years, the dominant narrative about Universal Design is a post-ADA phenomenon. Since the late 1990s, Universal Design proponents have debated the concept's relationship to the ADA and, by extension, to the notion of disability itself.[12] These debates are at an impasse, however, because the term is used to describe a wide range of approaches, from design that begins from a focus on disability (and has added value to others) to design that begins by focusing on a range of users to design that is just intuitive, common sense, and usable. *Building*

Access resolves this impasse by historicizing the debates themselves in relation to shifting understandings of disability rights, good design, and human variation. By treating Universal Design as a shifting historical discourse, a tool for making distinctions to create meaning and shape material realities, rather than a stable idea or practice, this book disentangles the aspiration for a more accessible world from the ideologies and values used to promote it.

Although the ADA popularized the discourse of Universal Design, the meanings of this term soon proliferated. Builders' magazines, newspapers, textbooks, and conference workshops began to tell a new story about Universal Design: that this approach was not about accessibility for disabled users at all but rather about a commonsense approach to "good design" for everyone.[13] Even prominent disabled people, such as journalist John Hockenberry, a wheelchair user, adopted the post-ADA narrative. Describing accessibility renovations to his home kitchen, Hockenberry wrote,

> In the end there was nothing "special" or "handicapped" about it. This kitchen was merely made to work with the real people who lived there. Its universality came not from abstract specifications but from the lives of real people, creating spaces for their daily lives. No detailing or style or luxury could possibly be more precious than this simple quality. Universal design is perhaps just an overly clinical name for something we think we know but perhaps we don't—good design.[14]

This new story, a crucial part of the post-ADA narrative, implied that accessible design was easy to achieve and simple to practice. It was good business as the population aged. It had little to do with disability. It was commonsense, good design.

Despite Universal Design's origins in the work of disability activists and in disability rights efforts preceding the ADA, the term has become a popular discourse in the post-ADA world—not by centering disability as a category of marginalization but by disavowing it. But how did Mace's concept come to signify a disability-neutral approach? In 1997 the Center for Universal Design at North Carolina State University in Raleigh, North Carolina, released "The Principles of Universal Design," a guide for inclusive and flexible design (Figure I.3).[15] Since 1997 the "Principles" have become the most-often-cited reference to Universal Design, shaping public perceptions of its theory. Although the "Principles" used terms such as "equitable" and "flexible," references to specific users, such as disabled people, do not appear in the text. Consequently, the public perception of Universal Design since the late 1990s has been shaped by what I term "barrier work," or claims that Universal Design is not about disability at all but rather about good design for everyone.

Widely cited as a representation of Universal Design writ large, the "Principles of Universal Design" has spread beyond architecture and industrial design into Web design, education, and even critical humanistic scholarship. As it spreads, however, Universal Design claims are largely taken as common sense. The concept remains largely

THE PRINCIPLES OF UNIVERSAL DESIGN

Principle 1: Equitable Use

The design is useful and marketable to people with diverse abilities.

Principle 2: Flexibility in Use

The design accommodates a wide range of individual preferences and abilities.

Principle 3: Simple and Intuitive Use

Use of the design is easy to understand, regardless of the user's experience, knowledge, language skills, or current concentration level.

Principle 4: Perceptible Information

The design communicates necessary information effectively to the user, regardless of ambient conditions or the user's sensory abilities.

Principle 5: Tolerance for Error

The design minimizes hazards and the adverse consequences of accidental or unintended actions.

Principle 6: Low Physical Effort

The design can be used efficiently and comfortably and with a minimum of fatigue.

Principle 7: Size and Space for Approach and Use

Appropriate size and space is provided for approach, reach, manipulation, and use regardless of user's body size, posture, or mobility.

Figure I.3. "The Principles of Universal Design," Version 2.0 (4/1/97). Courtesy of the Center for Universal Design, North Carolina State University.

ahistorical and undertheorized as a result. With few exceptions, critical methodologies from the humanities and social sciences have not been applied to exploring Universal Design's interventions, possibilities, and strategies. *Building Access* reaches below the surface of post-ADA narratives to parse Universal Design's barrier work, marketing discourses, and public circulation from its more critical, material, and epistemological contributions, unearthing a range of heterogeneous justifications, material practices, and finely graded interventions into dominant modes of knowing and making.

Global attention to Universal Design has heightened since the late 1990s. Translated into at least eleven languages, including Dutch, French, German, Bahasa Indonesia, Italian, Japanese, Korean, Norsk (Norwegian), Portuguese, Spanish, and Swedish, the "Principles of Universal Design" and the concept they elucidate appear as mandates in the United Nations Convention on the Rights of Disabled Persons.[16] International conferences attract networks of experts, designers, and researchers from Japan, Norway, and India, among other countries, to explore Universal Design alongside approaches termed "Inclusive Design," "Design for All," and "Design for the Lifespan." Advocates claim that these terms provide nonuniversalist alternatives for the philosophy that Universal Design describes. But like the barrier work of distinguishing between Universal Design and the ADA, the purported equivalency of these terms presupposes an ideal concept and approach that simply awaits a better title. Significant empirical questions remain, however, about whether these terms are constant in their meaning, scope, and practice as they circulate globally.

While all these approaches may aspire toward a more accessible world, their justifications, strategies, and conceptions of users transform across historical and geographic contexts. *Building Access* argues instead that the very notions of accessibility, inclusion, all, and lifespan are as contested, historically contingent, and value-laden as the design processes that materialize and dematerialize built worlds. Situating these concepts within the historical evolution of access-knowledge, I show that Western and often distinctly U.S. American ideas have shaped how experts, lawmakers, and designers understand the figure of the user. To mark the unmarked, I use the capitalized form "Universal Design" to designate a specific discourse, which congealed from U.S. material cultures, medical and scientific discourses, civil rights laws, racialized patterns of spatial planning, consumer ideologies, class relations, and gender systems. When I discuss Universal Design, then, I am referring not to an abstract ideal but to a specific phenomenon and the networks of social relations, expertise, and design experimentation that produced it. By focusing on the United States, *Building Access* excavates a geographically and historically specific range of hegemonies and resistances, enabling future research that decenters the U.S. American narrative about this phenomenon.

Building Access investigates the regime of legibility and illegibility at the heart of the U.S. liberal democratic project. That access to public space is a variety of freedom is hardly a contemporary idea, but in the twentieth-century United States, movements for race, economic, gender, sexuality, and disability rights focused their efforts on desegregating public space. While the segregationist causes they opposed were often distinct, these movements shared a demand for meaningful spatial citizenship: the right to occupy homes, workplaces, universities, restrooms, courthouses, and cities. Tactics of taking up space, such as marches and sit-ins, made these movements publicly legible. But when it came to legislating civil rights to housing, employment, and education, lawmakers and designers tended to treat the categories of race, class, gender, sexuality, and disability as discrete. Although the idea of "intersection-ality" came after the passage of major civil rights legislation in the 1960s and '70s, there is another reason that laws and environmental design did not consider that people at the intersections of systems of oppression face unique barriers to exercising rights. The reason had to do with the systems of knowledge and expertise that policy-makers enrolled in defining human variation and prescribing ways of containing it. This book shows that the liberal project of including an ever-widening range of human variation was inseparable from processes of objectification, surveillance, and standardization. As race, gender, class, and especially disability became objects of expert study, scientific legibility shaped the political legibility of architectural inhabit-ants, users, and citizens.

Across twentieth-century social justice movements, however, another type of poli-tics, often illegible and below the surface of public perception, focused on knowledge as a site of engagement and transformation. It may appear odd to characterize knowl-edge as a "site," implying that it is a place. As we typically understand it, knowledge is abstract, immaterial; knowledge describes the world rather than being within it. But what activists knew, and what many academic disciplines eventually came to under-stand, was that knowledge is social, relational, material, and spatially situated. *Know-ing* both reflects and shapes the world. Knowledge, in other words, is a kind of design. Treating knowledge as a contested domain for shaping the world, twentieth-century activists pushed against scientific and liberal conceptions of legible personhood, chal-lenging the neutral, disinterested objectivity of Cold War–era science and asserting alternative ways of knowing, which tethered accounts of lived marginalization and analyses of historical, political, and cultural systems.[17] These strategies, which I term "epistemic activism," rematerialized not only the built arrangements of segregated space but also the structures of knowledge production itself.

Access-knowledge challenged the norms of embodiment around which architec-tural design coheres. In the post–World War II era, proponents of barrier-free design argued that the world had been designed with an average user in mind, but the chang-ing nature of human embodiment through war, industrial accidents, and medical advances demanded a new strategy. Unlike High Modernist architects, who defined "good design" in terms of standardization and uniformity, proponents of barrier-free design argued that if architects design a world with disability in mind, this built-in access would benefit "all" people, even adding value for nondisabled users. *Building Access* traces these concepts of *anticipatory access, broad accessibility,* and *added value* as they shaped the regime of access-knowledge.

Despite claims that accessibility benefits all users, however, barrier-free design was firmly situated in twentieth-century notions of productive citizenship, which defined liberal belonging through the capacity for productive labor, as well as through the evident fruits of that labor: wealth accumulation, homeownership, and consum-erism. Midcentury advocates for barrier-free design claimed that accessible built environments would help to rehabilitate injured soldiers and workers, contributing to the common good, public safety, and national capital. Public universities and the private, single-family home—two sites of pervasive racial segregation, gendered divisions of labor, and economic accumulation—served as the primary foci of barrier-free design research.

The post-ADA narrative about Universal Design tells a different story, however. Contemporary advocates distinguish Universal Design from barrier-removal, arguing that the former is a broad, creative, extralegal approach to design for everyone, while the latter is situated in legal codes and standards and focused only on disabled users. Before barrier-free design became a bureaucratic term for codes and standards, its discourses and claims were nearly identical to those of contemporary Universal Design. It was only in the post–civil rights era, when laws such as the ADA emerged to mandate and enforce barrier-free design, that it became possible to frame it as narrow and bureaucratic. *Building Access* proposes that Universal Design did not emerge as an alternative to barrier-free design. These mutually constitutive approaches and their shared proponents, experts, and knowledge bases were instead part of a broader experiment with how to frame, negotiate, and deploy the project of design with disabled users in mind. But is Universal Design a critical project, and if so, what is its intervention? *Building Access* explores this question through several lines of thought, considering Universal Design's relationship to norms, the concept of disability, and the entangled dimensions of race, class, and gender, which intersect the politics of environmental design.

CRIPPING UNIVERSAL DESIGN

How does Universal Design relate to the concept of disability? Post-ADA narratives insist that Universal Design is disability-neutral: the focus is not on disability but rather on everyone.[18] This claim is confusing, however, because it does not clarify what "everyone" means in a world that devalues particular bodies. Similar to the idea that we live in a post-racial society, wherein race is a fiction and civil rights laws have mandated equality, rendering oppression immaterial, terms such as "everyone" give the impression that legible belonging in a population is unmediated by historical, political, or social ways of knowing. Accordingly, it is often taken as common sense that because aging is a form of impairment, everyone is or will be disabled at some point. It follows that better design will benefit not only our present, youthful, able-bodied selves but also the bodies that we will be in the accessible future.

But for those of us whose bodies do not follow these smooth, predictable temporalities, whose ways of being and moving find friction with our social and built environments, and whose present and future belonging has been shaped by past conditions of inequality, the idea of universal disability is perplexing at best. For scholarly fields, such as disability studies, this idea and its prominence in Universal

Design discourse calls into question foundational models, epistemologies, and ethical positions.

The history of access-knowledge, of which Universal Design is a part, is also the history of the field of disability studies. Around the time that Mace first wrote of Universal Design in the mid-1980s, the field emerged as a kind of epistemic activism, working within academia to challenge dominant medical and rehabilitation models of impairment and pathology. The generative intervention of disability studies paralleled (and later allied with) the rise of critical race, feminist, and queer studies from social movements.[19] At the core of disability studies, the field's foundational "social model" translated the insights of U.S. and UK disability activists into an academic theory.[20]

As the social model is often described, disability is a construct of built and social environments rather than pathology requiring cure or functional limitation demanding rehabilitation. Two decades earlier, however, rehabilitation experts developed a similar understanding of disability as an environmentally produced phenomenon, arguing that inaccessible built environments exclude disabled people from accessing necessary services, work, and public participation.[21] These experts emerged from within the rehabilitation profession, used established research methods in their field, and worked with architects and builders to produce the first U.S. accessibility standard, ANSI A117.1. Barrier-free design was a rehabilitation project, aimed at engineering more productive workers and citizens. In the 1970s, disability activists pushed back against rehabilitation researchers and their assumptions that disability is a failure of human performance, and thus a problem in need of elimination. While they agreed that disability is a socially and architecturally produced disadvantage, activists asserted that their lived experiences made them better experts on the subject of disability and challenged the rehabilitation norm of compulsory productive citizenship.

What distinguished the social model from rehabilitation, then, was not its focus on environmental precipitants of inequality but rather a new disability epistemology. Disability studies grew around this epistemology, deemphasizing medical and scientific knowledge in favor of critical theory, qualitative data, and humanistic texts. But in the early twenty-first century, around the time that Universal Design became a predominantly disability-neutral discourse, critical and crip theories of disability emerged to challenge the social model for overemphasizing the environmental construction of disability oppression over embodied experiences of disablement.[22] "Crip," a reclamation of the term "cripple" dating to the 1970s independent living movement, resists imperatives for normalization and assimilation.[23] Crip theories contribute that disability is a valuable cultural identity, a source of knowledge, and a basis for relationality.[24]

Rather than focusing exclusively on environmental inequality, the critical disability turn addresses ideology, political economy, and cultural systems responsible for characterizing disability as disqualification.[25] *Building Access* approaches Universal Design through the framework of crip and critical disability knowing-making. Unlike

crip theories, disability-neutral Universal Design discourses often reference rehabilitation notions of human performance and functional limitation, taking for granted
that restoring function improves productivity and is thus a self-evident good. But by
framing Universal Design as a productivity-enhancing feature of built environments,
these discourses reduce the critical project of access-knowledge to the status of a
rehabilitation technology for disabled users and an enhancement for nondisabled
people. Accordingly, constructs such as limitation and enhancement, far from neutral
or self-evident, produce a "depoliticized" perception of disability, which, Alison Kafer
explains, treats as common sense the notion that disability is a "problem to be eradi-
cated."[26] Paradoxically, depoliticized and neutralized approaches to disability make
it possible to imagine a world without disability in it. Shifting toward a more value-
explicit, intentional, and crip understanding of disability, *Building Access* situates
access-knowledge in relation to the liberal project of normalizing public space, assimilating misfit bodies into public life, creating reserves of productive labor, segregating
the unproductive, and, as in the case of eugenics, eliminating the physical presence of
disability in the world.[27]

Crip theory, too, requires a more robust account of the politics of knowing-making.
A core assumption persists that accessibility and rehabilitation are epistemologically
discrete.[28] Well-rehearsed arguments—that the problem is not unrehabilitated bodies but the lack of access—have reproduced the social model as a kind of common
sense and Universal Design as a metaphor for meaningful access. In one sense, these
arguments demand accountable knowing-making. As Jay Dolmage has productively
explored it, meaningful access should go beyond piecemeal efforts at "retrofit" and
"accommodation," addressing knowledge, values, ideologies, and systems.[29] This idea
resonates with the generative notion of "collective access," offered by contemporary
organizers in the disability justice movement, which is led by disabled people of
color.[30] Universal Design's open-ended, creative promise, its unfinished qualities and
"ongoing negotiation[s]" inspire projects of both individual and collective access,
in the sense of going beyond the technical aspects of inclusion to address broader
systems and ideas.[31] The sticking point here, however, is that the material world and
the social arrangements within it are not just abstract ideals. Working toward meaningful inclusion does not make the conditions of its materialization any less reliant on
the politics of knowing. The social model, along with crip theories that treat accessibility as an alternative to medical knowing, offered a first wave of disability theorizing that I call "access studies." *Building Access* extends this work into what I term
"critical access studies," a relatively new field that challenges the treatment of access
as a "self-evident good."[32]

Black disability scholar Chris Bell argues that disability studies fails to "engage
issues of race and ethnicity in a substantive capacity, thereby entrenching whiteness
as its constitutive underpinning."[33] Bell's critique applies to both access studies and
critical access studies in their current formations. Despite unsettling medical norms

of embodiment, access studies frequently centers liberal disability rights perspectives toward race, class, and gender oppression, and critical access studies has largely failed to address issues of whiteness, gender normativity, or class privilege, despite rejecting the mandates of able-bodiedness. *Building Access* centers the intersections of disability with race, gender, class, and aging in its historical study of how concepts of spatial access materialized in the twentieth-century United States. Although access-knowledge was a critical project aimed at unsettling norms of the user, I argue that our contemporary understanding of access has been shaped by historical perceptions of the user as a white, middle-class, productive citizen. Pushing crip theory toward a more robust account of the politics of knowing-making, *Building Access* argues for accountability toward these histories and their manifestations in contemporary post-disability and post-racial narratives.

MAPPING ACCESS-KNOWLEDGE

Building Access traces the work of knowledge and ignorance, legibility and illegibility, transparency and opacity in the phenomenon of access-knowledge. At the core of the commonsense refrain that "the world was not designed with disability in mind" is the notion that *making* built environments is an exercise of power entangled with the politics of *knowing*. But what kinds of knowing would make it possible to design a world with disability in mind? The twentieth-century regime of access-knowledge emerged to answer this question. In the quest to make a diverse range of users beyond the average legible to architects and designers, this regime of legibility and illegibility often defined the user in relation to productive work, recognizable citizenship, and political agency.

The User and the Norm

Building Access contributes to a growing field of inquiry that historicizes and theorizes the figure of the user as a site of architectural, technoscientific, and cultural meaning-making. Science and technology studies (STS) scholars and architectural historians propose that in the twentieth century, the user was both a subject and an object of knowledge.[34] Since antiquity, architects imagined the inhabitant as an ideal or universal body reflecting cultural ideals of beauty and proportion. Unlike the universal architectural *inhabitant,* the nineteenth- and twentieth-century figure of the *user* signified a range of variation. Statisticians, industrial scientists, and engineers identified this wide-ranging variation, termed the "human factor," as an unpredictable threat to industrial, military, and other technological systems. Studying this threat would enable its smooth assimilation into the machinery of production. As a scientific understanding of human diversity enabled the design of increasingly productive, efficient systems, flexible design for a range of users became the stuff of standardization and normalization.

Concepts of human variation, disability, and injury configured the user as a site of human engineering and rehabilitation. Scientific managers such as Frank and Lillian Gilbreth turned their attention to the injured soldier as a body amenable to productive citizenship, a unit of nation, industry, and war carried from one engineered system to another. Human factors research followed the disabled veteran into postwar civilian life. Before the twentieth century, the need for accessible design as a matter of public policy was unthinkable because disabled people were segregated from public space by eugenicist "ugly laws" (as historian Susan Schweik has shown), confined in institutions, and hence illegible as public citizens.[35] Access-knowledge bridged human factors research, ergonomics, and postwar rehabilitation cultures, which brought particular disabled bodies—often white, male, physically disabled soldiers rather than people of color, women, or mentally disabled people—into public legibility as both users and citizens. As Anna Carden-Coyne, David Serlin, and Beth Linker have argued, rehabilitation brought the disabled user into public view by marrying bodily reconstruction to postwar efforts to rebuild the nation.[36]

Access-knowledge was an experimental project. At every phase, experts and users engaged in new types of research, experimented with design features, and debated standards of practice that could shape mainstream design discourses. In the midtwentieth century, U.S. industrial engineer Henry Dreyfuss ushered in a new paradigm of "human engineering," borrowing human statistics gathered by military sources, physical anthropologists, and eugenicists to offer designers data as a tool for design. But as *Building Access* reveals, flexible design for a range of users always referred to standardized forms of knowledge and conceptions of a vulnerable and manipulable body, whose disabilities required elimination through better environmental design. As a postwar intervention, barrier-free design challenged the idea that physical ablebodiedness is a prerequisite to occupying built space, but proponents did not challenge the imperatives of normalization. This was evident in the experts enlisted to create accessibility guidelines: architects and builders worked with rehabilitation scientists, industrial designers, and scientific managers in tandem to produce barrier-free environments that would enhance productivity and human performance. Disabled soldiers entering universities as students under the G.I. Bill, most of whom were white disabled men, became natural objects of research for early accessibility guidelines. A rehabilitation program for students at the University of Illinois at Urbana-Champaign served as the testing ground for these guidelines. A second prototypical user, the white, disabled housewife, followed, as rehabilitation research turned to the home as a domain of engineerable labor.

Midcentury access-knowledge tethered the project of inclusive public space to the objectification of disabled people in scientific research. But soon, users began to push back. In the 1960s, the independent living movement challenged the authority of nondisabled experts to know and design *for* disabled people. But rather than reject rehabilitation or architecture outright, activists worked within these fields to position users as experts, experiment with new technologies of access, and reject productivity as a requirement of citizenship. Where the independent living movement intervened into rehabilitation practice, a new field of environmental design research (EDR) injected the architecture profession with more critical approaches to the user. Although these strategies of epistemic activism took place below the surface of legible protests and sit-ins, their tactics, frames, and design practices redesigned the normative basis of access-knowledge. *Building Access* shows that Ronald Mace's notion of Universal Design emerged from critical access-knowledge, particularly efforts in the 1970s and '80s to challenge the prototypical white male and white female wheelchair users as emblems of barrier-free design.

As this brief history shows, the user is a value-laden figure with significant history and politics. Commonsense claims that Universal Design is simply a form of good design tend to ignore that the legibility of disabled people as users has been contingent on their historic legibility as scientific objects, citizens, and workers, whose white, middle-class privileges remained unmarked. These claims also tell us very little about the entangled experiments and reiterations through which Universal Design materialized, or how these sedimentations made it a seemingly coherent, static, and namable practice in the late twentieth century.[37] This history matters not only for disability studies but also for the broader fields of American studies, science and technology studies, and design studies because the figure of the user has been a node around which normalcy, fitting, productivity, and national belonging are articulated.

The Politics of Knowing-Making

Science, argues feminist philosopher Sandra Harding, is "politics by other means."[38] *Building Access* develops the concepts of "crip technoscience" and "epistemic activism" as analytics for understanding the ambivalent relationships between disability activism, scientific research about disabled users, and liberal political discourses in the project of creating a more accessible world.[39] These concepts extend the work of feminist science and technology studies to histories of disability and design. Because disability studies emerged from activists' critiques of medical expertise, the field on the whole has not explored technoscience as an arena of world-building and meaning-making. In addition to studying the normative dimensions of science, however, *Building Access* provides an account of knowing and making as social and political practices. Refusing the terms of productive citizenship, disability activists of the 1960s and '70s turned to research and design as politics by other means. If liberal citizenship demanded smooth belonging and rehabilitation, crip technoscience involved strategies of friction, disorientation, and nonconformity. Activists engaged in self-taught design practices, creating their own tools, curb cuts, and ramps with repurposed materials, learning to code and hack computers, and tinkering with the structures of everyday life. For crip technoscientists, disability was the basis of shared culture and identity, a valuable resource for environmental retooling, and hence not a de facto disqualified condition.

Crip technoscience thus took shape as a politicized, world-altering practice with overt and subtle manifestations. In this sense, crip knowing-making redesigned the terms of legibility and illegibility in relation to liberal inclusion or economic citizenship. In public, disability protests such as the Capitol Crawl represented the struggles of illegible users to become legible. But for others, including Ronald Mace, illegibility served as a productive resource for challenging norms of the user. In tactical but imperceptible ways and within mainstream domains of power, epistemic activists like Mace chose scientific research, architectural education, accessibility code development, disability policy, and other seemingly mundane, often bureaucratic domains as arenas of political contestation.

Building Access unearths this epistemic activism as Universal Design's politics by other means. Examining legal documents, technical guidance, handbooks, media publications, design curricula, and user research methods, I show that Universal Design's interventions and critical practices have been largely illegible to scholars and contemporary advocates. But Universal Design is not a uniform practice. As a flexible discourse, it holds in tension the disability activist and the rehabilitation scientist, the human engineer and the noncompliant body, the accessibility standard and the resistant designer. It is within these entangled arrangements of knowing and making that Universal Design materializes, both in the sense of the built forms of curb cuts, automatic lights, and lever-style door handles and in the sense of appearing to cohere as a practice that we can reproduce, negotiate, and remake.

A USER'S MANUAL

This book begins a critical historical discussion about Universal Design, but it is not meant to serve as a conclusive, all-encompassing narrative of this history-in-the-making. The story told in this book is still materializing. Examining the very recent past presents many challenges and opportunities. In our digital age, the vast archive of Universal Design history can enrich our understanding of this phenomenon, but there are limits to what a single book can include. Many of the people, designs, and encounters that were part of this story are not included here.

For context and critical distance, I have designed this book to convey a long-term history of access-knowledge. Although organized chronologically, each chapter offers a genealogy of a key idea, claim, or refrain of Universal Design: equity (chapter 1), flexibility (chapter 2), design for "everyone" or "all" (chapter 3), the curb cut (chapter 4), design with users in mind (chapter 5), the term "Universal Design" (chapter 6), and the "Principles of Universal Design" (chapter 7). While my focus is on the history of ideas and discourses, this book is also a study of material culture, including how objects, advertisements, photographs, design documents, and ephemera coalesce to shape our understanding of Universal Design, as well as the questions that we are willing to ask about it.

Part of the material culture of accessibility and user-centered design has been an emphasis on the primacy of the wheelchair user as an embodiment of disability.[40] Another part of this material culture has been an emphasis on visual rhetorics. Images throughout the book tell a story about the optical material culture of access-knowledge, particularly regarding the shifting figure of the user. But there are many ways to engage with these illustrations, whether as evidence, landmarks, or guides to the narrative. Working with them on their own without the text tells a story, but engaging with the details and descriptions embedded in the narrative text does the same.

Building Access spans the nineteenth, twentieth, and twenty-first centuries. Ending at the "Principles of Universal Design," the arc of the book spans the rise of design for users, first normate (chapter 1) and later more particular (chapter 2). The middle chapters offer a prehistory of the concepts, strategies, and epistemic communities through which the Universal Design principles materialized, from barrier-free design (chapter 3) to crip technoscience (chapter 4) to epistemic activism (chapter 5). The final two chapters focus on Universal Design since 1985, tracing its rise in relation to the ADA (chapter 6) and its primary document, the "Principles of Universal Design" (chapter 7). Finally, the conclusion examines the present and future trajectories of Universal Design, given contemporary trends in urban development, population change, and disability politics. While *Building Access* is a history of the Universal Design movement, it is perhaps even more importantly understood as a critical history of epistemology, politics, and the built world as mutually enacted.

Chapter 1

Normate Template

Knowing-Making the Architectural Inhabitant

> Until universal/inclusive design is infused in pre-professional and continuing education, the attitudes of designers will limit their understanding and appreciation of diversity. They will continue to shape their designs for a mythic average norm, creating barriers that exclude the contributions and participation of people all over the world.
>
> —ELAINE OSTROFF, "Universal Design: An Evolving Paradigm"

Ask an architect about their work, and you may learn more about the style, form, materials, structure, and cost of a building than the bodies or minds meant to inhabit it. Examine any doorway, window, toilet, chair, or desk in that building, however, and you will find the outline of the body meant to use it. From a doorframe's negative space to the height of shelves and cabinets, inhabitants' bodies are simultaneously imagined, hidden, and produced by the design of built worlds. Since the mid-twentieth century, supporters of more accessible, inclusive, and user-centered design have contended that design for the "mythic average user" shapes architects' default practices. For any of us who have failed to fit, even temporarily, into the ready-made structures of clothing, furniture, workplaces, homes, and other designed things, this point is rather unsurprising. The related idea that "the world was not designed with disability in mind" is, in one sense, a statement about omission and ignorance as ways of knowing and thinking. In another sense, however, it is a statement about omission and ignorance as material arrangements, ways of making and unmaking the world's inhabitants through unintentional but accumulated practices.

Although it is easy to claim that the world was designed with an average user, rather than a disabled one, in mind, this claim tells us very little about the norms, habits, and practices that have shaped our historical and current built environments. To understand the projects of accessible and inclusive design, we must understand the world into which these projects were born. This chapter considers how architectural design for an unmarked, normate inhabitant materialized from historical habits of perception and practice. I offer the concept of the "normate template" as a useful abbreviation for the complex, critical notion that the world was designed with normate inhabitants in mind. Despite historical shifts in scientific understandings of the valued body and aesthetic standards of good design, I argue, the normate template has served as a historical pattern language for Western traditions of architectural design since antiquity, and it was these patterns that the twentieth-century phenomenon of access-knowledge emerged to unsettle.

HISTORICAL NORMATES

A universal body has served as a template for the architectural user for centuries.[1] This "mythic average norm" is not a neutral body but rather a particular white, European, nondisabled, youthful, and often masculine figure whose features remain unmarked.[2] But to understand how the mythic average norm or normate became an unmarked template for good design, we have to engage more closely with histories of knowledge. Disability studies scholars and historians of science have argued that the concepts of "normal" and "average" are relatively recent phenomena, appearing in the nineteenth century with the birth of statistics to produce modern forms of power.[3] As Lennard Davis concludes, the norm has a prescriptive function, which stems from its reference to real population data, unlike the earlier, classical notion of the "ideal" body, which referenced mythic figures divine in form.[4] For Davis, this is what makes the figure of the norm insidious: when norms purport to represent "real" populations, it becomes possible to attempt to align those populations with the average, consequently making normates appear as natural or neutral.

   In other words, norms do not simply reflect probabilities within populations. In shaping the "real" population, norms become prescriptions for normalcy. For architectural design, however, these distinctions between the impossible ideal, the descriptive average, and the prescriptive norm are not as salient. Because architecture is a world-building practice, references to ideal and average inhabitants have shared a prescriptive function. These prescriptions, I will show, have been central to ideas about architects as knowers and makers.

Classical Normates

In the first century BC, Roman military architect Vitruvius prescribed an ideal body as the template for beautiful architecture.[5] In apparent reference to Greek mathematician Protagoras's precept that "man is the measure of all things," Vitruvius declared that as within the body ("designed by nature"), "there is a kind of symmetrical harmony between forearm, foot, palm, finger, and other small parts; and so it is with perfect buildings."[6] The evidence of this natural harmony appeared in the body's internal and external proportions: parts of the body, such as the palms, corresponded to other measures, such as height, and by extending its appendages into space, the ideal body would have its naval at the center of a circle, leaving the head, arms, and toes to create a perfect square.[7] Vitruvius naturalized a classical, ideal body by locating the human body in relation to nature and the cosmos but also prescribed this body as the template for beautiful architecture.

Ideal embodied proportions were not merely the stuff of imagination, however. These proportions *materialized* in classical architecture modeled after the ideal body.[8] Buildings likewise materialized the existence of certain *bodies*—presumably white, masculine, nondisabled citizens—as the most likely inhabitant of public space. Knowledge of such a body and its proportions further defined architectural work itself: authoritative architects, for Vitruvius, were those who had mastered knowledge of human life, culture, and embodiment, and not just the geometries or functions of built and engineered forms.[9] Classical models of body-knowing thus engendered normative, authoritative knowing-making.

Scientific Normates

Vitruvius's account of the universal body, eclipsed in the Middle Ages, reappeared in the Renaissance, alongside the birth of modern science.[10] In 1490 Leonardo da Vinci depicted the "Vitruvian Man" as a white, youthful, masculine, muscled, and standing body, arms and legs extended into space, with a flowing mane of hair (Figure 1.1). While Da Vinci retained Vitruvius's interest in the body as an instrument of measurement, its specificities were obscured by its transcendent appearance.[11] The drawing soon became a new, shared iconography for both medicine and architecture, which referenced antiquated truth claims about bodily proportions.

The Vitruvian Man's status as a scientific object was short-lived, however. In the nineteenth century, positivist standards of knowledge, premised upon the validity of statistical data, gained traction within architecture. Modeling itself after scientific disciplines, the discipline of architecture established standards of practice and perception, which distinguished the creative work of artists and the technical labor of drafters and builders from the architect's professional authority regarding style and form.[12] Architects discredited the Vitruvian Man as a depiction of classical proportions, and historians criticized Vitruvius for conflating ideal bodies with material realities, challenging the accounts of mathematical proportionality that da Vinci had illustrated.[13] In its visual, material manifestation, the Vitruvian Man's proportions were thus revealed as myth and illusion. As a misfit, the figure became an untruth.

Yet representations of bodies resembling the Vitruvian Man became new epistemic objects in the nineteenth century. Positivist statisticians, criminologists, physical anthropologists, and early eugenicists reproduced similar figures in the new material culture of anthropometry, or the measurement of human populations with calipers and rulers for statistical calculation (Figure 1.2). Although claiming to be distinct from practices such as phrenology, anthropometry deployed similar representations and truth claims (Figure 1.3). In this sense, the practice was engaged in what Foucault calls "games of truth," trained at producing new arrangements of knowing-making.[14] Its

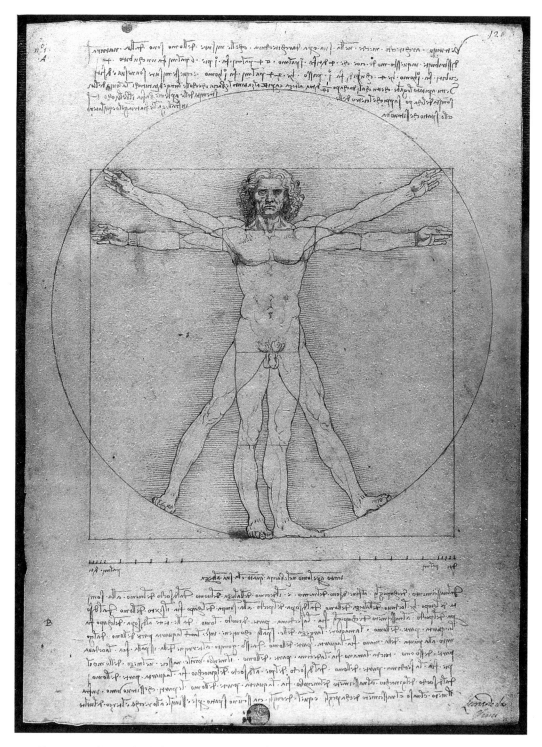

Figure 1.1. Leonardo da Vinci, *Vitruvian Man* (ca. 1490). Courtesy of Luc Viatour / www
.Lucnix.be.

initial, direct application was a new racial science, which sought to provide conclusive and comparative evidence of the supposed degeneracy of nonwhite, disabled, poor, and "feeble-minded" people.[15] Anthropometric data made it possible to calculate population averages (or norms), as well as standard deviations (or ranges of difference from the norm).

A positivist practice par excellence, anthropometry rendered the Vitruvian Man as fully normate: calculable, legible, a standard against which difference could be measured, and frequently, as in criminological and eugenic discourses, evidence of the supposed moral and aesthetic truths of normate bodies.[16] Despite claiming to be a new science, anthropometry shared many of the aesthetic and epistemological conventions of the classic, universal body. Vitruvius had claimed, for instance, that the body was a reflection of proportions of the universe. Although astronomical science had shifted, anthropometrists such as Adolphe Quetelet borrowed astronomers' methods of plotting data about cosmic events (such as planetary movements) to measure, model, and depict human bodies at the population scale.[17] The Gaussian curve, or "bell curve," thus became a well-known technology of demarcation between average and deviation, normate and misfit. At the curve's center, Quetelet's "average man," the most statistically probable body, resembled da Vinci's Vitruvian Man, a

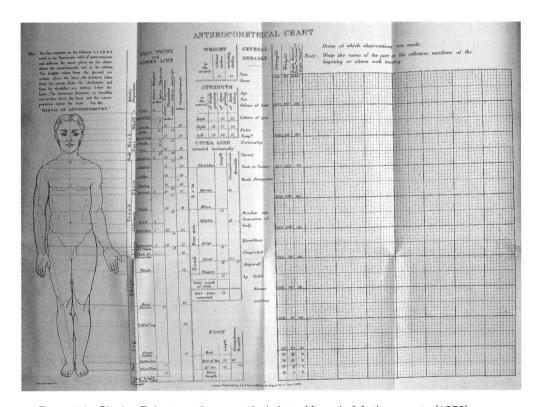

Figure 1.2. Charles Roberts, anthropometrical chart, *Manual of Anthropometry* (1878).

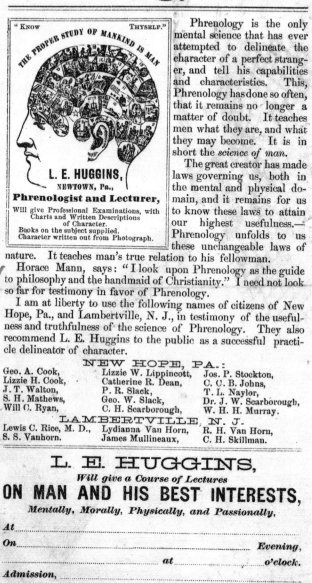

Phrenology is True

"KNOW THYSELF."

THE PROPER STUDY OF MANKIND IS MAN

L. E. HUGGINS,
NEWTOWN, Pa.,
Phrenologist and Lecturer,

Will give Professional Examinations, with Charts and Written Descriptions of Character.
Books on the subject supplied.
Character written out from Photograph.

Phrenology is the only mental science that has ever attempted to delineate the character of a perfect stranger, and tell his capabilities and characteristics. This, Phrenology has done so often, that it remains no longer a matter of doubt. It teaches men what they are, and what they may become. It is in short the *science of man.*

The great creator has made laws governing us, both in the mental and physical domain, and it remains for us to know these laws to attain our highest usefulness.— Phrenology unfolds to us these unchangeable laws of nature. It teaches man's true relation to his fellowman.

Horace Mann, says: "I look upon Phrenology as the guide to philosophy and the handmaid of Christianity." I need not look so far for testimony in favor of Phrenology.

I am at liberty to use the following names of citizens of New Hope, Pa., and Lambertville, N. J., in testimony of the usefulness and truthfulness of the science of Phrenology. They also recommend L. E. Huggins to the public as a successful practicle delineator of character.

NEW HOPE, PA.:

Geo. A. Cook,	Lizzie W. Lippincott,	Jos. P. Stockton,
Lizzie H. Cook,	Catherine R. Dean,	C. C. B. Johns,
J. T. Walton,	P. R. Slack,	T. L. Naylor,
S. H. Mathews,	Geo. W. Slack,	Dr. J. W. Scarborough,
Will C. Ryan,	C. H. Scarborough,	W. H. H. Murray.

LAMBERTVILLE, N. J.

Lewis C. Rice, M. D.,	Lydianna Van Horn,	R. H. Van Horn,
S. S. Vanhorn.	James Mullineaux,	C. H. Skillman.

L. E. HUGGINS,
Will give a Course of Lectures
ON MAN AND HIS BEST INTERESTS,
Mentally, Morally, Physically, and Passionally,

At _____

On _____ *Evening,*

_____ *at* _____ *o'clock.*

Admission, _____

Private examinations given at _____

Families and parties visited when invited.

Clark Pierson, Printer, THE RECORD Office, Lambertville, N. J.

Figure 1.3. Phrenologists claimed the truth of their practice to establish authority. L. E. Huggins, "Phrenology is True" (ca. 1870). Courtesy of Warshaw Collection of Business Americana, Archives Center, National Museum of American History, Smithsonian Institute.

former depiction of universal nature and harmonic proportionality: white, youthful, masculine, and able-bodied.[18] The bell curve, like Vitruvius's prescriptions for architecture, married description with prescription, rendering the most statistically probable bodies (i.e., the average or norm) as natural.[19]

Modernist Normates

While on its own, a statistical average may be an object of knowledge, a fact reflecting evidence of a population, normative prescription (or standardization) involves aligning a population or practice with norms of embodiment or behavior. If the normate template came into contact with standards of "good knowledge" in the nineteenth century, in the twentieth, it became an instrument for prescribing particular forms of knowledge in relation to Modernist architects' standards of "good design." An unmarked subtext for these standards was the "ideology of ability," which disability theorist Tobin Siebers defines as the societal "preference for able-bodiedness."[20] Modernists recapitulated earlier notions of geometric harmony and beauty through the new language of positivism, emphasizing an objective view of good design as premised upon the standardization of production. Design historian Stephen Hayward argues that while determinations of good design are often couched in seemingly neutral, descriptive terms, frequently in relation to generic values such as "common sense," they produce new arrangements of space, power, and knowledge.[21] Working as an instrument of what Foucault terms "games of truth" and sociologists of science describe as "boundary work," the normate template played an essential role in delineating "good design" from "poor design" in reference to dominant political, economic, and aesthetic interests.[22]

"A standard," wrote Le Corbusier (Charles-Édouard Jeanneret) in 1923, "is necessary for order in human effort. A standard is established on sure bases, not capriciously but with the surety of something intentional and of a logic controlled by analysis and experiment. All men have the same organism, the same functions. All men have the same needs."[23] Le Corbusier's figure of the "Modulor" followed the Vitruvian Man in conflating classical and scientific conceptions of the body and depicted the "harmonious measure" of the spatial inhabitant deemed "universally applicable to architecture and mechanics."[24] Similar to the apparent impartiality of Western science, figures like the Modulor portrayed a particular body, arranged from historical and contemporary ways of knowing-making, as a universal, impartial "view from nowhere."[25] In one sense, Modulor appeared to conflate (and thus misunderstand the distinction between) the ideal and the norm. In another, the figure complied with a long tradition of conflating real and ideal bodies to realize universal geometric harmonies in material form.

To claim authority and advance particular social, aesthetic, and industrial projects, Modernists appealed to the normate template's "scientificity," or what Foucault describes as the perceivable qualities of contemporary standards of what counts as science.[26] Put simply, describing something as scientific grants it the power and authority of supposed truth and objectivity. In Modernist games of truth, highly rationalized, standard forms served as currencies for determining the aesthetics and function of so-called good design. In 1932, for instance, Buckminster Fuller calculated that good design was premised upon the integration of aesthetics with standardizing modes of knowing-making, or as he put it, "*Science + Art + Industry = Universal Architecture.*"[27] This technoscientific standard (centered on what could be knowable, beautiful, and efficient) was purported to have the timeless quality of universality. Scientificity, in this case, appended references to nature, harmonic geometries, and the cosmos as a source of authority.

While Modernist notions of good design referred to early twentieth-century practices of industrial efficiency, they combined references to classical concepts of universality and modern notions of standardization to solidify the architects' role as a design authority. Echoing Vitruvius, the modernist Congrès internationaux d'architecture moderne (CIAM) wrote in 1933 that architecture should be "placed at the service of man," "facilitate all of [man's] actions," and be produced by architects possessing "perfect knowledge of man."[28] Modernist architecture fulfilled the expectation of "perfect" knowledge by positioning architects as experts on both design and universal human needs.[29]

The expectation of a universal white, male, nondisabled body continued to represent the default, normate inhabitant, with severe consequences for nonnormate populations. In the United States, where the overlapping demographics of people of color, women, and disabled people faced discrimination and segregation, the normate template reinforced the effects of Jim Crow laws, immigration policies, gender discrimination, and institutionalization.[30] The social project of eugenics, which was determined to cull supposedly defective bodies from the population, also changed the nature of spatial inhabitation: public space, often associated with freedom, became a site of management, surveillance, and control for vulnerable populations. Disability and design historians Christina Cogdell, Susan Schweik, David Mitchell, and Sharon Snyder have documented wide-ranging mechanisms of eugenic environmental design: early twentieth-century "ugly laws" prohibited people with atypical bodies from entering public space, eugenicists measured the traits of "feeble-mindedness" according to an individual's ability to cope with urban environments, and eugenic ideologies of "streamlining" influenced the aesthetics of industrial and product design of the 1930s.[31] Denying nonnormates access to public space created the illusion of their nonexistence, which consequently resulted in less-accessible environments.

The standardization of architectural inhabitants both resulted from and produced twentieth-century standards of professional architectural knowing-making. Normate bodies became legible to architects through professional handbooks, such as Ernst Neufert's *Architect's Data* in Europe and Charles Ramsey and George Sleeper's *Architectural Graphic Standards* in the United States (first published in 1936 and 1932, respectively), which offered standard "orthographic" conventions for depicting features such as doorways, windowsills, stairs, and roofs.[32] Orthographic drawing, a convention of architectural drafting, sought the ordered representation of architectural space. But the Latin "ortho-," meaning upright or correct, also captures the dual function of architectural standards: orthographic drawings both defined and prescribed the typical features of built environments.[33] Alongside standard doorways or roofs, depictions of the standard inhabitant, decorated with notations of measurement and size, staged the legibility of normate spatial users.

Representations of normate bodies followed the Modernist synthesis of classical representations and concepts with contemporary scientific standards.[34] Beginning with the third edition (1941) of *Graphic Standards* and persisting until its seventh edition in 1981, a set of black-and-white drawings titled *The Dimensions of the Human Figure* (Figure 1.4) appeared near the end of the book. The drawings referenced the conventions of da Vinci's Vitruvian Man, with arms extended into space and unmarked race, gender, and disability status, which together communicated their intended use as universal figures. The abstract, shaded bodies stood, sat, climbed, and crawled, while dimensional lines and numbers around their periphery provided what appeared to be average measurements.

The Dimensions of the Human Figure was a reproduction of an earlier set of identical drawings titled *The Geometry of the Human Figure,* which appeared in 1934 in *American Architect and Architecture* magazine.[35] On the surface, the function of these depictions appears translational: for architects without advanced mathematical training, the drawings seemed to provide a quick reference to average spatial dimensions. But while artist Ernest Irving Freese noted that the dimensions provided were "based on an average or normal adult" (implying the addition of statistics), architectural historians such as Hyungmin Pai have pointed out that the numerical values did not match any anthropometric data available at the time.[36] What, then, was the function of Freese's drawings, if not to serve as data-delivery devices for architects?

Combined with supposed dimensional data, the figures and their classical proportions were performing other material-epistemic work. One indication is the discursive shift from "geometry" to "dimensions" in the drawings' title, which suggests an equivalence of ideal and normate bodies, a conflation of seemingly historically distinct concepts that found easy relation due to their shared prescriptive status. The numerical dimensions added a hint of scientificity, creating the illusion that these figures were grounded in anthropometric data. But scientificity here is an aesthetic element with a persuasive function, lending architectural practice the appearance of standardization and order.

It would be easy to characterize Freese's dimensional notations, and the anthropometric data that they appeared to reference (however fictively), as pseudoscience. After all, averages are mathematical calculations, not representations of existing, living bodies. This suggestion presumes, however, that there is a real, objective truth about bodily size and proportion awaiting discovery by superior methods and proper

DIMENSIONS of THE HUMAN FIGURE

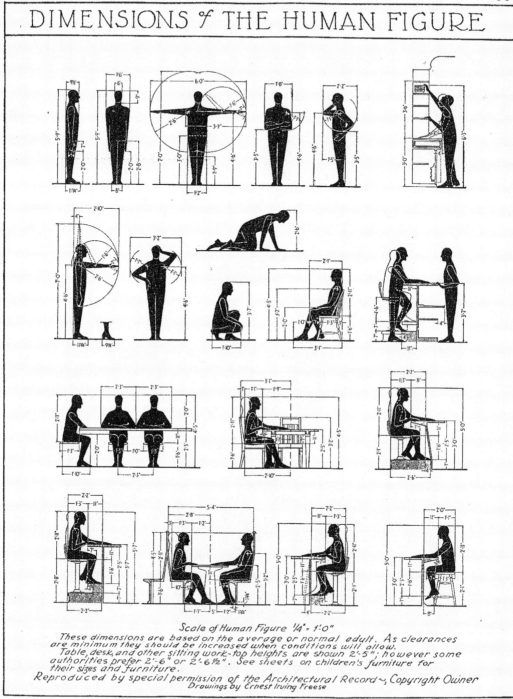

Scale of Human Figure 1/4" = 1'-0"

These dimensions are based on the average or normal adult. As clearances are minimum they should be increased when conditions will allow.
Table, desk, and other sitting work-top heights are shown 2'-5"; however some authorities prefer 2'-6" or 2'-6½". See sheets on children's furniture for their sizes and furniture.
Reproduced by special permission of the Architectural Record~, Copyright Owner
Drawings by Ernest Irving Freese

Figure 1.4. Ernest Irving Freese, *The Dimensions of the Human Figure, American Architect and Architecture* 145 (July 1934): 57–60.

notations. A different possibility is that architectural knowledge, like laboratory science, is inherently partial, historical, and mediated, whether through tools, representations, sociopolitical contexts, or aesthetic choices. In the case of the normate template, Freese's drawings in *Graphic Standards* highlight the ways that claims about the "truth" of the inhabitants' body are also exercises of power that convey the desirability of particular bodies (and their being-in-the-world) over others, and consequently materialize a world built with an aesthetic ideal in mind.

THE NEW NORMATES

The universal, the objective, and the scientific are all concepts that work as persuasive devices, even when material forms cannot meet their impossible standards. Freese's figures materialized an early twentieth-century reclamation of classical aesthetics and representations of the body in U.S. culture. Consider that just a year after Freese's figures appeared in *Graphic Standards,* eugenicist Robert Dickinson commissioned sculptor Abram Belskie to create two white, marble sculptures of human figures derived from average anthropometric data. He called these figures Normman and Norma. The classical ideal of the white, masculine, able-bodied citizen materialized in Normman's sculpted form.[37] But Norma's seemingly progressive inclusion reveals shifting norms of the ideal citizen, namely the introduction of the figure of the white, presumably reproductively fit woman as a standard-bearer of the nation, an acceptable prototype of embodiment in an era of racial anxieties about immigrant populations. A 1945 eugenics competition in Cleveland, Ohio, used the Norma sculpture as a reference when it called for a woman whose measurements most closely approximated the average American woman. Although none of the contestants matched Norma's chest, waist, hip, and height measurements, the winner (who most closely approximated the statistical average) was also one who manifested the cultural and aesthetic figure of ideal, white womanhood.[38] The competition, Belskie's statues, and the broader eugenic project served as a normate template for human populations—a kind of "eugenic world building," as feminist disability theorist Rosemarie Garland-Thomson describes it—revealing the close proximity between imagined architectural users and cultural requirements for standardized citizens.[39]

The normate template for architecture defined valuable citizens through more subtle relations of knowing and making. Regimes of legibility and illegibility, in particular, shaped how architects came to create buildings and public spaces with particular inhabitants in mind. Like the process of defining legible *citizens* under law, the project of making architectural inhabitants *legible* to designers entailed defining the center and margins of the population, often through visual representations of at least some of these bodies. While these public, nation-shaping practices shaped the normate template's public face, the standardization of normate world-building often hid them in plain view. The typical understanding that architects only understand

and anticipate the most legible, public bodies requires qualification, however, because the normate template also imbued particular forms of invisibility and illegibility with power.

The unmarked normate and its purported neutrality resembled the unmarked harmonic body and its purported relations to a fundamental nature.[40] Freese's figures, for instance, appear unremarkable: they stand, sit, and crawl using two arms and two legs; their dark shade does not appear legible as a racial category; their gender is largely unannounced.

Adjacent to one normate figure, who stands with arms extended forward in profile, Freese depicts a single, high-heeled shoe (see Figure 1.4). Architectural critic Lance Hosey argues that the shoe, with its higher heel and smaller dimensions, is meant to represent female embodiment as simultaneously an object of knowledge and a deviation from male norms.[41] To make the female inhabitant legible, Freese engages in an act of seemingly benign differentiation, achieving a marginal gain in diversity while reinforcing the standard, normate body as the template for architecture.

Read another way, however, the shoe illustrates the trappings of normate legibility modeled on aesthetic visibility, scientific calculability, or political citizenship. The high-heeled shoe is easy to miss. But it alone raises questions about the presumed universality and objectivity of the other figures. If we take Freese's drawings as a historical artifact, rather than an objective prescription of good design, the shoe offers a subtle hint of ways of being, moving, making, and knowing that standard architectural representations fail to provide.

ACCESS-KNOWLEDGE

The high-heeled shoe is a marginal, imperfect crack in a broader artifice of the "mythic average user." But if it scores the normate template's smooth surface to reveal other possibilities of knowing-making, we might wonder, what were these possibilities, where were they located, and what new worlds did they configure? In the twentieth century, a new regime of legibility and illegibility began to take shape in the normate template's shadows. This regime, which I call *access-knowledge,* was at first undetectable. By design, it worked below the surface of material forms, such as buildings, streets, or cities. Its purpose was to disrupt the normate order of things. And its public face, its most visible elements, appeared to be integrated into, rather than in disruption of, this order.

Legible Users

In 1981 Freese's drawings disappeared from *Graphic Standards,* where for forty years they had resided at the back of the book, between entries for "Metal Gauges," "Abbreviations," and "Modular Coordination." The handbook's seventh edition replaced *Dimensions of the Human Figure* with new anthropometric drawings of a man and a woman (Figure 1.5).[42] By appearance, the two figures closely resembled Norma and Normman in their white, standing, rigid, dimensional bodies. Their names were Joe and Josephine and the dimensional data attached to their bodies represented decades of research on human engineering and performance, culled by Henry Dreyfuss Associates, specifically industrial designer Niels Diffrient and human factors researcher Alvin Tilley.[43] Two other figures appeared on adjacent pages, representing a wheelchair user and a person using crutches—both without other identifying characteristics. The accompanying text offered suggestions for designing for blind, deaf, and hard-of-hearing people (Figure 1.6). For all these figures, dimensional data indicated upper and lower percentiles, in addition to the average.

Following the civil rights era, the figures appeared to represent social progress toward a greater diversification of architectural inhabitants—a new design approach directing architects away from the normate template and toward diverse ways of knowing-making. Printed at the handbook's beginning, the new figures seemed to

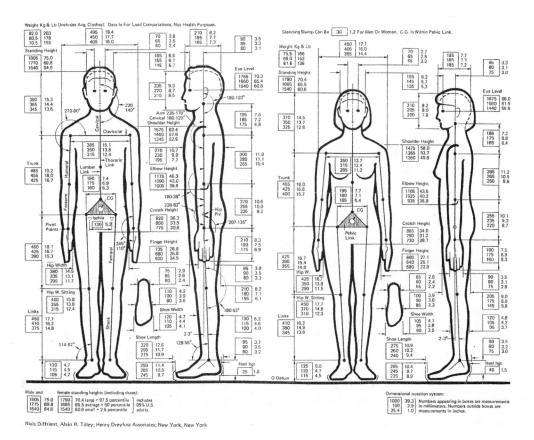

Figure 1.5. Anthropometric figures, such as Joe and Josephine, offer dimensional figures with added statistical data. Charles Ramsey and Harold Sleeper, *Architectural Graphic Standards*, 7th ed. (New York: Wiley, 1981). Courtesy of Judy A. Crookes, Henry Dreyfuss Associates.

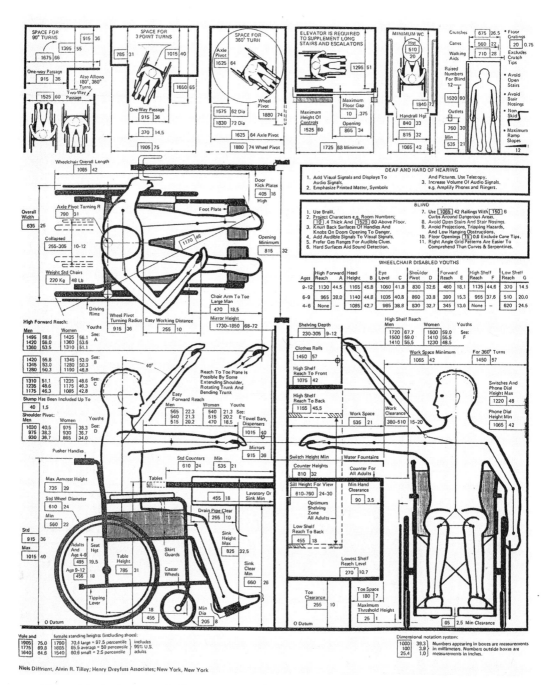

Figure 1.6. Anthropometric figures representing disability often depict a wheelchair user and, to a lesser extent, figures using canes or crutches. Charles Ramsey and Harold Sleeper, *Architectural Graphic Standards,* 7th ed. (New York: Wiley, 1981). Courtesy of Judy A. Crookes, Henry Dreyfuss Associates.

suggest that architects could finally design with a range of users in mind, not as an afterthought but throughout the entire design process. But these figures did not appear from thin air. They were not an indication that well-intentioned architects had simply sought out better information about users. Nor did they unseat the normate template. What happened, then, between 1941 and 1981 to produce such a significant shift in the representation of the architectural user? To understand this shift and its relation to access-knowledge, we must consider how these new figures materialized, what they represented, and why they appeared in *Graphic Standards* at this particular moment.

In the early twentieth century, the U.S. military employed industrial designers to create machines, vehicles, and uniforms, which they designed by drawing on the military's vast collections of anthropometric data about male soldiers' bodies. Influential American industrial designer Henry Dreyfuss continued to work in this capacity in the post–World War II era, bridging military and civilian applications of data with "human engineering," a new paradigm for creating products and tools by "designing for people."[44] This practice, later termed "ergonomics," merged the evidence base of military "human factors" research with the aesthetic and functional practices of industrial design.

While human engineering aimed to enable designers to create with users in mind, the practice was also, as its name suggests, involved in "configuring" the prototypical users of products and technologies.[45] Dreyfuss's development of human engineering reveals the surprising parallels between the projects of solidifying the normate template, in one sense, and unsettling it, in another. He recalls, for instance, the process of developing the first anthropometric drawings for use by industrial designers following World War II.

> Our office was working on the interior of a heavy tank for the Army. We had tacked a huge, life-size drawing of the tank driver's compartment on the wall. The driver's figure had been indicated with a thick black pencil line and we had been jotting odds and ends of dimensional data on him as we dug the data out of our files. Surrounded by arcs and rectangles, he looked something like one of the famous dimensional studies of Leonardo. Suddenly, it dawned on us that the drawing on the wall was more than a study of the tank driver's compartment: without being aware of it, we had been putting together a dimensional chart of the average adult American male.[46]

As this narrative unfolds, the user's body appears to materialize as if by magic. But the final form, an early prototype for the figure of "Joe," shares with Freese's figures its appearance of harmonic geometry, appended with dimensional notations. Dreyfuss invites the reader into this scene of discovery but quickly qualifies it by laying bare the firm's ad hoc research process. "Here and there," writes Dreyfuss, we found a book or article with some data we could use.... Many were old, out of print and probably inaccurate.... Over the years, our pile of books, pamphlets, clippings, and dog-eared index cards grew higher and more jumbled. When World War II came, the pile grew even faster. The armed forces and their suppliers undertook some very ambitious human engineering and published their findings. But still no one assembled these data into a single package that a designer could refer to and save spending days wading through his library and files.[47]

By scientific standards of the time, these research methods would have appeared disorganized, riddled with epistemological leaps, unlikely to yield a truthful representation of the user. But, as Dreyfuss illustrates, compiling research was an experiment in new ways of knowing-making: the process did not adopt a designerly view from nowhere or seek a one-to-one translation of data into form but rather injected a concept of "evidence" into fields of practice that were not necessarily wedded to an objective standard of truth. This position relative to more established sciences made human engineering a "switchpoint" at which new concepts, truth claims, and exercises of power could infiltrate the norms of design practice.[48] Dreyfuss's publication of *The Measure of Man* and its laying bare of the messiness of knowing-making animate the work of access-knowledge. Behind the scenes of major design projects and their final built form, access-knowledge was at work reconfiguring how designers make and know.

Joe came first, followed by Josephine.[49] The pair were intended as tools for "Tailoring the Product to Fit."[50] Alvin Tilley, a human factors specialist employed at Henry Dreyfuss Associates, completed the first iteration of the drawings in 1959 (Figure 1.7). They appeared the next year in a special issue of the journal *Industrial Design,* for which Dreyfuss wrote the introduction, and were followed that same year by *The Measure of Man,* a portfolio-style packet of dimensional drawings completed by two life-sized posters of Joe and Josephine.[51] Despite the portfolio's specialized use, however, Joe and Josephine were meant to appeal to a broader audience than industrial designers alone. In 1961 Dreyfuss appeared on television to promote the portfolio.[52] The images and data, though borrowed from military researchers and rehabilitation engineers, entered the mainstream. Joe and Josephine circulated as material-epistemic hybrids: generalized data, abstracted from other bodies, appeared alongside these line-drawn figures, who were in turn rendered as fleshy bodies through their appearance as life-sized drawings. This conflation of data and flesh took shape again when the portfolio was reprinted as a revised and expanded hardcover book in 1967. At Dreyfuss's insistence, the reprint displayed a "split human figure": half anthropometric normate diagram, half fleshy but normate man (Figure 1.8).

Dreyfuss's tank driver, and later Joe and Josephine, were objects, tools for designers to use. But they were also *enacted* through the ways that industrial designers synthesized various ways of knowing how bodies stand, sit, crawl, work, breathe, and feel.

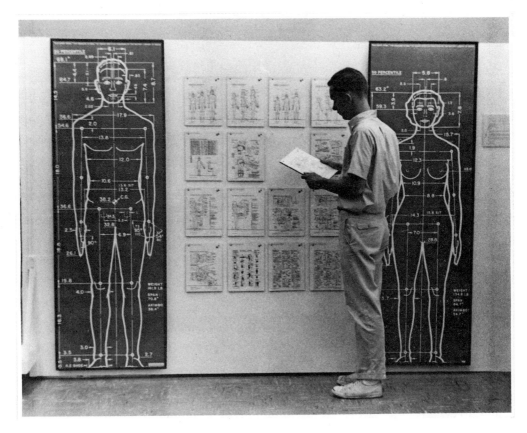

Figure 1.7. Real and imagined bodies: researcher Alvin Tilley stands before life-sized drawings of Joe and Josephine (ca. 1973). Courtesy of Cooper Hewitt, Smithsonian Design Museum / Art Resource, NY.

Joe and Josephine joined the scientific efforts of industry, medicine, and war into singular, legible configurations—arrangements that industrial designers could imagine as (and use to predict) an enfleshed, living user and employ as points of departure for investigating more particular users. Dreyfuss's accounts of these enactments, quoted above, were laid out in the introduction to the second edition of *The Measure of Man*, published in 1967.

Data provided inside the portfolio reflects several decades of ergonomics and human factors research in military design, factory engineering, fashion, psychology, and other fields for which statistical data could provide useful population-scale generalizations in an era of mass production.[53] Compared to Modernists touting standardization, however, the human engineering approach to industrial design emphasized the dynamic nature of human users and consumers. This was exemplified in Henry Dreyfuss Associates' firm motto: "We bear in mind that the object being worked on is going to be ridden in, sat upon, looked at, talked into, activated, operated, or in

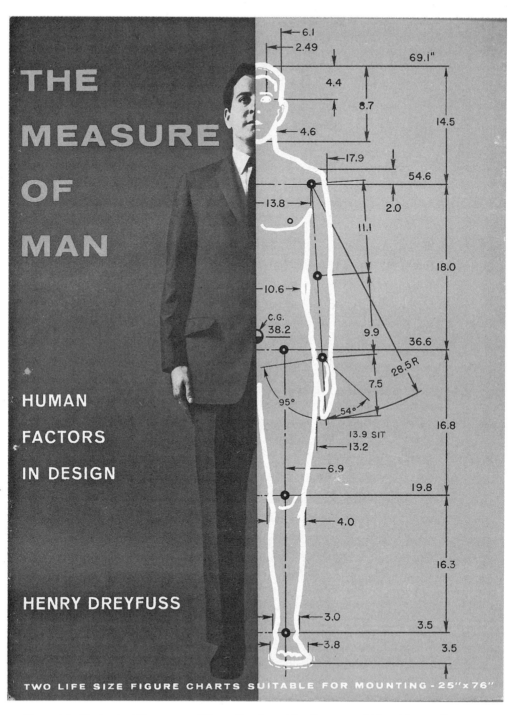

Figure 1.8. Revised edition cover of Henry Dreyfuss, *The Measure of Man: Human Factors in Design* (1967).

some other way used by people."[54] Designing for users was thus contingent upon knowing and predicting a multiplicity of uses, even for a single product. Far more than a data repository, *The Measure of Man* shaped user-centered design as a formal methodology—a tangible integration of knowing-making—that designers could employ in the service of more usable products. The imperative to design with users in mind served as a material and methodological critique of Modernist design principles, particularly their flattening of human users and failures to address human use.

A discourse arose within the design professions, likely in converse with the rise of social protest movements in the 1960s, to challenge the primacy of singular normate representations of the user. In the revised *Measure of Man* (1967), published amid the passage of major civil rights legislation for disabled people and people of color, Dreyfuss's description of Joe and Josephine addressed the normate template as a habit of perception.

> The published drawings included the dimensions of the small, average and large men, but only the average man was drawn. We found that people referred to the charts as "Dreyfuss' average man," which indicated that many people had misunderstood the diagrams and probably misused them. A good design must "fit" not only the theoretical average, but his large and small brothers. We had thought this was obvious in the charts, but we seemed to be wrong.[55]

Dreyfuss was aware that normate figures representing statistical averages were often taken as real bodies. Despite shifts in the content of statistical data, designers had continued to imagine the average body through a default habit of perception. But for Dreyfuss, the standard of the prototypical user was moving in another direction: away from the normate body and toward one that appears (in his description) nonnormate, even disabled.

Joe and Josephine, Dreyfuss claimed, have "numerous allergies, inhibitions, and obsessions. They react strongly to touch that is uncomfortable or unnatural; they are disturbed by glaring or insufficient light and by offensive coloring; they are sensitive to noise, and they shrink from disagreeable odor."[56] By Dreyfuss's account, Joe and Josephine's ways of being resemble symptoms of certain types of cognitive disabilities, such as autism or sensory processing disorders. These diagnostic categories, however, would not exist until the 1990s.[57] Nor was Dreyfuss apparently aware of the deinstitutionalization movement, which sought to transition mentally disabled people from institutions to community-based care. Although Dreyfuss appeared to understand Joe and Josephine's traits as statistically atypical, his attribution of these standards of human cognition for designers was central to devising a theory of good design as premised on the most nonnormate, misfit, and vulnerable bodies.

Yet Joe and Josephine's "allergies, inhibitions, and obsessions" were not necessarily atypical to the population, nor were they born of disability rights or social justice discourses. Instead, Joe and Josephine's described sensory characteristics reflected industrial designers' preoccupations with mechanical danger, chemical and thermal vulnerability, and sensory overwhelm in an era of Cold War science. Because Dreyfuss drew on available data from military and industrial sources and had begun his inquiries into body-environment interactions through military contracts, he had at his disposal a set of practices relating to engineering the user's safety, limiting exposures to mechanical vibrations, sounds, lights, and chemical exposures. A diagram of "Environmental Tolerance Zones" in *The Measure of Man* showed a human body viewed from above, at the center of concentric circles delineating degrees of environmental comfort in relation to atomic radiation, atmospheric pressure, heat, acceleration, carbon monoxide, and shock waves.[58] Notions of interface safety, in turn, informed human engineering as a vulnerability-mitigating method and set the baseline of good design according to military-industrial notions of the body.[59]

Despite attention to these sensorial dimensions of the human body, however, the primacy of dimensions and scale endured in the firm's new projects. Beginning in 1974, two years after Dreyfuss's death, Henry Dreyfuss Associates' Niels Diffrient, Alvin Tilley, and Joan Bardagjy published a series of portfolios titled *Humanscale* that incorporated newly available anthropometric, anthropological, human factors, and medical data on women, children, elders, and wheelchair users.[60] Although apparently marketed toward industrial designers, the new data and diagrams began to cross into the realm of architecture. In the early 1980s, legal requirements for accessible architectural design, particularly wheelchair users, had become enforceable in the design of federal buildings, increasing the urgency of a more inclusive knowledge base for architects.[61] Accessibility standards defined specific desirable outcomes in the built environment, such as the ideal slope of a wheelchair ramp. Disabled architect Ronald Mace had developed illustrated depictions of such codes.[62] Yet *Graphic Standards* turned to *Humanscale 4/5/6* (published in 1981) for its new diagrams of the human user, including the disabled user.[63] Although the new accessibility codes focused on disability (and not explicitly gender or age), the 1981 (seventh) edition of *Graphic Standards* replaced Freese's dimensional figures of the universal man and feminine shoe with an array of newly legible figures, including Joe, Josephine, a child, a wheelchair user, and a person using crutches—all depicted as white, featureless figures (see Figures 1.5 and 1.6).

These intertextualities suggest that in the twentieth-century project of access-knowledge, designing with particular types of users in mind entailed intersecting disciplinary and professional approaches to knowing, as well as making. One detail deserves reiterating: the legal impetus for disability access (code-based requirements that took hold in 1980) led to a wholesale diversification in *Graphic Standards* of the figures of the architectural inhabitant, an expansion of gender representation, as well as disability inclusion. Disability inclusion, in other words, enabled inclusion for a wide range of bodies. This was not because accessible features for wheelchair users, for instance, would be beneficial to the other users depicted but because the legibility of disability in the twentieth century was fundamentally entangled with the structures of knowledge governing legible human variation. Why the legal impetus for disability access led to such an expansion of representation, and how this relates to the growing intersections of industrial, scientific, and architectural knowledge, are explored in the next two chapters.

Chapter 2

Flexible Users

From the Average Body to a Range of Users

"Work" . . . is purposive human activity. It includes not only labouring for monetary gain but all similarly demanding activities such as war, sport, games, hobbies, and housework.

—W. T. SINGLETON, *The Body at Work: Biological Ergonomics*

Universal Design . . . defines the user as all people, not specifically disabled people. Ron Mace emphasized that we will all have disabilities at some point in our lives, whether from an illness, a temporary disability from an accident or just aging. If designers would take this into consideration, it could influence their designing for the full range of human variations over a lifespan. This perspective is much wider and more flexible by considering a broad range of possibilities.

—KRYSTYNA GOLONKA, "Ronald Mace and His Philosophy of Universal Design"

Examine any device labeled "ergonomic" and you are likely to find at least one feature that adapts to its user. From ergonomic desk chairs and standing desks with hydraulic lifts and tilt-inducing levers to modular workstations with insertable shelves, flexible design is a quality of products made to anticipate a broad range of users rather than a singular normate. Advocates for social diversity and inclusion often cast the concept of flexibility as openness to nonnormate ways of inhabiting built worlds.[1] Proponents of accessible and Universal Design, for example, offer "Flexibility in Use" as a method for eliminating frictions, signaling openness, and integrating misfitting bodies more seamlessly into designed environments.[2] There is another way to understand flexibility, however: as an instrument of standardization, normalization, and fit. In our late-capitalist moment, flexible products appear in specific spaces: sites of labor at all scales, from factories to office buildings, adopt flexible design to prevent injuries and discomfort related to repetitive motion, posture, and energy expenditures that arise when bodies meet machines. The successful ergonomic object reduces these frictions, blending the body and machine seamlessly to enable efficient and comfortable work.

This chapter traces the rise of "flexibility" as a multivalent concept, arguing that in military, scientific, and industrial discourses, this concept has been entangled with related ideas of the "user," the "human factor," and, most importantly, with disability. In ergonomics and human engineering, flexibility has been a design strategy aligned with preventing injury and disability, in one sense, and enhancing human performance, in another. Once rendered calculable in scientific, military, and industrial systems, human variation was understood as a threat necessary to contain. In the nineteenth and twentieth centuries, a belief that human variation places inevitable constraints upon engineered systems yielded flexible *making* (or design that considers a range of embodiments beyond the norm) as well as flexible *knowing* (or ways of keeping the range of embodiments in mind). Flexible knowing-making, in turn, shaped the twentieth-century phenomenon of access-knowledge.

KNOWING-MAKING FLEXIBILITY

Design for users, by most accounts, is a twentieth-century preoccupation. Historians locate the rise of the "user"—its legibility to designers—in Cold War–era efforts toward human factors research, ergonomics, human engineering, and spatial planning.[3] These methods of knowing-making combined the insights of new human sciences (such as psychology); new forms of rehabilitation, architecture, and industrial design expertise; and earlier natural, biological, anatomical, and physiological sciences.[4] The resulting ways of knowing the user's needs, behaviors, and embodiments appeared to materialize in the twentieth century. Yet the methods and epistemologies enabling user-centered design coalesced a century earlier in scientific, military, and industrial regimes concerned with disability. Even prior to Dreyfuss's human engineering or British aviation scientist K. F. H. Murrell's work on ergonomics, perceptions of supposedly deficient humans (termed "cripples," "feeble-minded," "injured," "handicapped," or, more recently, "disabled") shaped the figure of the user and methods of designing carried out in its name.[5]

The User and the Human Factor

Before federal laws could mandate accessibility for disabled users in all public buildings, before manufacturers could produce and market products to offset the effects of aging, before industrial designers could employ terms such as "ergonomics" and "human engineering" to address human vulnerabilities, and before designers could imagine the user as multiple—beyond the average, a range rather than a norm— the figure of the user was understood as a wildcard, a vulnerability-producing instrument that must be studied and controlled. For the nineteenth-century science of work, the "user" and the "human factor" were terms that described inevitable human vulnerability—and therefore the uncertainties and complications that workers would invariably introduce into systems. Fears of the user's vulnerability were entangled with concerns about industrial efficiency. As early as 1818, European engineers discussed the role of the "human factor" in promoting national "industrial supremacy" through standardization.[6] Whereas the "user" implied the individual-scale material relationships between bodies and technologies, the "human factor" represented uncertainty at the systems scale.[7] In *The Human Motor*, historian Anson Rabinbach argues that in the mid- to late nineteenth century, physiologists, industrial engineers, and physicists alike began to understand machines, bodies, and societies as analogous systems, modeled around the structures of nature and driven by energy.[8] Accordingly, in 1857 Polish botanist and inventor Wojciech Jastrzębowski introduced the term "ergonomics," describing it as the "Science of Work."[9] For Jastrzębowski, "work" encompassed the human imposition of force, whether "physical, kinetic, or *motory*," on natural resources, which would in turn translate human efforts into the "common good."[10] He clarified that in a broader sense, work also included "physical, aesthetic, rational, and moral" labor—ways of knowing, making, and relating to the world.[11] The inevitable outcome of work, as Jastrzębowski termed it, was "ability": the more one labors, in other words, the easier and more satisfying work becomes.[12] As an instrument of labor, the able, working body was thus understood as a machine that produces and consumes energy.

As the concepts of the user and the human factor came into circulation for industrial science, they also began to influence architecture. In the mid-nineteenth century, mechanical and functionalist metaphors for architecture emerged to describe buildings as bodies, the organs of which worked via mechanical relations.[13] References to the user and the human factor rendered both machines and buildings as sites for engineering and studying efficiency. For the most part, the architectural user remained an undifferentiated figure. Before architects could mark distinctions between users, they required an understanding of design as a functional, rather than only aesthetic or formal, practice. Surprisingly, industrial engineers sought to influence architects' understandings of the user. In 1864, for instance, Scottish steam engineer Robert Scott Burn called for architects to think about how clients use buildings throughout the design process rather than after the design has been set in stone. Architects must know, he wrote in his book *The Grammar of House Planning,*

> how much of his time a man has to spend in his house, and how often, therefore, he
> is to be pleased with its comforts or annoyed by its defects, it does not seem odd that
> he should rarely know whether he has to enjoy the one or endure the other until he
> takes possession, when knowledge comes too late for remedy. For it should never be
> forgotten, that the mistakes made in the planning of a house cannot be rectified when
> the plan is perpetuated in stone or brick and mortar.[14]

Although steam engineering and architecture are apparently distinct areas of expertise, the two fields of knowledge shared conceptions of energy, structure, and use.

Particularly in "house planning" and other vernacular architectures, Burn argued that foresight and attention to users were as crucial as solid structural engineering. Consequently, when the terms "user" and "human factor" began to appear together in nineteenth-century texts, they appeared in reference to industrial energy production, notably steam.[15] A decade before writing *The Grammar of House Planning*, in the 1850s, Burn developed his work on architecture and the user, which included texts on architectural geometry and applied ventilation for architectural structures, at the same time that he penned his major work *The Steam Engine*.[16] By the 1890s, Burn and other steam engineers were applying the term "user" to laboring bodies, whose work produced energy in steam plants, similar to the way that scientific managers such as Frederick Winslow Taylor conceived of workers as productive units expending energy.[17] Viewed by industrial managers as extensions of factory machinery, users' bodies became manipulable and engineerable. Body, energy, and labor were entangled in the possibility of a compliant and malleable user, who would be responsible for the smooth functioning of the industrial system.

Flexibility and Standardization

Although the human factor was a confounding factor in industrial production, mid-nineteenth-century engineers took the user's uniformity for granted. All users were potential disruptions to engineer and standardize, but *specific* types of users had not yet come to matter in the discourse of the user or the human factor. One project of human differentiation, the nineteenth-century science of anthropometry, made the variety of human forms legible. Recalling the last chapter, the practice of anthropometry had been integral to projects of scientific racism, colonialism, and positivist science.[18] Physical anthropologists, criminologists, and statisticians collected anthropometric data and differentiated populations based on race, physical impairment, and other factors. But anthropometrists also debated the usefulness of this data, particularly as a representation of populations.

War, like industry, draws upon bodies as resources for certain types of labor but also *produces* these bodies through repetitive training, arrangement, and rational ordering. Military anthropometric studies made use of large, available populations, and the studies resulting from military data consequently shaped how designers and engineers could know and apply the "human factor." In 1861 the U.S. Congress established the Sanitary Commission, an agency akin to the Red Cross supporting injured Union soldiers fighting in the Civil War.[19] Although tending to injured soldiers was the commission's primary purpose, it also gathered statistical data about U.S. soldiers fighting for both the Union and the Confederacy. At the time, statistics was a relatively new science and Sanitary Commission officials debated its strategic uses for military knowledge. One issue was whether data gathered from particular populations of soldiers' bodies could be generalized for application beyond the war machine. Charles Stillé, a historian and employee of the Sanitary Commission, explained that with statistical data, "the experience of thousands or hundreds of thousands of men may be substituted for that of one man, and the accuracy of numerical computation may thus supply the place of the rude estimate of personal opinion."[20] These claims embodied nineteenth-century positivism and its emphasis on the primacy of statistical data.

It was not just that military statistics would enable more accurate representations of the soldier population, however. Nor was it primarily in the name of general knowledge or scientific advancement that the commission's Bureau of Vital Statistics amassed data on soldiers. New anthropometric tools and methods, coupled with census data collection, were strategic for the military because they could help distinguish—at the population level—between the most robust, successful fighters and those whose bodies were less likely to successfully win in armed combat. Making distinctions along lines of ability and impairment rendered particular categories of human variation legible as features of the "human factor" in military systems. The Bureau of Vital Statistics claimed to lead the cutting edge of statistical research in the United States with its plentiful data about the "character, number, and health," as well as "physical peculiarities," of Union Soldiers.[21] Demographic and anthropometric data differentiated soldiers by nationality, race, "birth-places, ages, strength, capacity of lungs, statures, dimensions of chest, bodily proportions, pulse, [and] respiration," with "those in good health being distinguished from those not in their usual vigor."[22] Regarding this evidence, Stillé wrote, "It would be difficult to say whether their value in a medical, military, or physiological point of view should be regarded as the greatest."[23] Differentiation between health and sickness, whiteness and racial otherness, and all manners of bodily function and size thus became central to military statistical research. This was not simply a research endeavor. By allowing researchers to cross-reference data on physical disability, race, and age with character, number, and health, the database enabled statistical calculations of valuable users on the basis of specific traits.

A foundational study of the human factors field differentiated Civil War soldiers based on race and bodily ability. The focus of Benjamin Apthorp Gould's *Investigations in the Military and Anthropological Statistics of American Soldiers* was to catalog the presence of physical impairments that could potentially disqualify soldiers from service.[24] The analysis covered large-scale user surveys of Civil War enlistees. Drawing upon census catalogs of soldiers' bodies, Gould calculated their physical fitness, health, lung capacity, morphologies, and dimensions, and merged statistical science with medical categories. Variations in stature across geographic regions, for instance, served as evidence for the comparative fitness of soldiers from these regions.[25] On the whole, Gould's research was entrenched in the tradition of scientific racism.[26] It relied on and produced stable categories of difference to assess the impacts of race, disability, and class on soldiers' war-fighting capabilities. The soldiers' bodies under analysis—all male—were both normate and nonnormate, citizens and noncitizens, white and nonwhite bodies.

Making differences legible across these categories required calculations of probable human types, but the study's research design also produced such types. Even their tools of measurement reflected military anthropometrists' normate ideals of the upright, male soldier. Physical anthropologists had used tools such as the "andrometer" to study the Mi'kmaq First Nations people (whom Gould pejoratively labeled the "Savage Natives of New Holland"), who were colonized by the French and the Dutch in present-day Quebec.[27] Gould's study appropriated this tool to measure soldiers. Subjects were required to stand in an upright posture as if at attention (Figure 2.1). But unlike Stillé, Gould was skeptical that such measurements could provide reliable data, given that "the absence of rigidity of the flesh" and "the real fluctuations of the dimensions in consequences of respiration and other involuntary motions" would increase the "magnitude of errors" in measurement, with only a sufficiently large population sample producing accuracy.[28] Any averages calculated in the study, Gould followed, were not to be applied to predictions of actual people: "though correct for the type or the mean of all, they are by no means necessarily correct for individual cases."[29] Likewise, the categories to which statistics were assigned, Gould noted, were no more than rough calculations. The conditions under which soldiers were measured, "under circumstances sufficiently varied, upon a significant number of subjects," only produced knowledge "of the form to which all individuals are approximations, although no one of them may ever have attained, or hope to attain, its accurate impersonation."[30] Although Gould's studies were embedded in scientific racism, these were hardly the claims of a positivist devoted to the unerring truth of statistical reduction.[31]

Like architects' professional expertise, scientific authority often emerges from experimental knowing-making. Many of the nineteenth-century researchers we have learned of so far had broad, nonspecialized expertise. They dabbled in new, seemingly unrelated fields. Their credentials derived from experience rather than formal degrees. Gould, too, qualified his nonexpertise as an astronomer in the relatively new field of human statistics, reporting that the results of the study were "offered with the diffidence and distrust which must necessarily accompany the results of investigations in a field entirely new to the inquirer, and regarding subjects with which the tenor of his previous pursuits had left him completely unacquainted."[32] These disclaimers illustrate epistemic flexibility, an acknowledgment that scientific knowledge refuses standardization and generalization as universal truth but may be useful for particular, applied purposes nonetheless. Gould's comments also highlight another point: that describing human differences through statistical calculations often requires distilling variation into predictable but imperfect categories, which in turn produce new ways of being.[33]

Whereas nineteenth-century anthropometrists were involved with epistemological experimentation, efforts to formalize the method in the late nineteenth and early twentieth centuries yielded conflicting imperatives toward difference and standardization. Anthropometry became formalized as a research discipline in the 1870s, with

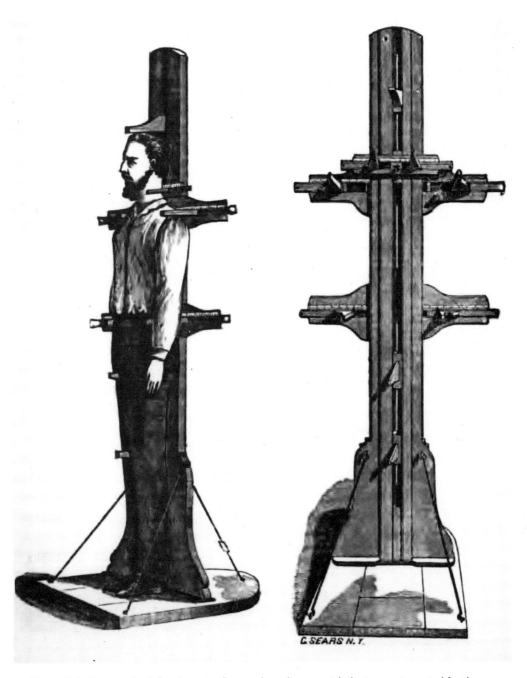

Figure 2.1. Purpose-built "andrometer," an early anthropometric instrument created for the U.S. Sanitary Commission. Benjamin Gould, *Investigations in the Military and Anthropological Statistics of American Soldiers* (1869).

international committees working to standardize statistical concepts, as well as anthropometric tools and methods.[34] The precision of measurement was the central concern of anthropometric practice at a time when international measurements, such as the meter, were only recently standardized and access to precise instruments of measurement was still limited.[35] Stadiometers, craniometers, skinfold calipers, measuring tables, and anthropometers standardized the spatial distance between body parts at increasingly sensitive scales: meter, centimeter, and millimeter, carefully marked on manufactured instruments.[36] Statisticians such as Quetelet and Galton developed "purpose-built" instruments according to needs as varied as measuring small children or skeletons.[37] These instruments of measurement, in turn, confirmed long-held beliefs about valuable embodiments.

Specific anthropometric measurements and tools demanded specific types of bodies and thus constrained research to particular "epistemic objects."[38] Standardized tools, in turn, naturalized the "military position" as the most reliable posture for linear anthropometric measurement (Figure 2.2).[39] The upright military position served as a tool of reliable measurement but also disciplined pliable and fleshy bodies into standardized anthropometric instruments.[40] This scope of military anthropometrics produced an evidence base that was entirely populated by male bodies that could stand, appear soldierly, and be amenable to discipline.

As anthropometry became increasingly scientific and professionalized in the early twentieth century, experts debated whether scientists could accurately measure non-normate bodies. Physical anthropologists and eugenicists—experts studying comparative racial anatomies—became professionalized as anthropometric experts due to their institutional and scientific legibility as dealers of precision and accuracy. Eugenicist statisticians, particularly Charles Davenport, found employment performing army anthropometrics.[41] Several studies in the early 1920s catalogued one million World War I army soldiers—"the first million drafted men sent to mobilization camps"—along with a study of "Defects Found in Drafted Men" numbering 2,510,591.[42] They documented conditions as varied as mental deficiency, astigmatism, deafness, tuberculosis, venereal disease, and pronated feet, combining the methods of military anthropometry and medico-physical examination to catalog the range of variations among soldiers, including those rejected for service.[43] Although the physical examiners at mobilization camps had not indicated soldiers' racial identification, Davenport and Love made explicitly racialized connections between the geographic distributions of certain measurements or conditions and the supposedly defective racial populations comprising those locales.[44] In the coming decades, the military hired teams of physical anthropologists from Harvard University and elsewhere to aid human factors researchers in establishing new types of measurement with functional uses for military equipment and machinery.[45]

Physical anthropologists believed that as a matter of scientific methodology, reliable anthropometry must use linear measurement of certain landmarks on the body,

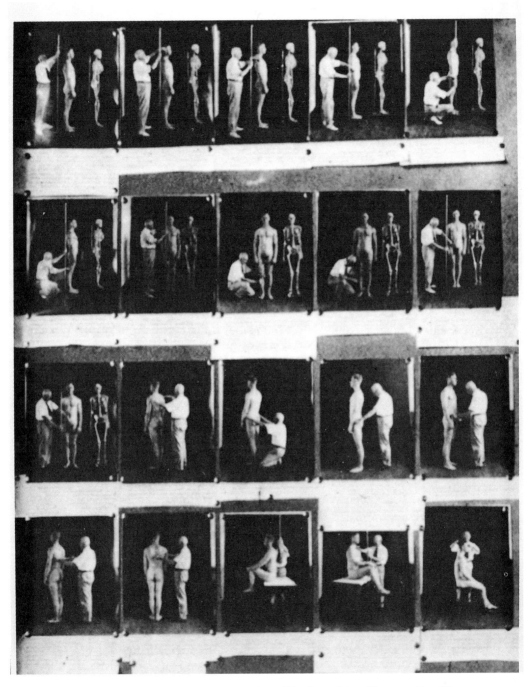

Figure 2.2. Anthropometric measurements of a solider in upright military position. Harry Laughlin, *The Second International Exhibition of Eugenics Held September 22 to October 22, 1921* (Baltimore: William & Wilkins, 1923). Wikimedia Commons.

such as the tip of the elbow or the heel of the foot. But in their estimation, bodies that did not stand, remain upright, or have these standard landmarks were not measurable with available tools or of interest for more generalizable data. Unlike military anthropometrists seeking to cull the weakest soldiers, prominent physical anthropologist Aleš Hrdlička argued that physically disabled bodies with "pathological condition[s]" and "defective constitution[s]," such as syphilis, giantism, dwarfism, microcephaly, arthritis, or other conditions affecting posture, size, and gait, would skew the measurement results and should not be anthropometric objects at all.[46] In statistical calculations of civilian populations, this omission reinforced the notion that disabled bodies simply did not exist as users.

Late twentieth- and early twenty-first-century anthropometry served as an evidence base for the emerging fields of human engineering, ergonomics, and human factors research. The more anthropometric data could reveal about variations within specific human populations, the more those populations were subject to standardization. Like industries that sought to control the unpredictable "human factor," military engineers designed weapons, armor, and uniforms that would fit specific soldiers' bodies (often by approximation) and thus reduce human error in war-fighting.[47] Flexible knowing (knowledge of a range of embodiments) and flexible design (designing for those embodiments) produced the foundations of access-knowledge.

REHABILITATING THE USER

Before exploring access-knowledge further, I want to return to the mid-nineteenth century, when another way of thinking about the user was taking hold beyond military statistical research. Nineteenth-century human sciences such as statistics, sociology, criminology, anthropology, and psychology are often understood in relation to normalization and objectification.[48] By taking statistical averages for granted as polemical norms, these fields appeared to prescribe against disability, racial otherness, and other devalued, nonnormate ways of being in the population as a whole. Another notion of the norm, which took the individual as its metric, circulated in the nineteenth century, particularly in relation to health and disability. Georges Canguilhem, in *The Normal and the Pathological,* describes this norm as concerned with the individual organism's homeostatic state.[49] Whereas statistical norms sought to align users with population standards, individual norms were more flexible, seeking only each person's return to an individual state of health. If medical diagnosis and cure enforced population norms, a return to individual homeostasis approximated the practice of rehabilitation.

When the two norms were conflated, however, returning the body to a state of normalcy would make flexibility a practice of normalization. Just before and during the U.S. Civil War, medical advancements such as antiseptics and anesthesia were increasing survival rates for bodies injured in war or work.[50] Human variation in the form of physical disability gained widespread legibility. A rehabilitation regime emerged in response, employing flexible knowledge in service of standardization.

In the 1850s the rehabilitation regime focused on assistive technologies, such as artificial limbs, which could help injured workers return to productive labor. Where simple technologies, such as peg legs, had existed before, the new artificial limbs normalized amputees' appearances with mechanical parts and aesthetic elements.[51] These new technologies also drew on emerging mechanical conceptions of human physiology, which understood bodies as energy-producing and energy-consuming machines and as objects of knowledge that experts could know in increasingly standard ways.[52] The U.S. Orthopedic Institute proclaimed in 1851 that it was "fully prepared to *invent and adapt* machinery to *every* variety of *deformity*," suggesting that prosthetics could be functional and mechanical extensions of the working body.[53] Some inventors, such as surgeon Douglas Bly, criticized mechanical knowledge as inferior to anatomical replications. Bly, who was not himself an amputee, asserted that his medical knowledge (acquired by "frequent dissections" and study of the "principles of the natural leg") made his "Bly leg" (Figure 2.3) a superior replica of the fleshy leg's natural anatomy than competing prosthetics produced by "common mechanics, and those who have undergone amputation."[54] The key was not in his medical knowledge, per se, but in the materials: rubber, ivory, cords, and an enamel finish replaced the cold, metallic interiors of other legs.

Following the Civil War, the U.S. federal government offered subsidies for the invention and manufacture of artificial limbs for injured soldiers, creating a marketplace for new innovations in prosthetics.[55] As the new technologies proliferated, inventors advertised their products by claiming their authority to know and make these devices. A primary marketing strategy emphasized the inventor's skill and knowledge of human bodily function rather than knowledge of comfort and usability (two concepts that would dominate twentieth-century user-centered design). In advertisements for artificial limbs directed at civilians reentering work as well as social life, assertions about mechanical knowledge and skill were common. Prominent New York City prosthetics manufacturer A. A. Marks advertised its artificial limbs as tools for amputees to pass as nondisabled, showing in advertisements that amputees could use prosthetics to conceal their bodies and instead convey middle-class status (Figure 2.4).[56] Before the company rose to prominence, it first developed standards for measurement and functional fit based on emerging human factors and rehabilitation principles. In an 1867 pamphlet directed at users of its "India rubber hands and feet," the company explained that well-fitting limbs required precise and standard measurements. "Persons cannot be too careful in taking measures," the company warned, "and they cannot well make mistakes if they adhere STRICTLY to the directions which are PLAINLY stated upon every blank."[57] With proper measures,

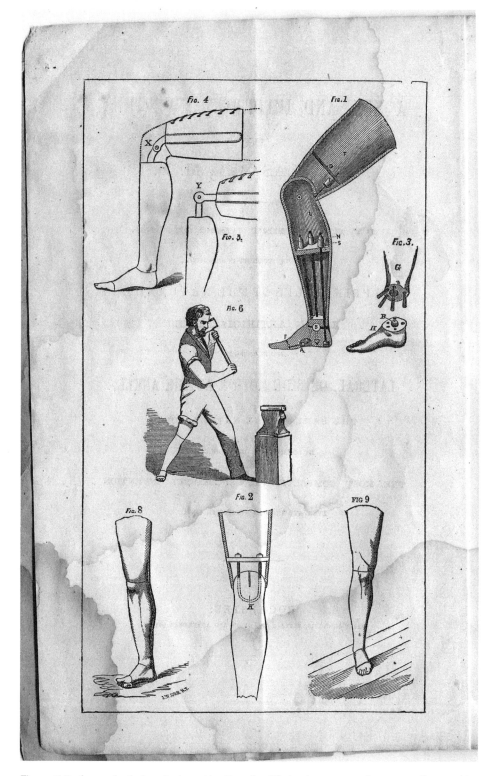

Figure 2.3. A prosthetic leg designed by Douglas Bly is shown worn, bent, standing, and in section (1858). Courtesy of Warshaw Collection of Business Americana, Archives Center, National Museum of American History, Smithsonian Institute.

A. A. Marks could fit artificial limbs to even the most geographically distant users ordering by post, suggesting that standard measurements enabled bespoke fit without a user appearing in the flesh.

While nondisabled inventors such as Bly argued that their designs followed cutting-edge scientific knowledge, and whereas A. A. Marks encouraged amputees to fit into standardized increments of size and shape, amputees also invented artificial limbs, appealing to their own experiential knowledge with amputation as evidence that their designs were superior to those of competitors. These inventors identified disability as a resource rather than a deficit. Disabled inventor James Foster wrote:

> I claim to be the only PATENTEE and MANUFACTURER in America (perhaps in the world) who wears a full length artificial leg and who was a practical mechanician

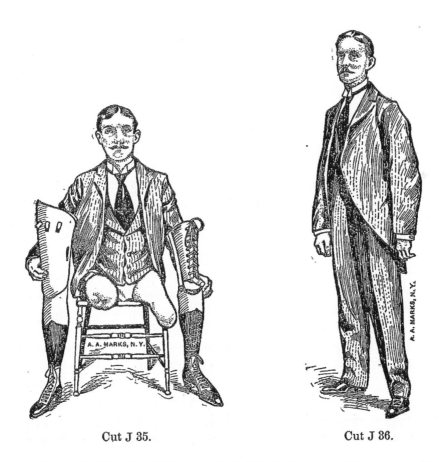

Cut J 35.   Cut J 36.

Figure 2.4. Upright citizenship: "Before" and "after" illustrations of a white man, a double amputee displaying his prosthetic legs and then concealing them beneath a three-piece suit. A. A. Marks, *Manual of Artificial Limbs: Copiously Illustrated* (New York: A. A. Marks, 1905), 112.

at the time of amputation, and that no other manufacturer has had the same facilities for experimenting with and improving artificial limbs that I have had, for I served a regular apprenticeship and was a practical mechanic before I lost my limb (which was amputated in February, 1860), and since which time I have had a thorough practical experience with other manufacturers of artificial limbs.[58]

Responding to the sentiments of Bly and others, Foster argued that disability credentialed him in mechanical knowledge, as well as the lived experience of being a prosthetics user. Disabled people, in other words, were not mere objects for inventors and physicians to study; they were also inventors with superior knowledge of the body. Foster's counterknowledge to the dominance of anatomical paradigms, measurement practices, and biomedical expert cultures reveal the fine gradations of medical, functional, and social knowledge in the rehabilitation regime. These were subtle but powerful distinctions that carried forth in the twentieth century as knowledge about the disabled body would become contested terrain in human factors research, industrial design practice, and the rise of the disability rights movement.

A shift came at the beginning of the twentieth century, when manufacturers used social and aesthetic appeals to market artificial limbs as consumer objects. The legibility of single categories of users (such as soldiers, workers, or amputees) gave way to an expansive understanding of difference as the rehabilitation regime merged with civilian life. A. A. Marks' prosthetic devices had been an early example of flexible designs without direct military or industrial application. As mentioned above, in previous decades, the company worked to standardize ranges of measurement for mail order prosthetics sent primarily to Civil War veterans, its early clients. From this data, the company designed prosthetics fitting ranges of stump sizes and locations. Data on disabled veterans' stumps consequently informed their late nineteenth- and early twentieth-century designs, which were personalized to individual users based on approximation to these standard measurements.

While prosthetics functioned mechanically and required fitting to individual users, they also performed other kinds of social and aesthetic work. By 1905 A. A. Marks claimed to be the nation's largest manufacturer and mail order supplier of artificial limbs. In its *Manual of Artificial Limbs: Copiously Illustrated,* a book-length, "exhaustive exposition of prosthesis," the company advertised "artificial toes, feet, legs, fingers, hands, arms for amputations and deformities," and "appliances for excisions, fractures, and other disabilities of lower and upper extremities."[59] User testimony, coupled with lifelike drawings (often from photographs) of both actual clients and imagined users, comprised the bulk of the catalog. Many of A. A. Marks' advertisements claimed that rehabilitation devices could render amputees as upright citizens of "polite society," as Stephen Mihm has shown (see Figure 2.4).[60] Disability technology consequently became a form of fashion and a desirable marker of social status—in other words, a lifestyle brand. This branding took for granted, however, that disability is a deficit in need of correction. Its advertisements suggested that a fashionable prosthetic could remedy the supposed deficit of disability by offering enhancement beyond a user's prior socioeconomic coordinates.

Despite reaffirming norms of able-bodiedness and middle-class status, however, the A. A. Marks catalog exploded the representation of normate white, male, and previously able-bodied types, as if to suggest that there was a prosthetic device for everyone. Promotional illustrations suggested that every type of person—not just male soldiers—could benefit from A. A. Marks' designs by regaining access to public life and recreation. For instance, young men could ride bicycles and ice skate and women could regain access to preparing food (Figure 2.5). But the catalog relied on typecast legibility and reductive, often stereotypical depictions of race, gender, and class. Wearing A. A. Marks, it promised, would enable white women to enact the supposedly gender-appropriate activities of cooking and letter-writing. The growing legibility of disabled (white) women as users of assistive technologies thus married the cultural understanding of women as homemakers and consumers, nearly always depicted using kitchens.[61] Likewise, (white) men were depicted as engaging in stereotypically masculine activities, such as chopping wood with axes, rowing boats, serving drinks, bicycling, ice skating, and playing cards.[62] As A. A. Marks' depictions of amputees extended the reach of rehabilitation into social life, they simultaneously reinforced cultural dynamics of power and privilege.

Particularly vexing are the *Manual*'s representations of race. While most of the amputees depicted appear white, the catalog's most conspicuous image shows Ceca Yammi, a Sioux Indian man, wearing an A. A. Marks leg on his left side (Figure 2.6). The line-drawn portrait depicts Yammi in a full headdress, holding both a tomahawk and a pistol. The accompanying testimony, attributed to Yammi, celebrates the artificial leg as "an example of what the 'White Medicine Man' can do for [the Sioux] people."[63] This striking image of racial diversity, however, likely reinforced white audiences' expectations of indigenous people as both inherently warlike and (when assimilated) thankful for the "White Medicine Man." While every other testimony in the *Manual* was written directly by its user, Yammi is spoken for by his physician, the "White Medicine Man," in a double-imposition of medical and racial authority. Given that practices such as anthropometry and comparative racial science were still prevalent during this time, Yammi's status as an object of description by a self-identified white male medical expert reveals that hierarchies of race and ability influenced assistive technologies and their marketing, despite their attention to individuals rather than populations.

DESIGNING PRODUCTIVE CITIZENS

Early twentieth-century technologies of mass production relied on knowledge of users as a diverse range rather than an average. This reliance was as much material as

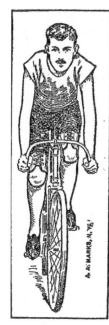

Cut J 26.

Cut J 27.

* MRS. E. E. ABEL—Housewife, Ontario. Knee amputation.
I am very thankful for the leg made me·from measurements last

October. I do all my housework and a lot of walking and I have
never used a cane or anything, and I can walk without any trouble.
April 25, 1904.

Figure 2.5. Male prosthetics users are depicted as engaged in leisure, such as
cycling, and women, such as Mrs. E. E. Abel, are shown cooking food on the
stove while wearing an artificial leg. A. A. Marks, *Manual of Artificial Limbs:
Copiously Illustrated* (New York: A. A. Marks, 1905), 109, 258.

Figure 2.6. Ceca Yammi, a Sioux Indian man, wears a headdress and an artificial leg. A. A. Marks, *Manual of Artificial Limbs: Copiously Illustrated* (New York: A. A. Marks, 1905), 289.

it was epistemological. A. A. Marks disclosed its production processes via a section drawing of its factory, which proclaims, through a quote from the *Scientific American*, the company's international industrial leadership (Figure 2.7). A potential disabled consumer—an amputee on crutches—stands on a sidewalk peering into the factory's ground-floor shop window. The building appears in section, cut down the middle, revealing seven floors of other users: workers, along with machines, in the complex choreography of efficient labor. Whether engaged in productive labor or dutiful consumption, A. A. Marks' depiction of bodies, machines, and architectural space makes legible the relations of knowing-making at play within the "black box" of the factory.

While the factory produces technologies for a diverse range of users, the drawing also illustrates the entangled work of other late nineteenth- and early twentieth-century regimes of standardization: architectural functionalism, mechanical and biomedical conceptions of the body, and scientific management. Built to return disabled soldiers to productive labor, many early twentieth-century prosthetics were "industrial tool holder[s]," which plugged workers' bodies directly into factory machines.[64] These devices also symbolized the place of the worker (as itself a machine) in the design of industrial labor. Scientific managers and industrial engineers, such as Frederick Winslow Taylor, believed that more effectively designed systems of labor could overcome differences between workers and create more standardized products. Taylor, a mechanical engineer, described the practice of efficient industrial production as "true science, resting upon clearly defined laws, rules, and principles" and "applicable to all kinds of human activities."[65] Like their eugenicist contemporaries, Taylor and his followers were disinterested in the average person or worker, who they considered to be slow-moving and lazy. Instead, they sought to transform environmental contexts and systems to create more efficient, productive workers.[66] Knowing such a worker would require quantifying labor itself.

Early twentieth-century mechanical engineers considered the human factor and flexible design for users as necessary points of intervention in industrial systems.[67] In the 1910s, James Hartness (president of the American Society of Mechanical Engineers and Taylor's contemporary) called for attention to the "human factor" in order to guarantee "success of the organization, or industry, or nation"; scientific management, he believed, could achieve these goals through "proper use of the human being, especially as regards modes of employment of mind and body."[68] Hartness considered users' bodies as engineerable tools (similar to machines). But human factors engineering was not an unfeeling practice of inserting cogs into a system. The human user's "welfare" and "relationship to other men and his environment in general," Hartness emphasized, were necessary for the efficient operation of productive machines.[69] The "human factor" thus became synonymous with the effective mobilization of social and built environments to produce more efficient users.

But what does it mean to "engineer" human needs and their differences? For Hartness, users were not an undifferentiated mass of bodies, nor was their standardization

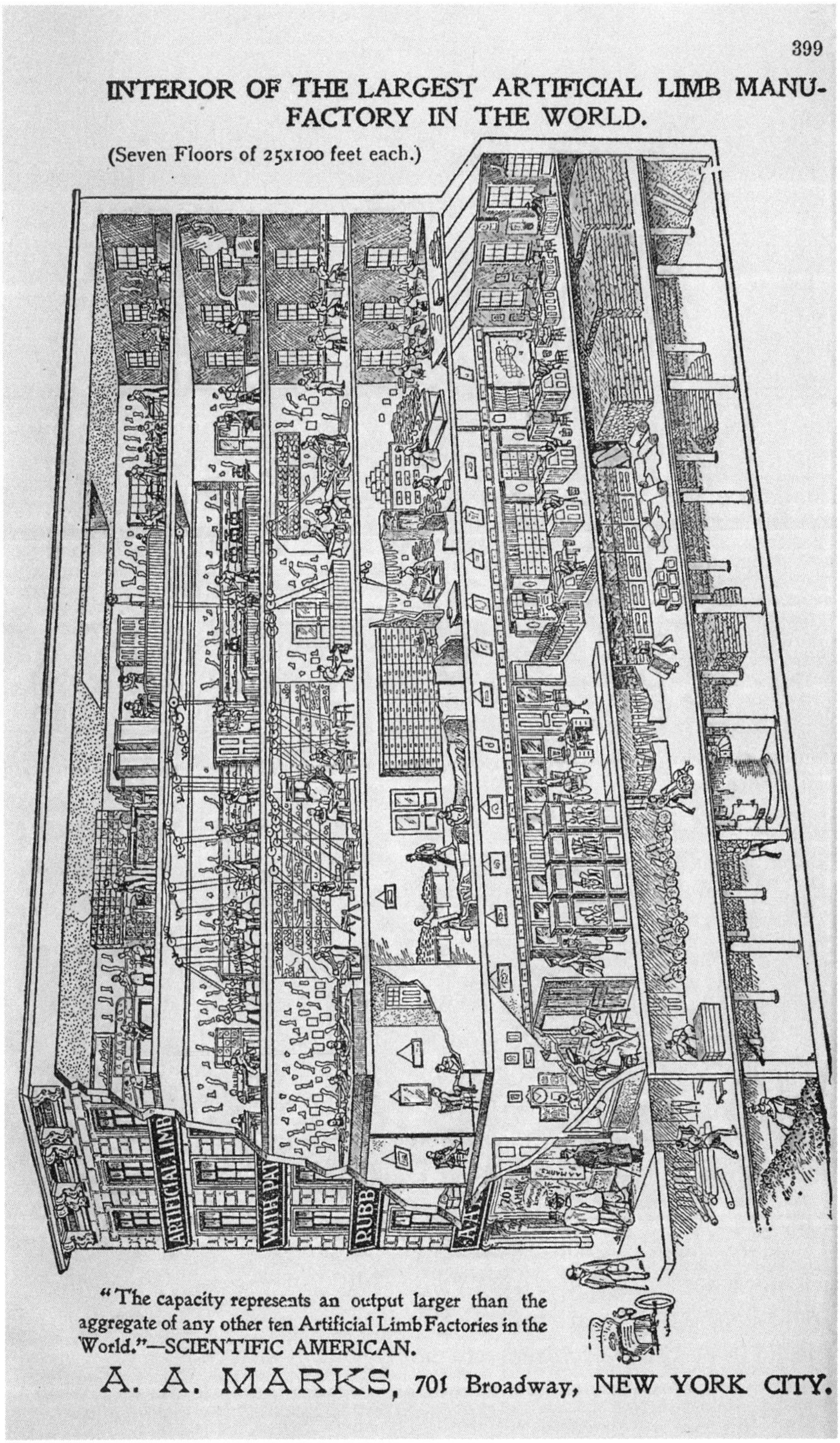

Figure 2.7. Section diagram of the "Interior of the Largest Artificial Limb Manufactory in the World," showing various stages of the production process across seven floors. A. A. Marks, *Manual of Artificial Limbs: Copiously Illustrated* (New York: A. A. Marks, 1905), 431.

necessarily desirable. In response to Taylor, who mechanized labor and increased the speed of work, Hartness believed that users operated on inherently different temporalities. They had their own normal states. "We know," he argued, "that there are all kinds of minds and all kinds of bodies. . . . Both the so-called lazy and energetic are alike following nature's law. . . . Both extremes are on the earth, and there should be a way by which each might be placed where his peculiar characteristics will render the best results to himself."[70] The answer to such divergence was not to invest in the average or typical "set of habits of users" but to allow users to "get back to [their own] nature" through design that is better attuned to users' perception and cognition.[71]

Harkness was apparently in the minority, however. As World War I began, time and motion became concepts through which users' bodies could be studied and engineered. Industrial engineers Frank and Lillian Gilbreth employed time-motion studies of workers that documented the temporalities of tasks to propose "methods of least waste"—a middle ground between Taylor and Hartness.[72] Standardizing movements across all bodies was not the goal. Rather, methods of least waste produced efficiency according to individual norms.[73] Lillian Gilbreth proposed that the unit of measurement for scientific management should be "the individual and his work"; she noted that "functionalization is based upon utilizing the particular powers and special abilities of each man. Measurement is of the individual and his work."[74] But flexibility toward a worker's peculiarities also relied on standardization. The Gilbreths understood the user's body as "a subject for scientific study and for scientific administration," with individual "idiosyncrasies" serving as legible categories of "efficient deviations," which managers repurpose into other parts of the system.[75]

Toward the end of World War I, scientific management extended its flexible orientation regarding individual workers toward the changing face of human embodiment, particularly disability.[76] The "war cripple" and the "industrial cripple," Frank Gilbreth argued, "constitute elements seriously to be considered in the great problem of [military and industrial] preparedness."[77] Scientific managers adopted elements of both flexibility and standardization to transform disabled people (whom they understood as ready and malleable bodies) into more productive workers through practices of vocational rehabilitation,[78] or what Henri-Jacques Stiker calls "vocational redeployment."[79] Consequently, assistive devices, such as prosthetics, were employed in the service of standard mechanical labor.[80] If disabled veterans could access these technologies and have fewer barriers in their work environments, Frank Gilbreth argued, they would be become full citizens and participants in society.[81]

In the interwar period, scientific management, military human factors research, and rehabilitation were nearly indistinguishable.[82] The Gilbreths led the push for integrating disabled users into human factors research, which they believed would enable home-front industrial production for the war machine.[83] As they described it, "No definite and permanent advance is made with any kind of work, whether with materials or men, until use is made of measurement. This is especially true of the advancement of the human factor in industry."[84] In their *Motion Study for the Handicapped,* the Gilbreths' concepts of the "One Best Way" and "methods of least waste" espoused the values of standardized work and uniformity.[85] But rather than frame a single, normate body as the ideal laborer, the "One Best Way" sought enhanced human performance for disabled and nondisabled people.[86] The Gilbreths argued that the best methods of vocational and industrial efficiency "were similar for all handicapped—soldiers and civilians alike. They apply equally well to the maimed and the blinded. They involve determining the One Best Way to do work and teaching it through the most efficient learning process."[87] Disabled workers could use adaptations, such as those described in a "Simultaneous Motion Cycle Chart," to align their productivity with the "One Best Way."[88] These acknowledgments of the inevitability of human variation recalled earlier notions of the "human factor" as an unpredictable element of industrial systems, as well as rehabilitation practices of using adaptive technologies to fit the user to the system. While the Gilbreths portrayed these concepts as objective and scientific, standard methods of production were closely linked to the political and cultural goals of assimilating disabled veterans and civilians into mainstream life, an agenda driven by the imperative to overcome the supposed deficits of disabled embodiment and not by acceptance of difference.[89]

Citizenship became contingent on productive labor, as determined by the science of work, in the early twentieth century. At the intersection of human factors, rehabilitation, and scientific management, early disability rights discourses were entrenched in notions of productive citizenship, as defined by a person's amenability to both rehabilitation and enhancement. The worker, the machine operator, the soldier, the consumer, and the citizen of leisure shared this status as engineered, malleable sites. And many experts in scientific management, rehabilitation, and human factors came to understand themselves as disability rights advocates. When the rehabilitation regime introduced new preferred terminology for impairment, the Gilbreths promoted the (now-defunct) term "handicapped" in place of (the Civil War–era term) "crippled."[90] The difference between "cripples" and the "handicapped," they explained, was that the latter "ha[d] become a recognized part of the industrial community,—welcomed and admired, an element that stands for both progress and maintenance."[91] The price of belonging was mere productivity.

In liberal democracies, citizens often receive qualification based on their demonstrated independence and autonomy. Disqualified citizens are often those whose perceived dependency and simultaneous failure to assimilate cast them as nonproductive and therefore failing to uphold the duties of citizenship.[92] Near the end of World War II, Lillian Gilbreth expanded the insights of the "One Best Way" by collaborating with others to write self-help texts for disabled civilians and emphasizing employment access as crucial to disability rights and equality.[93] Rehabilitation specialists, such as Howard Rusk and Eugene Taylor, echoed the Gilbreths' insistence on the citizenship of populations framed as "war cripples" and "industry cripples," arguing that "comprehensive rehabilitation programs have been established in the armed forces and the veterans administration. The disabled civilian, in a democracy, deserves the same opportunity."[94] In the discourse of self-help, citizenship involves taking advantage of the opportunities one is provided, particularly medical therapies and vocational rehabilitation. National belonging, in other words, is the right to be rehabilitated.

DESIGNING FOR USERS

If rehabilitation is, as disability historians David Serlin and Anna Carden-Coyne suggest, a project of postwar economic and spatial construction, premised on returning the body to a supposed state of normalcy in order to "restore," "rebuild," and "reconstruct" the nation, then what cultural preferences did this regime inject into U.S. environments and political economies? How did these preferences relate to established ways of knowing human variation and making in response to it? And what role have those preferences had in shaping twentieth-century discourses of disability rights and user-centered design?[95]

By the post–World War II era, the discourse of the "user," the "human factor," and "ergonomics" had existed for over a century in U.S. and European industrial, scientific, and military contexts. Wars had introduced new types of embodiment and funded new research in increasingly specialized areas of expert study, and the results of this research had shaped not only the engineered systems of work but also the social relations of liberal belonging. Users could now be workers, consumers, housewives, men of leisure, and citizens, but the price they paid was flexibility toward regimes of human engineering.

The two world wars, like the Civil War, produced new fields of scientific expertise in relation to the body and disability. "Human performance" experts, including the Gilbreths, served as consultants for research on the operational management of military bodies.[96] Along with its preference for able-bodied and able-minded soldiers, the military adopted an industrial emphasis on efficiency and productivity.[97] Bridging military, industry, and civilian consumption, human factors researchers drew on a wide range of disciplinary knowledge before the field formalized in the 1950s. In the 1930s, for instance, "the functional specifications for the first pressure-cabin aircraft were written by a flight surgeon."[98] But as the effects of aviation technologies on the body, particularly in relation to gravity, acceleration, and altitude, became measurable, new fields of expertise emerged to study these effects on specific bodies, generalize them to wider populations, and devise better practices for design and engineering.[99]

Although human factors research apparently sought the greater good, the fields' ties to eugenics—a project of culling so-called defectives from the population— remained close. Industrial managers and eugenicists alike influenced the development of human factors as a science, which laid claim to users' bodies as sources of evidence about human variation.[100] In the 1920s, military-funded university laboratories led by Charles Davenport and Albert Love aided in the collection of human factors data about soldiers' bodily dimensions, data that extended Gould's studies to one hundred thousand twentieth-century users.[101] Population-level knowing, in turn, enabled flexible, user-centered design. Military anthropometrics translated, for instance, into a flexible range of twenty-two clothing sizes for soldiers based on height, chest, and waist measurements but also enabled the army to fully standardize equipment, uniforms, and training environments across users.[102] By the late twentieth century, human factors research would expand into all U.S. military branches, each proliferating efforts to harness the human factor for maximum efficiency and warfighting capability.[103] Donning bellicose names such as the army's "MANPRINT," the air force's "IMPACTS," and the navy's "HARDMAN," new research programs would require that contractors "increase their staffs to include [human factors] specialists."[104] The boundaries between military and civilian human factors research, blurred in previous decades by the involvement of eugenicists and rehabilitation researchers, would become further entangled with the introduction of research into civilian commercial uses, such as aircraft design.[105] In effect, the project of *knowing* users for the purpose of *engineering* efficient systems would become its own expert industry.

Similar to nineteenth-century industrial research, twentieth-century human factors research was entangled with industrial trends (namely the rise of consumerism). Civilian-focused industrial designers in the interwar period called for a "broad conception of consumer desire" and argued that designers ought to "know who the ultimate consumer is likely to be."[106] Consequently, anthropometric measurements of women's bodies determined clothing sizes based on standard deviations.[107] World War II anthropometrics had an even more potent effect on civilian design, however. In the late 1940s, data on soldiers' aptitudes and uses of technology were published for general civilian application.[108] American industrial designer Henry Dreyfuss used this data to craft a new approach for user-centered design in *The Measure of Man* (1960), a portfolio that translated statistics into diagrams of the human figure, first Joe and then Josephine.[109] Just five years later, in 1965, U.S. audiences gained access to K. F. H. Murrell's "human performance in industry," which detailed ergonomics as design for the "range of the population for which the equipment is intended," including design that considers particularities such as the "sex of the user."[110] Murrell understood the user as flexible and adaptive. "Unlike a machine," he wrote, "a person can change his role rapidly and frequently."[111] This was the hallmark of "man's flexibility" to the environment, a flexibility that put the onus of change on the body rather than the environment itself.[112] While Murrell's view of flexibility appeared to contrast with flexible consumer-oriented designs, such as ready-made clothing, these perspectives were two sides of the same coin: efforts to know the range of diverse users in turn standardized the knowable universe and yielded multiple, but standard, user-centered designs.

Chapter 3

All Americans

Disability, Race, and Segregated Citizenship

All standards which will be recommended to benefit the permanently handicapped will be of benefit to everyone.

—TIMOTHY NUGENT, "Design of Buildings to Permit Their Use by the Physically Handicapped"

What has changed since the collapse of Jim Crow has less to do with the basic structure of our society than with the language we use to justify it. . . . We have not ended racial caste in America; we have merely redesigned it.

—MICHELLE ALEXANDER, *The New Jim Crow*

On February 12, 1946, Isaac Woodward, an African American World War II veteran on his way home to Goldsboro, North Carolina, was arrested for disorderly conduct. His crime was asking a bus driver to stop for a restroom in the Jim Crow South. As police officers transported Woodward to the rural South Carolina jail, they beat him so severely that he became blind.[1] National attention to the beating of Isaac Woodward framed the racist violence of Jim Crow laws through the tragedy of incapacitation. The consequence of racism, in other words, was disability. Following pressure from the NAACP, President Harry S. Truman delivered a public address supporting civil rights for African Americans. "It is more important today than ever before," he said, "to insure that all Americans enjoy these rights. When I say all Americans I mean all Americans."[2] Truman's words referenced the tensions between "separate but equal" citizenship and the foundational premise of the U.S. liberal rights regime: that "all men are created equal." But while his rhetoric acknowledged a divided nation, Truman's "all" appeared to reference Woodward's race as a category of identity and citizenship but not his disability.

In 1948 the University of Illinois at Galesburg established a vocational rehabilitation and education program for injured soldiers, funded by the G.I. Bill.[3] Thirteen white, disabled students lived in a barely used, one-story army rehabilitation center for one school year, until plans to establish a medical institution for "the aged and infirm" threatened to close the program (Figure 3.1).[4] In response, the students organized a march at the Illinois state capitol.

The march utilized symbols of disabled veterans' belonging in normal, U.S. consumer and civilian life: "twenty-plus paraplegic-driven cars," accompanied by prominent disabled veterans' organizations, approached the capitol building with their demands.[5] A police motorcade guided the protestors, stopping to "salute" the cars at every block.[6] Upon their arrival, most of the students could not access the building's staired entrance and had to use a side door to attend meetings with state officials.[7] Considered by some as one of the first public disability protests in the United States, just two years after police brutality against Isaac Woodward, the protest hid in plain view the racially divided consequences of demanding access to public space.

Although the protesters' demands were not immediately met, the Galesburg program, and the Rehabilitation Education Center at the University of Illinois at Urbana-Champaign that followed, were part of the postwar reorganization of disabled belonging in built environments, a national project of expanding citizenship for some in the name of access for all. Initially, access-knowledge produced through fields such as rehabilitation and gerontology pinpointed disabled users as *objects* of research. In the late 1940s, rehabilitation experts at the University of Michigan's Institute for Human Adjustment began holding national conferences on rehabilitation and labor for the "Handicapped Worker over Forty" and "Housing the Aging."[8] Rehabilitation and gerontology extended the regime of the flexible user into civilian life, joining disability and aging into a category of "functional limitation," which referenced the body's misfitting relationship to its milieu as a deficit. The new category and the field of rehabilitation research enabled a new practice of barrier-free architectural design. But while "functional limitation" appeared to be a very specific category, advocates for barrier-free design argued that "all Americans" would benefit from more inclusive environments.

This chapter traces the rise of barrier-free design in the mid-twentieth-century United States. Approaching this phenomenon through histories of systemic racism, the human sciences, and architecture, I argue that in the civil rights era, the growing political legibility of particular nonnormate users was contingent upon their scientific legibility as productive, white spatial citizens. Histories of barrier-free design tend to address the rise of accessibility codes and standards, laws, or examples of designed products and spaces. Instead, I address material rhetorics, or how words, claims, documents, research practices, and images accumulate in (what appear to be) static laws and hegemonic standards. Using the idea that barrier-free design benefits "all Americans" as a touchstone, I examine how the term "all" shaped the figure of the disabled user in relation to norms of race, gender, class, and age.[9]

A contemporary narrative insists that barrier-free design revolves around a limited population of users with "functional limitations," often through "narrow code compliance to meet the specialized needs of a few [disabled people]," while Universal Design

THE GALESBURG ILLINI

VOLUME 3—NUMBER 20   THE UNIVERSITY OF ILLINOIS, GALESBURG—FRIDAY, MARCH 25, 1949   EIGHT CENTS

DIVISION TO CLOSE

Tim Nugent, representative for the disabled students of the Galesburg Division, confers with Dr. Andrew Ivy, vice president of the University of Illinois and Fred K. Hoehler, state director of public welfare in the State House at Springfield in a futile attempt to gain access to the Governor. Hoehler's department will head the medical center for aged and infirm which will occupy the present site of the Division. Those present in the photograph reading from left to right are Tim Nugent, Dr. Andrew Ivy, and Fred Hoehler.
—Photo by Gil Salter.

WHEELCHAIR VETS TREK TO SPRINGFIELD IN VAIN EFFORT TO KEEP DIVISION OPEN

By KEITH ROBERTS and RAY CRIGGER

A group of more than thirty students, including fifteen paraplegic and poliomyelitis wheelchair victims, travelled in convoy to Springfield last Wednesday to plead with the governor to consider their future schooling opportunities in light of the fact that the Division is soon to be converted into a Public Welfare Medical Center.

Although the Division representatives were escorted to the governor's mansion and later to the State House by the screaming sireens of the Springfield Police department, all they received in return for their efforts was Governor Stevenson's flat refusal to listen to their views.

The Governor left the mansion while the Divisionites waited on the sidewalk outside and later appeared on the second floor of the State House where the students were waiting nearby in a departmental office. However, in neither instance did Governor Stevenson greet the group which consisted largely of disabled veterans.

Previous Engagements

Because of the press of previous engagements, Governor Stevenson, who spoke Monday at the dedication of a new building of the Pabst brewery in Peorin, assigned the task to one of his executive secretaries, Mr. Lou Conn, who turned the group over to Fred K. Hoehler, director of the Public Welfare Department which will maintain the medical center replacing the Galesburg school in June, and to Dr. Andrew Ivy, vice president of the University.

In answer to question from the student representatives, Mr. Conn revealed that the Governor was not well acquainted with the rehabilitation program here for disabled students. Consequently, he was also completely unaware of the tremendous progress that has been made through the medium of

the program since its initiation in October, 1948. Nevertheless, it decision regarding the closing of the Division and the consequent termination of the only complete program in the nation of corrective therapy and rehabilitation that is integrated with a collegiate institution and is available to wheelchair cases.

Results Unsatisfactory

When the results of this meeting proved unsatisfactory to the Division students, a sub-committee was formed to further consult the representatives of the administration on this matter and to again try to bring the case before the Governor rather than one of his executive secretaries.

This committee, consisting of Don Swift, president of the Disabled Students Organization; Harold Scharper, George Steinmann, Rurss Gates, president of the Student Senate; Al Kuhn, representative of the student body; Tim Nugent, director of the Galesburg Division rehabilitation program; and Keith Roberts, news editor of the Galesburg ILLINI, met with Mr. Koehler and Dr. Ivy, vice president of the University.

Dr. Ivy indicated that although there are approximately one thousand cases of paraplegia each year as a result of civilian accidents or various types in addition to the present large number of such cases as a lt of the recent conflict, tha   need for the college educatio of these individuals

is the responsibility of the federal government rather than that of the state of Illinois.

Plans Discussed

Mr. Hoehler declared that arrangements will be made if possible for those disabled students now in attendance at the Division. Various plans discussed included the completion of two years of college work by correspondence or the establishment of an "isolated ward" for paraplegic students in conjunction with the new medical center for the aged and infirm which is to be established on the present school site.

Such a program is only designed to meet the needs of those disabled students who have already begun their education, not ot provide facilities for other handicapped students who not yet entered school.

Ivy Suggests

Dr. Ivy suggested that there might be a possibility that the Navy Pier branch of the university would at some future date be able to handle disabled students on its campus. He further recommended that the Division paraplegic students attempt to make some arrangement for their further schooling through a federal agency.

The representatives of this campus were told that the Governor's refusal to see them was partly as a result of their failure to secure an appointment with him in advance. However, after this group had been denied the opportunity of consulting with the Governor even briefly, Representative Kenneth Peel stated that he had spent three hours Tuesday attempting to secure such an audience for the group. Senator Wallace Thompson, a local resident, also unsuccessfully attempted to obtain a appointment for the disabled students with the Governor.

LOUTTIT ANNOUNCES DIVISION CLOSING TO STUDENT BODY

By BARBARA MADDEN

In his speech Wednesday, announcing the July, 1949, closing of the Galesburg Division, Dean C. M. Louttit urged, "You members of the student body should not allow yourselves to slack off on your studies just because the Division is closing. By doing so you may jeopardize your standing when it comes to transferring to Champaign next fall."

At the beginning of his speech, Dean Louttit expressed regret at the closing, but later explained that the circumstances had pointed to no other solution. Although three weeks ago, President George D. Stoddard of the University had announced that the Division would continue in operation until June, 1950, the situation had been changed by a phone call from Gov. Adlai Stevenson.

Governor Requests

Stevenson asked President Stoddard last week if it would be injurious to the University of Illinois to close the Galesburg branch in June, 1949. Since Stoddard's answer was no, the Governor stated that he would have to ask the U. of I. to withdraw because pressure to do something about the crowded conditions of state institutions was so strong.

The Welfare Department of the State of Illinois is planning to use this plant to relieve some of the burden carried by our over-crowded state hospitals, as a research center for medical care of the aged.

Students Have Priority

It was at this point in the address that Dean Louttit remarked that he believed that the trip by the paraplegic students to Springfield in a last-minute effort to have the Division continued was a lost cause. Louttit quoted Stoddard as saying that special teachers would be hired to help the disabled students to complete their two-year courses, if they were not able to attend classes at Urbana.

As a note of cheer, Louttit announced that Galesburg students with satisfactory grades will have priority in Urbana. Details concerning transfers will be released as soon as possible, probably through advisors.

He also reasured the married students living in the blockhouses that they would not be required to vacate their apartments immediately at the end of school, but would probably be allowed to remain until the end of the summer.

Stoddard Cites Evidence For Div. Closing

The Governor discussed with me the proposed closing of the Galesburg Undergraduate Division as of June 30, 1949. I had previously suggested as preferable the closing of Galesburg in June, 1950. Under agreement with the War Assets Administration and the Department of Public Welfare, the University acquired the facility in the Fall of 1946 on a three-year lease, subject to a two-year renewal provided a six months' warning were given.

As the Governor has pointed out, the need for more space in the hospitals of the State is critical. It is recognized that the facilities at Galesburg are adapted to the care of aged and infirm patients.

It should be possible to reduce the operating budget of the University by nearly $2,000,000 for the coming biennium. All the staff members on tenure will, of course, be transferred to the University at Urbana-Champaign or to Navy Pier. A high priority will be given to other staff members who desire to transfer to one of these campuses. It is probable that the students who have finished one year at Galesburg can be taken care of at the Navy Pier Division or Urbana-Champaign. There is, however, a small number of disabled veterans who cannot use the facilities in Chicago or Urbana. Dean Louttit is working on a special plan whereby such veterans may complete the second year's work by correspondence or extension if they so desire.

George D. Stoddard, President,
University , ,Illinois.

Galesburg Division representatives, including wheelchair students, assembled outside of the Governor's mansion Wednesday morning immediately after trip from Galesburg. Police escort stands by.
—Photo by Winston

Figure 3.1. Cover of the *Galesburg Illini* reporting that the program for disabled students is to close. Pictured at bottom right are students and faculty from the University of Illinois at Galesburg waiting outside the governor's mansion. *Galesburg Illini*, March 25, 1949. Courtesy of the University of Illinois Archives.

offers "a more inclusive design process for everybody."[10] These claims presume the historical stability and internal coherence of both approaches, while also treating the question of antinormative design as racially neutral. Terms such as "all" and "everyone" are not mere mathematical calculations or conditions of thoughtless ignorance, however. They are material rhetorics that appeal to ideas of valuable scale and population. From design for a "broad" range of human variation to calls for eschewing "narrow" or "singular" approaches to accessibility, these scalar distinctions define who counts as a user and through what forms of evidence designers purport to know.

THE PARTICULARITIES OF "ALL"

A common understanding of racism in the late twentieth and early twenty-first centuries dictates that oppression is a bias—something in the mind—that greater awareness and education can alleviate. But historians have shown that racism, often attributed to attitudes, is also a material arrangement, a pattern of "racial making," as Elizabeth Hale puts it, which produces whiteness as a neutral, unmarked default through a "culture of segregation," two key aspects of which have been rules and symbols in the built environment, such as Jim Crow–era "whites only" signs.[11] Integrated with racial making, however, is racial knowing. As Chris Bell and other scholars of race and disability have pointed out, default, neutralized, and unmarked presumptions of whiteness often characterize how disability and its history are known.[12] How we think about and study disability, in other words, often takes for granted that disabled people are white and that whiteness is a neutral condition of contemporary life.

As a reference to included or potentially includable populations in the twentieth century, the term "all" was entwined with racialized ways of knowing-making. In Truman's example, we find that the term "all" unsettles a presumed norm, and thus serves a critical purpose. In this sense, "all" is an epistemological category, a term that shapes a population to be known as more than singular. As a category describing populations, the term almost always appears in reference to either political populations (such as citizens and nations) or embodied populations (characterized through shared biological or physical traits). In the nineteenth and twentieth centuries, for instance, proponents of scientific racism positioned race as an indelible biological category, understood as nature, but geneticists and anthropologists in the 1940s challenged these biologically essentialist views of race by proposing that "All Mankind Is One Family."[13] Here, "all" served as a neutralizing term, which sought to smooth out the effects of historical differentiation, but in doing so imposed a more universal category of sameness. The scientists' responses embodied what critical race scholars such as Michelle Alexander characterize as post-racial ideologies, often termed "race-neutral" or "color-blind."[14] In their insistence upon biological sameness as evidence that race is a myth, these ideologies often elide the historical, material, and sociocultural frictions of racialized experience, particularly as they manifest in unequal accumulations of wealth and power. Whether racial difference can be measured in biological terms, racial inequality has materialized through systems of colonialism, slavery, and segregation, which produce racial difference as a mechanism to control and exploit nonwhite bodies.[15] The use of the term "all" to describe genetic sameness, then, is a way of knowing-making a certain understanding of race. Similar to what Charles Mills terms an "epistemology of ignorance," the term "all" is a materially arranged condition of knowing that renders the privileged status of whiteness as smooth, neutral, illegible, and unmarked.[16] In its nonspecificity, the limitations of "all" appear as mere omission or forgetting rather than as a tactic within a regime of illegibility shaped by systemic racism.

Inseparable from the marked racialization of U.S. citizenship, the term "all" has a history and set of meanings that require unpacking. In the twentieth century, "all" frequently referenced shifting understandings of human community that nonetheless maintained whiteness as a norm. This was especially true in nationalist discourses. The early twentieth-century discovery that blood types do not correspond to racial phenotype made blood donation possible and, as Sarah Chinn narrates it, framed national discourses of blood banking in the 1940s through the language of "all."[17] Blood drives called for "all" people, regardless of race, gender, age, or class, to donate blood in the name of democracy. The "universal donor" took shape as a patriotic and democratic body, whose sacrifice of fluids and tissues could save and rehabilitate the nation's soldiers.[18] But blood banking simultaneously became a project of racialization, which constructed whiteness as a neutral category and blackness as deviance. Although the Red Cross and other organizations called for all citizens to donate blood, Chinn writes, "blood donated by whites . . . was unlabeled, unmarked. Only the blood given by blacks was labeled as such," leading to disparities in access to blood banks that in turn precipitated protests by African Americans declaring "I Am an American, Too!"[19] These protests reveal that African American struggles to count as full U.S. citizens were both political and epistemic: holding the state and white citizens accountable for false promises of universal equality involved contesting the presumed boundaries of "all" and "American." While the term "all" treated whiteness as an unmarked category of smooth belonging, however, proclamations of universal equality *redesigned* the language and methods of demarcation rather than neutralizing the frictioned material vestiges of racial difference.[20]

In response to the overtly racist beating of Isaac Woodward, Truman's use of "all" gestured toward correcting historical disenfranchisement and legally mandated inequality. But his repetition ("When I say all Americans I mean all Americans") also suggests the ambivalences of the term "all" as an instrument of legibility in liberal rights regimes. A basic presumption of such regimes is that legal legibility (or nominal citizenship) sets in motion progress toward substantial inclusion, often by smoothly enveloping each new, legible identity into the community of citizens. But as postcolonial disability theorist Nirmala Erevelles argues, liberal citizenship is a historical-material arrangement produced through political economies, not a pregiven or natural cate-gory.[21] Because slavery, for instance, built the nation and its industries, liberal indi-vidualist values of citizenship, defined by "productivity, efficiency, and autonomy," are intimately wedded to histories of white property ownership, the "racial division of labor," and other material arrangements that, in turn, rely upon norms of able-bodiedness (and able-mindedness) to "decide who could or could not be a citizen."[22] Much like the insistence that "All Mankind Is One Family," liberal rights regimes dic-tate that once marked as formal citizens, rights recipients can assimilate smoothly, become neutral and normate, if they prove their worth as productive citizens. By this logic, any remaining inequalities that communities of color face, particularly those resulting from the legacies of slavery, historical patterns of racial segregation, or on-going state violence, are not caused by systemic racism but rather problems inherent to those communities. The assumptions of U.S. liberalism (and the individualized sys-tem of capitalism on which they are based) reveal the connections between the dis-course of "all" and the regime of the flexible user, which approached the citizen as a labor unit within broader systems of management and control. Within those systems, the category of the productive citizen shaped imperatives for users to become effi-cient, rehabilitated workers and soldiers. But as the examples above illustrate, when "all" are called to sacrifice bodies for the nation, those with unmarked racial and eco-nomic privileges as citizens often benefit at the expense of those whose racialized, disabled, and otherwise "misfit" bodies are treated as extractable labor.

PRODUCTIVE SPATIAL CITIZENS IN THE JIM CROW ERA

Design for a range of human variation was the goal of the access-knowledge regime, and yet legible variations and determinations of valuable difference were frequently racialized, gendered, and classed. Where the legibility (and illegibility) of categories of race, class, and gender intersected with disability in barrier-free design, the twentieth-century discourse of "all" aligned with the figure of the productive spatial citizen, a flexible user whose right to public and private space is contingent upon its amena-bility to productive labor.[23] Barrier-free design was enmeshed with state projects of granting inclusion to disabled people who proved themselves as good workers and citizens deserving of rights in a liberal democratic, capitalist order, and whose mem-bership in this order entitled them to spatial access as a condition of belonging. Since the 1910s, industrial managers had argued that removing environmental barriers for men injured in war and industry would promote the goals of vocational rehabilita-tion.[24] Similarly, following World War II, proponents of barrier-free design argued against the widespread institutionalization of disabled people, not as a matter of civil rights or economic equality but because institutionalization was a loss of "human resources," preventing the nation from absorbing citizens' labor; likewise, once made productive and provided environments that support their rehabilitation, disabled people would no longer be costly "burdens" to society.[25] As architect Leon Chatelain noted, "They may truly be a burden but frequently it is not their fault. It is the lack of awareness of the general public which has created this difficulty."[26] Typically, such comments regarding disability as deficit would be associated with rehabilitation, not accessible design. But as Chatelain and others imagined it, an accessible future would supply productive spatial citizens.

> Most important is the day when we can use the tremendous power of the rehabilitated physically handicapped that is now going to waste, for instead of being dependent on public assistance they will be gainfully employed in buildings which are freely accessible. The economic potential is enormous but more important we will have people who are happy because they are at work in productive, useful occupations.[27]

Productive spatial citizenship was thus the dominant discourse of rehabilitation, conceived in spatial terms. The rise of barrier-free design between the 1940s and '60s took place at the nexus of rehabilitation and architectural knowing-making, with close connections to regimes of scientific management. Because these regimes were all concerned with smoothing out the relations between laboring bodies and environments, the scientific legibility of the functional, productive user shaped the identification of citizens.

The imperative for productivity is central to liberalism, which defines citizenship through spatial conceptions of resourcefulness, whether in the case of colonialist geographies that designate land and bodies as standing reserves or in the treatment of racialized and disabled bodies as what philosopher Ally Day refers to as "labor-producing" sites.[28] The other side of this coin is that those deemed unproductive or incapable of navigating spaces of productivity were often subject to segregation from the population. In the eugenics era, particularly between the mid-nineteenth century and the end of World War II, spatial segregation was used to separate so-called defectives from the mainstream population, often through institutionalization.[29] These conditions, which disabled lawyer Harriet McBryde Johnson referred to as the "disability gulag," were particularly severe for black and indigenous disabled women of color, who were subject to both segregation and sterilization.[30]

Born from the combined effects of scientific racism, white supremacist ideologies, and state power, legally mandated racial segregation in homes, schools, and other public places was a project of knowing-making. Segregation took shape through the isolation of black communities in cities, controls on immigration, the isolation of indigenous people in reservations, and the internment of Japanese people, which federal policies and courts upheld as consistent with the spirit of national goals.[31] Taking up space (and the wrong kinds of space) under segregated conditions had grave consequences. White police officers' perceptions that Isaac Woodward was out of place, and therefore justifiably violable, had brutal consequences. Unlike white, war-injured soldiers, Woodward's disablement as a result of police brutality did not make him a prototype of national identity, nor were there programs of national rehabilitation fashioned in his name. While black soldiers like Woodward were called to sacrifice their bodies for the good of "all" citizens, they did not receive the racial, economic, and political privileges of admission to the category of "everyone."

Disability and race are hardly discrete categories. As historians such as Douglas Baynton have argued, racial difference is often marked by perceptions of disability and defect, and markers of infirmity or poor health have been used to justify racism against communities of color.[32] It is important not to discount, however, the race and class privileges of white, middle-class disabled citizens, who were the focus of barrier-free design. A "sharp intensification" of the polio epidemic in the United States after World War II produced a significant population of civilian disabled children and adults.[33] Like institutionalization and residential segregation, the response to polio was racialized. As historian Naomi Rogers argues, rehabilitation centers for polio survivors, such as Franklin Roosevelt's Warm Springs, were "whites only" facilities, and the relatively low incidences of polio in the U.S. South created a presumption that black populations were not susceptible to the disease.[34] Rather than intensify institutionalization, however, legible polio outbreaks in predominantly white communities led to the creation of new architectural and urban spaces, premised upon the rights of (white) citizens to access public space.

In a similar fashion, barrier-free design and its attention to specific (though unmarked) disabled people—white, middle-class, injured veterans or elderly disabled women—was entangled with nationalist discourses, as well as the funding sources and social agendas that consolidated racial hierarchy in the post–World War II era. The G.I. Bill, for instance, was to provide soldiers funding for access to housing, education, and services that would enable their integration into postwar life. But as numerous historians have documented, the bill's benefits were often extended to white, male veterans in heterosexual couplings and denied to veterans of color and unmarried civilian women.[35] Consequently, the wealth-generating privileges of access to state-funded education, labor, mortgages, and suburban homes in planned communities were afforded to predominantly white populations. These conditions, along with the rehabilitation imperative to smooth out the frictions between disabled bodies and their environments, contributed to an illusion of disability as a race-neutral phenomenon.

Access-Knowledge in the U.S. University

It was against the backdrop of systemic racial exclusion and violence in the Jim Crow era that rehabilitation experts began developing barrier-free design in the late 1940s. Barrier-free design took shape at the intersections of post–World War II rehabilitation, architecture, and industrial design. Its central premise was that built environments, including products, buildings, and even cities, constituted a major barrier to vocational rehabilitation for disabled people, who (once rehabilitated) could resume other practices of citizenship. Other barriers, such as social attitudes limiting access to housing and employment, manifested in the choices that architects, industrial designers, engineers, and builders made as they fashioned the world.

The rise of barrier-free design responded, in part, to pervasive institutionalization.[36] But its primary impetus was the rehabilitation of the World War II soldier. In 1947 Congress established the President's Committee on Employment of the Handicapped to investigate and make recommendations for disabled veterans' vocational rehabilitation.[37] The subcommittee on barrier-free design worked with the Veterans Administration and a rehabilitation program at the University of Illinois to conduct human factors research toward the first accessibility guidelines in the United States. This research enlisted hundreds of (mostly white and male) disabled students, many of whom attended the university through funding from the G.I. Bill, who engaged in experiments with accessibility technologies and building features.

Despite being located in the Midwest, rather than the South, the University of Illinois at Urbana-Champaign was a site of severe racial segregation. In 1948 only 0.01 percent of its thirty thousand students were African American.[38] Not only were these students denied access to campus housing, but efforts toward so-called urban renewal were also increasing segregation in the surrounding community; in 1948 restricted covenants increased, despite the U.S. Supreme Court's ruling in *Shelley v. Kraemer*, which found these segregationist housing agreements to be unconstitutional.[39] Some students of color gained admission to the rehabilitation program in later years, but it is important to point out that each experimental accessibility feature and site of access, such as campus housing, Greyhound buses, and basketball teams, was likely either racially segregated or majority white.[40]

The legibility of disabled people such as wheelchair users within these spaces required using research methods, such as anthropometry, which had been (and continued to be) used for the sciences of racial differentiation and military-industrial efficiency. Accessibility research at the University of Illinois culminated in the first attempt at defining best practices for accessibility through a set of voluntary guidelines: American National Standard A117.1 (ANSI A117.1), a six-page document first published in 1961 to describe basic features of accessible built environments.[41] The guidelines included considerations for public sidewalks, parking lots, entrances, ramps, doorways, floors, restrooms, water fountains, public telephones, elevators, and technological features (such as sounds and flashing lights to communicate to visually and/or hearing-impaired people).[42] The committees devising the guidelines initially addressed disability, understood as physical impairment, but later in the process added considerations of aging.[43] They omitted "modifications to old buildings," known as retrofits, focusing instead on "minimal performance standards" for the "design and construction of new buildings."[44] Private homes were also excluded by virtue of not being public spaces.[45]

Born of an interdisciplinary process, the standards reflected advocates' belief that accessible design was not solely a task of rehabilitation professionals but "rather the responsibility of the architect, engineer, designer, builder, manufacturer, and also legislators, municipal leaders, and community planners."[46] While rehabilitation professionals remained experts regarding the concept of disability, the concept also opened up an interdisciplinary field in which other professionals could also claim access-knowledge. Among the experts who devised these guidelines were architects, builders, civil engineers, rehabilitation scientists, and even representatives of the telecommunications industry, who offered guidance on accessible public telephones.[47] Deciding that it would "add strength and dignity to the standards," the committee members listed their fields of expertise in the final document.[48]

From the beginning, the A117.1 standard was portrayed as accessible to all users. Throughout the process of crafting the A117.1 standard, Timothy Nugent, director of the University of Illinois Rehabilitation Education Center, emphasized that accessibility would benefit "all," regardless of disability.[49] He reinforced this message in public talks about the standard, stating, "All standards which will be recommended to benefit the permanently physically handicapped will be of benefit to everyone."[50] Likewise, he called upon rehabilitation professionals, designers, and builders to contribute more accountable and accessible built environments to the project of postwar reconstruction.[51] Other advocates of A117.1, including prominent Philadelphia builder William Lotz, reiterated that while builders are often "thoughtless in our regard for the one out of every seven persons who is physically handicapped," "we should all benefit" from barrier-free design.[52] These claims prefigured the discourse of Universal Design, which would arise in the 1980s, by situating accessibility as beneficial for "everyone" from the outset. These were not neutral claims, however. In portraying accessibility as broadly beneficial, barrier-free design supporters treated access to public space as a reward for being a productive citizen.

Barrier-free design aspired to become inconspicuous in built environments. Like the figure of the productive citizen, once it began to "work," access would become unmarked, assimilated, part of the norm rather than opposed to it. The flexibility of designs was crucial to achieving this smooth integration. Echoing the notion of disability as a resource that could contribute to the value and usability of design, Nugent noted that broad accessibility could occur "without the loss of space or function to the general public" and "without extra cost."[53] Moreover, disabled and nondisabled people alike would be able to use accessible public buildings and spaces "independently and without distinction."[54] The spirit of such claims was that barrier-free design had something to offer to all users, but beneath them was an appeal to count disabled people as productive citizens and workers, the omission of whose "human resources" from the national economy was of "considerable significance."[55] To maximize and capture these resources, Nugent's basic research at the University of Illinois addressed a range of disabilities, including those related to mobility, sight, hearing, nervous systems, aging, and heart disease.[56] The smooth integration of built-in accessibility features, or accessibility by-design, for a broad range of users was therefore a project in service of vocational and social integration.

A surprising early discovery of accessibility research was that features created with disabled people in mind sometimes unintentionally improved usability for nondisabled people—a discovery that also supported the claim that designing for the average user decreased usability for everyone. In the university's dormitories, for instance, accessible folding shower seats had been "expected to last several years" but quickly "wore out in less than six months" because the majority of nondisabled students were using them with such regularity that they exhausted the hinges and materials.[57] "Able-bodied students," Nugent reported, "preferred to use the showers with the seats down."[58] Stories like these provided powerful narratives for justifying accessibility according to its added value for mainstream consumers.

The empirical finding that wheelchair ramps or shower seats with certain technical specifications benefit nondisabled students justified the claim that such features benefit "everyone." By "everyone," Nugent appeared to mean the average white postwar U.S. consumer, student, or worker. It was unclear that barrier-free design would be available for someone like Isaac Woodward, whose race would likely have excluded him from attending the University of Illinois and whose disability had served as a tragic representation of police brutality but had not elevated him to the status of a war hero or productive spatial citizen.

The characterization of shower seats as accessible to "everyone" presumed (but did not name) the norm of the white student-as-user. Barrier-free design research began at the height of the black civil rights movement, in the midst of the Supreme Court's hearings on *Brown v. Board of Education* (1954), the Montgomery Bus Boycott (1955), and the desegregation of Little Rock, Arkansas (1957)—all major events in the politics of desegregation, inclusive design, and urban planning alike. These events made public spaces such as schools, restrooms, and public transit into material and symbolic sites of protest. ANSI A117.1 was thus inseparable from the privileges of white citizenship, including (but not limited to) access to safe and comfortable housing, suffrage, elementary and secondary education, healthcare, and transportation. These privileges were the material conditions that allowed white able-bodied normates access to the University of Illinois, its dormitory restrooms, and its shower seats. As feminist architectural historian Barbara Penner points out, however, ANSI A117.1 offered guidance for wheelchair-accessible public spaces at a time when restrooms, schools, and public transit remained racially segregated.[59] The premise that accessibility should be available to all citizens thus failed to distinguish between the relative degrees of power and privilege between members of the population in an era of explicit racial segregation.

A relic of the rehabilitation regime and its treatment of disability as a discrete, embodied phenomenon, the presumed white user was also youthful and strong.

While barrier-free design later addressed both aging and disability, two conditions that gerontologists, rehabilitation researchers, and even architects were understanding as medical problems, the initial research assumed that young, white, wheelchair-using college students at the University of Illinois were representative of the broader population of disabled people. In 1963 British architect Selwyn Goldsmith noted, "The disabled people whose characteristics and capabilities had helped inform the design prescriptions were translated into the world beyond the University of Illinois."[60] These particular bodies set accessibility standards that were replicated in other states, eventually instituted in U.S. federal law, and served as an international model.

Engineering Access in the Suburban Home

Few spatial domains were closer to the epicenter of mid-twentieth-century constructions of whiteness as normal and blackness as difference than the suburban home. In the late 1940s, the G.I. Bill and Federal Housing Authority loan processes (such as "redlining" and restricted covenants) enabled white U.S. citizens to migrate from urban areas to middle-class suburbs.[61] This process consolidated the spatial patterns known as "white flight" and entrenched the racial and economic segregation of African Americans through a disinvestment in cities and an accumulation of white suburban wealth. Segregation was not simply a problem in southern states. In Levittown, New York, a model community for new suburban architectures, redlining policies formally excluded African American, Latino, and other people of color from buying homes beginning in 1948, initiating decades of legal battles for protection from housing discrimination.[62] Consequently, the consolidation of wealth and privilege in white suburban populations produced a tendency to market barrier-free design toward these populations as consumers. Although ANSI A117.1 did not provide guidelines for domestic space, advocates promoted the guidelines by appealing to the racialized, gendered, and classed norms of suburban, white, middle-class society. One article by two ANSI A117.1 committee members, architect Leon Chatelain and social worker Donald Fearn, focused on accessibility in churches, spaces that were arguably even more strictly segregated than suburban neighborhoods.[63] A ladies' tea event, they wrote, lost nearly half of its attendees because it was held in a second-floor room. "Those not attending the Tea felt it was too difficult, not safe, or just impossible for them to climb and descend this staircase because of age, physical disability, or a medical condition."[64] Consequently, the planning committee had decided to adopt the ANSI A117.1 guidelines. "In the future," they noted, "the Tea will be held in churches *that all may enter*."[65] For churches considering modifications to their buildings, Chatelain and Fearn assured that accessibility for "the handicapped and the aged will accrue benefits to all who attend. The specifications which eliminate architectural barriers for them will increase the safety, comfort, and ease in use for everyone. Plan for the future now. Look forward to the day when everyone—the able-bodied, the aged and the handicapped—can use your church to attend worship services and to participate in the total church program."[66] These assurances and repeated emphases on the term "all" were polite, nonaccusatory strategies for encouraging more accessible church spaces. But like the segregated home and university, they were inseparable from the context of segregated churches.

Appeals to "safety" and freedom from risk also justified the benefits of accessibility for "all." Ronald Junius, assistant director of the A117.1 project, described the risk.

> By 1980, for every able-bodied citizen, there will be one person with chronic disease, one person with a physical disability or one person over sixty-five whom the able-bodied will have to support unless they are given an opportunity to be productive.[67]

Other advocates emphasized safety by describing ANSI A117.1 as a "boon to insurance," a benefit to worker's rehabilitation that decreases workers' compensation claims, reduces "public liability," promotes health, and reduces fire risks.[68] Jayne Shover, chair of the National Safety Council's Committee on the Safety of the Aging, wrote in 1962 that ANSI A1171.1 would allow "greater independent safe use of public facilities by the crippled, the aged, and the infirm" and compared it to practices of "safety engineering."[69] Unlike Chatelain and Fearns, Shrover adopted a more urgent political tone: unless the guidelines were adopted, Shrover warned,

> workers in the field of accident prevention will be faced with a distasteful choice. Either they can seek to prevent injuries among the elderly and disabled by advocating that they adopt a mode of existence which would exclude them from independent participation in community life; or they can continue to total the accidental injuries incurred by these brave souls who endeavor to surmount the architectural barriers in public buildings in order to live rather than exist.[70]

These civil rights imperatives begged the question, however, of who could reliably expect to access public life without fear of, for instance, racially motivated violence. The very notion of safety was a privileged concept associated with white, middle-class, suburban existence and framed not for the good of disabled people or to advocate for deinstitutionalization but in the name of government and industry.

The social legibility of the suburban home as an arena of safety was also related to the epistemic legibility of white, disabled women in rehabilitation and gerontology. In the 1940s and '50s, the categories of disability, aging, and gender were becoming legible categories of difference for user-centered design. As scientific managers expanded their focus from the factory floor to more diffuse sites of productive labor, economized and gendered domains such as the private home became sites of economic and physical rehabilitation, production, and efficiency.[71] In the 1950s, architectural experiments in mass-producing standardized single-family houses to accommodate these migrations further entrenched the whiteness of the suburban home, with entire industries, regimes of knowledge, and manufacturing practices emerging to support these developments. For instance, architects designed suburban homes as technologies for white, middle-class women whose labor they translated into "homemaking,"[72] a designation that both identified women's bodies as sites of efficient, extractable labor and reinforced the status of white women as model citizens.

The rise of the suburban home and the figure of the white, disabled housewife as sites of intervention for rehabilitation experts were also inseparable from the material arrangements of racially segregated built space (Figure 3.2). Less recognized by scholars but just as significant were efforts to render the privileged white, suburban, middle-class, heterosexual home as a disability domain. David Serlin has argued that in the 1950s, the meaning of rehabilitation and the design of prosthetics shifted from war-related injury to masculine norms of labor and productivity.[73] Concurrently, rehabilitation professionals turned to engineering disabled housewives, spatially bound bodies whose gender roles, perceived inherent weakness, and designated belonging in suburban homes made them appear as natural sites for scientific management. The visual and material rhetorics of rehabilitation interventions into the mid-century home recalled a longer history of depicting assistive technologies and built environments as enablers of white, middle-class women's comfort agency, productivity, and quality of life. For instance, recalling prosthetics manufacturer A. A. Marks' display of women wearing prosthetics while cooking in kitchens (see Figure 2.5), prominent rehabilitation expert Howard Rusk devoted several of his 1950s rehabilitation monographs to accessible and adaptive homemaking for disabled housewives, particularly white, elderly, physically disabled women.[74] For these users, rehabilitation through self-help entailed becoming autonomous consumers rather than productive factory workers or independent citizens. Consequently, white women's aging and gendered bodies became model organisms for the study of disability as a relationship between bodies and environments; in coming decades, experts in physical rehabilitation and ergonomics would understand older, white, disabled housewives as the baseline of standards of physical ability for all people.

While contemporary preoccupations with the access needs of the aging "baby boomer" generation lend the impression that such concerns are specific to recent population trends, proponents of barrier-free design in the 1950s and '60s (the period when today's baby boomers were born) were equally concerned with the growing population of people over sixty-five years of age.[75] The legibility of aging as rehabilitation concern naturalized the extension of scientific experts into the domestic life of white, middle-class, aging women. Concerns with women as users began to surface in barrier-free design manuals for disabled and elderly people, with particular attention to wheelchair-accessible kitchens.[76] In 1960 architect and ergonomist Alexander Kira (who would later become famous for his ergonomic studies of the bathroom) published guidelines for the "Housing Needs of the Aged," with emphasis on "Functional Planning for the Elderly and Handicapped."[77] Like Rusk, Kira believed that

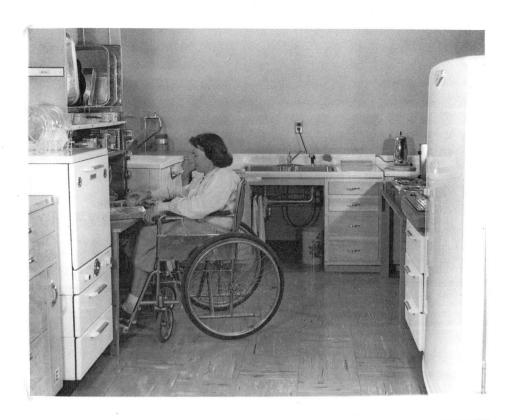

Figure 3.2. Barrier-free design research in the domain of the home focused on the figure of the white, disabled housewife using the kitchen (ca. 1961–74). Courtesy of the University of Illinois Archives, images 4030.tif and 4028.tif.

adapted housing could serve a rehabilitative function. But his focus was the structure and planning of housing itself rather than the use of adaptive and self-help devices, as disabled housewives' manuals promoted. Although individual self-help devices and buildings operated at different scales, Rusk and Kira's efforts toward accessible housing were simultaneous to Nugent's development of ANSI A117.1. The project of accessible domestic space reveals the broader reaches of access-knowledge beyond the university context, which rehabilitation, human factors research, scientific management, and architecture converged to share knowledge for mutual benefit.

The single-family, white, middle-class suburban home was thus much more than a container for private, heterosexual, nuclear family life. For the figure of the white disabled woman to become legible for rehabilitation practices, the home had to appear as a public domain amenable to expert manipulation and productive spatial citizenship. When gerontologists and rehabilitation experts explored methods of enhancing productivity for aging housewives, their attention fell disproportionately upon elderly white women.[78] Rehabilitation experts offered adaptive housework to women who not only occupied white, suburban spaces but who also had the white privilege of long life, or access to aging. Epidemiological data from the Jim Crow era shows that African American people had significantly higher rates of premature death than white people and were 20 percent more likely to die before the age of sixty-five in spaces of Jim Crow segregation, even when accounting for class and income.[79] While these figures may not have been immediately legible to those inhabiting privileged, white communities, racialized expectations of what kinds of people were likely to be in the world nevertheless shaped the imagination of the home itself as a privileged domain of labor and aging.

It was by claiming expertise about the seemingly neutral, objective, biologized, and often-conflated categories of disability, aging, and gender that rehabilitation specialists and architects (workers in predominantly white, nondisabled, cisgender male-dominated professions) enacted early barrier-free design.[80] Although the site of the suburban home shifted these experts' attention away from the normate male figure, the legibility of aging, white, disabled women as housewives was not a recognition of their race, gender, class, or disability as connected to systems of oppression. Nor was the rehabilitation regime concerned with women of color, whose labor often took place outside the home, whether in factories or in the homes of others.[81] Rather, the figure of the white, disabled, aging woman fit vocational expectations of the particular types of users performing labor in private, domestic space, as well as cultural expectations of white womanhood as representative of the nation.

THE QUESTION OF SEGREGATION

On February 1, 1960, four young African American men sat at a "whites only" Woolworth's lunch counter in Greensboro, North Carolina, and refused to leave.[82] Their sit-in embodied a notion, central to twentieth-century social justice activism, that access to public space is a litmus test of freedom. A national movement of sit-ins and protests led by students of color followed, and Greensboro became an epicenter of civil rights organizing in the South. When widespread arrests of protesters overran the capacity of local jails, police repurposed the abandoned Central Carolina Rehabilitation Hospital, an old polio treatment facility, as a site of incarceration.[83]

A decade earlier, on August 28, 1950, Ronald Mace, a white, middle-class, nine-year-old boy from Winston-Salem, North Carolina, entered the same building (then known as the Central Carolina Convalescent Hospital) after contracting polio (Figure 3.3).[84] Although polio outbreaks were relatively uncommon in the South, Greensboro was an epicenter of the disease between 1948 and 1950, and the local news reported each diagnosis, rehabilitation, and death.[85] On August 31, 1950, a front-page story in the Greensboro Daily News reported Mace as one of several recent cases admitted to the hospital.[86] On the same day and page, the newspaper reported the state of North Carolina's strong resistance to admitting four black students to North Carolina State University's law school.[87] The resistance followed the U.S. Supreme Court's holdings in two cases, *Sweatt v. Painter* and *McLaurin v. Oklahoma State Regents,* which preceded *Brown v. Board of Education* in challenging the segregationist doctrine of *Plessy v. Ferguson* by finding that racially segregated law schools provide unequal services to students of color. The contrast between these cases—the polio epidemic and the rise of the civil rights movement—on the front page of the local news hinted at two types of perceived danger in the early 1950s and in the Jim Crow South: the dangers of legible, medicalized disability and the dangers of legible challenges to white racial hegemony.

In its heyday, the Central Carolina Convalescent Hospital had been one of the largest polio rehabilitation facilities in the United States. The local outbreak's severity had also given the facility a rare quality: from its staff to its patients, it was racially integrated (Figure 3.4).[88] Like another local disability space, the Guilford Industries for the Blind broom factory (a sheltered workshop for blind people), there appeared to be "no color line": white and black people worked and engaged in rehabilitation practices together.[89] Both the rehabilitation hospital and the sheltered workshop offered ordered, institutionalized, and efficient spaces for the production of flexible users, whose bodies were later displayed as inspirational. A 1951 article reporting on the polio epidemic pictured Mace in crutches and leg braces, held up by a nurse, with a wheelchair sitting in the background.[90] Accompanying the photo, a triumphant caption read: "He Can Stand Alone." A belief in disability as tragic deficit, rather than anti-racist motivations, integrated the Central Carolina Convalescent Hospital. Consequently, the hospital's rehabilitation activities shaped its perception as a space that was neutral of history or politics, such that when the state reused it ten years later to incarcerate black civil rights activists, the building was not legible as a former space of institutionalization. Nor was the hospital's reuse as a jail recognizable as part of a

Figure 3.3. The entrance to the Central Carolina Convalescent Hospital (1950). Courtesy of Joy Weeber.

new pattern: the transitioning of institutional spaces such as hospitals and asylums into prisons. Nevertheless, this pattern began the phenomenon of mass incarceration, or what Michelle Alexander refers to as the "New Jim Crow."[91] The spatial segregation of racial minorities and disabled people was clearly linked in these cases, but while racism and ableism shared spatial dimensions and certain mechanisms, the populations most vulnerable to these oppressions were not often imagined as related.

At the same time that Supreme Court cases such as *Sweatt* and *McLaurin* were chipping away at the Jim Crow regime, the social and cultural forces surrounding segregation did not disappear with challenges to laws. Resistance to federal civil rights by states such as North Carolina made achieving racial justice a process of struggle

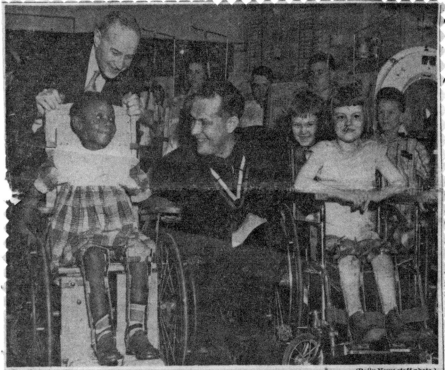

MAYOR CONE AND VAUGHN MONROE AT POLIO HOSPITAL

Mayor Benjamin Cone stands behind Shirley Boone while Vaughn Monroe, center, entertains patients at the polio hospital. Right of Monroe is Amanda Greene, John Pridgen looks over Amanda's shoulder.

Smiles Repay Vocal Star For Show At Hospital

Vaughn Monroe and members of his orchestra gave two shows at the Central Carolina Convalescent Hospital yesterday afternoon. And they got a show in return.

At first, Monroe's pianist and Ziggy Talent were absent. So Mayor Benjamin Cone gathered a number of little polio patients around and sang "Pop! Goes the Weazel."

Monroe looked around at the eyes of some of the patients. He couldn't let them down and didn't. Over at the piano he stood and accompanied himself to "While Irish Eyes are Smiling" and "Brown Eyes."

Beds Seesaw

"Gotta go now," he said. And the Shriners accompanying him and the mayor and the patients filed out. The four rocking beds began seesawing.

At the entrance to the polio hospital, Monroe met the rest of the group from the orchestra. So Monroe, the Shriners, the mayor, Talent, the pianist, and the four Moonmaids returned to Ward 2. In the meantime, all the patients and staff members had returned, too.

Join In Singing

Talent was joined by the patients in singing the yah-yah-yadi-yadi-yah-yah-yah-yah refrain in "The Maharajah of Magadore." And they applauded when Talent, on his knees, sang a ditty about a little boy who wanted to be a G-man.

Monroe and the Moonmaids harmonized with "Mockingbird Hill" and ended the program with "Racing with the Moon."

The entertainers played last night for a dance sponsored by the Shriners.

The show Monroe's group got in return? the broad smiles of the polio patients. He won't forget that.

Figure 3.4. The Central Carolina Convalescent Hospital's patients and staff were racially integrated. This image shows a young African American girl in a wheelchair, posed with two white adult men and other (white) children. A young Ronald Mace appears on the far right. *Greensboro News & Record*, May 5, 1951, 9. All Rights Reserved.

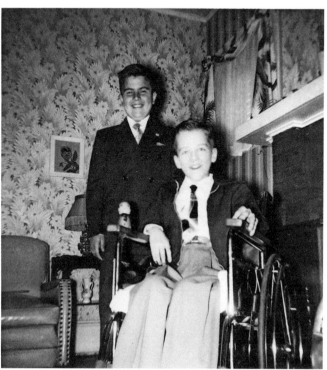

Figure 3.5. Ronald Mace returned to his family home in 1951. Here, he is depicted near a wheelchair ramp and with his brother. Courtesy of Joy Weeber.

and labor, and in 1951 the Civil Rights Congress, a U.S. civil rights defense organization, filed a 237-page petition with the United Nations detailing evidence of genocide, defined as systematic violence and discrimination, against African Americans in the United States.[92] The same year, Mace reentered life in his family home, despite his doctors' recommendation of prolonged institutionalization (Figure 3.5).[93] Disabled peoples' resistance to institutionalization was not yet a significant force in the early 1950s, but the prevalence of polio among white, middle-class populations enabled some, like Mace, to access life beyond institutions. The Maces' home in Winston-Salem acquired a wheelchair ramp, and Mace was able to continue his former hobbies of tinkering with soap box derby cars and model airplanes. His status as a "polio victim" and apparent prowess with designing model airplanes even won him an all-expenses-paid trip to Detroit, Michigan, which he attended with his father.[94] Similar opportunities were unlikely to have been available to lower-income disabled people, who did not have the resources to access home life, nor would they have been available to disabled people of color, such as Isaac Woodward.

It is unlikely that Mace would have been cognizant of these privileges as a young child, but his early life in the segregated South no doubt shaped his understanding of space as an instrument of exclusion. He had attended segregated public schools, which remained white at the time of his high school graduation in 1959, five years after *Brown v. Board of Education.*[95] Without a doubt, he encountered signs reading "whites only" and "colored only" in public spaces such as restaurants, where he faced other types of environmental barriers.[96] Mace was also part of a generation that became disabled in the pre-ANSI A117.1 world. Staired entrances and inaccessible restrooms at his schools prevented his regular attendance.[97] But with the resources of his family (for instance, his mother, who carried him up the stairs of his school every day), Mace navigated inaccessible spaces for most of his life.[98] These adaptations were both resourceful and isolating, however. In 1960 Mace matriculated at North Carolina State University in Raleigh, North Carolina, where he studied architecture at the School of Design (despite the reservations of the school's dean).[99] Unlike the University of Illinois campus where barrier-free design research was taking place, NC State was inaccessible. Mace lived and performed his studio exercises from a mobile home, where his mother also resided. At NC State, he began a lifelong career of researching housing access for marginalized users. Mace's senior architectural thesis on housing design research, which studied Chavis Heights, a segregated black public housing facility in Raleigh, highlighted what he described as a chasm between the architect and the user.

> Mass housing has placed the architect in the awkward position of having to design for a statistical person usually ethnic, cultural and economic worlds away from his own position in society. Thus the planner and the architect must operate with assumptions about how people live, how they want to live, and how they would live if possible.

Assumptions frequently unfounded based upon middle class values and prejudices
having [sic] little relevance for people of other cultures and economic classes.[100]

By building for others, in other words, professional architects often failed to understand the cultural (here, indicating racial) and classed lived experiences of their users.
This idea, which activists and scholars in many fields would echo in the 1960s, served
as a driving factor in Mace's career, which he concentrated on shifting the relations of
knowing-making for architects and users.

The shifting landscape of disability rights laws in the late 1960s and early '70s
molded Mace's career. Following his graduation in 1966, Mace's social consciousness
about the architecture profession developed around his experiences of employment
discrimination.[101] Potential employers often treated his disability as a disqualification, pathology, or nuisance. At the time, there was no legal recourse for this discrimination. ANSI A117.1, which applied only to the design of built environments, remained
a voluntary standard, and according to a 1965 survey of three thousand architects,
most were unaware of its guidance.[102] Congress had only passed the Architectural
Barriers Act, the first legislation requiring accessible design in federally funded buildings, in 1968. Mace finally found employment at a small firm in Greensboro, North
Carolina, in 1972, and worked on projects such as designing the local civic center.[103]
The following year, Congress passed major civil rights legislation, Section 504 of
the Federal Rehabilitation Act, which made access to federal buildings and services
a civil right for disabled people, leading Mace to establish his own consultancy, Barrier Free Design.

Mace's early life in North Carolina, from his time in the Central Carolina Convalescent Hospital to his work at NC State, illustrates the complexities of the concept
of "segregation" in the mid-twentieth century, when removing structural barriers for
disabled users was slowly becoming legible and black civil rights struggles remained
public and contentious. While Mace faced severe discrimination on the basis of his
disability, it is also important to note that the architecture profession in which he was
trained was almost entirely white and male.[104] Although space was a common denom-
inator of both disability and race segregation, Mace's white middle-class status gave
him access to resources and opportunities in posthospital life that were denied to
people of color. These complexities would later shape Mace's work regarding the concept of Universal Design.

Post-racialism and the Emergence of Disability Access Laws

As a relation of knowing-making, spatial segregation remained a target for antiracist (as
well as feminist and disability rights) activism in the 1960s and '70s.[105] When Congress
passed major civil rights legislation in the 1960s, including the Civil Rights Act of
1964 and the Fair Housing Act of 1968, the laws both marked a major victory for activists and initiated intense struggles over enforcement. In response to the post-racial

position that these laws had solved the problem of racism, however, black intellectu-
als such as Stokely Carmichael and Charles Hamilton argued that racism is a system-
wide pattern of discrimination that is illegible in mundane, everyday life (even in the
absence of overt malice).[106] These ideas made racism legible as something that occurs
beyond the reaches and mandates of the law, within diffuse culture and material
arrangements that must be addressed in order for change to take hold.

By insisting that racism had disappeared, however, an emerging post-racial narrative elided the differential impacts of oppression on the basis of race, gender, or
disability. It was within a post-racial framework that it became possible to use racial
segregation as a parallel case or metaphor for disability exclusion.[107] In 1965 architect
and ANSI A117.1 committee chair Leon Chatelain wrote, "A little coordinated planning can open up whole new worlds to millions of people, and all facilities will truly
be open to everyone regardless of race, creed, color or physical handicap," implying
that ending discrimination in built environments was an issue that cut across race,
religion, or disability.[108] A race-neutral discourse on disability, underscored by an
emphasis on "all" and "everyone," emerged.

> I look forward to the day in the not too distant future when every building and facility
> will be usable by everyone, the able-bodied as well as the physically handicapped....
> When all people can truly work, play and live together.... When an individual in a
> wheelchair can attend the church of his choice.... When he may enjoy a football or
> baseball game or attend a concert or the opera.... When there will be no need to have
> specially built schools to be used by physically handicapped children, for all of these
> buildings will be open to all who desire to enter.[109]

Chatelain's framing of "everyone" highlighted nondisabled users' privileged access to
choice and agency: the choice to engage in leisure or attend a mainstream school, he
argued, should be available to "all." Yet it was only *after* the passage of race-focused
civil rights laws, such as the Civil Rights Act of 1964 and the Voting Rights Act of 1965,
that advocates like Chatelain drew parallels between race and disability and that
"physical handicap" appeared alongside race as a qualifier of "everyone." It was also
only after the passage of race-focused civil rights laws that a "freedom of choice" discourse appeared in reference to disability, often in concert with the notion that the
struggle against racism had now ended and that the time for addressing disability
had arrived. While Chatelain replicated the discourse of making facilities open to
"everyone," the world he imagined consisted of the highly segregated and contested
spaces of schools, churches, and sporting events. That barrier-free advocates did not
acknowledge racial segregation prior to these laws suggests that it was expedient to
appropriate the momentum and success of black civil rights after Jim Crow but not
to ally accessibility to anti-racism then or thereafter. Two sites of spatial reform in the
1960s highlight the presumed whiteness of barrier removal for "all."

Knowing-Making Racial Desegregation

From the 1940s to the 1960s, barrier-free design attached itself to the tastes and preferences of white, middle-class consumers in privileged, safe, and seemingly neutral spaces of the suburban home and the public university, where the design of new products and buildings would enable access to the material practices of normal life. These white geographies of accessibility contrasted with the stigmatized spaces of inner cities, which were sites of racial desegregation. In cities, desegregation required a range of practices, including integrating transit, housing, and urban redesign, but unlike market-led interventions and voluntary compliance standards for barrier-free design, efforts toward racial desegregation met resistance from law enforcement and the "carceral state."[110]

Despite civil rights protections for people of color, access to formal equality and citizenship through civil rights and antidiscrimination laws failed to produce needed material changes in built environments, wealth accumulation, or widespread disenfranchisement, resulting in riots and uprisings in Detroit, Los Angeles, Chicago, and Newark. Rhetorics of disability and pathology shaped the federal response to these uprisings and the material conditions upon which they were based. In 1967 President Lyndon B. Johnson formed the National Advisory Commission on Civil Disorders—the Kerner Commission—to study the causes of these riots and how they could be prevented, employing a cadre of expert sociologists, psychologists, and anthropologists, as well as law enforcement and defense officials, to discover the causes of and means of preventing expressions of black rage in segregated urban environments.[111] The resulting Kerner Report found that the structural and material effects of white supremacy—particularly unequal housing, education, and access to work, in addition to racially targeted police violence—produced uprisings in U.S. cities and was not something inherent to black communities themselves.[112]

The detailed report outlined the historic and current conditions of systematic racism and poverty in inner cities, particularly mass housing, finding that these conditions drove uprisings (termed as pathological "civil disorders"). It highlighted that "what white Americans have never fully understood—but what the Negro can never forget—is that white society is deeply implicated in the ghetto. White institutions created it, white institutions maintain it, and white society condones it."[113] The powerful claim that race riots were products of white supremacy (as they took shape in built environments) located the "problem" of racial inequality in the milieu rather than individual people or communities. Despite this strong criticism, however, the report ultimately concentrated on preventing and responding to the violence of race riots carried out against "white Americans" by the "Negro" (whose American citizenship was unnamable) because these riots constituted threats to the nation.

The Kerner Report used pathologizing understandings of disability to justify the need for expert surveillance and control in black communities.[114] Pathologizing blackness was a twentieth-century medical, social scientific, and eugenic project. In the 1960s, scientists and experts such as sociologists, anthropologists, and psychologists used the language of diagnosis to characterize black rage as a pathological civil disorder. The role of these experts was to grant an air of scientificity to what was ostensibly an ideological and historical question.[115] The Kerner Report relied upon representations of black rage as a disease that inflicted the bodies of cities and required swift treatment and prevention.[116] Concluding that racial barriers to economic access were making the nation vulnerable, the commission wrote, "Our Nation is moving toward two societies, one black, one white—separate and unequal. . . . Discrimination and segregation have long permeated much of American life; they now threaten the future of every American."[117] These provocative claims seemed to raise the collective stakes of desegregation through the language of threat and risk, but they also characterized black rage as a pathological threat, a "racial disorder" to the nation's body, and particularly its white citizens.[118] The response to pathologized black rage was carceral confinement rather than spatial freedom or greater access. Psychiatrists, Jonathan Metzl has argued, justified confining black activists in mental institutions on the basis of their perceived pathological minds and bodies.[119] Constructing resistance to racial segregation came to rely, then, on representations of disability, illness, and pathology as in need of incarceration. Even further, this resistance reinforced for black people the segregationist arrangements of institutionalization that disability activists had fought in the post–World War II era.

With diagnoses of black pathology came prescriptions for cure. Concurrent with the Kerner Report, the Department of Housing and Urban Development established a "Model Cities" program as an antipoverty and antiriot measure devoted to creating comprehensive, federally controlled, and easily surveilled communities in urban centers, which consequently became laboratories for carceral experimentation.[120] Ultimately, Johnson ignored the Kerner Report's recommendations, which included "treating" riots with increased economic opportunities, ending housing discrimination, ordering greater police protections, and training police to avoid using excessive force against civilian rioters, but the Model Cities program progressed. The institutional and systemic violence of white supremacy, which communities of color felt in the widespread denial of access to work, housing, and civic belonging, remained just as potent in the coming decades.

Knowing-Making All Americans

When strategies for barrier-free design moved beyond research or accessible homes to seek legal enforcement in the late 1960s, disability, age, and race became separate categories of civil (and therefore administrative) rights, government welfare, and citizenship under President Johnson's Great Society reforms. The trope of the productive spatial citizen continued circulating as barrier-free design acquired bureaucratic and legal backing. Accessibility advocates, such as Edmond Leonard, framed barrier removal as a saving grace for physically disabled people whom "medicine and rehabilitation [had] salvaged . . . from an otherwise barren past," echoing Chatelain

> these rehabilitative advances are meaningless when the disabled person is shut out from the mainstream of public life by the frustration of public barriers. . . . When we can use the tremendous manpower of the rehabilitated physically handicapped who will be able to be gainfully employed in buildings which are freely accessible. The economic potential is enormous, but more important we will have people who are happy because they are at work in productive, useful occupations.[121]

In policy discourses, the productive spatial citizen thus acquired legibility as a political agent and a citizen. In 1964, the same year that Congress passed the Civil Rights Act and the Voting Rights Act, it began hearings on the enforcement of barrier-free design through an antidiscrimination regime.[122] The crux of these hearings was that disabled citizens required access to government services, such as rehabilitation therapies and employment training (not to the whole of society or public space, as activists and disabled people themselves demanded). Senators argued, for instance, that disabled people would be discouraged from practicing basic rites of citizenship in government-owned office buildings without barrier removal.[123] As disability rights became institutionalized in law, the concept of disability became somewhat distinct from aging. In 1965 the Older Americans Act mandated community-based services for elders. Simultaneously, Congress amended the Vocational Rehabilitation Act of 1965 to establish a new National Commission on Architectural Barriers to Rehabilitation of the Handicapped, charged to investigate the efficacy of state- and local-level voluntary accessibility regimes.[124] In rehabilitation discourses, however, disability and aging remained tethered concepts.

National policy attention to disability rights came to a head within the flurry of Johnson's Great Society reforms and civil rights laws, making the whiteness of its presumptions and rhetorics all the more severe. In 1967, the same year that Johnson commissioned the Kerner Report, the National Commission on Architectural Barriers to Rehabilitation of the Handicapped (established by Congress) released *Design for All Americans*, a report arguing that disabled and elderly people qualified as members of the general public to whom spatial access should be afforded as a right of citizenship.

> The modern man-made environment is designed for the young and healthy. Yet almost everyone, sooner or later, is handicapped by a chronic or temporary disability or by the infirmities of old age. By designing for the ideal human body, we bar real people from getting an education, earning a living, becoming a part of active community life. More than 20 million Americans are built *out* of normal living by unnecessary barriers: a stairway, a too-narrow door, a too-high telephone. At the right moment,

their needs were overlooked. In time, the last vestiges of such thoughtlessness will disappear from the American scene.[125]

By this point, barrier-free design had been forwarded as a project of productive spatial citizenship for nearly two decades but had not yet received federal attention under law. Following the report, however, Congress passed the Architectural Barriers Act in 1968 and adopted ANSI A117.1 as the basis of barrier-free design for all physically disabled people, enforceable in spaces housing federally funded services and programs.

It is clear from the timing of these laws and the hearings supporting them that spatial access was a legible social justice demand in the legislative consciousness of the mid-1960s. Recall that the 1968 Kerner Report characterized black racial uprisings in segregated cities as pathologized disabilities threatening "every American." In the same political and cultural milieu, barrier-free design justified itself as "design for all Americans." Born from the expert testimonies of white rehabilitation experts regarding the labor value of disabled bodies, accessible design appeared as a nonthreatening alternative to what rehabilitation experts characterized as the perpetuation of injustice against disabled citizens by mainstream architects and builders. The crux of *Design for All Americans* was a 1967 study by the American Institute of Architects (AIA), which found that architects, manufacturers, and builders were largely ignorant about issues of disability and access.[126] Federal legislation was necessary, the report argued, because the voluntary nature of ANSI A117.1 did not provide incentives or requirements to design with disability in mind. The commission recommended new federal legislation requiring that any new public, federally funded buildings be "designated to accommodate the elderly and the handicapped," two categories that had become legible through white rehabilitation conceptions of space and belonging since the 1940s.[127]

A closer examination of *Design for All Americans* reveals that both its rhetoric and substantive content explicitly framed disability access through presumptions of white citizenship. The title referenced the postwar rhetoric of "all," which called upon all bodies to make themselves available for productive spatial citizenship, and "Americans," recalling earlier civil rights declarations, such as "I Am an American, Too!," which black activists deployed to challenge the whiteness of blood banking and other somatic nationalist practices. By defining disabled and elderly people as citizens belonging in the cohort of "all Americans," the report appeared critical of the normate template and its false universality.[128] For instance, the report framed the segregation of disabled and elderly people in institutions and nursing homes as "inhumane and costly."[129] But rather than advocate for closing these institutions, it insisted that "accessibility [must be] made an integral part of all design" for all citizens without acknowledging racial and economic structural barriers that constrained the category of "all Americans" (including the Kerner Report's failure to name black people as

Americans or citizens).[130] The conflation of disability with older age was another unmarked presumption, as was the association between disability and feminized gender
(as in the case of supposedly feminine housewives and supposedly emasculated,
injured male soldiers).[131]

While the language of "all" failed to ensure that law, policy, or the built world
included everyone, it nevertheless succeeded at constructing design for some as
design for all and conflating the particular with the universal. Presumptions of whiteness also appear in apparent references to the Kerner Report and the Model Cities
program.

> The pressures for creating a more livable environment have mounted. Not only the
> handicapped but all Americans are demanding environmental improvement. Air and
> water pollution, slum housing, unsafe streets and highways have become the themes
> of countless conferences. The creation of model cities has become a national goal,
> backed by Federal legislation and funds. Environmental improvement is indeed "an
> idea whose time has come."[132]

Here, white-centered priorities of safe streets, building highways, and ending slum
housing (a euphemism for aggressive urban redevelopment) appear as national goals.
Barrier-free access (in terms of "environmental improvement") is presented as a logical
next step in their endorsement of aggressive urban restructuring. These statements
actively materialized "design for all Americans" as a commitment to the unnamed
privileges of whiteness, and hence to an actively post-racial politics of design.

Neither the Architectural Barriers Act nor the Civil Rights Act addressed the disproportionate health disparities and institutionalization of disabled people of color
in the 1960s, two issues related to segregated housing.[133] Shortly after the assassina-
tion of Dr. Martin Luther King Jr. (one month after the Kerner Report was released),
Congress passed the Fair Housing Act of 1968, a bill enforcing the Civil Rights Act
of 1964 by prohibiting housing discrimination on the basis of race, religion, nationality, and sex. While *Design for All Americans* had recommended revising existing housing standards to include barrier-free requirements, its aim was to establish disability
as a housing issue, not to address race in barrier-free design.[134] And it was not until
two decades later—in 1988—that Congress amended the law to include disability
and age-related discrimination (through Mace's advocacy).[135]

Ultimately, rights legislation treated disability as a medical and rehabilitative category. While disabled peoples' rights of citizenship were becoming more legible, these
rights were contingent upon evidence of productivity and amenability to rehabilitation. Barrier-free design discourses thus married rehabilitative access-knowledge to
bureaucratic and ablenationalist regimes, continuing to justify access through ideologies of ability. Advocates testified in Congress that accessibility would produce more
"self-sufficient, productive" workers, or as Peter Lassen, executive director of Paralyzed

Veterans of America, put it in 1969, more "complete human being[s]."[136] Barrier-free advocates framed equal access to government resources as a right of public citizenship: "the handicapped," noted Jack H. MacDonald, a Michigan Republican and member of the House of Representatives, "represent a tremendous potential asset for the Nation. It can only be fully utilized, however, by insuring that all facilities constructed with public funds are readily accessible to them, whether for work, recreation, or residence."[137] If productive spatial and public citizenship materialized through a field of access-knowledge dominated by rehabilitation experts, ideologies of ability, and views of disability as tragedy or deficit in need of elimination, barrier-free design merely redesigned the language through which architectural and cultural norms of embodiment were enforced. There can be no doubt that these conditions came at a cost to those bodies that were deemed unproductive, incurable, or unamenable to rehabilitation. But as a grassroots disabled peoples' movement emerged in the following decade to challenge compulsory productivity, rehabilitation, and inaccessible environments, the question remained: would access-knowledge problematize the false neutrality of "all" or would it remain committed to the narrows of white, middle-class, and gendered norms?

Chapter 4

Sloped Technoscience

Curb Cuts, Critical Frictions, and Disability (Maker) Cultures

Responsibility flows out of cuts that bind.
—KAREN BARAD, "Intra-actions"

In the late 1960s, disability activists and their allies drove around Berkeley, California, under dark of night, smashing sidewalks with sledgehammers and pouring new curb cuts with bags of cement or asphalt—or so the rumor goes.[1] While those allegedly involved describe the circumstances surrounding activist curb cuts as far more mundane, heroic stories about sledgehammer-wielding activists have taken shape as the primal scenes of U.S. disability activism, securing the movement's place within the broader memory of civil rights–era direct action and portraying disability as a social and cultural rather than medical category (Figure 4.1). These stories have, in turn, shaped the national narrative about disability rights and U.S. citizenship. The Smithsonian's National Museum of American History in Washington, D.C., for instance, houses in its permanent collections a concrete fragment from an activist-made curb cut in Denver, Colorado, from 1978 (Figure 4.2). At their core, artifacts and narratives of activist curb-cutting express the central ideas of the 1960s and '70s independent living movement, through which disabled people rejected their status as objects of knowledge for rehabilitation professionals and architects, asserting disability as a kind of expert knowledge and critical making.[2] When disabled people enact politics, these narratives suggest, they also design and build new worlds.

"The social life of city sidewalks," wrote Jane Jacobs in 1961, "is precisely that they are public."[3] The curb cut is often understood as a post–World War II technology of barrier-free design, a design feature enabling access to the public sidewalk. Accordingly, the curb cut has also served as a storytelling device in liberal narratives of inclusion and good design. In 1946 lawyer Jack H. Fisher wrote to the mayor of Kalamazoo, Michigan, arguing that curb cuts and ramps "were instrumental in allowing disabled veterans, disabled non-veterans, aged and infirm persons and mothers with baby carriages more freedom of movement."[4] Productive disabled citizenship

Figure 4.1. Flat sidewalks and curb cut at the corner of Dwight and Dana, an alleged site of DIY curb cuts, in the present day. Photograph by author.

Figure 4.2. A fragment of a concrete sidewalk, which disability activists in Denver smashed as part of a protest in 1978. Courtesy of National Museum of American History, Smithsonian Institution, Division of Medicine and Science.

and the liberal narrative surrounding it were central to these particular user categories and the stories they told. Fisher continued:

> These cement ramps in many instances mean the difference between disabled veterans and disabled non-veterans having employment, as with the ramps a person confined to a wheel chair, on crutches or wearing an artificial limb is able to get to a place of employment unaided. The ramps thus enable many so called unemployable persons to become employable persons, and not only benefits the disabled person alone, but benefits the community at large as well.[5]

To suggest that curb cuts reflect the idea that accessibility benefits everyone requires accepting that the universe of users encompasses particular, legible forms. While curb cuts would not appear in most U.S. cities until the 1970s, Fisher's assertion that these features would increase employment for disabled veterans and have added value for others resonates with the claims of rehabilitation experts that barrier-free design benefits "all." Reinforcing the nondisabled, normate status of the "community," Fisher's explanation presents as fact that "everyone" benefits from the curb cut, a fact that dematerializes the racialized, gendered, and classed dimensions of difference—even within the category of disability. And even within the category of disability, this story obscures the diverse physical, sensory, and mental access needs of different disabled users. Much like disability activists' political claims that "every body needs equal access" (Figure 4.3), claims that "everyone" benefits from curb cuts are historically materialized conditions of legibility and illegibility.

Materiality is messy, but the optics of concrete can be misleading. On the surface of Berkeley's streets, curb cuts appeared to materialize en masse after 1973, following high-profile acts of Congress that provided a political mandate and government funding.[6] A year earlier, however, in 1972, the city of Berkeley adopted an official mandate to install curb cuts at every corner—a major victory that symbolized disabled peoples' legibility as users.[7] Once integrated into the urban fabric, the curb cut became a material device for securing the place of disability in public space, as well as a metaphor for the smooth integration of misfit users into social, economic, and material life. Yet this victory erased any physical evidence of guerrilla curb-cutting and other crip interventions into the social life of Berkeley's sidewalks. By repaving Berkeley's sidewalks, the official curb cuts rewrote the history and theory of curb cutting.

Reproduced for nearly a century, the liberal curb cut narrative has become a quintessential explanatory device for the claim that accessibility benefits "everyone." As disability rights leader Ed Roberts framed it in the early 1990s,

> We secured the first curb cut in the country; it was at the corner of Bancroft and Telegraph Avenue. When we first talked to legislators about the issue, they told us, "Curb cuts, why do you need curb cuts? We never see people with disabilities out on the

Figure 4.3. Disability activists used the term "everybody" strategically. Here, a protester holds a sign that says "Every Body Needs Equal Access." Raymond Lifchez and Barbara Winslow, *Design for Independent Living: The Environment and Physically Disabled People* (Berkeley: University of California Press, 1979), 10. Courtesy of Raymond Lifchez.

streets. Who is going to use them?" They didn't understand that their reasoning was circular. When curb cuts were put in, they discovered that access for disabled people benefit[s] many others as well. For instance, people pushing strollers use curb cuts, as do people on bikes and elderly people who can't lift their legs so high. So many people benefit from this accommodation. This is what the concept of universal design is all about. Now Berkeley is a very accessible city. We [people with disabilities] are visible in the community because we can get around everywhere fairly easily. . . . I look around, and I notice that a lot of us are getting gray. As we get older, we realize that disability is just a part of life. Anyone can join our group at any point in life. In this way, the disability rights movement doesn't discriminate. So those of us who are temporarily able-bodied and working for access and accommodation now get older, and the changes they make will benefit them as well.[8]

Much like the barrier-free design regime that framed accessibility through its benefits for "all," Roberts's narrative of curb cuts as benefiting "everyone" or "many people" reproduces an often-told story about accessible design and disability. In this story, the curb cut's treatment as a metaphor, historical object, and material frame represents the values of unmarked assimilation into public space and promotes a notion of disability identity and community as indiscriminate, uniform, and united in its goals and needs.[9] Far from neutralizing the curb cut's symbolic and material work, however, these valences suggest that the foundational objects and origin stories of the independent living movement, of barrier-free design, and of Universal Design contain manifold ways of understanding disability, varied positions on assimilation and resistance, and wide-ranging approaches to access-knowledge. These complexities require unpacking.

Smooth belonging, the crux of the liberal curb cut theory, contrasts with rumors of guerrilla curb-cutting by dark of night to animate one of the central tensions within twentieth-century access-knowledge: the friction between liberal demands for compliance, productivity, and assimilation and radical, anti-assimilationist, and crip methods of knowing-making the world. This chapter historicizes these frictions by tracing the rise of what I term "crip technoscience."[10] Emerging from within disability cultures and communities, these experimental practices of knowing-making challenged hierarchies and power relations within the field of access-knowledge by shifting expertise to those with lived experiences of disability and away from the outside experts often designing in their name. Unlike most accounts of assistive and adaptive technologies, which focus on conforming the user to its material environment, I argue that curb cuts are politically, materially, and epistemologically adaptive technologies around which two distinct approaches to disability inclusion—liberal, assimilationist positions and crip, anti-assimilationist positions—have cohered.[11] Tilting and reconsidering the historical archive of the curb cut and other disability-made technologies, crip technoscience reveals a field of critical labor, friction, leverage, noncompliance, and disorientation that materialized within access-knowledge as a response to dominant medical, scientific, and rehabilitative ways of knowing the user.

THE POLITICS OF SURFACE TEXTURE

Curb cuts (and their close cousins, wheelchair ramps) often signify the notion that disability is a social and environmental construction, produced in the relationship between bodies and built environments, and thus not something innate to the body. Frequently referenced as the "social model" of disability, this idea was central to the regime of knowing-making that I am calling access-knowledge. In the mid-1960s, rehabilitation professionals and medical sociologists developed a notion of "functional limitation" to describe the environmental production of misfit, or the discrepancy between what a body *can* do and what it *ought to* be able to do (by normate

rehabilitation standards).[12] Simultaneously, a growing movement of physically disabled, D/deaf, and blind people challenged the authority of rehabilitation experts
and their claims to know disability, offering instead a politicized and cultural understanding of disabled people as resourceful, creative, nonnormative, and interdependent.[13] Disability activists produced a set of ideas that later influenced an academic
theory of the "social model," which is often taken to argue that disability is a system
of disadvantages that societies produce, and not solely embodied pathology.[14] But as
disability activists articulated it, the notion of environmentally produced disability
was not the social model's primary contribution. Instead, activists were concerned
with creating a new standard of knowledge, offered as an alternative to medicine and
rehabilitation. In 1972 the UK-based Union of the Physically Impaired Against Segregation (UPIAS) proclaimed:

> We as a Union are not interested in descriptions of how awful it is to be disabled. What
> we are interested in, are ways of changing our conditions of life, and thus overcom-
> ing the disabilities which are imposed on top our physical impairments by the way
> this society is organised to exclude us. In our view, it is only the actual impairment
> which we must accept; the additional and totally unnecessary problems caused by the
> way we are treated are essentially to be overcome and not accepted. We look forward
> to the day when the army of "experts" on our social and psychological problems can
> find more productive work.[15]

Treating disability as deficit and disqualification, in other words, failed to understand
the broader social and cultural contexts of disability, which included lived experiences of oppression and disability communities forged from acceptance of disabled
embodiments. This epistemological and political argument appropriated the rehabilitation language of productive citizenship, using it to characterize rehabilitation
experts as engaged in the *unproductive* labor of normalization.

As a metaphor for disability's social construction, the liberal curb cut metaphor
often reproduces the rehabilitation notion of body-environment misfit in concert
with ideas of equal rights and universal disability. Yet this metaphor says little of the
politics of knowing-making disability.[16] For instance, theorists invoke the frictioned
dynamic between wheels and stairs to argue, as feminist philosopher Iris Marion
Young has, that "moving on wheels is a disadvantage only in a world full of stairs."[17]
Metaphors of "ramping" or curb cutting to a better world suggest overcoming barriers,
reorienting values, and achieving broad accessibility through flexible design.[18] Such
metaphors circulate beyond architecture in the "electronic curb cut," a metaphor for
built-in accessibility, and even "curb cut feminism," which explains that everyone benefits from feminism, not only women.[19] Prevalent uses of the curb cut as a metaphor
for broad inclusion refer to the historical "fact" of its usability to multiple types of

users, including wheelchair users, cyclists, or people pushing strollers and shopping carts, to emphasize the necessity of unmarked, smooth disability integration into U.S. public space.

> Unusual things happen when products are designed to be accessible by people with disabilities. It wasn't long after sidewalks were redesigned to accommodate wheelchair users that the benefits of curb cuts began to be realized by everyone. People pushing strollers, riding on skateboards, using roller-blades, riding bicycles and pushing shopping carts soon began to enjoy the benefits of curb cuts. These facts are good examples of why sidewalks with curb cuts are simply better sidewalks.[20]

These supposed facts appear as commonsense yet miraculous findings discovered in the process of enacting more inclusive built environments. They attest to the nature of barriers as constructed rather than pregiven. They convey the notion that more thoughtful design can remake the world. Yet, by treating disability as a universal, environmentally produced experience of misfit, curb cut metaphors align more closely with *rehabilitation* models of disability and barrier-free design than with the social model's articulation of disabled peoples' resourceful, interdependent knowing-making as a form of politics.

Like Berkeley's city-sponsored curb cuts, liberal curb cut metaphors pave over the history of crip resistance to the normate template, rehabilitation, and expert logics of environmental knowing-making that guerrilla curb cutting embodied. There is another way to understand the curb cut, however. Illustrating a crip theory of the curb cut, which professes the antinormative work of noncompliant users empowered as makers, Robert McRuer writes,

> The chunk of concrete dislodged by crip theorists in the street—simultaneously solid and disintegrated, fixed and displaced . . . marks the will to remake the material world. The curb cut, in turn, marks a necessary openness to the accessible public cultures we might yet inhabit. Crip theory questions—or takes a sledgehammer to—that which has been concretized; it might, consequently, be comprehended as a curb cut into disability studies, and into critical theory more generally.[21]

Curb cutting disrupts, in other words, the concretized status quo through acts of rematerialization. Understood as simultaneously productive and disruptive, cutting and rebuilding, the crip curb cutting narrative suggests that misfitting can be a resource for redesigning not only the *place* of disability in the built world but also our ways of *knowing* disability. Curb cutting, in other words, is crip technoscience.

Seamless, smooth, a cross-cutting plane from point A to point B, paving over physical and attitudinal barriers—these are some of the ways that liberal curb cut theories understand the materiality of this feature. Liberal curb cuts embody simple, effortless common sense and flexibility. Crip curb cuts, by contrast, are instruments of friction, disruption, and countermaterial rhetoric. They propose access as negotiation, rather than as a resolved, measurable end. Taking curb cuts to signify friction, as opposed to smoothness, has implications for how we understand the strategies and tactics of disability activism. Curb cuts can signify critical labor rather than productive work, explains Eric Dibner, a nondisabled ally of the independent living movement and early ramp designer.

> A ramp is a bevel between two elevations.... In order to reach something you need location—you might have to move it closer—and ease of operation—it has to turn easily. So you extend it to make it a lever, which gives you greater force and also brings it down closer to you. To me, the ramp is really symbolic, in a way, of how I see proceeding through the system. You're trying to get from point A to point B and you need to figure out how to lever your way—a ramp is a lever—and you need to figure out how to move objects that are blocking your path.... People aren't really trying to make a different world; they're just trying to build ramps.[22]

Dibner's theory of the ramp as a leverage-producing device references Galileo's notion of ramps as "simple machines" that move objects from one plane to another and thus create a more advantageous mechanics.[23] The operative work of ramps as levers is not an *ease* of use but the generation of *force.* Ramps generate friction and leverage toward particular outcomes or goals. In other words, they materialize politics.

For Galileo, simple machines fell into one of two categories. Frictionless, "ideal" machines required almost no force to set them into motion (relative to what they produced). "Real" machines," however, required some energy to work, producing frictions that reduced their leverage.[24] Like the ideal machine, liberal curb cuts are purportedly neutral, smoothing out tensions between users and ramping over the frictioned work of critical knowing-making. Elision, rather than friction, is their surface texture. But apprehending the significance of curb cuts for access-knowledge requires challenging these associations, not because they are inaccurate but because they risk depoliticizing and oversimplifying the material, epistemic, and technological force of designing ramps and curb cuts for disability access.

Crip curb cutting (or ramping) is not assimilation, Dibner seems to suggest, nor does curb cutting remake the world by displacing dominant norms. As a frictioned, leverage-generating device, the curb cut represents noncompliant labor within an existing system, discourse, or built arrangement. As in political struggles for systemic change, critical, interrogative, and "adversarial" design practices leverage material disruption and contention as productive forces.[25] In *Slope:Intercept,* designer Sara Hendren captures the "interrogative" work of curb cutting as public noncompliance.[26] A series of portable, inexpensively produced plywood ramps can be carried, stacked, and arranged in urban environments to produce surfaces on which wheelchair users and skateboarders (both urban misfits) can roll, maneuver, and occupy space. The temporary curb cuts require neither productive labor nor assimilation into existing material arrangements, but their presence generates friction and their use multiplies force. *Slope:Intercept* suggests that the political work of curb cuts rests upon the production of friction and disorientation rather than smooth, neutral belonging.[27]

"Functional estrangement" is a term that critical design theorist Anthony Dunne uses to describe the interrogative work of certain material forms, which can unsettle the user's experience of the designed world.[28] In some respects, critical design resembles so-called empathic simulation exercises, prevalent in rehabilitation education, which enroll nondisabled users in observing impaired experience through temporary use of a wheelchair or blindfold. Often conducted in the name of disability awareness, these exercises presume a user that is normate and open to temporary experiences of estrangement.[29] And like the rehabilitation promises that accessibility reduces functional limitation and relieves frictions between bodies and environments, Dunne contrasts functional estrangement with user-centered design, which appears as purely functional and rarely social, interrogative, or agonistic.[30] Hence, the critical design theory of functional estrangement takes for granted that disability is a depoliticized experience and that accessibility is a neutral solution to functional limitation.

But power and privilege shape critical design and its means of enactment. My concept of "crip technoscience" takes a different approach, investigating the critical design work of how misfit disabled users, for whom estrangement is already a pervasive experience, draw on the sensibilities of friction and disorientation to enact design politics. Reading the curb cut as crip technoscience centralizes disabled people as critical knowers and makers, extending the work of feminist technoscience scholars, who frame technoscience as an interface between critical ways of knowing and iterative practices of world-making.[31] Crip technoscience understands ramps and curb cuts as frictioned "real machines," to use Galileo's term, often operating in tension with their users, rather than as frictionless, "ideal machines," integrating seamlessly.

Crip curb cutting is a friction-producing concept through which accessibility materializes "slantedly," to borrow from Sara Ahmed, through disorienting, tense negotiations of the categories of "knower" and "maker."[32] While disabled people are often imagined as cyborgs with "seamless" relationships to technology, Alison Kafer explains, these relations are often tense, frictioned, and subject to other forms of economic and embodied privilege.[33] Following Kafer, this chapter centers disabled peoples' "ambivalent relationship to technology," informed by histories of failure and denials of access, as well as iterative, political design practices.[34] Rather than centering assistive technologies that aim to cure or rehabilitate bodies, then, I focus on how disability design and politics co-materialize. If we take a sledgehammer to the seemingly concretized sidewalks of disability rights history, what layered sedimentations of resistance do we find below?

DISABILITY MAKER CULTURES

Ronald Mace half-smiles at the camera (Figure 4.4). He sits in a high-backed hospital wheelchair, one arm in a sling, the other using a tool to tinker with something on the table surface before him. In the background, glimpses of the Central Carolina Convalescent Hospital, where nine-year-old Mace was committed in 1950, are fuzzy but visible. The wheelchair configures him as disabled, a body acted upon in this rehabilitation hospital, but the tool and Mace's gaze suggest that he, too, makes and knows.

Diffuse networks of disabled youth, adults, and their families in the postpolio maker community of the 1940s and '50s practiced "self-help" citizenship, employing do-it-yourself tinkering and engineering to access built environments. Concentrated in white, middle-class communities, for whom the rehabilitation regime sought access to private homes and public universities, the disability maker culture both

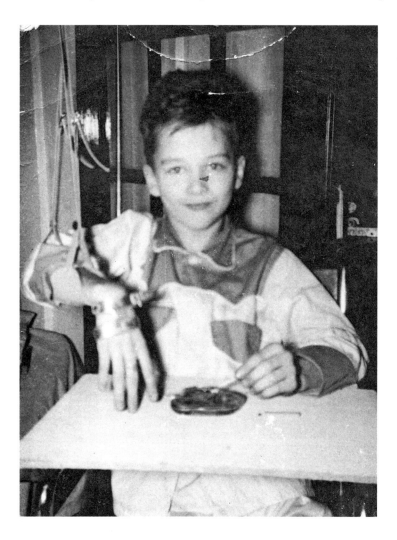

Figure 4.4. Ronald Mace tinkering with a tool at the Central Carolina Convalescent Hospital (1950). Courtesy of Joy Weeber.

embraced and resisted the demands of productive spatial citizenship. In "Electric Moms and Quad Drivers," design historian Bess Williamson captures the postpolio maker community of this era, which designed adaptive technologies as consumer goods and also produced small-scale architectural features such as ramps.[35] Through newsletters such as the Ohio-based *Toomey Gazette* (later the *Rehabilitation Gazette*), families shared information gleaned from other sources, including prominent rehabilitation proponents and popular magazines, built their own wheelchairs from spare parts, designed everyday household tools with found materials, and offered techniques for hacking automobiles, beds, and wheelchair ramps (Figure 4.5). One of many postwar disability cultures, the postpolio maker community reflected the white, middle-class norms of the era.[36] As Williamson points out, the only people of color apparent in the *Toomey Gazette* were representatives of institutionalized populations.[37] Despite opposing institutionalization, Williamson argues, postpolio makers were engaging in "acts of integration, not resistance into the normative roles for men and women of their class and race."[38] Tinkering with homemade tools, automobiles, and the architectures of single-family homes contributed to smoothing out the frictions between physically disabled bodies and compulsory white, middle-class, heteronormative able-bodiedness.

Figure 4.5. Disabled makers shared tips for designing features such as homemade wheelchair ramps. *Toomey Gazette* (Spring 1961): 11. Courtesy of Post-Polio Health International.

Disabled Knowing-Making in Private

Although disabled makers were not engaging in public acts of disobedience, and while their domain was often the privileged white, middle-class home, subtle acts of critical remaking were taking place. The interdependent, networked nature of the postpolio maker culture, wherein disabled people and their families connected to others with similar experiences, made disability a resource for grassroots social networks. Through these networks, postpolio makers shared strategies for creating mundane tools of daily life, and not just technologies that would enhance their productivity. Alice Loomer, a white disabled woman and wheelchair user who had polio as a child, described these activities as "hanging onto the coattails of science" in a time when disabled people were often excluded from schools and had "been given little knowledge of science and technology" but instead "learn[ed] to improvise, invent, supervise, or do more of our own construction."[39] Mace, for instance, created a device for squeezing his wheelchair into a narrower profile so that he could access the restroom of his family home. Loomer developed "all kinds of things: kitchens, hand controls, van lifts, even urinals" over her lifetime by using everyday materials, such as "a paper coffee cup, a small garbage bag, a bunch of Kleenex, and a rubber band."[40] While the public face of access-knowledge—rehabilitation experts, legislators, and architects— defined an experimental field of knowledge in public, many disabled makers operated through these nonapparent, distributed networks of knowing-making, remaining unrecognized as engineers or researchers.

Because it operated in the illegibly political sphere of the private home, the postpolio maker culture of the 1940s and '50s did not appear explicitly resistant to rehabilitation norms. But for many postpolio makers, tinkering with and adapting technologies was a way of enacting access, either through disabled expertise or through interdependence with nondisabled allies such as family members. Loomer's first wheelchair, for instance, was an assemblage built from "a kitchen chair and [her brother's] old bicycle."[41] Another, a rigged power chair, combined a manual wheelchair frame with electrical controls and motorized wheels; "its craftsmanship is deplorable," she said of the chair, "but it's the only wheelchair that could have kept me away from nursing homes and attendants. . . . I made it. So I know how to fix it. . . . I may have failed almost as often as I succeeded, but I have equipment that fits me."[42] This ethos of reinvention was not the individualistic endeavor of single engineering geniuses in their workshops but a product of the interdependent networks of disabled people, families, and assistants who co-materialized a disability maker culture in the mid-twentieth century, often without formal training in engineering or architecture.

While Loomer was not subverting the white, middle-class norms of the midtwentieth century, she also did not embody the white disabled housewife that rehabilitation engineers and scientific managers sought to transform into a productive worker. Nor was she (or Mace) a disabled cyborg, whose relationship to technology operated as a well-integrated, smooth circuit.[43] Loomer's experiences tinkering with wheelchairs disclose a technological ambivalence, which holds in tension the need for access or function with the frictions, limitations, and failures inherent to techno-scientific design processes. Unlike the Cold War–era hopefulness toward technology as a solution to human problems, technologies such as prosthetic limbs, wheelchairs, or canes could nevertheless be awkward or painful to use, ineffective in the absence of ramps and curb cuts, or simply prone to error. Ambivalence toward these technologies, then, is itself a disabled way of knowing-making, born from the iterations of lived experience, technological failure, and ambivalence toward the fantasy of normalization. In this sense, postpolio makers were imagining access as a beginning, what Jay Dolmage calls a "place to start," rather than a measurable or imaginable outcome.[44]

Disabled Knowing-Making in Public

Public accessibility, through barrier-free design, also contributed to the rise of disability maker cultures. In public, ambivalence toward technology presented opportunities for political friction and contestation. Take, for example, the disability maker culture that materialized around access to public universities. In 1949 the governor of Illinois threatened to shut down an educational program for disabled students at the University of Illinois at Galesburg, intending to repurpose the building as an institution for the elderly, where the state would transfer people housed in other, overcrowded "mental wards."[45] The program's thirteen students and their director, Timothy Nugent, organized a series of demonstrations to protest the move (see Figure 3.1). The first protest took place at the inaccessible Illinois state capitol building. With the support of a local police motorcade, paraplegics drove adapted automobiles (like those created by postpolio makers) from Galesburg to Springfield, where they circled the drive in front of the building and attempted to visit the governor at his mansion before speaking to state officials.[46] These officials offered students the options of completing "two years of college work by correspondence" or remaining at Galesburg in an "'isolated ward' for paraplegic students in conjunction with the new medical center for the aged and infirm."[47] Opposing the options of isolated coursework or reentering a public university-turned-institution, the students organized a second demonstration, this time to put pressure on the University of Illinois's administration. Tactics for the second protest drew upon the resourcefulness of disability maker culture. Some students wheeled around campus to gain public visibility, while others demonstrated access-in-action by placing "two-by-ten planks from a paint scaffolding ... over some steps to show that these guys in wheelchairs could get into that building."[48] Constructed in situ with repurposed supplies from the campus landscape, these informal ramps were material-discursive arguments, which made the case for disabled students' belonging in mainstream built environments.

At stake in these demonstrations of disabled knowing-making was the admission of students with disabilities, the majority white and male, to a major public university. In one sense, the students resourcefully demanded access to a rehabilitation program that would extend their normalization into productive citizenship. In another sense, however, the students made their nonuniform belonging legible and demonstrated its value by producing friction. The rough, noticeable presence of disabled bodies, technologies, and design forms in the campus environment was an argument for belonging but not necessarily sameness. While the student protests were not immediately successful, the state government eventually decided to allow a program for physically disabled students to continue at the Urbana-Champaign campus "as an experiment."[49] It was within the context of this disability maker culture (and its relatively privileged location) that the Rehabilitation Education Center and the city of Champaign became experimental sites for access-knowledge.[50]

Physically disabled students, particularly wheelchair users, who attended the University of Illinois in the 1950s and participated in the Rehabilitation Education Center would have been enrolled as designers in experiments with accessibility technologies. Some would have lived in adapted dormitories and others in buildings that were "designed and constructed so that they are equally usable by the able-bodied and the physically disabled."[51] Some would have used an informal ride system, organized through word of mouth, to get to class on time, and others would have helped to design new accessible buses, outfitted with hydraulic lifts resembling machines for loading trucks with heavy materials, which would serve as an alternative transit system in Champaign.[52] If they were athletes, they would have ridden these buses to nearby wheelchair basketball or cheerleading competitions.[53] Some would have been involved in lobbying Emerson Dexter, a vocational rehabilitation counselor and the city's mayor, to install curb cuts in Champaign, and because few precedents for such features existed, some disabled students would have helped to design them (Figure 4.6).[54] For the predominantly white, physically disabled students in the program, the new curb cuts would have enabled participation in the surrounding community.

In all these spaces, technologies, and design features, accessibility was continually being remade. There were not, at this point, any standards for accessible universities, public buildings, or city streets. Nor was accessibility understood as an objective set of circumstances that would benefit all users. The material conditions of access had to be studied, tested, and enacted. But in this space of vocational rehabilitation and productive citizenship, the frictions of access-experimentation channeled into efforts to standardize accessible knowing-making. In 1959 the Rehabilitation Education Center received federal and private funding for the American National Standards Project A117, which would create standards for barrier-free design based on the center's research and experiments.

Like design, research is an iterative material practice, and like public protest, it involves negotiation, material symbols, and generative frictions. Accessibility research at the Rehabilitation Education Center would not have resembled, on its surface, the protests that, nearly a decade earlier, had enabled the program to continue. In one major study, researchers used well-established methods of rehabilitation and human

Figure 4.6. The city of Champaign, Illinois, adopted wide curb cuts (ca. 1956–66). Courtesy of the University of Illinois Archives, image 4022.tif.

factors research, such as anthropometry, to measure wheelchair users' space requirements. But similar to the student demonstrators, who had repurposed scaffolding
planks to build ad hoc ramps for a campus protest, researchers repurposed methods,
such as anthropometry, and in the process reinvented them. Even their experimental tools were appropriated and remade. A primary apparatus of measurement was a
"thirty-four foot long" adjustable ramp with a flexible design: it was "adjustable to
length and pitch" and served as an experimental space, as well as a tool for spatial
measurement (Figure 4.7).[55] Bearing little resemblance to anthropometric calipers
and rulers, which quantified the body as a discrete unit with standard landmarks, the
adjustable ramp measured the body, technology, and space together in the generation
of force and leverage. According to Nugent, "hundreds of paraplegics and quadriple-
gics, men and women, young and old"—in other words, people with varying degrees
of strength and stamina—rolled up and down the ramp, their measurements serving
as a new evidence base for barrier-free design.[56]

Figure 4.7. An experimental ramp for accessibility research at the University of Illinois (ca. 1950s). Courtesy of the University of Illinois Archives, image 5301.tif.

Although concerned with measures such as energy and fatigue, the researchers approached the ramp as a "real machine," in Galileo's terms, a lever operating flexibly in recognition of far-ranging abilities. While the ramp was experimental, flexible, and adjustable, however, the research project required a final set of standards, which would dictate ideal practices for ramp construction. But the researchers acknowledged that their sample, the majority of whom were young, physically rehabilitated wheelchair users, would likely skew the results, and their suggestion for the final ANSI A117.1 standard recommended a modified ramp with a "shallower" slope of 1:12 to account for users with less upper body strength and stamina.[57] Highlighting the entanglements of legibility and flexibility in the work of experimental access-knowledge, the process of designing ramps and curb cuts for accessibility standards repeated in the Rehabilitation Education Center's efforts to include students with a broader spectrum of sensory, mobility, and cognitive disabilities and chronic illnesses in coming decades.[58] Where these efforts to develop access-knowledge remained within the rehabilitation regime, however, disability activists in other locales would soon enter into disoriented relations with this regime.

CRIP TECHNOSCIENCE

"John uses an electric powered wheelchair, writing brace, raised tables, Handihook, specially devised door knobs for radio, television, recorder, etc. Ed uses an iron lung, mouthstick. Both use a microswitch speaker phone with a direct line to the operator; Stenorette with special controls, and keys to the campus elevators."[59] The two University of California, Berkeley, students were Ed Roberts and John Hessler, and the account of their commercially available and self-made technologies appeared in a *Toomey Gazette* article on quadriplegic students across the United States, who were accessing public life beyond institutions by enrolling at universities. Although Roberts and Hessler eventually became leading disability activists in Berkeley, the article provides a snapshot of these two disabled men as makers, sharing their experiences and expertise with a community of people with similar disabilities. The optimistic account of Roberts's and Hessler's technologies echoed, in some respects, the rehabilitation narrative: with the right technologies, quadriplegic students could attend universities and receive the privileges of education. But the two were also part of emerging opposition to this narrative, through a radical, anti-assimilationist culture sometimes called "crip."[60] As one activist put it, the independent living movement sought to "reverse the history of rehab within rehab itself."[61] Even before the movement adopted its best-known strategies of direct action and public protest, independent living activists made creative use of friction and subtlety as they sought to shift the rehabilitation regime, and the broader field of access-knowledge, from within.

Cripping Rehabilitation

Berkeley's crip culture shared features of earlier disability maker cultures. According to historical records, the majority of its participants were white and many were middle class.[62] Some had postpolio disabilities while others had experienced disability since birth or as a result of injuries in late adolescence. This community was also sited in the privileged geography of a university, within which a marginalized residential community of quadriplegic students housed in the campus's Cowell infirmary became a space from which activism would emerge. Recalling the early days of the University of Illinois program at Galesburg, disabled students at Berkeley lived in the infirmary's third floor, which was established in 1962 as a "residence program for severely physically disabled students" with funding from the Department of Vocational Rehabilitation.[63] Demographically, the Cowell students embodied the imagined demographics of rehabilitation's focus: most were male and white, a few were (white) women, and there was one disabled man of color as part of the group of nine.[64]

Isolated from Berkeley dormitories and student life, Cowell became a seedbed for crip community and activism through the independent living movement. Although the term "independent living" had originated within vocational rehabilitation to describe rehabilitation for those deemed unemployable, the movement appropriated this term to define a political position against compulsory productivity.[65] Espousing principles of self-determination, rather than rehabilitation-oriented self-help, the movement argued that everyone (regardless of their productivity) should have equal access to housing and care in the community rather than in nursing homes or institutions. Despite its title, the movement invested in an ethics of interdependence; personal assistants included nondisabled people hired to help with daily activities, as well as other disabled people who provided one another formal or informal services.[66] This subtle shift from independence to interdependence challenged dominant rehabilitation norms, which dictated that nonproductive bodies were dependent and dysfunctional misfits in need of correction.

Prior to the movement, options for severely disabled people were bleak: many were institutionalized, placed in nursing homes, forced to rehabilitate, or even sterilized or killed through eugenics programs.[67] Disability charity organizations confirmed a view of disability as a problem in need of cure. Rather than promoting access or acceptance, organizations such as the March of Dimes portrayed the lives of children with polio as pitiful and used ableist imagery in fundraising marathons promoting cure.[68] Although disability communities had formed around maker practices and at public universities, a cultural notion of disability was not yet legible within the dominant rehabilitation frame.

Consequently, many of the disabled students entering universities in the 1960s were leaving situations of institutionalization, medical paternalism, or isolation. Independent living intercepted these conditions of confinement, isolation, and normalization by producing a new epistemic culture surrounding disability, centered on experiments in access-knowledge.[69] Similar to the feminist women's health movement driven by texts such as *Our Bodies, Ourselves,* disabled people organized knowledge and expertise around their independence from medical authority and interdependence with one another.[70] Knowledge about and by disabled people became the stuff of political friction. Resisting their patient status, the Cowell students formed an activist group called the Rolling Quads. One of their first actions was to "revolt" against Cowell's rehabilitation counselor, whose strict insistence on attending classes did not often account for their access needs.[71] When the counselor was removed, the students became further politicized, advocating for changes to the campus environment.

Numerous historical accounts of the independent living movement, including Ed Roberts's earlier in this chapter, attribute the rise of disability culture to Berkeley's urban infrastructure, with its curb cuts, ramps, and independent living services. Few accounts consider the role of crip technoscience in the *making* of Berkeley's accessible infrastructures or its disability culture. Cowell was a site of crip epistemic culture-in-the-making, where disabled students shared space, formed mutual aid networks, transferred knowledge, and experimented with adaptive technologies of everyday life. Much of this ingenuity manifested in small, ephemeral designs, such as "pips," or rubber grips fitted with levers for turning doorknobs, and "Balkan frames" engineered by students to lift themselves out of bed without the help of attendants.[72] Through these experiments, the Cowell students amassed user-generated access-knowledge and advocated for the university to build ramps in new buildings and retrofit older entrances to their specifications.[73]

Although the disability rights motto "Nothing About Us Without Us" would not circulate until the 1990s,[74] the independent living movement adopted an epistemology of self-determination that presaged this motto. In Illinois, ramp-invention and barrier-free design research had focused on creating standardized forms of access. At Berkeley, crip technoscience centered disabled students' authority as experts about their bodies and surrounding environments. But the movement did not understand medical, technoscientific, and rehabilitative knowledge as inherently normalizing (as later crip theories and some articulations of the social model of disability would do). Nor did it view rehabilitation knowledge and user experiences as inherently conflicting. Independent living activists claimed a kind of "strong objectivity," which feminist epistemologists describe as the idea that one's own lived experiences, though situated, are also more objective than the dominant frame.[75] Put simply, medical and rehabilitation experts did not have a monopoly on objectivity. As John Hessler and Michael Fuss put it in a 1969 proposal for independent living beyond Cowell,

> One of the greatest sources of information on self-care will be the disabled themselves. Having been disabled for a long time, they have gained a great amount of invaluable knowledge on self-care that they can pass on to those recently disabled, who in turn can teach valuable information on newer techniques learned at rehabilitation centers.[76]

Thus, the independent living movement's epistemological claims were grounded in the politics of knowing-making: the problem with rehabilitation, they implied, was the exclusion of disability expertise and agency from the arenas of medical care and decision-making and the consequent exclusion of (what they deemed) *more* objective self-knowledge of disability grounded in life experiences. As Fuss and Hessler make clear, the Cowell residents did not reject liberal autonomous values, such as "self-help."[77] Instead, they insisted on disabled peoples' unique *technoscientific* literacies, with relevance for the politics of everyday life. In their proposal to expand the Cowell program, Fuss and Hessler recalled,

> One young man, after many years of having to have his leg urinal drained, talked to students at Cowell who were either able to drain their own urinals or who were developing their own methods. They were able to show him how he could wear his urinal bag above his knee so that he could reach it. He added this knowledge to his own— where he had designed a pair of pants where he could open up the seams—and now is able to drain his own urinal. The importance of such an ability can be measured in many ways. What draining his urinal means for this man is that he is able to leave his

living residence and remain outdoors all day long. He can go to classes. When he has
to drain his urinal he can go to a public lavatory. This contrasts with what he had to
do before—that was, each time his urinal filled (which was every two or three hours),
he would have to come back to Cowell Hospital, unless he could find a friend, or was
willing to ask a stranger to drain it for him. Also, it means that several times a day he
no longer has to ask someone to help him. . . . Another thing that it has done for him
is to make him realize that with the appropriate equipment and with the right frame
of mind he may even be able to do more things for himself such as fixing his own
meals, doing his own dinner tray, and perhaps, even putting himself to bed.[78]

The young man described was not a seamless cyborg with an easy, frictionless relationship to technology. Everyday practices of remaking the world, however, were
infused with a disability politics of independence *from* expert medical knowledge
and interdependence *between* disabled students. As they moved toward establishing
a more permanent and expansive program for disabled students, the Cowell students
proposed that the program reserve central leadership positions for disabled people,
whose expertise in navigating inaccessible environments and healthcare systems
would be an asset.[79]

By the time that Berkeley students proposed a formal Center for Independent
Living (CIL) in 1972, they had developed a theory of the user tied to an epistemological critique of expertise, authority, and objectivity.[80] Activists framed rehabilitation as a hegemonic system of medical expertise, in which biased "'professionals,'
'experts,' and 'specialists'" are "more likely to be knowledgeable about a person's limitations than about his capacities."[81] As an alternative, the CIL proposed putting disabled people in the role of service providers in order to infuse the system with user
perspectives. It proposed an independent living program that was

designed and will be implemented by blind and disabled people who at one time were
consumers of rehabilitation services and now, because of the nature of their experiences as consumers, have decided it is time for them to become providers. It represents an effort to create something which at present does not exist, namely client
participation in the rehabilitation system.[82]

The CIL's early objective was not to reject rehabilitation but to transform its medical
expert cultures and paternalistic power from within. These transformations of the
rehabilitation regime drove the paradigm shift that the CIL intended to produce.[83]
For instance, rather than shutting down rehabilitation hospitals, in 1974 CIL members acted as consumers, providers, and social workers in a rehabilitation program at
Herrick Memorial Hospital in Berkeley.[84] At Herrick, disabled people constituted the
majority of the hospital advisory board, leading movement leader Ed Roberts to
report, "The clinic meets the needs of the disabled because we helped design it. . . .

The doctors learn from us and we receive medical care from them. Here, it is not a superior-inferior thing."[85] This political focus on hierarchies of knowledge justified claims to strong objectivity but did not eschew rehabilitative or medical science altogether. The role of nondisabled allies was to provide physical or emotional support to disabled peoples' leadership.[86]

Visitors to the CIL in the 1970s would have witnessed blind people using Braille typewriters and books, wheelchair users fixing chairs and retrofitting vans with lifts, and many people engaged in sign language, computer programming, and independent living skills courses.[87] The space became a training ground for other forms of activism. Disabled designer Ralf Hotchkiss, who later won a MacArthur Award for his work with do-it-yourself wheelchair building in developing countries, established a wheelchair and van repair shop (modeled after bicycle self-repair shops) at the CIL.[88] Computer programming courses, which offered vocational skills, were seedbeds for later computer activism by disabled children and their families, who (in the 1980s) would tinker with and hack computers to create assistive technologies.[89] These activities could be considered a type of epistemic activism, which sought to transform access-knowledge from within.[90]

Positioning itself "not [as] a political action program" but as an effort to "plug into the operations of the present rehabilitation network and observe the new relationships which are developed in the course of its existence," the CIL aimed to influence "the greater milieu of which we are a part."[91] Strategically, the organization appropriated the term "independent living" from the rehabilitation field in order to access funding. Previously, the term "independent living" referred to rehabilitation activities for those who were not eligible for vocational rehabilitation and thus required attendant care.[92] The CIL's focus on access, wheelchair repair, and technological training addressed vocational employment, in one sense, but also challenged the imperative for productive citizenship by providing skills that would benefit disabled people regardless of their employment status. Consequently, the California Department of Rehabilitation, on which the CIL had expected to rely for funding, initially objected to the nonvocational nature of access activities.[93] Despite philosophical differences, however, the CIL eventually received a $50,000 grant in 1972 from the regional office of the Rehabilitation Services Administration, initiating a flurry of activity that included connecting disabled people to service providers, finding accessible housing, and doing community advocacy.[94] Between 1972 and 1979, the CIL served 6,600 people and provided 813 different services, including attendant referral, blind services, computer training, counseling, D/deaf services, legal resources, housing assistance, job assistance and training, mechanical training, technical assistance, architectural barrier-removal, transportation, and wheelchair design and repair.[95] The approach also created a national model: by 1978, only six years after its establishment, approximately sixty to seventy Centers of Independent Living had been established across the United States.[96]

Intercept Activism

Curb cut and wheelchair ramp experiments materialized the independent living philosophy of gaining access to public life beyond the dictates of rehabilitation and productivity. Between 1969 and 1970, the Rolling Quads lobbied the city of Berkeley to install curb cuts on sidewalks, requesting an annual budget of $30,000 for "wheelchair ramps in existing curbs" and for adding ramps "in all new construction as a matter of course."[97] Although funding was allocated, installation was slow. It centered on the main strip of Telegraph Avenue and did not always cover desired intersections. Consequently, members of the CIL used asphalt to pave some of their own curb cuts as they waited for the city to complete its project.[98] While these activist-made curb cuts were not forged from activist anger carried out under cover of night, their intervention was no less significant as an experiment in crip access-knowledge, which operated in the spaces where municipal curb cuts had failed to materialize.

Crip technsocience experiments with curb cut materials, sizes, shapes, slopes, and construction methods reveal that in environmental design, as in other forms of technoscience, objectivity and authority are materialized rather than pregiven. Two designers—Hale Zukas and his attendant, Eric Dibner—developed some of the earliest iterations (Figure 4.8). Zukas was a power chair user with cerebral palsy who worked on public advocacy for curb cuts for the CIL. The two met in 1968, when Dibner worked at the Disabled Students Program at Berkeley, which grew from Cowell.[99] While Dibner was not himself disabled, he had worked for several years as a personal attendant to Cowell residents John Hessler and Scott Sorenson.[100] In 1968 Dibner traveled with Hessler to France, where he crafted ad hoc ramps and experimented with slope and materials such as wood planks.[101] When Hessler and Dibner returned from their trip, some curb cuts had appeared in Berkeley and enabled chair users to navigate the streets "without needing assistance at each curb."[102] Consequently, Hessler and Dibner lived together in an apartment in the community, where Dibner built a ramped entrance to the door.[103] It was by supporting the leaders of the CIL as an attendant, rather than by acting as an expert architect, that Dibner became interested in accessibility.[104]

Initial curb cut experiments addressed issues such as slope and materials. Zukas developed a curb cut prototype that Berkeley used for a decade until curb cuts entered building codes.[105] This prototype, initially created with plywood and duct tape, was "four feet deep by eight feet wide, which in a standard six-inch curb is obviously much steeper than the one in twelve [1:12]" standard developed by research in Illinois.[106] While fairly simple, the prototype allowed power chair users access to Berkeley sidewalks and streets. The rough, do-it-yourself nature of these curb cuts suggests a crip understanding of access as a critical project in inaccessible cities but also as an always unfinished effort requiring further iteration.

Activist-made curb cuts introduced critical frictions into built environments. Beyond their functional value, they also drew attention to the failures of existing

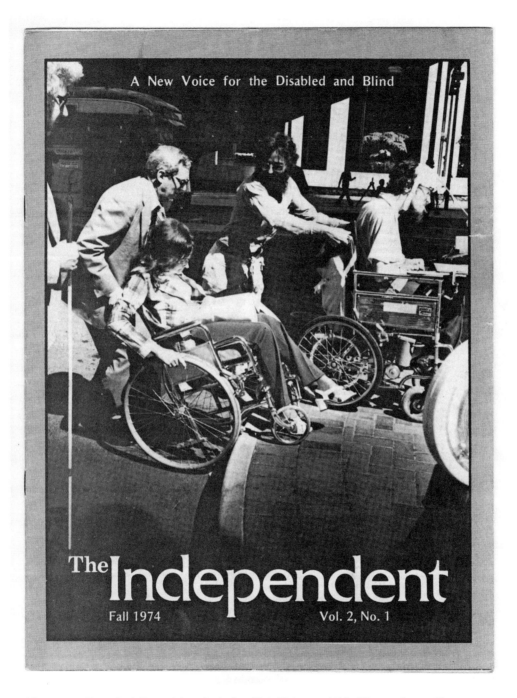

A New Voice for the Disabled and Blind

The Independent

Fall 1974   Vol. 2, No. 1

Figure 4.8. Four disability activists, including Hale Zukas and Eric Dibner, along with two unidentified people in the foreground, roll up Berkeley's first official curb cut, which maintained a high lip. *The Independent* 2, no. 1 (Fall 1974). Courtesy of the Bancroft Library, University of California, Berkeley, and the Center for Independent Living, Berkeley.

material arrangements to account for the presence of wheelchair and power chair users. Design considerations regarding materials and slope were important for disabled users because the curb cut served as a lever, moving wheeled technologies between street and sidewalk. But the process of developing curb cuts also produced frictions when it became evident that access needs are not uniform across users. Blind people, in particular, pointed out that when a curb cut smoothly intercepted the street and the sidewalk, it disoriented their learned sense of the city's layout. These concerns had not been legible when the focus had been on chair users and walking people, both presumed to be sighted.

Objections to the curb cut's universality disoriented the movement's presumption of chair users as the prototypical disabled body. Activists reiterated the curb cut through a growing "cross-disability consciousness."[107] As Zukas explained it, the initial solution was to create curb ramps "outside the crosswalk. So there would continue to be a curb in the regular path of travel to alert blind people that they were about to step into the street."[108] But where gutters, parking meters, or fire hydrants interfered with placing curb cuts immediately to the side of a street corner, they had to appear in the middle of a block.[109] This compromise created navigation problems for chair users, who were faced with the choice of navigating street traffic to reach a crosswalk or crossing at an offset location where drivers may not see them. Getting the curb cut right for both chair users and (walking) blind people required several more iterations.

Rather than opting for a smooth curb cut to resolve tensions between chair users and blind people, activists experimented with materials that would produce more friction on curb cut surfaces. Tactile paving, such as the yellow dots that appear on contemporary curb cuts, had been a subject of experimentation around accessible housing (see Figure 4.1). Nondisabled ally and Cowell attendant Charles Grimes recalls a steep ramp attached to an apartment building.[110] The plywood ramp's steep slope and two-by-four beams of wood made it difficult to climb and dangerous to egress. In response, Grimes added tactile paving by spreading a mixture of cat litter and paint on the ramp to "giv[e] the tires some purchase."[111] These material frictions made using the intercept possible. The tactile paving eventually became a technology with cross-disability application, slowing down wheelchairs on steep ramps and indicating changes in surface and slope to blind or visually impaired people.

Through the CIL's experiments with tactile paving, slope, and curb cut placement, the organization became a recognizable source of expertise for accessibility standards. In 1976 California state architect Edwin Shomate requested feedback from the CIL on the state's accessibility code. The CIL's thorough response, written by Zukas, detailed suggestions related to the organization's experience and research. One recommendation translated experiments with rough surface textures into the design of concrete ramps.

We recommend specifying grooving the final 36 inches of the surface *only* and eliminating a "substantially more rough" surface as an option. Our experience indicates that
the commonly used methods of roughening surfaces almost always fail to produce a
texture that is sufficiently differentiated to be readily detectible by the blind.[112]

Zukas also recommended adding language to the code that would read, "Wherever
possible, curb ramps should be located outside the main stream of pedestrian traffic
so as not to present a hazard to blind persons."[113] Other recommendations emphasized the broad scope of disabilities that the new guidelines should include in addition to blind people and wheelchair users, such as people with hearing impairments
and "those with limited arm movement" who may not easily reach control panels
at elevators."[114] Although focused on impairment categories, Zukas's suggested technical specifications went beyond the typical treatment of functional limitations (as
isolated in the body). Instead, Zukas infused the technical specifications with the
independent living movement's broad understanding of disabled users and disability culture. Zukas's recommendations to Shomate ended with a strong suggestion
that "in the final version of the regulations, copious use be made of diagrams and
graphic illustrations. It may be an exaggeration to say that one picture is worth a
thousand words; nevertheless, illustrations can be a tremendous aid to understanding."[115] Accompanying the letter, Zukas attached a page from Ronald Mace's *Illustrated Handbook of the Handicapped Section of the North Carolina State Building Code*.
This emphasis on the optics of accessibility disclosed another CIL strategy of using
drawing, mapping, and visualization to make arguments for access, particularly for
normate sighted architects.

As the independent living movement grew, activists devised new methods of
producing access-knowledge in addition to designing technologies and products.[116]
Collaborating with university faculty, the CIL created courses based on the independent living movement's user-led approach to disability. Courses on "Unhandicapping Design" were offered at the CIL, while Berkeley faculty taught "Barrier-Free
Design for Disabled Persons" (in the Department of Architecture), "Independent Living Arrangements" (in the Department of Environmental Design), "The Disabled
in Society" (in the Department of Education), "Legislation for the Disabled" (in the
School of Law), and independent studies for field work conducted while working
as an attendant (a joint independent study course of the departments of Architecture,
Environmental Design, and Social Welfare).[117] Of these courses, those focused on
architecture had perhaps the greatest impact, serving as training grounds for a more
general practice of accessibility auditing.

Accessibility audits were a design methodology through which independent living
activists challenged dominant ways of knowing disability. These surveys of existing
buildings used predetermined metrics to determine their accessibility. Participants in

the CIL's architecture courses conducted building audits, which taught students to detect and design accessibility features.[118] CIL audits "identifying buildings as accessible or rampable"[119] utilized experimental standards and guidelines from research conducted elsewhere, including ANSI A117.1 research in Illinois, the North Carolina accessible building code developed by Ronald Mace, disabled UK architect Selwyn Goldsmith's influential *Design for the Disabled,* and early research from Edward Steinfeld, an architect and gerontologist who would later become involved in Universal Design.[120] Throughout the 1960s and '70s, teams of wheelchair users and nondisabled architecture students conducted massive environmental audits under the auspices of a new type of architectural survey method called "performance testing" to gather data about building accessibility at Berkeley.[121] By recording architectural barriers on the campus and surrounding community, disability activists grew the practice of "performance evaluation" and helped to refine protocols for future audits as forms of citizen survey work. This work entailed "critical assessments" of the built environment alongside establishing the terms of these audits' validity through conversations between users and designers.[122]

Accessibility audits drew from the existing ANSI A117.1 guidelines as well as other tools in human factors and ergonomics research, such as the use of time-lapse cameras, to study the built environment.[123] Although time-lapse research originated in scientific managers' "time motion" studies, the focus of accessibility research was not bodily movements alone but how bodies move through the environment. Researchers mounted cameras to each user's wheelchair at eye level.[124] Photographic documentation created an evidence base of legible inaccessibility, such that architects and facilities managers at Berkeley could "analyze each building from the perspective of the user, and not simply from a manual, a checklist."[125] Crip technoscience thus enabled a cripping of access-knowledge itself, as a regime otherwise focused (at the time) on rehabilitation and normalization. Experiments in architectural education became part of the CIL's work when the organization collaborated with Berkeley professor Raymond Lifchez and designer Barbara Winslow to bring disabled "user-experts" into the design studio.[126] CIL members acknowledged these efforts as building architects' knowledge base through a more accurate study of user-environment relations.[127]

Based on experiences with disabled experts in the design studio, Lifchez and Winslow conducted ethnographic research for their 1979 book, *Design for Independent Living: The Environment and Physically Disabled People.* The book studied disabled people as a resourceful maker culture, translating the authors' observations of the independent living philosophy into potential design applications.[128] Its depictions of diverse disabled people went far beyond the trope of the white, disabled housewife to portray both white and nonwhite disabled people of many genders adapting domestic spaces and engaging in all manner of political, social, and cultural activities, including protesting, wheelchair dancing, having meetings, engaging in intimacy, and socializing. The book was the first to distinguish between rehabilitative and crip cultural approaches to environmental design. Provocatively, Lifchez and Winslow concluded the book by asking,

> Is the objective to assimilate the disabled person into the environment, or is it to accommodate the environment to the person? . . . Currently, the emphasis [in barrier-free design] is on assimilation, for this seems to assure that the disabled person, once "broken-in," will be able to operate in a society as a "regular person" and that the environment will not undermine his natural agenda to "improve" himself. . . . This assumption can be counterproductive when designing for accessibility. It may serve only to obscure the fact that the disabled person may have a point of view about the design that challenges what the designers would consider good design. Many designers have, in fact, expressed a certain fear that pressure to accommodate disabled people will jeopardize good design and weaken the design vocabulary. Though certain aspects of the contemporary design vocabulary may have to be reconsidered in making accessible environments, one must also look forward to new items in the vocabulary that will develop in response to these human needs—ultimately leading toward more humane concepts of what makes for good design.[129]

By emphasizing disabled people as experts about their own lives and needs, Lifchez and Winslow challenged an implicit assumption that accessibility will harm the aesthetics or form of "good design." They also contested the assumption of barrier-free design advocates that good design should seek to eliminate disability and assimilate disabled people into the mainstream. These arguments made disabled people's "nonconforming uses" of built environments legible as political practices that could challenge designers' and rehabilitation experts' assumptions about disability.[130]

In contrast to disability simulation exercises, research methods such as mapping and environmental surveys made the distribution of accessible and inaccessible spaces in the city more legible in aggregate. In 1973 Ruth Grimes, a planning student at Berkeley, created a map of the city's curb cut route on Telegraph Avenue and parts of Shattuck Avenue.[131] The following year, Grimes, Dibner, and others collaborated on a survey of accessible housing for the city's Master Plan.[132] In accordance with the independent living philosophy, these surveys integrated disabled people into the evaluation process, even when nondisabled people were involved.[133] Once sites for improved access were identified, the CIL wrote letters offering ramp design services to businesses and homeowners at the rate of fifteen dollars per hour.[134] A local carpenter built most ramps for approximately $200.[135] Design drawings (informed by the ANSI standards and Mace's North Carolina code) showed homeowners and businesses that wheelchair accessibility in their space was possible (Figure 4.9a, b, and c).[136]

Although they referred to existing accessibility standards, the CIL's ramp designs and drawings experimented with the optics of architectural representation. For

a

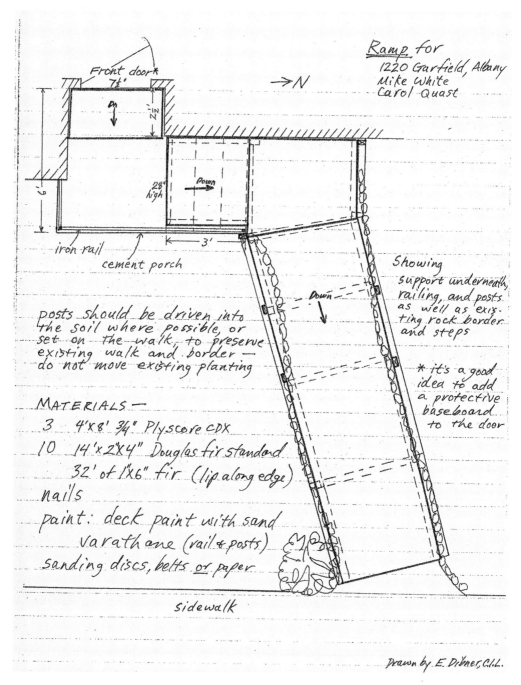

Ramp for
1220 Garfield, Albany
Mike White
Carol Quast

→ N

Front door
7½'

2'2"

6'

28" high

Down

Down

iron rail

cement porch

3'

Showing support underneath, railing, and posts as well as existing rock border and steps

* it's a good idea to add a protective baseboard to the door

posts should be driven into the soil where possible, or set on the walk, to preserve existing walk and border — do not move existing planting

MATERIALS —

3   4'x8' ¾" Plyscore CDX
10 14'x2"x4" Douglas fir standard
    32' of 1"x6" fir (lip along edge)
nails
paint: deck paint with sand
    varathane (rail & posts)
sanding discs, belts or paper

sidewalk

Drawn by E. Dibner, C.I.L.

Figure 4.9a, b, and c. Wheelchair ramps for private homes and businesses, drawn by Eric Dibner as part of a CIL initiative (ca. 1978). Courtesy of the Bancroft Library, University of California, Berkeley.

Concrete ramp to auditorium, E. Oakland Center

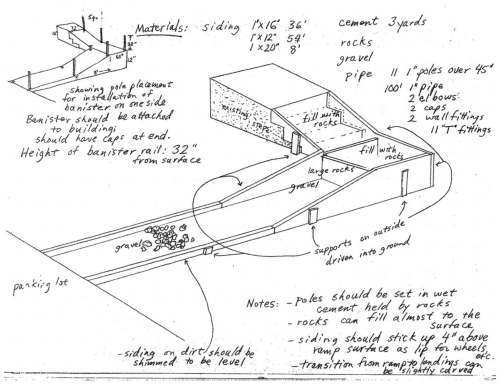

Materials: siding 1"x16" 36'   cement 3 yards
                 1"x12" 54'   rocks
                 1"x20" 8'   gravel
                               pipe   11 1" poles over 45"
                                       100' 1" pipe
                                       2 elbows
                                       2 caps
                                       2 wall fittings
                                       11 "T" fittings

showing pole placement
for installation of
banister on one side
Banister should be attached
to building; should have caps at end.
Height of banister rail: 32"
                  from surface

existing steps

fill with rocks

fill with rocks

large rocks

gravel

gravel

supports on outside
driven into ground

parking lot

- siding on dirt should be
  shimmed to be level

Notes: - poles should be set in wet
           cement, held by rocks
        - rocks can fill almost to the
                                surface
        - siding should stick up 4" above
             ramp surface as lip for wheels, etc.
        - transition from ramp to landings can
                be slightly curved

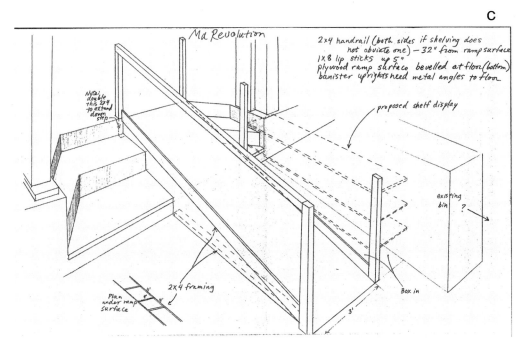

Ma Revolution

2x4 handrail (both sides if shelving does
         not obviate one) - 32" from ramp surface
1x8 lip sticks up 5"
plywood ramp surface bevelled at floor (bottom)
banister uprights need metal angles to floor

proposed shelf display

Note: double
this 2x4
to extend
down
step

existing
bin ?

Box in

2x4 framing

Plan
under ramp
surface

3'

instance, they shifted the visual and technical norms of architectural drawings in order to make accessibility imaginable for owners, designers, and builders. In some cases, these illustrations defied the standardized architectural representations, notations, and handwriting that texts such as the *Architectural Graphic Standards* prescribed. Dibner, who had formerly taken architectural drafting courses but shifted his focus to disability and design issues when he began working as a personal attendant, drew a series of architectural ramps to accompany the CIL's evaluations of potential accessible housing and public spaces. These drawings obeyed few of the conventions of architectural drawing. Many materialized on lined paper, drawn with a ballpoint pen. Casual handwriting, rather than standard capitalized letters, appeared on each plan. Each drawing illustrated the ramp in enough detail to establish its function and internal workings. In place of an architect's professional seal, Dibner signed each drawing, "Eric Dibner, CIL."[137] In material and textual form, the ramp drawings made crip technoscience legible as a visible credential, field of work, and source of expertise. No doubt, the signature also raised questions and invited interrogation.

Dibner's ramp illustrations, their dimensional and material notations, and drawings of the surrounding landscapes disclose the experimental nature of ramp design, particularly in spaces with unusual constraints that would prevent a standard, 1:12 slope.[138] Private residences, for instance, received designs that specified supports, structures, and materials for a relatively small California front yard (see Figure 4.9a). A directive to include "deck paint with sand" for traction recalls Grimes's earlier paint and cat litter mixture, and possibly others that were part of a slow accumulation of knowledge and best practices around ramp design.

For public spaces, such as community centers and grocery stores (see Figure 4.9b and c), where illustrating the possibilities of access required more of a rendering than a technical drawing, the ramps acquire more detail. One proposal, for the Oakland community center, appears made of concrete. Existing steps, along with interior and exterior features, are visible, and specifications for plywood siding held up with external supports and filled with rocks and gravel make visible the ramp's interior frictions. Shifts in materials—from wood to concrete—suggest the emerging solidity of ramp designs within the built environment, as well as the improvised and accumulated knowledge of plywood structures as supports for concrete and gravel surfaces. The tactic of mixing sand and paint to create surface friction on an inexpensive plywood ramp translates directly into the choice of concrete as a material that maintains a pebbled surface while allowing the user the benefit of a longer ramp with a landing for rest, and reinforced side railings. Together, the assemblage of proposed materials and structures illustrates the material and metaphorical work of friction in producing leverage for CIL activists seeking access to public resources such as the community center.

Playing with ideas of public and private, the proposed ramps suggest that accessibility is necessary in domestic space, and not only the public life of street commerce.

Other designs suggest the necessary presence of disability within Berkeley's radical political milieu. Ma Revolution, a local Berkeley co-op grocery store aligned with anti-racist prison activism, was located at the corner of Telegraph Avenue and Dwight Way, on the same block as the CIL and just a block away from one of the sites at which activists allegedly created do-it-yourself curb cuts (see Figure 4.1). The store primarily hired people of color and former prisoners and supported the San Francisco People's Food System, an alternative to corporate food distribution.[139] A proposed ramp for the store's interior was a simple plywood intercept without a landing (see Figure 4.9c). Its three-dimensional representation appears the most solid of the three illustrations shown here, with geometric proportions, solid lines indicating the foreground, and dashed lines marking structures behind a section cut. The ramp appears to address internal structures of the store, connecting itself to the floor and surrounding shelving. The proposal of a ramp for Ma Revolution's interior was part of a campaign to remove sidewalk signs and turnstiles at grocery stores in Berkeley, beginning in 1976.[140] But placed in the broader context of public space in Berkeley, the proposal highlights the possibility that chair users could be grocery store shoppers, as well as supporters of food justice and prison abolition, which shared an anti-assimilationist politics with advocates of deinstitutionalization and independent living. Disabled peoples' lack of access to these and other activist spaces underscored a frequent claim that disability was not recognized as a civil rights issue. Visualizing the possibilities of ramp design in such spaces, then, was a way of emphasizing disability activism as a radical political force.

KNOWING-MAKING DISABILITY HISTORIES

Relations of knowing-making, these iterative design processes suggest, are sites of activism, leverage, and friction. Subtle, mundane projects of crip technoscience served as a training ground for later, more public and legible disability protests. On April 5, 1977, disability activists began a twenty-five-day occupation to protest the federal government's failure to enforce Section 504 of the Federal Rehabilitation Act of 1973 and its mandates of barrier-free programs and services. Protesters sought the enforcement of measures that would ensure ramps, Braille materials, accessible bathrooms, sign language interpreters, and other forms of access in buildings housing federally funded programs and services. A cross-disability coalition, made up of majority-white disability activists who included chair users, D/deaf people, and blind people, staged "the longest occupation of a federal office by protesters in U.S. history" with support from black civil rights and labor activists.[141]

A turning point for U.S. disability activism, the protests made the resourcefulness and collective power of disabled people more public and visible. Although the 504 sit-in has been memorialized as an overt display of power, however, more subtle forms of crip technoscience and ingenuity created structures of support and survival within the space of the sit-in. As activist Corbett O'Toole recalls it, "Somebody went out and scrounged an old refrigerator box, and taped it to the director's air conditioning machine to create a refrigerator for people that had medications that needed to be refrigerated."[142] When phone lines to the building were cut off, D/deaf people would sign from windows to friends below on the street.[143] These strategies recalled crip experiments with repurposing materials, building alliances, and working within existing constraints, often behind the scenes of what is legible as politics, to produce social change.

While the protest embodied these frictions, activists involved in the 504 sit-in framed their intervention as a sort of ramp or curb cut, which would transition disabled people from their presumed, stigmatized status as patients or wards of the state to full citizens under law. They derived this legibility from the black civil rights movement tactic of the "sit-in." Kitty Cone, a white disabled woman activist who organized the 504 protest in Berkeley, later recalled,

> A sit-in was a tactic of the civil rights movement, and it was a way of drawing parallels between the issue [of disability rights] and the civil rights movement of the sixties. People all over the country were not thinking of people with disabilities as an oppressed minority or deserving of civil rights; they were thinking of people with disabilities as objects of charity, objects of pity, probably a group of people who were very weak. So a sit-in was a really good tactic to show that we were a civil rights movement and part of the whole history of struggling for progress for our community.[144]

Legibility involved visual and conceptual parallels between disability rights and black civil rights struggles against spatial segregation, but by treating ableism and racism as parallel structures of oppression, the sit-in (and the discourse surrounding it) ramped over the presumed whiteness of disabled people as a neutral dimension of disability community. Parallels cast black civil rights as a thing of the past while disability rights remained a present concern.

In disability activism, the notion of "cross-disability consciousness" marks awareness of power and privilege within disability communities such as the CIL. The cross-disability coalition of activists understood that as "descendants of the [black] civil rights movement of the '6os, we learned about sit ins from the civil rights movement, we sang freedom songs to keep up morale, and consciously show the connection between the two movements. We always drew the parallels. About public transportation we said we can't even get on the back of the bus," Cone recollected.[145] These claims were strategic: they borrowed and appropriated from one movement's successes to frame another, and even made comparative claims to establish the uniqueness of disability as an experience of spatial misfit, evident in Cone's insistence that "we can't even get on the back of the bus." Yet the shared focus on desegregation or access to space did not necessarily mean that these movements recognized the collective stakes of spatial oppression (such as making the racial desegregation of cities a disability rights issue or the deinstitutionalization of disabled people of color a racial justice issue related to mass incarceration).[146] The pervasive but unmarked whiteness of disability leadership reinforced the notion that invoking civil rights tactics and strategies was a neutral practice. Despite highlighting the frictions of nondisabled belonging as a resource for activism and protest, the sit-in also obscured the frictions of racialized nonbelonging in public space.

In the 1970s, white disability rights advocates drew frequent parallels between ableism and racism to justify the need for "a Federal Civil Rights Law, with appropriate sanctions, directed against the discriminations which are daily practiced against the physically handicapped, and whose effects are every bit as demeaning and as incapacitating as they are when directed against other citizens because of the color of their skin."[147] The term "civil rights," like "barrier-free" or "citizenship," was neutral toward the identities of marginalized people it sought to strategically include or exclude. Disability was termed a "civil rights" issue, however, in reference to racial equality. The implied argument was that racial antidiscrimination laws had not addressed disability as a civil right, and that the time had come to recognize disability within regimes of liberal democratic protection afforded to "all" others. This narrative, however, presumed that the fight for black civil rights was not a disability rights issue and that the struggle for black equality had reached completion. Claims that the time for disability rights had finally arrived, then, embodied a "post-racial" assumption that framed disability rights as the agenda of the future, a seamless integration of disability into existing civil rights narratives.

Temporal distinctions have been central to liberal disability rights narratives, which presume the smooth functioning of rights regimes more generally. Consider, for instance, Joseph Shapiro's claim:

> In the black civil rights movement, people put their lives on the line to assert their moral claim to laws that guaranteed their inclusion in society. When public attitudes about race changed, African-Americans won civil rights protections. Disabled Americans got their civil rights protections before the same kind of sea-change in public understanding.[148]

These comments suggested that the struggle for black civil rights had ended when rights were won but that disability rights were a continuous, more difficult, continually frictioned struggle. Framing this perception, civil rights legislation had offered the palliative effect of obscuring ongoing white supremacy in material environments. The neutral and unmarked status of whiteness as a presumed norm engendered the perception that civil rights laws had cured the racial disparities of cities.[149] But despite the Fair Housing Act of 1968 and other federal legislation directed at addressing the harms of racial segregation for black communities, barriers to accessing housing, education, and work in fact ballooned in the 1970s.[150] Few U.S. cities saw meaningful decreases in segregation in that decade. As Douglas Massey and Nancy Denton have argued, a "distinctive feature of spatial organization in American cities" remained in the 1970s, as it does today, the pervasive (yet unmarked) isolation of black communities, with all of the attendant barriers to education, work, and public life that result from residential segregation.[151] Where segregation appeared to decrease, the causes were sometimes in service of antiblack racism. For example, in the San Francisco Bay area where the 504 protests took place, white movement back into the city resulted in an early wave of "white-black displacement through gentrification rather than a true move toward integration" and left African American people disproportionately isolated from resources compared to Latino and Asian people.[152]

Parallels, like smooth, frictionless curb cuts, tell us little about the intercepting, frictioned work of intersections. In the same year as the 504 sit-in, the Combahee River Collective, a group of black socialist feminists, articulated an idea that legal scholar Kimberlé Crenshaw would later term "intersectionality."

> The most general statement of our politics at the present time would be that we are actively committed to struggling against racial, sexual, heterosexual, and class oppression, and see as our particular task the development of integrated analysis and practice based upon the fact that the major systems of oppression are interlocking. The synthesis of these oppressions creates the conditions of our lives. As Black women we see Black feminism as the logical political movement to combat the manifold and simultaneous oppressions that all women of color face.[153]

Intersectionality called attention to the particular and situated perspectives that constitute what appears as neutral and accordingly made it possible to think and speak about the tensions and overlaps between these systems.[154] The point was to affirm that racism and sexism, among other systems of oppression, were not discrete and that the intersections of these systems had material effects on the oppressions faced by women of color. But like 1960s civil rights laws focused on race, the discourse of intersectionality would not acknowledge disability as a category of oppression for some time.

One reason that the concept of intersectionality has been generative for scholars and activists is that by pointing out that systems of oppression overlap, this concept debunks the liberal idea of a post-oppression world. Accordingly, this concept asks us to think about how disability activism in the late 1970s was relating to the concept of race, to anti-racist movements, and to disabled people of color. While activists' narratives about 504 often gave the impression that the struggle for racial civil rights had ended, and that a new era of disability rights was thus beginning, more recent historical accounts have explored the often discounted and overlooked presence of disabled people of color in the movement, as well as the disability movement's relationships to black and Chicano activist organizations. These narratives also inform a more racially accountable narrative of crip technoscience in the 504 sit-in.

The Black Panthers, who had recently allied themselves with efforts to remove disabled and elderly people of color from nursing homes, and a Chicano group, the Mission Rebels, both provided food to sustain the 504 occupiers.[155] It is very clear that this support was crucial to sustaining the occupation through its twenty-five days. Yet accounts of the coalition between the Black Panthers and CIL activists sometimes reiterate the parallels or analogues between anti-ableist and anti-racist struggles to explain the emergence of this coalition.[156] Recall that liberal curb cut theories insist upon the "interest convergence" of wheelchair users, parents pushing strollers, and cyclists while ignoring the potential intersections and shared identities between these categories. Similarly, accounts of parallel struggles against spatial segregation often fail to produce intersectional analyses of power and privilege within and across disability and racial justice movements.[157] Complicating the liberal curb cut theory that disability design benefits "everyone" by providing a smooth transition to an equal future, the racial histories of the 504 sit-ins and public displays of crip friction suggest that "everyone" continued to be a majority-white designation.

Black crip activist and scholar Leroy Moore argues that disabled activists of color did more than serve food at the occupation, yet their leadership and presence has been largely ramped over in disability histories (and, I would add, histories of barrier-free design).[158] What I am proposing here as a crip curb cut theory provides a different way of understanding the sit-in and the roles of activists of color: not as interest convergence but as leverage and boundary work. Disability historian Susan Schweik has analyzed the coalition between the CIL and the Black Panthers as a "frame extension," which captures the internal tensions between the two groups (around issues such as ableism within Black Panther discourses and whiteness in disability rights discourses) while accounting for the work of overlapping membership.[159] Dennis Billups, a young blind Black Panther, called for black activists to support the sit-ins: "We need to do all we can. We need to show the government that we can have more force than they can ever deal with—and that we can eat more, drink more, love more and pray more than they ever knew was happening. . . . We shouldn't have to fight for our rights, . . . they should already be there."[160] Billups emphasizes the ongoing, frictioned struggles of disabled and black communities to gain legal recognition of their rights. Similarly, Schweik argues, disabled Black Panther Bradley Lomax and his caregiver Chuck Jackson (also a Panther) were unacknowledged leaders in 504. Whereas disability was not initially part of the Black Panthers' consciousness, Lomax influenced an emerging intersectional analysis that then led to the Panthers' support for the sit-in. Based on these accounts, black activists appeared to believe that the ongoing, tense, and difficult work of racial justice was being enacted through disability activism, contra the post-racial understanding of racial justice as a thing of the past and disability rights as the struggle for the future.

The significance of the 504 sit-in for disability rights to accessible transportation, government buildings, and other public spaces cannot be overstated. Successful sit-ins across the United States initiated a new era of barrier-free design, which focused on reiterating accessibility standards and compliance strategies. Once Section 504 became enforceable in the late 1970s, the messy, experimental practices of crip technoscience were slowly eclipsed by a new form of objectivity, premised upon standardized and quantified accessibility. The CIL began consulting on accessibility with organizations such as the Oakland Housing Authority, Bay Area Rapid Transit, the Urban Land Institute, and local museums and hospitals.[161] In the following decades, Zukas, Dibner, and others involved with crip technoscience experiments would lend their expertise to the emerging barrier-free design compliance regime. Along with these successes remained questions of frictions, disorientation, and elision: What are the perceived stakes of accessibility? What issues count as accessible design issues? How can designers know?

Chapter 5

Epistemic Activism

Design Expertise as a
Site of Intervention

Today's culture and society, by reason of increased size and heterogeneity
of the population, has produced new problems which are completely
unprecedented and for which the architect has no answers whatsoever....
The architect's working processes must develop simultaneously and
proportionally with the development of civilization itself. The working
processes of the majority of today's architects are not developing
proportionally, leaving the architect stranded, defeasible, or even defunct.
One of the major reasons that architects' working processes are not
developing is the fact that architects are not studying and designing for the
full range of human experience. It is the primary task of architects to respond
to human needs, both physical and emotional.

> —WILLIAM DOGGETT, RONALD MACE, WILLIAM MARCHANT,
> FRED TOLSON, and L. ROCKET THOMPSON, "Housing
> Environmental Research"

If followed by improved data and performance criteria in the years to come,
the vast amount of new building and rebuilding activity which lies ahead will
produce an environment that can be enjoyed by all of our citizens.

> —AMERICAN INSTITUTE OF ARCHITECTS, "Barrier-Free
> Architecture"

When ideals materialize as laws, knowing and making become contested grounds.
Following the 504 sit-ins in 1977, disability activists successfully pressured the Department of Health, Education, and Welfare (HEW) to enforce Section 504 of the Rehabilitation Act. Barrier-free design advocates celebrated this enforcement, claiming that
it "reflects the spirit of the law."[1] Beyond requiring accessible federal programs and
services, Section 504's enforcement initiated a new trajectory for access-knowledge.
Increasingly, barrier-free design became a matter of compliance with the ever-
broadening array of design standards and codes grounded in specific forms of empirical knowledge. Legal mandates for accessible design did not solely emerge from

activism, however; nor were independent living movement ideologies prevalent among architects. Rather, codes and their enforcement materialized from new fields of research and the social relations between experts who prepared the ground in which new forms of accessibility would later grow and flourish. These conditions, which I term "epistemic activism," are this chapter's primary focus.

Disability scholarship regarding social movements often focuses on overt tactics, such as the 504 sit-ins or the Capitol Crawl, which were geared toward public visibility and solidifying a shared sense of disability identity.[2] Epistemic activism, by contrast, takes place in the relatively illegible spheres of knowledge-production and dissemination. A glimpse of such practices appeared in the previous chapter, in the work of independent living activists to interject friction into built space, assert disabled users as design experts, and "reverse the history of rehab within rehab itself."[3] But while these practices circulate in the disability rights movements' origin stories, far less is known about how activism takes place *within* the privileged sites where knowledge is produced, bureaucratic decisions are rendered, and codes and standards are enacted. Reframing compliance regimes, professional fields, and knowledge itself as social and relational phenomenon, I argue that these seemingly mundane sites were no less sedimented, political, or interventionist than sit-ins and protests.

Disability theorists often invoke accessible design as proof that built environments and societies *materialize* disability oppression and that disability is not inherently biological or physiological.[4] Unlike biomedical and scientific models, which treat disability as an object of study, social and cultural understandings of disability consider scientific knowledge and accessible design as discrete enterprises. Yet a defining feature of twentieth-century access-knowledge was the entanglement of accessible design practices with dominant ways of knowing disability in fields such as rehabilitation and human engineering. These entanglements call into question whether the social model is indeed discrete from scientific and biomedical knowledge. Any oppositional framing between the two is suspect, given these histories of architectural knowing-making.

This chapter investigates how particular intersections of design and science coalesced around the regime of barrier-free design between the 1960s and 1980s and consequently became contested arenas in the politics of knowing-making. Approaching architecture and design discourses as a field of expertise and authority, much like more recognized natural and social sciences, I argue that accounts of the built environment as a materializing force of disability exclusion must attend to design knowledge as a site in which norms are produced and resistance is enacted. If crip technoscience works through friction and leverage, epistemic activism operates through critical torsions, subtle twists, and strategic turns of architectural discourse and law that generate leverage; proliferate the meanings of access; and produce momentum for achieving it.

DESIGNING ACCESS-KNOWLEDGE

With the professionalization of architecture in the mid-nineteenth century, architects configured the inhabitant by referencing scientific data, as well as classical geometries.[5] These ways of knowing, in turn, shaped the legibility of normate and average users as the most likely inhabitants of built space. But in addition to configuring inhabitants as objects of knowledge, the profession also configured the *uses* of professional expertise. In the era of Cold War technoscience, some Modernist architects established their authority by appealing to technical and scientific expertise.[6] Simultaneously, new epistemological arguments (captured in the above epigraphs) contended that architects had not integrated full knowledge of their inhabitants.

Access-knowledge grew from interdisciplinary research outside the architecture field, such as in rehabilitation and human engineering, as well as in arenas beyond the academy, particularly in disability maker cultures and the independent living movement. A third, hybrid domain of knowledge, however, enrolled architects, social scientists, and users to produce new modes of architectural knowing. Compliance-knowledge, this third domain, was concerned with what architects engaged in barrier-free design needed to *know*. Highlighting the limits and boundaries of responsible professional authority, proponents of evidence-based compliance approaches harnessed a robust evidence base to fill the gaps in architects' professional expertise.

Direct challenges to architectural knowledge and authority arose from within the profession. The American Institute of Architects (AIA), the field's professional licensing body, identified a need to convince architects that barrier-free design was valuable and necessary. Initial moves toward redesigning architectural education began in 1965, when Congress established the National Commission on Architectural Barriers, tasked with facilitating collaborations between the AIA, HEW, and the Vocational Rehabilitation Administration (later called the Rehabilitation Services Administration). Two architects—Leon Chatelain and Edward Noakes—served as the commission's chair and project director, respectively. The following year, the AIA granted nearly $60,000 toward research investigating strategies for barrier-free design promotion and education.[7] An AIA-employed research firm studied architects' attitudes about barrier-free design and identified steps toward a more widespread practice of design with disabled people in mind. In addition to a nationwide survey, the AIA developed and tested educational resources at its annual conference and local chapter meetings. These experimental materials framed accessibility to architects in two different ways, and compared their efficacy. The two frames were: "(a) designing and building for the real rather than the assumed average physical and mental characteristics of the population, and (b) designing and building for the 'physically handicapped' with its attendant emotional appeal."[8] According to the AIA's findings, architects reported understanding the needs of "high visibility" physical disabilities marked by the use of wheelchairs, canes, and other assistive devices; yet architects also believed there to be a "general lack of demand in the private marketplace for barrier-free design" and few recognized people with illegible disabilities such as "heart disease or a nervous disorder" as constituting a significant population.[9] These insights recalled the independent living movement's paths to developing cross-disability consciousness by challenging the wheelchair user's primacy in the optics of disability inclusion.

A new research agenda emerged, along with experimental objectives and terms of expertise. Concluding the AIA report included in the commission's 1967 publication, *Design for All Americans*, researchers recommended "long-range program[s] of research" in two areas: first, the "true physical characteristics of the population which constitutes the real market for barrier-free design"; and second, the value of accessibility features, including "desirable performance characteristics of space, products, and components."[10] These two new data sets would contribute to the organization's educational efforts and aid in the development of "concise instructional and reference materials," such as design handbooks and standards.[11] In the coming decades, the AIA's recommendations for long-term data collection on users, markets, and design features would define research and policy agendas, while the conclusions of its 1967 study (with respect to architects' lack of knowledge about disability) would shape strategies and perceptions for cultivating access-knowledge. Based on the AIA's research, *Design for All Americans* made the case for barrier-free design as an important matter of citizenship. While barrier-free design was not a dominant architectural practice in the 1960s, the report and its underlying research aligned with the zeitgeist of new evidence-based architectural practices, which called on architects to apply broad knowledge of the human sciences to socially and politically relevant design.

ENVIRONMENTAL DESIGN RESEARCH

In 1960 Ronald Mace matriculated at North Carolina State University's School of Design. A lifelong tinkerer, he initially planned to major in industrial design, but after a meeting with the school's dean, who "felt that a person with a disability could not make it through the program, and did not have any business trying," Mace felt discouraged and changed his major to architecture.[12] But guidelines such as ANSI A117.1 were only released during his second year in school and had no legal binding. Unlike Champaign and Berkeley, Raleigh did not have a large student disability community, nor did the School of Design have accessible restrooms, elevators, or studio spaces.[13] As in secondary school, entering the School of Design's inaccessible building required Mace to be carried up and down the stairs. During the week, he lived and worked in a rented trailer with his mother, and on weekends he returned home to Winston-Salem.[14] While Mace was no stranger to architectural barriers, his experience at the School of Design compounded his social isolation and lack of independence.

Daily micro-aggressions and continued isolation intensified Mace's view that architectural discourse and professional culture were oblivious to disability. Mace developed an analysis of architects' ignorance, which he described as a materially and historically conditioned arrangement resulting from the public invisibility of disabled people and from norms within the profession. Yet disability activism was not a primary influence for Mace, at least not of the variety concentrated in Berkeley and Champaign. He would not meet other disability activists or develop a political consciousness around disability until the late 1970s. But his social and epistemological analysis of built environments appears to have emerged from exposure to 1960s-era epistemic activism within architectural discourses, particularly the critical field of environmental design research (EDR). Forged at the intersections of architecture and social science, EDR's focus on human experiences of the built environment shaped Mace's theories and strategies for intervention.

Coincidentally, NC State became an epicenter of EDR in the late 1960s, after Mace graduated. But leading up to this development, a shift toward design informed by evidence and ecological models of person-environment interaction was taking place around both student and faculty work. To conclude his undergraduate degree in 1966, Mace and several classmates produced a groundbreaking thesis project, which detailed the significance of social science research on architectural design, specifically in the case of housing.[15] Reviewing wide swaths of literature in urban sociology, environmental psychology, public health, and other fields, the thesis demonstrated that while vast amounts of knowledge about human behavior, cognition, and physical embodiment existed to inform architects' conceptions of inhabitants, these professionals relied instead upon intuition, rather than evidence, to understand the user. An impressively detailed and interdisciplinary literature review was followed by the students' own ethnographic research. Comparing two public housing sites, Chavis Heights and Walnut Terrace, both inhabited by African Americans, they studied the influence of building design, amenities, and layout for inhabitants' self-reports of psychological and social well-being, using surveys, in-home interviews, and drawing exercises with children to collect data.

"Housing Environmental Research," the thesis, offered surprising insights about the authors' views of the social effects of architectural practices. Architects, they proposed, should "treat all architectural projects as if they were experiments"; throughout the design process, they believed, architects should identify hypotheses and assumptions about a project's "bio-social-psychological effects" in order to create an evidence base for future practitioners.[16] In determining standards of good design, they warned against excessive reliance on "minimum standards produced under government control [that] tend to become irrefutable edits."[17] But their critique of minimum design standards, such as those in building codes, focused on social biases rather than the bureaucratic nature of standards: "Compilations of middle class desires and prejudices administered by conservative elements of the middle class bureaucracy do not automatically provide a 'decent home and a suitable living environment' for all people. . . . Few can deny that our knowledge of what constitutes a decent and satisfactory dwelling for a particular people is seriously limited. Minimum standards cannot be expected to fill the gap left by our lack of knowledge."[18] Here, Mace and his colleagues were weaving a theory that narrow building codes and standards produced through a privileged bureaucracy were biased in their content and required new empirical knowledge as a remedy. Together, the critique of minimum standards, the proposal for reflexive architectural practices, and the notion that assumptions should be interrogated throughout the design process foreshadowed key elements of Mace's later Universal Design philosophy.

Before Mace articulated this philosophy, however, similar ideas were shaping the environmental design research field, which contended that scientific knowledge could yield more robust design practices. Mace's thesis provides a surprising window into the rise of EDR, a field it prefigured by two years. In the 1960s architects and social scientists used insights derived from human experience, behavior, and embodiment to challenge Modernism and its emphasis on the standard inhabitant. Whereas Modernist architects presumed an average inhabitant, the interdisciplinary field of EDR coalesced from environmental psychology, urban sociology, history, philosophy, and ergonomics to study the varied qualitative dimensions of human life.[19] With human-environment relations at its center, EDR adopted an ecological understanding of built space as an assemblage of bodies, economies, and knowledge.[20]

In architectural historian Joy Knoblauch's words, EDR represented the "going soft" of architecture in an era of hard science.[21] Against the dominant architectural emphasis on neutrality and standardization, EDR proponents offered the concept of "value-explicit" design, with particular attention to "economic and political context."[22] In the sense that it challenged architects' objective authority and neutrality, EDR resembled independent living activism. But while activists challenged architecture from the outside, claiming authority precisely because they were *not* licensed architects, EDR pursued epistemic activism *within* the architectural profession: activism "not by the protesting crowds," as architectural historian Abigail Sachs argues, but "by *architects* for *architectural discourse,* which is the forum in which architects make claims to professional expertise."[23] EDR challenged High Modernist standardization, as well as the neutral objectivity of architects as space-makers. Proponents argued that architects' intuition failed to capture the complexities of misfit or atypical users.[24] Similar to feminist critiques of scientific objectivity, EDR characterized the mainstream of architectural design as embodying epistemologies of ignorance, understood in this context as the active production of not-knowing through historical arrangements (such as the normate template) as well as through habits of thought and practice (such as the taken-for-granted assumption of architects' expertise about users).[25] Epistemic activism adopted diverse tactics: challenging assumptions, producing new knowledge, and transforming the basis of previous knowledge-generation or interpretation were key sites of intervention.

Academic disciplines coalesce from geographically diffuse networks of knowers, but their real-time moments of encounter at conferences and meetings make it possible to trace these networks, their influence, and the new ways of thinking they produce. Such encounters suggest that epistemic communities and cultures, or networks of knowers and their habits of thought and perception, are also materialized.[26] Although EDR ideas had circulated for at least a decade prior, the Environmental Design Research Association (EDRA) formalized the field, providing a space in which its interdisciplinary epistemic community could share and remake ideas of person-environment interaction. Participatory design research expert Henry Sanoff established EDRA in 1968, at the height of global social protest and domestic political concerns about urban inequality.[27] Writing with his colleague Sidney Cohn, Sanoff made the stakes for EDRA explicit.

> There is a tendency [among designers] to be strong on relevancy and weak on scientific rigor. There is a tendency to be unaware of a body of knowledge relevant to their problems and the need to rediscover and re-argue epistemological issues long since resolved or declared un-resolvable in the social and behavioral sciences. As a result they contribute little to resolving the major conceptual problems and simultaneously add to the total source of confusion and disarray which has pervaded this movement.[28]

Recalling Mace's thesis, quoted at the start of this chapter, Sanoff and Cohn's argument identifies architects' ignorance in their failure to be interdisciplinary, to read beyond their field. The human sciences, both social and behavioral, apparently held the key to more robust architectural practice. Framed as a social and epistemic intervention, the objective was to inject an epistemological notion of "evidence" into a field that lacked a scientific notion of discernible research or rigorous truth.

EDRA consolidated ideas about architecture and science that, if Mace's thesis is any indication, had been brewing for quite some time in diverse fields. Mace's 1966 thesis prefigured EDRA's rise and the beginning of Sanoff's career as an NC State professor (which took place months later). But "Housing Environmental Research" was very much of the epistemic culture that the organization promoted. Mace and his colleagues wrote, for instance, that the "most basic and important problem facing architecture today" is that "scientifically grounded knowledge about the effects this man-contrived environment has on its inhabitants is absolutely minimal."[29] Later, they argued that the architect must "use social scientists as consultants ... in order to discover the real needs of his clients," noting that "there is no reason that architects should not set up and direct their own research in order to discover answers to their own particular questions."[30] These emphases on the "real" (as opposed to imagined or fabricated) needs of clients also foreshadowed the 1967 AIA findings, which emphasized the need for data about "true characteristics" of disabled users.

EDR proponents positioned the field as epistemic activism within architectural discourse, an alignment of architectural theory and practice with social justice.[31] Rather than adopt mainstream standards of rigor and objectivity, EDR experimented with a complex understanding of good knowledge for good design. A central assumption was that most architects substituted their own intuitive knowledge, based on embodied experiences, for the user experience. EDR, by contrast, "portend[ed] linkages between research-driven evidence and environmental design."[32] While it challenged architects to adopt a more rigorous evidence base, EDR was not rooted in statistics or positivism. Key sources of data included social science research on "environmental knowing," which was rooted in phenomenological traditions.[33] Some researchers were influenced by cybernetics and general systems theory.[34] The field enabled researchers concerned with person-environment relations in the disciplines of design methodology, environmental psychology, urban sociology, rehabilitation, history, and phenomenology to connect with practicing architects through a shared interest in spatial relations.[35] The resulting epistemic community brought nonarchitectural expertise to bear on the making of built environment.

But the EDR paradigm was also a microcosm of civil rights–era epistemological and political debates. Whereas liberal frames position legibility as a sudden discovery, the making-visible of invisible bodies, legibility can also occur through imperatives for gradual data collection, whereby surveillance becomes an acceptable solution to social problems. For psychologists studying buildings and cities, the effects of built environments on issues such as "undesirable behavior," "social ills," and "mental illness" caused concerns that intersected new arenas of policing.[36] Despite its apparent progressivism, EDR was entangled with the social projects of surveillance, containment, and incarceration. In response to urban riots in the late 1960s, for example, the Kerner Report identified stressful urban environments as a factor producing black rage. In response, however, sociological, psychological, and criminological research on urban conditions proliferated, enabling targeted solutions for monitoring and controlling urban communities of color.[37] Presentations at EDRA meetings addressed issues of how to contain and discipline urban populations through built environments, a seemingly benign response that buttressed the phenomenon now known as mass incarceration.[38]

Within the EDR framework, scholars, designers, and activists also explored strategies of epistemic resistance to hierarchy and control. As design researcher Charles Burnette described it, the field represented a shift in design knowledge from industrial and military human factors research to an expanded field that was "inherently more humanistic and relevant to the broader concerns of environmental design."[39] Disability research was a key "humanistic" area for the field as it developed its concepts of evidence and expertise (and consequently contributed to access-knowledge).[40] Many of the field's early leaders, including environmental psychologist Gary Moore (who cochaired EDRA's Steering Committee with Sanoff) and influential sociologist

John Zeisel, focused their research on the built environment and its effects on disability across the life span.[41] Psychologist Carolyn Vash, who worked in vocational rehabilitation for the state of California, introduced the politicized language of disability rights to EDRA in 1972 when she presented on "Discrimination by Design: Mobility Barriers."[42] Like other rehabilitation specialists including Nugent, Vash emphasized that barrier-free design such as ramps benefit nondisabled and disabled people alike.[43]

Participatory action research on disability and aging pushed the field beyond medical and rehabilitative models toward social understanding. Drawing on Sanoff's influence, scholars such as Edward Steinfeld and Elaine Ostroff, both of whom would become leaders in Universal Design, presented their work on participatory design research at early EDRA meetings and continued to be involved in the organization.[44] Steinfeld promoted participatory research on health in low-income housing for elders, which informed his later accessibility research.[45] Ostroff, a Massachusetts-based artist and researcher who was involved in the deinstitutionalization movement, described her attempts at epistemic activism within the field of special education.[46] In the early 1970s, Ostroff had promoted disability maker practices within mental institutions and special education, two areas that she found excessively focused on controlling rather than supporting mentally disabled children.[47] Her "Do-It-Yourself Kits for the Handicapped" and other projects provided disabled children and special education teachers recycled or repurposed materials, which they would use to redesign classroom education.[48] Whereas top-down mandates from experts and designers drove deinstitutionalization in the state of Massachusetts, where she worked, Ostroff adopted a different strategy, introducing ideas about disabled children as experts at the level of "adhocracies, temporary work groups," and other informal networks within the institutions that "promoted skill sharing and helped us to go beyond limited roles and disciplines."[49] Transferring authority from "elite consultants of the clinical, behavioral, and design world,"[50] Ostroff's strategy was to empower students with developmental disabilities, parents, and teachers to redesign their classrooms and understand themselves as experts.[51] These epistemic interventions into special education, from within its discourse rather than beyond it, were the basis of Ostroff's groundbreaking 1978 book, *Humanizing Environments*, a title that referred to the dehumanizing conditions of mental institutions in which she had worked.[52] Ostroff's interdisciplinary approach and unorthodox methods demonstrate the reach of the environmental design paradigm, which included both the imperatives of surveillance and top-down management as well as grassroots strategies for user participation.[53]

Similar strategies of epistemic activism bridged EDR with the independent living movement. Drawing on the EDR paradigm, architecture educators Raymond Lifchez and Barbara Winslow at the University of California, Berkeley, worked with the independent living movement to develop participatory design education practices.[54] The field's influence on *Design for Independent Living* is explicit in the book's section on how to conduct user research, which references sociological theories, such as symbolic interactionism, as well as ethnographic methodologies to describe methods of studying *with* disabled users.[55] Suggesting its legibility to EDR, Harvard environmental design expert Mayer Spivack hailed the book as "encouraging evidence . . . that designers can develop rich, verifiable, dependable data to support their design work."[56] That this conception of evidence was gaining legibility among architectural researchers in the 1970s also reveals the extent to which knowledge itself had become a field of political relations and activism. EDR's humanistic approaches toward disability, environmental behavior, and design shaped a capacious understanding of the concept of evidence, which mirrored the CIL's more visible and explicit interventions into knowing-making. *Design for Independent Living* translated the independent living philosophy into EDR language.

> For several decades designers have tried to understand what it is like for the child or elderly person to operate in a world designed almost exclusively for the able-bodied adult, in order to design more sensitively from that other perspective. Now there emerge other spokespersons for vulnerability—physically disabled people. They are truly articulate about their needs and expectations, and we do not have to second-guess their meaning. They offer a view of being in the world that truly challenges the designer's imagination.[57]

Here, reference to architects' attempts at understanding children and elders points to functional limitation research, which defined disability as a contextual but mechanically replicable phenomenon. Disability simulation practices, in which nondisabled people would wear blindfolds or use wheelchairs for a day, were commonplace in rehabilitation research but increasingly challenged by disability activists, who claimed that these practices captured neither the adaptive resourcefulness of life with disability nor the cultural dimensions of disability community.[58] Lifchez and Winslow's user-led design practices, rich ethnographic data, and scenario planning reinforced the sense that simulation exercises were unnecessary if architects recognized disabled people as experts about their own lives, whose knowledge challenges what rehabilitation professionals or designers assume about disability (Figure 5.1).

EXPERIMENTS IN COMPLIANCE-KNOWLEDGE

In the 1970s, disabled designers such as Mace took leadership roles in a new expert industry, which formed around compliance with barrier-free codes between 1973 (following the passage of Section 504) and 1980 (when ANSI published an updated version of A117.1). Mace was at the forefront of this code compliance milieu, which included generating compliance-knowledge to define and implement codes, as well as translating this knowledge into presentable information for designers, civic agents,

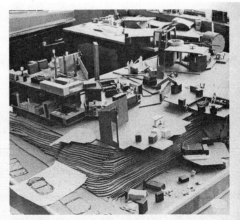

*The three-dimensional model: constructing the site
(foreground). In the background is the scenario map
in plain view as a reference.*

Development of the model.

The environment.

Discussions with user-clients.

Figure 5.1. "Scenario mapping" activities that Lifchez and Winslow undertook by bringing disabled people into the design studio. Raymond Lifchez and Barbara Winslow, *Design for Independent Living: The Environment and Physically Disabled People* (Berkeley: University of California Press, 1979), 144–45. Courtesy of Raymond Lifchez.

and community organizations. Mace's thesis and lived experiences of disability shaped his strategies for promoting barrier-free design. When he graduated from NC State in 1966, Mace had great difficulty with finding an architecture internship. Although he was eventually employed at a small firm in Greensboro, he could not find accessible housing in town and had to commute from his family home in Winston-Salem.[59] Throughout his career, Mace had to tinker with and remake technologies of architectural labor; to access the studio's drafting tables, he used a hydraulic stool of his own design.[60] Nevertheless, the firm's small size afforded opportunities to work on a number of public works, including "banks, schools, knitting mills, and an expansion for the Greensboro Coliseum."[61] Soon, Mace began infusing ideas about users and accessibility into his design projects.

Architectural education was his next area of intervention. In 1972 Mace was offered a job teaching architectural drafting at Fayetteville Technical Institute, where he found opportunities to infuse accessibility awareness into the technical dimensions of the design process.[62] Word of the disabled architect spread. Mace's professional networks in Fayetteville connected him to the North Carolina state government, which hired him to clarify and illustrate the state's new accessibility guidelines, the first state-level standards in the United States and a "national model" (Figure 5.2).[63] The guidelines had been in the making for several years. As the state's architect, Theresa Raper, described it, "legislation was not enacted overnight in North Carolina and implementation of these measures through the *State Building Code* was not instantaneous. The process of development, implementation, education and now amendment has been underway for about ten years."[64] In 1967, a year before the federal

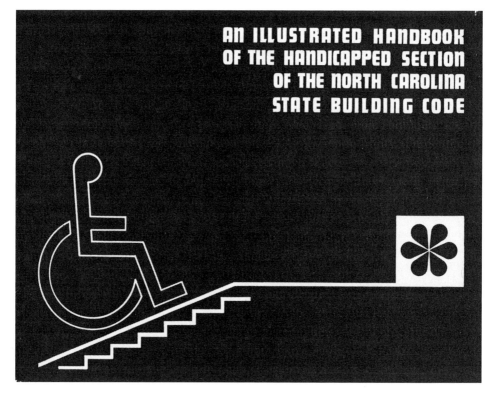

Figure 5.2. Cover of Ronald Mace, *An Illustrated Handbook of the Handicapped Section of the North Carolina State Building Code* (Raleigh: North Carolina Building Code Council, 1974), showing an abstract wheelchair symbol and a ramp.

Architectural Barriers Act, North Carolina committed to incorporating accessibility standards, based on ANSI A117.1, into state building codes.[65] Initially, the "*Code* was composed primarily of 'should's,' largely duplicating the ANSI Standard, instead of 'shall's'; hence, it was viewed as *recommending compliance.*"[66] More specific codes materialized from a process of "collective bargaining": builders demanded tax incentives in exchange for building accessible multifamily apartments.[67] But designers found the new regulations, published in 1973, confusing and unclear. The reason, as Raper described it, was that they were "forced to concentrate new effort on many traditional building elements."[68] These concerns spoke directly to Mace's idea that architects' training had not equipped them with the knowledge or skills to think beyond traditional building approaches.

Hired by the state to illustrate and explain the new code, Mace gained access to a privileged domain of power (the state's code bureaucracy) and utilized a strategy of epistemic activism to challenge architects' assumptions and practices. Referencing the *Architectural Graphic Standards* and other norms of architectural representation,

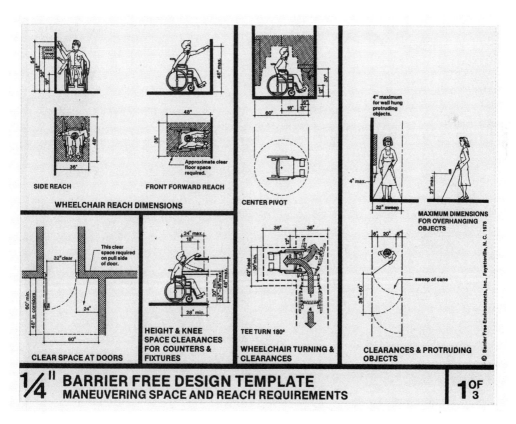

Figure 5.3. A design template showing anthropometric wheelchair users and space requirements for people using walking sticks (1978). Ronald L. Mace Papers, MC 00260, Special Collections Research Center, North Carolina State University Libraries, Raleigh, N.C.

some of the illustrations featured wheelchair anthropometrics (Figure 5.3). Others were more stylized and playful, using photographs to show wheelchairs and other devices in motion, conveying disability as dynamic and agentive (Figure 5.4).

Developing and disseminating the North Carolina accessibility code introduced Mace to an emerging industry of barrier-free design experts. In the code-development stage, he had met other disabled professionals, who the state had solicited for feedback. As Special Consultant to the Commissioner of Insurance, he produced visual aids, such as illustrations and a slide show titled "Are You Aware?," to educate nondisabled "code officials, design professionals, students and civic groups."[69] Illustrating the guidelines and creating the slideshow, with the help of his drafting students, propelled Mace and his accessibility expertise into a professional community concerned with barrier-free design. In his professional life, this community contrasted with experiences of isolation in school and university. Rather than working separately from

Figure 5.4. Mace used stylized images such as this one, layering a photograph of a wheelchair user to create the appearance of motion, in order to convey a more dynamic understanding of disability. Ronald Mace, *An Illustrated Handbook of the Handicapped Section of the North Carolina State Building Code* (Raleigh: North Carolina Building Code Council, 1974), 63, 78.

students and colleagues, Mace applied his professional expertise and lived experiences to redesigning everyday life, from the Fayetteville Technical Institute campus
to government buildings.

In 1974 Mace founded Barrier Free Environments (BFE), an accessibility consultancy and design firm working with local businesses.[70] Initially, BFE characterized itself as a firm specializing in "design for the disabled and elderly population"
(Figure 5.5).[71] The firm designed accessibility in spaces that were not yet subject to
building codes, particularly multifamily dwellings, group homes, and mobile homes
(Figures 5.6 and 5.7).[72] Although Mace had lived for most of his life in a single-family
home in Winston-Salem, his years living in a mobile home during architecture school
had given him direct, day-to-day experiences of tweaking the structure of such a
home for greater accessibility. His architecture thesis, which addressed mass housing in a still-segregated black neighborhood, likewise reflected his awareness of the
raced and classed dimensions of housing beyond the suburban, single-family home.
Similarly, Mace's work on multifamily dwellings broadened the scope of barrier-free
design beyond the idealized white suburban single-family home to include class and
race in designers' conceptions of users.

Despite reaching beyond middle-class users, much of BFE's early work reflected
the racialized and gendered norms of the disabled user in midcentury barrier-free
design. This was evident in the bodies that BFE's design publications depicted. A
mobile home accessibility guidebook, for instance, illustrated prototypical disabled
users as white women using wheelchairs in accessible kitchens. Other work on "site
considerations" for multifamily dwellings, such as apartments, also depicted disabled
people as neutral, white, often featureless. Mace's consciousness regarding race and
gender began to shift in the late 1970s as he met and later married Lockhart Follin,
a disabled woman, activist, and sociologist involved in feminist and racial justice
movements. Lockhart Follin-Mace was the director of the Governor's Council on the
Employment of the Handicapped and later the director of the Governor's Advocacy
Council for Persons with Disabilities.[73] She had been "instrumental" in the passage
of North Carolina's state disability rights legislation.[74] Her analysis of disability as a
minority identity very likely had a transformative impact on Mace's work at BFE,
which incorporated subtle challenges to architectural norms of embodiment.

Much of BFE's early work dealt with retrofits, or changes to the existing built environment. Nevertheless, the work was experimental, involving the types of iterative problem-solving to which Mace had become accustomed as a disabled designer.
Retrofits provided opportunities for marking up existing structures, drawing attention to their inadequacies, and experimenting with new building forms. Mace designed
a retrofit entryway for North Carolina's Justice Building, suggesting the buildings'
failures to address the rights of disabled citizens (Figure 5.8). To promote disabled
peoples' participation in higher education, he also completed several retrofit projects
for smaller colleges. These recalled the CIL's experiments with ramp and curb cut

a

DESIGN FOR DISABILITY

DURING THE NATURAL PROCESS OF AGING, FROM INFANCY TO DEATH,
PEOPLE EXPERIENCE PERIODS OF VARYING ABILITY AND DISABILITY.
BECAUSE OF HEREDITY, INCOMPLETE DEVELOPMENT, PREGNANCY,
DISEASE AND, INEVITABLY, OLD AGE, ALL PEOPLE WILL AT SOME
TIME BE DISABLED.

A DISABILITY DOES NOT RESTRICT ONE'S ACTIVITIES OR CAPABIL-
ITIES UNTIL THE ENVIRONMENT POSES OBSTACLES. ATTITUDINAL
BARRIERS COMBINE WITH ENVIRONMENTAL BARRIERS TO SEVERELY
LIMIT THE ACTIVITIES OF PEOPLE WITH DISABILITIES AND PERPET-
UATE THE MYTH THAT DISABLED PEOPLE ARE INFERIOR, DEPENDENT,
AND IN NEED OF CONSTANT CARE.

ARCHITECTS, ENGINEERS, ADMINISTRATORS, DESIGNERS AND OTHERS
WHO MAKE ENVIRONMENTAL DESIGN DECISIONS INADVERTANTLY CREATE
BARRIERS. THE PHYSICAL ISOLATION RESULTING FROM SUCH BARRIERS
HAS SEVERE SOCIAL AND PSYCHOLOGICAL CONSEQUENCES AND CONTRIB-
UTES TO MISCONCEPTIONS AND NEGATIVE ATTITUDES TOWARD THE
DISABLED WHICH FURTHER SEPARATE THEM FROM THE MAINSTREAM OF
SOCIETY.

BARRIER FREE ENVIRONMENTS, INC. IS AN ARCHITECTURAL AND DESIGN
CONSULTING FIRM SPECIALIZING IN THE ENVIRONMENTAL NEEDS OF
PEOPLE WITH DISABILITIES. BFE WORKS TO ELIMINATE ENVIRONMENTAL
BARRIERS IN ARCHITECTURE, PRODUCT DESIGN, AND PLANNING; AND
SEEKS THROUGH RESEARCH, AND THE DEVELOPMENT OF EDUCATIONAL AND
AWARENESS MATERIALS TO MAKE KNOWN THE ABILITIES OF DISABLED
PEOPLE.

architecture
planning
products
awareness
research

Figure 5.5. Barrier Free Environments offered technical design services geared toward disability (ca. 1974).

architecture

new facilities

BARRIER FREE DESIGN IS NO LONGER A CHARITABLE PHILOSOPHICAL CONCEPT BUT A LEGAL NECESSITY. AS A RESULT OF RECENT LEGISLATION AND RELATED COURT DECISIONS, SCHOOL BOARDS, UNIVERSITY AND CITY PLANNERS, ADMINISTRATORS, AND ARCHITECTS ARE BECOMING AWARE OF THE NEED FOR BARRIER FREE DESIGN.

SPECIALISTS IN DESIGN FOR THE DISABLED, BFE'S EXPERIENCE INCLUDES FULL ARCHITECTURAL PROGRAMMING AND DESIGN SERVICES, AS WELL AS CONSULTING SERVICES TO OTHER ARCHITECTS AND DESIGNERS ON ACCESSIBILITY CONSIDERATIONS AND FEATURES IN NEW FACILITIES.

WHEN CALLED IN AT THE PROGRAMMING OR SCHEMATIC DESIGN PHASES, WE CAN ADVISE ON THE PERFORMANCE LEVELS OF PEOPLE WITH DISABILITIES, RECOMMEND ECONOMICAL ALTERNATIVES TO CODE REQUIREMENTS, AND PREVENT POSSIBLE OMMISSIONS.

c

architecture

modifications
WITH RISING BUILDING COSTS AND
INCREASED EMPHASIS ON ECONOMY, EXTENDED BUILDING LIFE, RE-
STORATION, AND PRESERVATION, IT IS APPARENT THAT THIS COUNTRY'S
PRESENT STOCK OF INACCESSIBLE BUILDINGS COULD REMAIN IN USE
INDEFINITELY AND THEREBY CONTINUE TO PROHIBIT ACCESS AND DENY
EQUAL OPPORTUNITIES TO THE NATION'S DISABLED POPULATION.
RECENT LAWS AND TAX CREDITS ARE CAUSING MANY PEOPLE TO CON-
SIDER BUILDING MODIFICATIONS FOR ACCESSIBILITY.

BFE HAS HAD EXTENSIVE EXPERIENCE IN BARRIER REMOVAL PROJECTS
IN ALL TYPES OF FACILITIES. WE CAN ADVISE ON:

- LEGAL AND ADMINISTRATIVE PROBLEMS OF MODIFICATIONS

- POSSIBLE CONFLICTS BETWEEN ACCESSIBILITY MODIFICATIONS
  REQUIREMENTS, LOCAL AND STATE CODES, AND NATIONAL
  STANDARDS

- ESTABLISHING PRIORITIES, ESSENTIAL REQUIREMENTS, AND
  DEVIATIONS FROM ACCEPTED DESIGN STANDARDS

- COST ESTIMATING, FUNDING, AND BENEFITS OF RECENT TAX
  INCENTIVES

- MATERIALS AND PRODUCTS EVALUATION AND SELECTION TO
  ENHANCE AND SIMPLIFY MODIFICATIONS FOR ACCESSIBILITY

BFE CONDUCTS STUDIES TO EVALUATE THE ACCESSIBILITY PROBLEMS
OF EXISTING STRUCTURES, DESIGNS MODIFICATIONS FOR ELIMINATING
THE BARRIERS, AND DEVELOPS PLANS FOR BARRIER REMOVAL PROJECTS.
THE FIRM WILL ALSO ASSIST BUILDING OWNERS AND LOCAL ARCHITECTS
IN CONTRACTING TO IMPLEMENT THEIR BARRIER REMOVAL PROGRAMS.

BFE'S BARRIER FREE DESIGN CONSULTING SERVICES HAVE BEEN EMPLOY-
ED ON RESEARCH AND ARCHITECTURAL PROJECTS FOR FEDERAL AND STATE
AGENCIES, NATIONAL ORGANIZATIONS, AND PRIVATE INDUSTRY.

919·323-1718

Introduction

demonstration unit

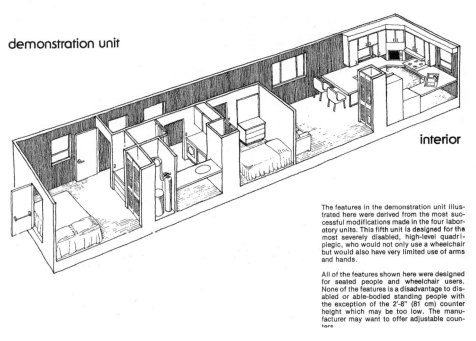

interior

The features in the demonstration unit illustrated here were derived from the most successful modifications made in the four laboratory units. This fifth unit is designed for the
most severely disabled, high-level quadriplegic, who would not only use a wheelchair
but would also have very limited use of arms
and hands.

All of the features shown here were designed
for seated people and wheelchair users.
None of the features is a disadvantage to disabled or able-bodied standing people with
the exception of the 2'-8" (81 cm) counter
height which may be too low. The manufacturer may want to offer adjustable coun-
ters.

Figure 5.6. Accessible mobile housing design represented a departure from the single-
family suburban home. Barrier Free Environments, *Mobile Homes: Alternative Housing for
the Handicapped* (Washington, D.C.: Department of Housing and Urban Development,
1977), 16.

design, which imagined reiterated possible configurations and materials. Early on,
Mace used photographs of these spaces as the baseline from which to retrofit, draw-
ing directly on the images to render accessibility thinkable under existing conditions
(Figure 5.9).

Retrofits were a necessary strategy in a world filled with inaccessible buildings and
design features. They also enabled experimentation toward future accessibility standards. Despite his critiques of minimal compliance standards, Mace became involved
in redesigning accessibility guidelines for new construction. This work was strategic,
offering him access to spaces and conversations in which he could challenge architects' assumptions about disability, in addition to the standards themselves. As he developed a more complex analysis of disability and techniques for retrofitting the built
environment, Mace also quickly rose as an expert within the compliance industry,

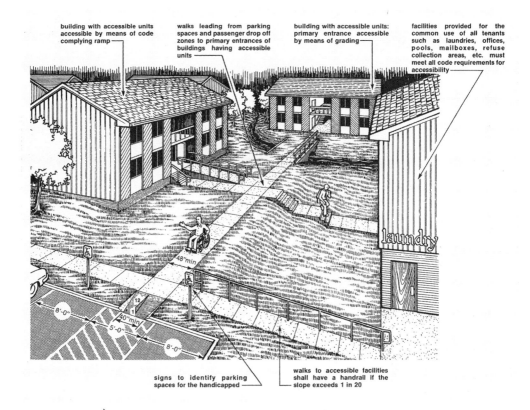

Figure 5.7. Accessible apartment buildings and multifamily dwellings not only focused on different users but also addressed new architectural and landscape features. Barrier Free Environments, *Accessible Housing: A Manual on North Carolina's Building Code Requirements for Accessible Housing* (Raleigh: North Carolina Department of Insurance, 1980), 35.

working on technical assistance for enforcing 504 and preparing accessibility reports for the National Academy of the Sciences, the HEW, the Architectural and Transportation Compliance Board, and the Department of Housing and Urban Development.[75] His experiences of developing and illustrating accessibility codes prefigured the development of compliance-knowledge in the coming decade.

Legal mandates for barrier-free design and the attendant need to enlarge the evidence base of accessibility had led to a proliferation of access-knowledge and compliance strategies in the late 1960s and early 1970s. According to the AIA's 1967 report and *Design for All Americans,* a better understanding of disabled users and performance standards would enable "legislative action" to enforce compliance.[76] As access-knowledge proliferated, data derived through flexible, capacious, experimental, and justice-oriented methods were translated into accessibility codes and standards. Codification was a constraining practice, in one sense, because it distilled a wide field of

PROPOSAL FOR RAMPED ENTRY
NORTH CAROLINA JUSTICE BUILDING
8/20/80

Figure 5.8. Suggested retrofits to add a ramp to the North Carolina Justice building, which had several small steps to its entrance (1980). Ronald L. Mace Papers, MC 00260, Special Collections Research Center, North Carolina State University Libraries, Raleigh, N.C.

knowledge into simple, measurable, and knowable dictates. Yet this process of distillation was relationally enacted, through specific geographies and epistemic communities that negotiate standards and uses of evidence.[77] While standardization appeared to tame the universe of possibilities that crip technoscience, disability activism, and EDR enabled, the process of creating a compliance regime made compliance-knowledge itself an arena of productive negotiation and contestation.

The compliance regime was no less socially constructed, epistemologically challenging, or political than the more legibly contentious milieus from which it emerged. Formed slowly in the last half of the twentieth century, the accessibility compliance regime emerged from a growing epistemic community, which generated theories of access alongside and through standards and guidelines. Take, for example, the discourse of design for "all," which was central to the theory of barrier-free design. The ambiguities of this discourse made it strategic, a currency through which to achieve particular goals. Coupled with the AIA's finding that voluntary barrier-free design

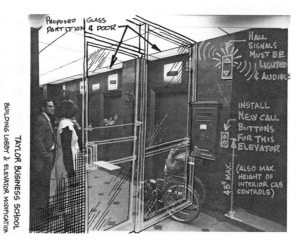

Figure 5.9. Suggested retrofits for the Taylor School of Business drawn directly on photos of door thresholds, sidewalks, and a lobby (where Mace himself appears in the photo, ca. 1978). Ronald L. Mace Papers, MC 00260, Special Collections Research Center, North Carolina State University Libraries, Raleigh, N.C.

measures, "while helpful, had not assured the total accessibility and utility of the federal government to disabled individuals," design for "all Americans" buttressed the case for legally mandated accessibility.[78] Without negating the problematics of design for "all" discussed in chapter 3, I want to address how this term circulated as a political currency within compliance-knowledge to shape code-formation.

An initial legal push for barrier-free design was the 1968 Architectural Barriers Act, a result of *Design for All Americans*. Unsurprisingly, this law remained unenforced. Congress followed up with the federal Rehabilitation Act of 1973, which established a national body, the Architectural and Transportation Barriers Compliance Board (hereafter, the Access Board), to enforce accessibility mandates.[79] Composed of representatives from each federal department, the Access Board was a community of experts charged with setting accessibility standards for federal buildings and monitoring their compliance. Following this legislation, the enforcement of disability rights became contingent on not only the removal of physical barriers to disabled peoples' social, political, and vocational participation in society but also the *codification* of particular types of architectural and product design as standardizable practices with measurable outcomes. While accessibility standards appeared bureaucratic, narrow, and rigid, they materialized from historical and social processes that took place alongside (rather than in replacement of) the theoretical development of accessibility. It is important to recognize that the compliance regime was an attempt at accountability, with the Access Board charged with ensuring compliance through interagency cooperation. Despite its legislative mandate, however, the Access Board failed to enforce 504.

The Access Board's failure was not a result of ignorance or a lack of political will, per se, but rather a specific arrangement of bureaucratic knowing-making. Parts of this arrangement, such as the lack of funds, leadership, and activity in the first six months of its existence, were material.[80] Others were epistemic and ideological. Translating the philosophy of barrier-free design into codes required revising its basic premises. The Access Board's executive director, James Jeffers, emphasized the need for "continual and concerted effort to seek the advice and counsel of disabled persons" and warned of compliance enforcement becoming "incestuous and illegitimate" rather than producing a "responsive and functional environment for all persons."[81] Nevertheless, codification reshaped the scope and meaning of barrier-free design. "Total" compliance—the goal that *Design for All Americans* identified—became "minimal" compliance as the Access Board defined administrative structures and jurisdictions to enforce the law.[82]

Unlike the EDR paradigm and its expansive approach to evidence, compliance-knowledge sought data about a limited, predictable range of users and solutions. The AIA's 1967 findings that architects need clear guidelines and standards dominated the discourse of compliance-knowledge. According to this discourse, access standards should correspond to provable, measurable, and definable outcomes based on evidence.[83] Standardization was purportedly a solution to the anxiety-producing immensity of human variation. As Lifchez and his colleague Cheryl Davis described it,

> It is when all buildings are made to be barrier-free, when all disabilities are to be taken into account, when the client is Any Person (able-bodied and disabled, child and eighty-five-year-old), that architects usually find the charge overwhelming. Where does one begin? What assumptions can one make about needs? What questions are to be asked, and of whom? One feels as if one were suddenly being asked to rethink the entire history of Western architecture, in which the able-bodied have been the sole perceived users.[84]

Minimal compliance guidelines were a compromise, intended to ease architects into barrier-free design. This compromise, however, was only one part of a broader constellation of access-knowledge strategies that emerged after the Rehabilitation Act of 1973. Barrier-free design advocates also began experimenting with legal and rhetorical strategies for addressing architects' resistance or ignorance.

Experiments in compliance-knowledge took place within the seemingly mundane, depoliticized space of code-construction. In 1971 the ANSI A117.1 committee had reviewed the standard and "reaffirmed [it] with no changes in the content."[85] But following the Rehabilitation Act of 1973, the federal government established the National Center for a Barrier Free Environment (NCBFE), with Edward Noakes, chair of the ANSI A117.1 committee, serving as its president.[86] The NCBFE was charged with supporting the Access Board through research, technical assistance, and information dissemination. Action at the state level, such as Mace's work on North Carolina's code, was part of a broader proliferation of more localized codes and standards that developed in the 1960s and '70s. Although some states were beginning to develop their own accessibility codes and often referred to ANSI A117.1, the scope of each standard was as varied as the states they represented. Each state code differed in its presentation of guidelines, data, and illustrations to architects and builders. Variations between state, federal, and even international standards created an impetus for even greater standardization, and with it, experiments in compliance-knowledge.

VISUALIZING COMPLIANCE

Barrier-free design advocates experimented with making guidelines clear and legible to architects unfamiliar with accessibility. As in Mace's *Illustrated Handbook* for the North Carolina accessibility code, the design of textual and visual information became a site for theorizing access itself. Experiments with the theory of access often took place in the geographic sites where epistemic communities formed: conferences, meetings, and other face-to-face social and professional interactions between those claiming access expertise. In 1974 an international epistemic community began to form around barrier-free design at the United Nations Expert Group Meeting on Barrier-Free Design, held at the UN Secretariat in New York. As its name suggested, access had been a growing, global field of knowledge and expertise in the mid-twentieth century, albeit with variations between practices and politics of access-knowledge in each country. In the previous decade, some non-U.S. advocates, including British disabled architect Selwyn Goldsmith, had been exposed to the work of U.S. accessibility experts (including Nugent).[87] The UN Expert Group meeting, by contrast, collected U.S. access-knowledge expertise, particularly in vocational rehabilitation, to make recommendations for international accessibility standards.[88] Rehabilitation International, a U.S.-based disability advocacy organization, convened the UN Expert Group meeting to establish an international epistemic community and share member states' experiences with designing accessible environments.[89] Delegates from France, Argentina, the United Kingdom, the Netherlands, Belgium, Italy, Canada, Yugoslavia, and the United States shared their national projects of barrier-free design.

Representing the United States, leaders of the HEW, the ANSI A117.1 committee, and the President's Committee on the Employment of the Handicapped were in attendance.[90] Edward Noakes, chair of the ANSI A117.1 committee, made the case that in promoting barrier-free design, "good design principles will result in access for all."[91] In creating accessible cities, he argued, the "greatest hurdle is to convince operators and manufacturers of mass transportation vehicles that by meeting the needs of the handicapped, they will be providing a superior, safer and more convenient service for everyone."[92] This framing of accessibility as a public good mirrored the discourse of *Design for All Americans* and turned the meeting's emphasis toward standardizing barrier-free design.[93]

Recommending a wayfinding symbol to demarcate "special facilities for the handicapped," the UN Expert Group and Rehabilitation International offered the now-ubiquitous wheelchair symbol, the International Symbol of Access (ISA), as a universal marker of disability.[94] As a wayfinding symbol, the ISA undoubtedly provided a useful, standard representation of barrier-free design, which would announce the presence of accessible features to disabled and nondisabled people alike. Likewise, the ISA represented international attention to accessibility as a policy matter. As part of broader moves toward standardizing access, the symbol announced disabled citizens' significance to Western states and provided visible verification of accessibility compliance. For some barrier-free design advocates, however, the ISA disclosed a narrow focus on special facilities for disabled users. Rather than promote a more accessible environment overall, some felt that the symbol caused segregation. As Mace argued at a 1977 White House conference on disability, "The symbol has been useful and helpful where standards require minimum numbers of facilities to be accessible," but if "all toilet rooms on every floor were equally accessible, there would be no need for such a symbol or sign. . . . Use of the symbol in new facilities will continue to be necessary as long as the standards do not call for all facilities to be accessible to all people."[95] Mace's argument highlights the nonuniversality of the ISA, particularly as a reflection of the ways in which standards and their legal enforcement were taking shape in the late 1970s. In this sense, the ISA countered the argument that barrier-free design benefits everyone, whether disabled or nondisabled.

As a regime of legibility, the ISA provided a legible, public face to barrier-free design, but much like liberal curb cut narratives, it also made less legible the frictions, experiments, and disorientations that were part of the ongoing critical project of access-knowledge. For instance, the 1967 AIA report had drawn attention to architects' limited conceptions of the category of disability, which often included wheelchair users and blind people using white canes but not invisible sensory or mental disabilities, heart conditions, or the effects of aging. Consequently, the ISA ignored the report's call for more research and public education on the broad range of users who would benefit from barrier-free design. Although the ISA appeared to emerge from the public visibility of disability rights on an international stage, it failed to capture the cross-disability consciousness growing through accessibility experiments, such as curb cuts. The icon arrived on the scene just as U.S. accessibility codes were becoming legally enforceable, contributing to the perception that barrier-free design itself was narrow in its approach to users and excessively mired in bureaucratic code compliance rather than more meaningful forms of accessibility.

CHALLENGING NORMS

Contemporary inclusive design proponents often characterize barrier-free design as a synonym for minimal code compliance with bureaucratic standards geared toward accessibility for a narrow range of legible disabilities. These characterizations of barrier-free design reflect a particular historical understanding of the compliance landscape in the 1970s and '80s. But this landscape was not as concrete as it appeared. Whatever access was or became, it was part of an ongoing set of enactments, within which advocates were experimenting with ways to know, frame, and promote design for a broad range of users. Below the surface of events such as the UN Expert Group meeting, even in spaces of privileged advocacy and expertise, epistemic activism was taking place.

Recall that the home had become an expert domain for rehabilitation specialists interested in barrier-free design in the 1960s and '70s. In September 1974 national accessibility experts convened at the National Conference on Housing and the Handicapped to develop barrier-free design in light of the UN Expert Group's recommendations. The meeting challenged the Expert Group's focus on standardization and introduced ideas from the independent living movement into housing policy. Dean Phillips, president of Goodwill Industries, began the conference by explaining, "The title of this conference is Housing and the Handicapped, not Housing for the Handicapped. The word 'and' was chosen carefully to emphasize the importance of the participation of the handicapped themselves in determining what type of housing is needed."[96] Noakes, who had expressed similar sentiments at the UN conference just a few months earlier, reiterated "the need for handicapped persons themselves and their advocates to take part in decision-making and to insist on their rights."[97] Other participants translated the merits of disabled expertise into the qualities of effective design. Advocates for integrating intellectually disabled people into mainstream settings argued against so-called special facilities and instead for flexible designs "with a number of models to accommodate individual choice and differences in lifestyles."[98] Against the UN Expert Group's calls for standardization, the National Conference recommended greater user input into housing design and new curricula about disabled users for architecture schools.[99]

Although interdisciplinary collaborations had been part of barrier-free design since its beginnings in the ANSI A117.1 committee, their continuation in periods of intensive code-formation reveals that creating standards is a collaborative, contested, and frictioned effort, not simply a purely technocratic process taking place in a far-removed expert realm. A new epistemic community was forming, however, at the intersections of traditional barrier-free design research (grounded in rehabilitation and functional limitation) and the emerging EDR paradigm. Some experts emphasized the need for interdisciplinary approaches to accessible housing standards. Rehabilitation Services Administration Commissioner Andrew Adams, for instance, argued for interdisciplinary alliances with "city planners, code experts, builders and land developers," as well as rehabilitation agencies, whose expertise could improve housing codes.[100] Both Mace and Steinfeld attended a breakout session on architectural and physical planning for accessibility (which Noakes facilitated).[101] Both were early career architects trained in EDR. Mace had just completed work on the North Carolina building code and was rising in recognition as an accessibility expert and disabled architect. Steinfeld had recently become an assistant professor of architecture and gerontology at Syracuse University in New York, after earning his PhD at the University of Michigan, where he worked with Leon Pastalan, gerontologist and advocate of "design for the lifespan." As a graduate student, Steinfeld had worked as a research architect at the National Bureau of Standards and served as secretary of the standards committee for ANSI A117.1.[102] The encounter between Mace and Steinfeld in 1974, particularly in the presence of Noakes, an advocate for barrier-free design as design for all users, entangled the domains of EDR and barrier-free design and established a relationship that would become even more significant in coming decades.

Evidence-based design for new accessibility standards aligned with the project of making a greater diversity of architectural users both scientifically and politically legible. In 1974 the U.S. Department of Housing and Urban Development (HUD) commissioned new research on populations that were not previously legible as architectural users. "Over the last decades," wrote Donna Shalala, assistant secretary for policy development and research at HUD,

Americans have been learning to see what we have never seen before. . . . People who have been hidden from us by prejudice, by custom, and by ignorance. Today, finally, we see the black population; we are only beginning to see other groups—women, the American Indian, the elderly, and the handicapped—see them both as national resources and as groups having claims on the national consciousness.[103]

To make disabled users legible, HUD commissioned Steinfeld, Steven Schroeder, and Marilyn Bishop, working with Syracuse University industrial design professor Rolf Faste, to update and expand ANSI A117.1 by including federal housing standards for wheelchair users.[104] This research was another practice of epistemic activism. Recalling that earlier anthropometric studies had focused on finding population averages or rehabilitating disabled users, this new research addressed underrepresented populations. Researchers conducted anthropometry studies of sixty wheelchair users, primarily elderly women, performing tasks in contemporary home spaces, elevators, and bathrooms (Figure 5.10).

White, disabled women using wheelchairs in kitchens had been a normative focus for barrier-free design research in previous decades. The study reproduced these norms, in part. But its reasons for doing so were specific epistemological challenges to conventional anthropometry. Earlier anthropometrists adopted proportionate sampling. For instance, if a population included 20 percent of individuals in one category, the study would include the same percentage of those individuals.[105] Proportionate sampling generalized from a small group of individuals to the broader population, much as normate bodies often appear to represent all bodies, persons, and citizens. Proportionate sampling also determined the extent of the population studied. Military anthropometrists of the late 1970s complained that it was "almost impossible" to design beyond the "middle 90–95 percent of the population," at least "without compromising the effectiveness of an item of clothing, personal protective equipment, or work place layout."[106] The 5th and 95th percentiles, they argued, were fictional "forms unrealized in nature" and "statistically impossible."[107] By contrast, Steinfeld's study "over-sampled" for a previously overlooked population of elderly women living in public housing, particularly those without additional rehabilitation training, because the researchers calculated that if design standards can be functionally accessible to users in this demographic, they will also be accessible for others.[108] While not rejecting the norm of the white, disabled woman kitchen user, the study's focus on mass housing introduced elements of class and housing research into the archive of anthropometry. The new wheelchair anthropometry study also expanded this range to the 2.5th–97.5th percentiles of bodily measurement.[109] Notably, this range went far beyond the typical 25th–75th percentile measurements presented in general population anthropometrics for architectural design and fashion. In doing so, it challenged what counts as a "broad range" of variation, showing that all ranges are statistical

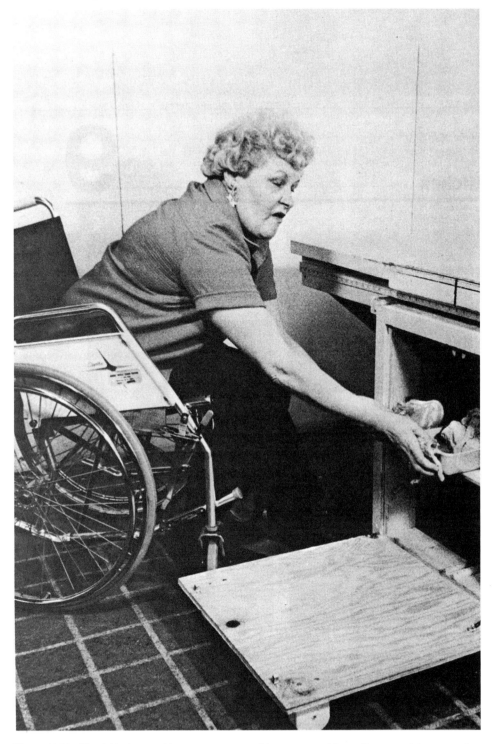

Figure 5.10. Mock kitchens with measurement grids were used for anthropometric research. Here, an elderly white woman seated in a wheelchair reaches into a mock oven. Edward Steinfeld, Steven Schroeder, and Marilyn Bishop, *Accessible Buildings for People with Walking and Reaching Limitations* (Washington, D.C.: U.S. Department of Housing and Urban Development, Office of Policy and Development Research, 1979), 109.

fictions. This epistemic flexibility and willingness to expand the range would presage later research on extreme population outliers.[110]

Earlier anthropometrics had also relied on the ideal of upright military posture for static measurements, or "structural" anthropometry, of bodies at rest, which were then made measurable with carefully calibrated rulers and calipers such that a researcher could capture the linear distance between so-called bodily landmarks.[111] The new wheelchair anthropometrics expanded the instrument of measurement to spatial enclosures or grids into which bodies could mark their spatial use. This meant that the legibility of users was not constrained by a requirement of able-bodiedness, predictably configured limbs or posture, or the ability to stand upright in difficult poses.

Although he was not formally trained in anthropometric methods, Steinfeld had been exposed to emerging rehabilitation models of person-environment relations during his education in social gerontology. Framing the study as an evidence-based design intervention, Steinfeld argued that although a "major goal" of ANSI 117.1 was "the use of technical criteria generated from reliable empirical research," existing barrier-free environment recommendations either lacked sufficient data or relied on "anecdotal" or "limited and ambiguous" sources of data.[112] Making sources of data explicit for designers, he suggested, would make intelligible "who was being included or excluded from access or use of buildings" in these standards.[113] The resulting data, published in 1979, enabled the first revision to the ANSI A117.1 standard in 1980 and influenced the development of evidence-based design as a practice.[114] In addition to expanding general standards for disability access, the inclusion of housing standards enabled barrier-free design to reach federally funded multifamily housing and hence more racial and economic diversity than barrier-free design in the previous decade.

While informing ANSI A117.1-1980, the study made clear that standards were but one part of a "complex system" of access.[115] The research expanded insights from the EDR paradigm to barrier-free design. Where environmental design researchers questioned the primacy of architects' intuition about users, Steinfeld challenged the lack of data underpinning the "technical criteria" for accessibility standards.[116] An expansive and oft-cited literature review accompanying the new research incorporated perspectives from anthropology, gerontology, urban history, and environmental psychology to propose barrier-free design as a knowledge-production practice concerned with a broad range of users.[117] The review likewise reframed the "functional limitation" model of disability, which rehabilitation researchers had introduced in the 1960s. Whereas this model typically offered a depoliticized understanding of person-environment relations, Steinfeld et al. offered an explanation of disability that mirrored independent living and social model ideologies.

> When [misfit occurs], the blame for the misfit is placed upon the environment and it
> is subsequently changed. Since the disabled person has different physiological norms,
> it is only natural that his relationship to the environment is different from that of the

able bodied person. He can no more be expected to adapt and develop competence in a misfit environment than can the able bodied person. However, when such a misfit occurs for the disabled person, the blame is placed on the person rather than on the environment. This shifting of blame from the environment to the person is an ideological position based on the value assigned to disabled people. Once this position is changed so that the environment is blamed, then responsive environments can be created in which disabled people can display competence and, by extension, overcome much of the dependency and stigma which stems from being environmentally incompetent.[118]

Although the terms "competent" and "incompetent" suggest norms of environmental behavior, the point here was that most built environments had not been created to demonstrate disabled peoples' resourcefulness and adaptation, whereas more accessible environments could be those that would highlight disabled peoples' ways of moving through the world. Yet the idea of environmental competence placed barrier-free design research in direct conversation with human factors and ergonomics, framing "buildings as task environments for access" and suggesting that accessibility is best understood through "an integrated framework of human performance."[119] A visual manifestation of this "human performance" understanding of accessibility was "The Enabler," a figure that Steinfeld and Faste introduced as a tool for designers to think about body-environment relations (Figure 5.11). Like the figures of the architectural inhabitant discussed in chapter 1, the Enabler was an apparently white, male, standing figure designed to appear neutral. Its name suggested compulsory normalcy or able-bodiedness. A list of possible functional limitations accompanied it, including "difficulty interpreting information," "limitations of stamina," "extremes of size and weight," as well as "complete loss of sight" and "difficulty using lower extremities." These terms and their emphasis on deficit and limitation recalled earlier research identifying functionally limited users for rehabilitation.

Independent living movement activists would have dismissed the Enabler as another manifestation of nondisabled expertise and judgment of disabled bodies, similar to products designed for "limited activity citizens" (Figure 5.12). Without discounting this criticism, I suggest that the Enabler's purpose was to intervene into a specific field of knowledge, marked by singular representations of disability. Unlike the ISA, the Enabler was multiply disabled. Notations of possible impairments challenged the existing evidence base of barrier-free design to move beyond prototypical wheelchair user and consider illegible disabilities. Even an apparently able-bodied person could be cognitively disabled, experience chronic fatigue, or be too small or too large for typical built spaces. These possibilities were acknowledged in earlier barrier-free design, but because they did not appear as legible as a wheelchair, they were illegible ways of being in the world. Unlike Freese's figures, the Enabler's framing and representation suggested that figures appearing normate could embody many

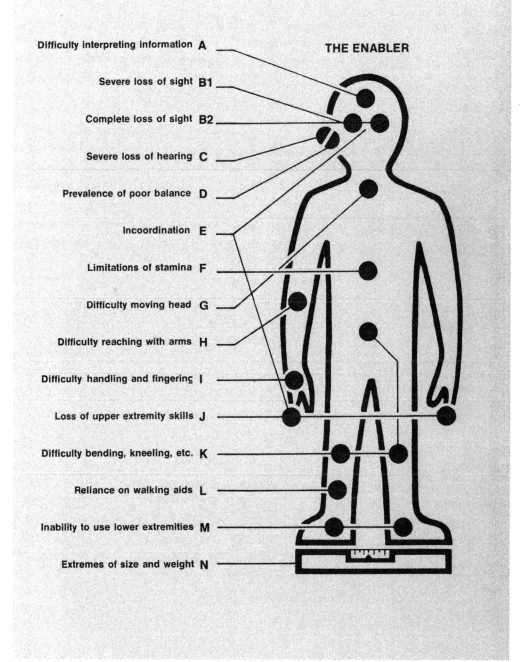

Difficulty interpreting information **A**

Severe loss of sight **B1**

Complete loss of sight **B2**

Severe loss of hearing **C**

Prevalence of poor balance **D**

Incoordination **E**

Limitations of stamina **F**

Difficulty moving head **G**

Difficulty reaching with arms **H**

Difficulty handling and fingering **I**

Loss of upper extremity skills **J**

Difficulty bending, kneeling, etc. **K**

Reliance on walking aids **L**

Inability to use lower extremities **M**

Extremes of size and weight **N**

THE ENABLER

Figure 5.11. The Enabler appears normate. The figure is accompanied by dots and a list of possible functional limitations that users could experience. Edward Steinfeld, Steven Schroeder, and Marilyn Bishop, *Accessible Buildings for People with Walking and Reaching Limitations* (Washington, D.C.: U.S. Department of Housing and Urban Development, Office of Policy and Development Research, 1979), 75.

Basic Kitchen Planning for Handicapped People and Limited Activity Citizens

- The vital point to consider is the comfort and safety of the occupant—whose movement is limited. Stock cabinets and standard appliances can be adapted to these conditions to bring customer satisfaction and allow the builder to keep optimum controls on his first installed cost . . .
- The plan shown is a good thought starter—it can guide you to a most acceptable final "handicapped" kitchen presentation.

GENERAL ELECTRIC

Figure 5.12. General Electric, "Basic Kitchen Planning for Handicapped People and Limited Activity Citizens" (1979). Ronald L. Mace Papers, MC 00260, Special Collections Research Center, North Carolina State University Libraries, Raleigh, N.C.

possible variations and deviations from the norm.[120] The Enabler manifested epistemic activism within the seemingly rigid domain of rehabilitation research and standards formation, introducing the possibility of both legible and illegible mobility, as well as sensory, cognitive, and strength-related disabilities, into a format of representation that otherwise portrayed itself as universal and neutral. In this sense, the Enabler both operationalized and challenged the average body represented by the normate template.

The Enabler was part of a broader cultural resistance within barrier-free design, which went beyond the sphere of code compliance to reframe cultural preferences for normalcy. In 1978 Edmund Leonard, an attorney serving on the President's Committee on Employment of the Handicapped, chided design for the majority of nondisabled users, particularly "design for persons with average dimensions, average powers, senses, limitations, and adaptability," as "a fallacy and an anachronism."[121] Built environments, according to Leonard, operate on the scale of populations, not individuals; thus, they need to keep the full range of human users, particularly disabled users, in mind. "Accessibility to the built environment for all people," Leonard contended, "can be achieved, with very few exceptions, without the need for special and separate provisions for persons with disabilities. Most modifications to achieve accessibility enhance the safety of everyone."[122] These claims echoed those of earlier barrier-free design proponents nearly two decades earlier, reiterating that the normate template fails to account for all users' needs and that barrier-free design can better enhance usability for all people.

While for architects, designing beyond the average user was a radical proposition, this practice was more mainstream in industrial and product design, particularly as a result of Henry Dreyfuss's influence. Some industrial designers, such as Richard Hollerith, president of the Industrial Design Society of America (IDSA), framed disability design as "design for all of us."[123] Other industrial designers made similar claims to promote accessible products to broader consumer markets.[124] Integrating flexible design for broad user groups into mass-produced consumer goods offered a profitable opportunity, but industrial designers also engaged in epistemic activism, not just by broadening the field's typical understanding of the user but also by challenging the concepts and frameworks designating valuable users and good design. James Mueller, a workplace ergonomist and industrial designer, worked alongside occupational therapists, biomedical engineers, and vocational rehabilitation counselors in the 1970s.[125] At a 1975 conference, he argued that rehabilitation

> suggests a "return to normalcy"; return to the "normal" population, the "normal" environment, a "normal" lifestyle. In truth, however, we are beginning to understand that the 50th-tile man and woman, the "normal" population, are as much a minority as those persons considered to be handicapped. The designers of homes, offices, elevators, kitchen appliances, automobiles, doorknobs, and countless other products are

awaking to the fact that the characteristics of these products which make them un-
usable for the disabled person are the same as those which make them difficult or
dangerous to use for the so-called "normal" population.... The malady of design then,
is not only that we have failed to consider the needs of the disabled, but that we have
not fully understood the variety of people who come in contact with these products.
Hence the constant need for modification, adaptation, and redesign of manufactured
products for the severely disabled.[126]

Like Steinfeld, Mueller was concerned with unsettling the normate user rather than
with promoting assimilated, productive citizens. While working as an ergonomist in
a rehabilitation center, Mueller found that his industrial design training could influence the path toward deinstitutionalization by removing the stigmatizing medical
and institutional aesthetics and specialized functions of many adaptive devices.[127] An
industrial design perspective could inform the aesthetics of workplace products, but
Mueller was also concerned with how industrial designers find evidence about disabled users. The field's evidence base would benefit, he suggested, from centering
the knowledge of disabled people who as "human being[s] and [as] user[s]" encountered and adapted themselves to hostile built environments.[128] With these epistemological critiques, the discourse of design for "all" or "everyone" began to torque away
from the seemingly neutral white, average, American disabled user (personified by the
disabled soldier or housewife), particularly within academic discourses, spaces, and
publications (Figure 5.13).

Challenging norms taken as common sense is an epistemic activist practice, but
it is also important to consider the new norms that take their place. In the case of
barrier-free design, unsettling the normate template gave way to the notion of disability universalism. In the late 1970s, barrier-free design advocates recapitulated the
claim that accessibility for disabled users benefits everyone by arguing that disability is a universal experience, which everyone will experience at some point in the life
spectrum. Disability universalism, which assumed that built environments are sources
of vulnerability that could disable virtually anyone through poor design choices, recalled collaborations between rehabilitation professionals, ergonomists, and gerontologists in the 1950s, who devised accessible homes for the aging.[129] The idea was also
beholden to functional models of disability, which ignored the racialized, classed, and
gendered dimensions of aging.

Disability universalism was a pervasive belief among proponents of barrier-free
design in the late 1970s. Take, for instance, James Jeffers, executive director of the
Architectural and Transportation Barriers Compliance Board, charged with setting
and enforcing federal accessibility laws. In 1977 Jeffers claimed, "Although barrier-free
design is commonly associated with the environmental needs of disabled persons,
it is a much more universal concept in its application."[130] He was quick to clarify,
however, that while environmental barriers could potentially impact any user,

some of us have the ability to adapt more readily than others. For the physically disabled person, however, the ability to adapt to nonfunctional design is severely limited. For this reason, disabled individuals, for the purposes of survival and participation, are demanding barrier-free design that will benefit all by ensuring functional, safe, and convenient design of our man-made environment.[131]

Jeffers's qualification recalled Lifchez and Winslow's recognition of disabled people as "spokespersons for vulnerability" whose knowledge architects need not "second-guess."[132] Reflecting the rise of legible disability activism in the late 1970s, particularly the 504 sit-in, Jeffers highlighted disability activists' leadership and knowledge. Other barrier-free design advocates, however, adopted rehabilitation discourses. Architect Michael Bednar's account of barrier-free design extended the notion of disability

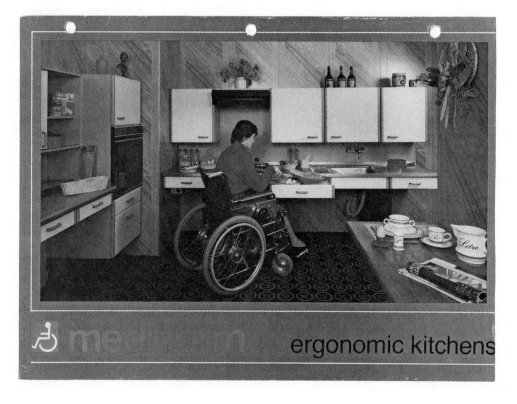

Figure 5.13. Manufacturers of accessible and "barrier-free" products used diverse aesthetic strategies. Some (such as Medinorm [ca. early 1980s]) emphasized ergonomic ideas of disability and reproduced the trope of the white, disabled housewife. Others (such as the manufacturer of the Huey Saturn drafting desk [ca. late 1970s]) offered more progressive depictions of race, gender, and disability, showing disabled people of color and women in professional settings. Ronald L. Mace Papers, MC 00260, Special Collections Research Center, North Carolina State University Libraries, Raleigh, N.C.

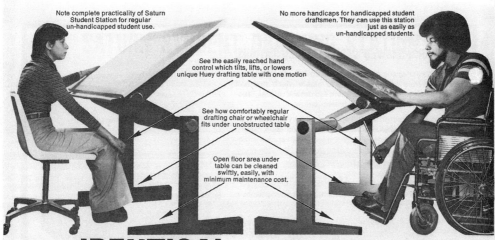

Note complete practicality of Saturn Student Station for regular un-handicapped student use.

No more handicaps for handicapped student draftsmen. They can use this station just as easily as un-handicapped students.

See the easily reached hand control which tilts, lifts, or lowers unique Huey drafting table with one motion

See how comfortably regular drafting chair or wheelchair fits under unobstructed table

Open floor area under table can be cleaned swiftly, easily, with minimum maintenance cost.

THE IDENTICAL UNIQUE HUEY SATURN STUDENT STATION TRAINS HANDICAPPED & UNHANDICAPPED WITH EQUAL EASE

No More Need to Buy Special Drafting Equipment for the Handicapped

PROBLEM
School administrators asked: is it possible to avoid the extra expense of buying special drafting equipment which only the handicapped can use?

Please see detailed specifications and other beneficial features on pages 2 and 3.

SOLUTION
Huey's answer: A unique, highly practical student drafting station precisely designed and engineered to fit the needs of *both* un-handicapped and handicapped with equal facility. Makes your budget go farther and gives you maximum flexibility by eliminating idle equipment sitting around waiting for handicapped students only. It no longer matters how the numbers of handicapped or un-handicapped students vary. Unique Huey Saturn Student Drafting Stations can be used constantly by any type of student. No budget waste, no time waste, no use waste.

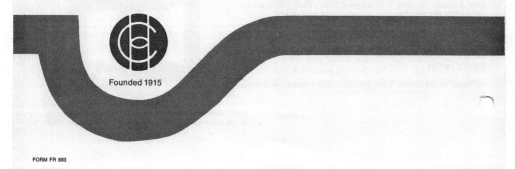

Founded 1915

FORM FR 883

universalism, decentering disability activism in favor of a more functional, geronto-logical view.

> These side effects of barrier-free design are a redefinition of this concept as a much broader and more universal one that involves the environmental needs of all users, not only the disabled. . . . We all pass through stages in our lives with varying degrees of ability and disability. An environmental design that is responsive to life's stages and the capabilities of all users can truly be termed *barrier-free.*[133]

Notice that the operative phrase here is "all users, not only the disabled" and not "all users, especially disabled people." Whereas in decades prior the discourse of "all" had excluded considerations of race, class, and gender, it now excluded disability as a category of oppression. Despite appearing to expand the range of possible users for barrier-free design, disability universalism was giving way to disability erasure.

BUILDING STANDARDS

Barrier-free design experts trained in EDR agreed that ANSI A117.1 was not a univer-sal, objective code: as the evidence base of accessibility shifted, the document required updating. A new ANSI committee, chaired by Nugent and with Steinfeld serving as its secretary, translated Steinfeld's 1979 research into a new version of A117.1.[134] While serving on this committee, Mace emphasized the position, first articulated by Nugent in 1961, that barrier-free design could benefit a broader population of users.[135] The com-mittee was tasked with revising the standards with consensus from federal agencies, architects, and builders. After facing resistance from these agents, Mace and Steinfeld were called upon to find a resolution, and ANSI published the new voluntary stan-dard in 1980, which expanded upon the 1961 standard by incorporating guidelines related to hearing and vision disabilities, as well as for spaces such as kitchens and bathrooms.[136]

Experts employed for the 1980 revisions were aware of the pitfalls of the minimal compliance approach. One disadvantage was that codes were rigid, while adaptive and flexible built environments were purportedly more inclusive. Even prior to bro-kering compromises on the ANSI revision, Mace was formulating his notion of Uni-versal Design as an approach that was distinct from narrow accessibility standards.[137] As he argued in his thesis, standards and checklists often represented the perspectives of majority bodies rather than the full range of users. Steinfeld appeared to agree with this position. Because standardization relies upon "the model standard [to be] truly authoritative and acceptable to all interest groups who are affected by the regula-tions," he wrote, it would be preferable to avoid treating barrier-free design guidelines as rigid, "inflexible 'gospel,'" lest inflexibility limit the "social change" that barrier-free design aims to produce.[138] Despite these critiques, the solution was not to abandon codes. Instead, Mace appeared to adopt a more subtle strategy of epistemic activism, which would translate accessibility from a "charitable philosophical concept" into a "legal necessity.[139] This strategy of social change within the compliance industry and design professions worked on multiple fronts to challenge assumptions as well as baseline requirements for accessibility.

Although barrier-free design began as a philosophy of access for "all," it had failed in significant ways; as the approach became synonymous with code enforcement, it began to fail in others. From Mace's perspective, a significant issue was the lack of a uniformity in federal codes, which left states and localities to adapt ANSI A117.1 "to meet local needs, pressures, or opinions," ultimately resulting in inconsistent standards with mitigated efficacy.[140] Consistent guidelines, Mace believed, were necessary to stop the "proliferation" of conflicting codes.[141] Additionally, the federal agencies charged with creating these standards had their own inconsistent internal guidelines, which "made universal application impossible."[142] These agencies, which were involved with the Access Board at the same time that they were subject to compliance with its guidelines, did not always comply to the full extent required by law.[143] These issues of bureaucracy and enforcement reinforced a notion of codes as both rigid and inadequate.

Another issue with codes, however, was what Mace perceived as a lack of transparency surrounding decision-making. Rather than adopt the new ANSI A117.1 without revisions, the Access Board offered it for comment from federal agencies and the general public.[144] The Access Board apparently excluded members of the ANSI committee from comment. Writing to Zukas, who was also on the Standards Committee, in 1980 Mace protested this exclusion.

> There are few people in this country who have the experience in developing design requirements for people with disabilities and who also have the professional qualifications as architects, engineers or regulatory officials as well as the necessary expertise of disability to effectively consider the complex technical, philosophical, political, and economic implications of such standards. With all due respect, I feel there is no one on the A&TBCB staff nor on the Standards Committee with such qualifications. I am therefore led to ask, "Whom did the committee hear from in making decisions to change technical specifications from those researched and tested in the ANSI Standard Project?" . . . To my knowledge, not one qualified person was consulted to provide information to the Standards Committee at critical decision points in the development process. Thus technical and policy decisions have been made that will affect the lives of disabled people for years to come without the benefit of some of the best information available.[145]

While materializing the standards was a seemingly routine bureaucratic process, in moments of tension and conflict, issues of expertise and knowledge came into play.

Mace's protestations illustrate his growing frustration that as barrier-free design became institutionalized, technical issues hindered substantive accessibility. They also revealed the place of expertise in the frictioned, contested politics of code production.

As code production anticipated legal enforcement, it remained a site of epistemic activism. References to data and best practices served as tools for theorizing what counts as accessibility. Mace strongly believed that the primary impediment to code compliance was the lack of uniformity between state and federal standards and not the standards themselves. He became frustrated with the Access Board's process, however, which he believed had diminished the benefits of predictable standards. Responding to recommendations that accessible pathways be widened from three to four feet to accommodate a greater turning radius, Mace charged the Access Board with "violating the accessible route concept and creating inconsistency," noting,

> In the past, the greatest hindrance to accessibility in construction has been the lack of consistency among the codes and standards and the confusion and litigation caused by it. During our years of work on developing standards and in teaching designers and others to use them, the most frequently heard appeal stated by every facet of the construction and regulatory industry is "Give us consistency in the standards, and don't keep changing our mind and we will be happy to make buildings, products, and equipment which are accessible."[146]

Here, Mace suggests that standardization is not synonymous with minimal compliance. Put simply, what counts as accessible design and how to convince architects to produce it are two separate issues, both at stake in the compliance debates.

Contemporary critics of barrier-free design often characterize this approach as compliance with onerous legal codes. The history of ANSI A117.1 suggests, however, that it was not simply the enforcement of access by law that made barrier-free design narrow or rigid. Rather, the contemporary perception of barrier-free design is likely shaped by the process of tightening, formalizing, and proliferating codes in the 1980s: a process that was as productive as it was constraining.

In 1982 the Access Board published a revised version of the accessibility standards, the Minimum Guidelines and Requirements for Accessible Design (MGRAD). It commissioned further accessibility research on issues such as tactile surfaces.[147] Federal agencies then, in an effort to align state and federal codes, developed a Uniform Federal Accessibility Standard (UFAS) based on the MGRAD in 1984.[148] As the Access Board revised these standards, their enforcement became confusing, even for experts such as Mace who had themselves helped to define the codes. In the midst of code revisions, Mace's firm, Barrier Free Environments, was commissioned to design a multifamily accessible housing facility in Asheville, North Carolina.[149] The project received federal funding from HUD and was thus bound to its accessibility standards, which were premised upon the MGRAD and ANSI A117.1. HUD rejected the initial plans for this building because while complying with the agency's internal guidelines, it did not comply with the 1980 revisions to ANSI A117.1 (revisions that Mace himself had helped to develop). HUD then rejected Mace's second iteration of the project because it did not comply with the North Carolina accessibility code, which Mace had also helped to develop. The North Carolina code, the ANSI A117.1 guidelines, and HUD's internal guidelines were only three of dozens of federal and state codes that had proliferated in the 1970s and '80s. Despite Mace's direct involvement in the development of these codes, and despite his expertise as a disabled user and architect, the experience of designing an accessible apartment building in his own state left him "exasperated."[150]

Despite these frustrations, it was *through* the development of codes, rather than beyond them, and through interactions with other experts, rather than alone, that Mace's early theory of Universal Design emerged. As he later recalled,

> I first got my hint for Universal Design . . . when I was participating in the revision of ANSI A117.1 of 1980 and the Development of the Architectural Standards for North Carolina. At the time, many people thought that "accessible" apartments didn't have much storing space, and handrails would be annoying to people without disabilities. Some even thought that they would actually become disabled if they lived in such places. Also, people thought that toilets with wheelchair symbols were only meant for wheelchair users. However, I started to realize that many people could benefit from our ideas. Think about the people pushing baby carriages, go-carts, bicycles, skateboards, whatever. I began to see that all the things that were considered necessary only for people with disabilities were really necessary for everybody. These ideals are not only good ideas for wheelchair users but were ideas that could help everyone. When I started saying this, others also started to voice their opinion that "accessible design is good for us, too."[151]

All of these ideas had circulated for decades in the rhetorics of accessibility, but what made them persuasive in the early 1980s was the contrast between messy bureaucratic compliance and the possibility of a world designed to be accessible from the beginning. Unlike the morass of accessibility codes, within which every measurement had become an embattled detail, the return to barrier-free design as design for "all" users became an opportunity for exploring access beyond the trappings of bureaucratic and institutional standards.

While frustrating, Mace's experiences with revising accessibility codes provided a point of contrast with his relationship to a growing network of like-minded designers and scholars who desired creative accessibility solutions beyond code compliance. This epistemic community coalesced through meetings and collaborations that intensified in the early 1980s. In 1980 Mace began working with the Disability Rights and Education Defense Fund (DREDF), the legal wing of the CIL in Berkeley, to design and implement technical trainings on Section 504.[152] This was likely his first exposure to the West Coast's independent living movement. He cultivated close friendships and personal connections with many of the movement's activists, including University of Illinois alumna Mary Lou Breslin.[153] The same year, the National Center for a Barrier Free Environment hosted an interdisciplinary conference promoting a "Cooperative Future in Barrier Free Design."[154] As participants imagined it, the future of barrier-free design would include establishing a self-reliant network of users, building a stronger evidence base regarding psychological and behavioral dimensions of built environments, and developing a uniform accessibility code for buildings, transit systems, and information technology.[155] These broadly imagined futures encapsulated the range of grassroots and institutional efforts that had characterized access-knowledge in previous decades. Unanimously, the group decided that the long-term goal of barrier-free design, particularly as promoted by the U.S. federal government, should be a "built environment that is enabling to all persons by mainstreaming barrier free design principles into the entire design process," a goal that subverted the rehabilitation goal of "mainstreaming" disabled people by placing the onus on designers to change built environments.[156] While Mace was familiar with some of the experts at the meeting, such as Nugent, others (including Hale Zukas and Eric Dibner, and emerging experts John Salmen and Cora Beth Abel) were new to him. In the next few years, Mace would meet with these and other experts as they worked collectively to define barrier-free design's trajectories.

Momentum for more meaningful and less bureaucratic barrier-free design drew a broad network of access-knowledge experts, researchers, politicians, high-profile architects, and activists to an international 1982 conference called "Designed Environments for All People" at the United Nations Headquarters in New York. The conference served as the "culmination of the International Year of Disabled Persons."[157] Compared to the UN Expert Group meeting a decade earlier, the conference revealed that barrier-free design was no longer the exclusive domain of rehabilitation experts. Nearly every recognizable expert in the barrier-free design field was present, including Mace, Steinfeld, Zukas, Lifchez, Salmen, and Gunnar Dybwad, a Brandeis University professor who had just helped to win a 1981 U.S. Supreme Court case that closed the infamous Pennhurst State Penitentiary.[158] Industrial designers James Mueller, Richard Hollerith, and Patricia Moore, who had all worked on issues of aging and disability in the built environment, were also present. Environmental design researchers Gary T. Moore, John Zeisel, and Craig Zimring attended, as did barrier-free design experts Polly Welch and James Bostrom, both of whom worked closely with Mace in the coming years.

High-profile speakers in the disability and design worlds used the meeting as an opportunity to exchange interdisciplinary concepts and ideas. Former Georgia senator and disabled veteran Max Cleland, newly employed at the Veterans Administration, gave a keynote advocating for an "Expanded Concept of the User." A roundtable

TEACHING DESIGN FOR ALL PEOPLE: THE STATE OF THE ART

Elaine Ostroff, Daniel Iacofano

Design Faculty Seminar
Adaptive Environments Center, Boston, MA

April 1-3, 1982

In cooperation with the Massachusetts College of Art Design Department and the MIT Laboratory for Architecture and Planning

Support by funds from the National Endowment for the Arts and the U.S. Department of Education

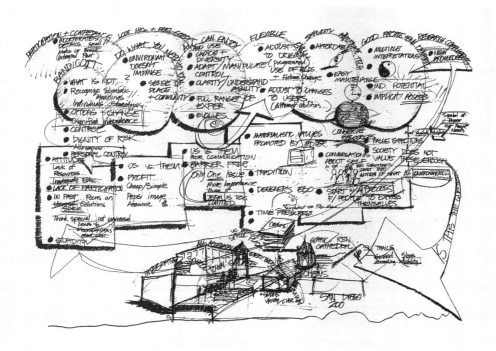

Figure 5.14. The "Teaching Design for All People" workshop (1982) served as an idea generator for accessibility experts. Courtesy of the Elaine Ostroff Universal Design Papers, Archives Center, National Museum of American History, Smithsonian Institution.

discussion of prominent designers placed accessibility within the purview of good, mainstream design. Its participants included industrial designer Victor Papanek, a leading advocate of design for social change; prominent Harvard-educated landscape architect Lawrence Halprin, a modernist who advocated for user-centered design; former Yale School of Architecture dean Charles Moore, an advocate of centering the body in architectural practice; high-profile MIT- and Yale-educated architect Stanley Tigerman; and architect Duane Thorbeck, an advocate of participatory design. The discourse of good design for all people had reached the mainstream, in other words, and had captured the attention of influential designers and cultural makers.

Just a few months after "Designed Environments for All People," Mace was invited to the small faculty seminar "Teaching Design for All People: The State of the Art," hosted by Cora Beth Abel and Elaine Ostroff at the Adaptive Environments Center in Boston, Massachusetts (Figure 5.14).[159] The meeting brought together designers and educators, including Mace, Lifchez, Salmen, industrial designer Marc Harrison, and Mace's North Carolina–based colleagues Robin Moore and Bettye Rose Connell, all of whom were interested in disseminating access-knowledge through design education. The seminar participants worked toward collective responses to basic questions, such as "what is an accessible environment?" and "why don't many new environments reflect these qualities?"[160] As participants answered these questions, theories of "good design" and accessibility formed. One participant noted, for instance, that "the design process encompasses knowledge. . . . To ignore knowledge leads to stupid design."[161] Another insisted, "Codes and regulations force designers to think about unique features for unique people rather than about the overall design problem-solving process."[162] These comments produced a sense of consensus that compliance regimes discouraged designers from thinking creatively, beyond average users or prototypical disabled users.

By sharing their qualms with accommodationism and code compliance, participants such as Mace were confiding in like-minded experts in a community of practice rather than intervening in expert discourses. But their shared frustrations produced a consensus that barrier-free design is synonymous with code and consequently disconnected accessibility from historical promises of benefiting "all" users. This consensus and the consistent emphasis upon design for "all people" prepared the ground for the discourse of Universal Design. But whether this approach would present a viable alternative to barrier-free design or merely reframe the language of accessibility remained to be made and known.

Chapter 6

Barrier Work

Before and After the Americans with Disabilities Act

> It is much more interesting to foster the development of innovation like a gardener
> than to audit compliance with laws like the police.
>
> —EDWARD STEINFELD, "Universal Design as Innovation"

Who benefits from a more accessible world, and how can designers know? In 1985 disabled architect Ronald Mace imagined "a way of designing a building or facility, at little or no extra cost, so that it is both attractive and functional for all people, disabled or not."[1] He called this idea "Universal Design" and offered it to architects as an aspiration for a more inclusive, functional built environment. The idea seemed straightforward, simple, common sense. It was easy to cite and quote. Nothing about Universal Design appeared radical, political, or confrontational. On the surface, Universal Design was just a new term for good design.

But Mace's concept was not simple. Its design was quite intricate, its logics thorny, its ideas pastiche. Complicating matters further, there was not one approach called Universal Design; there were many. Between 1985 and 1995, Universal Design's first decade as a term that appeared in print, this generative concept proliferated through experiments that addressed both its public framing and its internal theory. How these proliferations extended access-knowledge to new experimental sites and concepts, enlarged the legible range of users, introduced innovative modes of epistemic activism, and both multiplied and reigned in the meanings of Universal Design are the focus of this chapter.

BARRIER WORK

Since the mid-1990s, proponents of Universal Design have argued that the approach is distinct from barrier-free design. The latter they frame as a compliance-based strategy rooted in the Americans with Disabilities Act. These arguments are part of a broader discourse debating what Universal Design is and is not: depending on whom you ask, the term may describe design for everyone but not design for disabled users; built-in good design but not retrofits or accommodations; meaningful accessibility but not of the variety achieved through the law.

Despite these distinctions, a great deal of confusion exists about what counts as Universal Design. One reason for this confusion may be that in its philosophy, rhetoric, and community of experts, Universal Design has been nearly indistinguishable from the barrier-free design of the 1960s. Like Nugent, Mace argued that designing for disabled users also benefits nondisabled users. Mace and other Universal Design experts were involved with revising the compliance standards that laws such as the 1990 Americans with Disabilities Act enforce. Into the 1990s, many of these same experts continued to define these standards.

Drawing distinctions between one or more ideas can be a useful way of shaping a certain view of the truth. Another way to understand the work of drawing distinctions, however, is that when we say that two things are different, we actually create them as such. We make them seem whole, coherent, and discrete when they are really quite unstable and complex. Drawing distinctions, then, is not just about saying what is objective or true but also about producing a new order of things, crafting a strategic material-epistemic arrangement. What, then, was the strategy behind defining Universal Design as discrete from its predecessor?

Put simply, the strategy was one experiment among many. The most generative aspect of Universal Design was not Mace's explanation of it, per se, but its instability. Its apparent simplicity helped it to spread, but its hidden complexity also made Universal Design amenable to ongoing experiments in knowing-making. Between 1985 and 1995, the concept of Universal Design became a generative force for innovating the entire field of access-knowledge. Innovation in this case referred to slow cultivation, a long-term creative accumulation rather than quick, disposable, profitable change. These experiments took place in the material culture and social relations of access-knowledge: ideas, arguments, design charrettes, competitions, newsletters, architectural curricula, handbooks, and a host of other forms. As Universal Design proliferated within these sites, the idea was disseminated widely but at each turn also *remade* (Figures 6.1 and 6.2). In this chapter, I delve into the archive of Universal Design discourse, design documents, accessibility standards, and ephemera to investigate these experiments in access-knowledge and to situate the events of the late 1990s that followed.

Although I am arguing that Universal Design had a close relationship with barrier-free design, the very acts of drawing distinctions between the two are worth noticing. These acts of what I term "barrier work" had an important purpose, explored in this chapter and the next. Barrier work is similar to what sociologist of science Thomas Gieryn calls "boundary work," or acts of distinction between science and nonscience.[2] Barrier work also resembles what Karen Barad terms an "agential cut," or when an act of distinction makes ideas appear different and their differences appear meaningful.[3] If we understand that part of the Universal Design experiment was barrier work—to

Figure 6.1. A neighborhood curb cut in Raleigh, N.C. (2010). Photograph by author.

both cut and bind—then the question of Universal Design's relationship to barrier-free design becomes not about a pregiven idea of what either of these terms mean but rather about a historical idea of what they have meant, when, and for what purposes. Like my earlier explorations of critical friction and torsion, barrier work helps us understand Universal Design and barrier-free design as engaged in mutual reiteration, or what Barad terms "intra-action." Framed in this way, barrier work is a conversation about what Universal Design ought to be, where it should focus, and how it should proceed—an internal theory that is not always apparent in the public face and presentation of Universal Design.

UNIVERSAL DESIGN IN THE PRE-ADA ERA

Around 1985, Mace received a phone message from the world-renowned disabled violinist Itzhak Perlman: "I. M. Pei will be calling you to talk about [the Jacob Javits] convention center in [New York]. They are having problems with an 'accessible escalator'" (Figure 6.3).[4] In the vertiginous landscape of accessibility codes of the 1980s, mainstream architects called upon experts such as Mace to explain standards. Even so-called *star* architects such as I. M. Pei were not exempt from these legal requirements.[5] What Pei meant by "accessible escalator" may have been lost in the message's

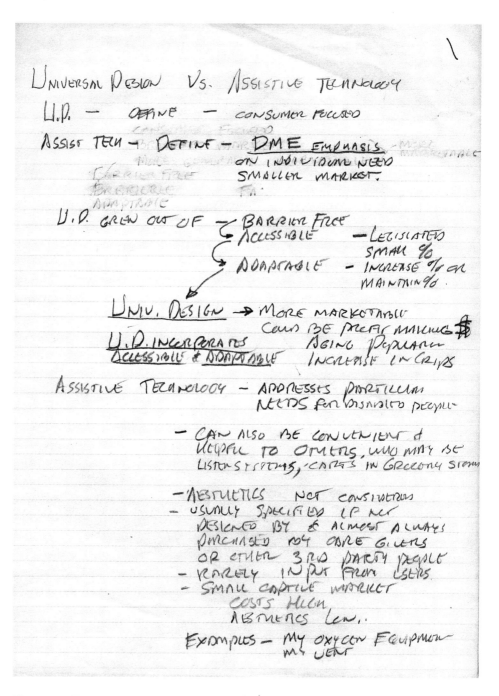

Figure 6.2. Ronald Mace's handwritten notes (ca. 1990) record a brainstorming session on the differences between Universal Design, assistive technology, and barrier-free design, using the disability movement term "crip" to describe the population of disabled users. Courtesy of Joy Weeber.

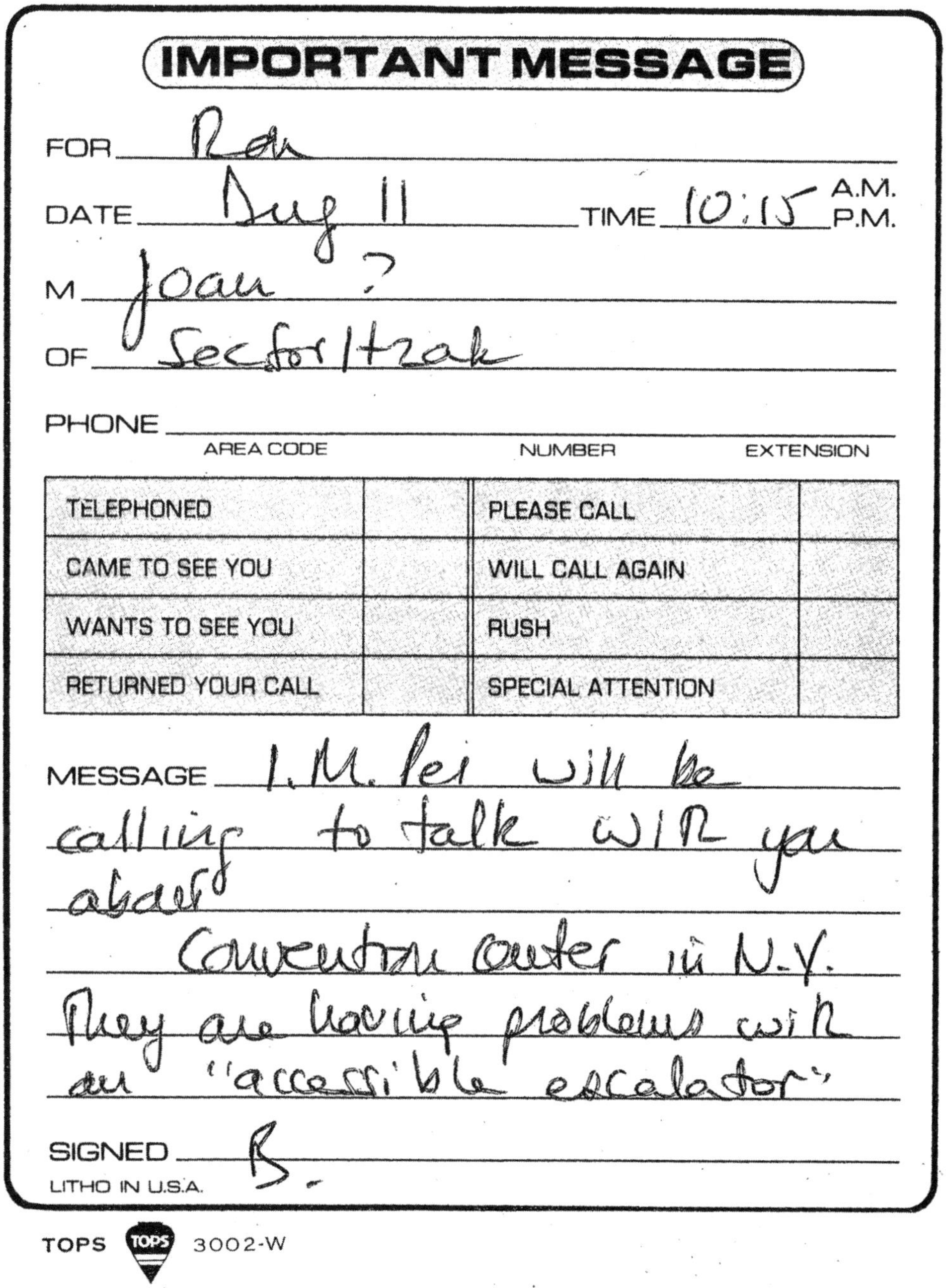

IMPORTANT MESSAGE

FOR _Ron_

DATE _Aug 11_   TIME _10:15_ A.M. / P.M.

M _Joan ?_

OF _Sec for Itzak_

PHONE _____
AREA CODE   NUMBER   EXTENSION

TELEPHONED		PLEASE CALL	
CAME TO SEE YOU		WILL CALL AGAIN	
WANTS TO SEE YOU		RUSH	
RETURNED YOUR CALL		SPECIAL ATTENTION	

MESSAGE _I.M. Pei will be calling to talk with you about_

Convention Center in N.Y.
They are having problems with
an "accessible escalator"

SIGNED _B._

LITHO IN U.S.A.

TOPS 3002-W

Figure 6.3. Disability culture created some of the networks through which accessibility experts connected. Message to Mace from Itzhak Perlman (ca. 1985). Courtesy of Joy Weeber.

transcription.[6] What is clear, however, is that legally enforceable codes, no matter how limited, were extending the influence of accessibility experts and the social networks of disability culture into the realm of "star architecture."

Although he was an accessibility expert, Mace was also one of the compliance system's greatest critics. There were benefits, however, to being one of the few disabled architects in the U.S. accessibility scene. Expertise brought both subtle authority and strategic influence. Mace speculated that if he could access high-profile architects and raise their awareness about accessible design, then their designs would have far more influence than innovations in less legible arenas.[7] Influencing star architects was one of Mace's many experiments in disseminating knowledge about accessibility and changing architectural culture, such that designers would be less resistant to code compliance.

In the early and mid-1980s, barrier-free design had become synonymous with compliance and regulation. While the underlying theory had been capacious and wide-ranging (albeit with significant limitations regarding race, class, and gender), it was only when accessibility practices became a matter of legal enforcement that barrier-free design came to signify a narrow, bureaucratic accessibility approach. Even prior to this legal enforcement, however, disability activists and accessibility experts contended with resistant architects, who insisted that accessible design was not "good design." As Lifchez and Winslow explained,

> Many designers have, in fact, expressed a certain fear that pressure to accommodate disabled people will jeopardize good design and weaken the design vocabulary. Though certain aspects of the contemporary design vocabulary many have to be reconsidered in making accessible environments, one must also look forward to new items in the vocabulary that will develop in response to these human needs—ultimately leading toward more humane concepts of what makes for good design.[8]

Accessibility proponents challenged mainstream standards of good design by introducing disability knowledge and theory as a valid interpretive framework. In doing so, they framed design as a value-explicit enterprise rather than neutral or objective. These were, in effect, epistemological arguments.

In the twentieth century, the discourse of "good design" was often deployed to advocate for a particular agenda. Design historian Stephen Hayward argues that since its emergence in the 1930s, "good design" often appeared as a kind of "common sense" but was actually an "exercise of power, concomitant with a hegemonic idea of progress or modernity, and the antithesis to a contrary world of 'bad' or 'uncultivated' design."[9] By offering a counternarrative to inaccessible "good design," barrier-free design supporters unsettled the norms that mainstream architects often took as common sense. These strategies of drawing boundaries between good and bad design suggest the overlapping work of "friction" (or resistance to the normate template) and "torsion" (or transformation of a discourse from within itself) could also be used to offer a design philosophy that went beyond barrier-free regulations.

Subtle Disability Politics

Mace had an experimental sensibility when it came to access-knowledge. His architecture thesis, "Housing Environmental Research," had proposed that designers should "treat all architectural projects as if they were experiments" by identifying their assumptions, testing them through several iterations, and adapting their future design strategies accordingly.[10] But because so much of Mace's work in the 1980s focused on writing texts and interpreting standards, it appears that he was also experimenting with ideas and language, in addition to architectural designs (see Figure 6.2).

If we approach Universal Design as a historical experiment, *designed* like any other kind of laboratory test, the complexities of this concept become easier to locate. Mace wanted to know how to promote accessible design to architects. He hypothesized that the best approach had to do with language and framing. The Universal Design experiment began with a control, which provided a baseline against which to compare future iterations. Mace's 1985 article, "Universal Design: Barrier-Free Design for Everyone," was precisely such a control. The key was in the language.

> Universal Design is a concept whose time has arrived. It is also on the cutting edge of progressive design, and offers designers the chance to challenge conventional design thinking by designing products, buildings, and facilities which incorporate new ideas, and embody the essence of good design: that which is practical and can be used by all.[11]

The words were enticing. Few would object to the public face of Universal Design as "good design," "practical," "cutting edge," and "progressive." In just fifty-six words, Mace captured and reproduced nearly every claim of earlier barrier-free design proponents and disability activists. Yet he emphasized that these ideas were fresh, new, progressive, and on the cutting edge. To read these statements literally, as empirical claims about Universal Design or as simple recitations of earlier discourses of design for "all," however, misses the rest of Mace's strategy.

What, then, was Mace testing? A distinguishing feature of the article was its approach to disability politics.[12] If the above claims served as controls, each of the experimental variables addressed a particular assumption about disability. First, Mace redesigned the language of accessibility. The article's title, "Universal Design: Barrier-Free Design for Everyone," suggested that barrier-free design was narrow in its focus and needed to be expanded. But unlike later definitions of Universal Design, Mace did not position the concept against codes or disability inclusion. "The prospect of universal design," he wrote, "advanced significantly in 1980 with the publication of the revised [ANSI A117.1]," enabling architects and product manufacturers to "produce new and more universally usable products."[13] Here, "universal" worked as both a seemingly neutral term and as a challenge to the previous efficacy of the normate template or the inclusiveness of barrier-free design for "all."

Also distinct was Mace's rejection of rehabilitation logics and compulsory productivity. In response to the view that disabled people are tragic, assimilation-seeking patients who aim to "'overcome' their disabilities and live active lives," Mace delivered a complex analysis of marginalization in built environments.[14] This analysis referenced language from his undergraduate thesis, which critiqued architects' white, middle-class values. Although he did not engage with race explicitly, Mace challenged the pervasive emphasis on access for middle-class and wealthy disabled people in earlier decades of barrier-free design. In an extended analysis of class privilege, Mace argued that wealthy disabled people were more likely to access the resources to "modify their environments to achieve a degree of freedom that other disabled people could not enjoy."[15] "Wealthy and famous disabled people kept themselves invisible by insulating themselves from society" in private homes, Mace explained, while "less affluent" people were often institutionalized, resulting in a perception of disabled people as a "small group of helpless people who made no decisions and had no buying power."[16] These ideological and epistemic claims directly addressed architects' objections that there were not enough disabled people to constitute a significant client base for accessible design.

Simultaneously, Mace redesigned the internal theory of barrier-free design by challenging recent trends toward ISA-marked "special" or "handicapped" products and spaces, which often had an "institutional appearance" and did not allow for a greater awareness of spatial misfit with disability at its center (Figure 6.4).[17] Code compliance approaches often required people seeking barrier-free access to convince others of the degree of their impairment through a process that critical disability theorist Ellen Samuels terms "biocertification"—for example, use of a wheelchair or assistive device or official proof of a diagnosis.[18] As examples of users who benefit from access but are often forgotten, Mace cited "young people with moderate mobility impairments [who] are placed in nursing homes," "older couple[s]," D/deaf and hard-of-hearing people, temporarily disabled workers, and even people without formal disability diagnoses.[19] These references offered architects perspectives on deinstitutionalization, disability rights, and culture. The point was to show that disability-focused design is not inherently distasteful, institutional, or aesthetically displeasing. Rather, it was stigmatizing attitudes toward disability that had made accessible design appear as such.[20]

In perhaps his most risky move, Mace highlighted disabled people as powerful knowers, political agents, and activists rather than treating them as passive, disempowered users. In the political economy of manufacturing and design, pervasive institutionalization and disability exclusion had made disabled people appear invisible and produced a "vicious cycle of denial and lack of use," preventing further developments in accessibility.[21] Despite historical income disparities and marginalization,

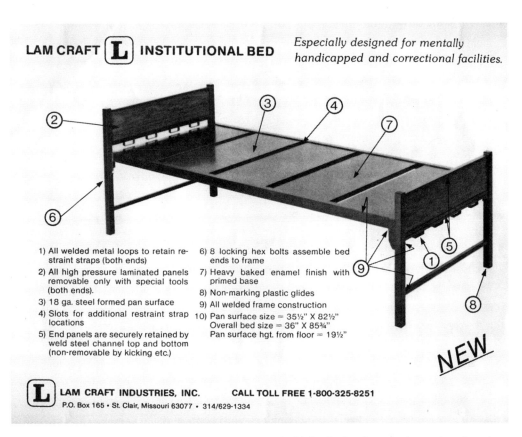

Figure 6.4. Mace was critical of products designed with institutional aesthetics and marketed toward disabled users in the 1960s and '70s. This advertisement (ca. late 1970s) of an institutional bed from Lam Craft Industries notes design features aimed at institutionalized populations, including loops for metal restraints. Courtesy of Joy Weeber.

powerful disability rights "activism has resulted in the development of new laws and numerous accessibility standards. These requirements *forced* upon the building in-dustry by disability advocates have had very positive results in getting at least minimal accessibility into buildings."[22] Accordingly, Mace argued that built-in accessibility would ensure compliance with codes and save architects and manufacturers from costly fines resulting from legal noncompliance.[23] These economic arguments treat disabled people as a profitable niche market. Mace's strong suggestion was rather that disabled people were now a powerful force backed by law. These claims sug-gested that Mace was integrating his background in environmental design research and compliance-knowledge with his more recent exposure to radical disability rights ideas through his wife, Lockhart Follin-Mace, and through collaborations with the Disability Rights and Education Defense Fund (DREDF), the legal organization of the independent living movement.

Mace's final variable involved disability universalism, which he introduced and swiftly subverted. Citing statistics that the number of disabled people is demographically significant and growing, Mace argued that the probability of experiencing disability while aging is high. But beyond this attention-generating citation, he also offered an argument rooted in the politics of knowing-making: many people experience barriers in built environments not designed with them in mind. The problem, he posited, is that "architects often do not have the correct information to make their buildings accessible, because design schools do not teach about disabled people, children, elderly people, or women and their differing abilities."[24] Unlike those who insisted that accessibility benefits "all users, not only the disabled," Mace experimented with foregrounding disabled users in their complexity.[25] His reinterpretation of disability universalism went beyond the claim that "everyone is disabled" to address intersectionality, particularly the disproportionate marginalization of disabled women, children, and elders who architects do not consider in design processes.

Later, in 1989, Mace and his colleague Ruth Hall Lusher, a disabled design expert trained in gerontology, extended the definition of Universal Design by framing it as a strategy for accountability toward a broad range of marginalized users.

> Instead of responding only to the minimum demands of laws which require a few special features for disabled people, it is possible to design most manufactured items and building elements to be usable by a broad range of human beings including children, elderly people, people with disabilities, and people of different sizes. This concept is called universal design. It is a concept that is now entirely possible and one that makes economic and social sense.[26]

It is significant to note that Mace and Lusher proposed that Universal Design *foreground* disability rather than arguing (as later proponents would) that Universal Design is distinct from disability access. While foregrounding disability, they also framed Universal Design as a resource for allyship between users that were marginalized by mainstream standards of good design (albeit in different ways and to qualitatively different degrees). In doing so, they adopted a cultural understanding of disabled people as a disadvantaged minority group that exists *in relation to* other spatially excluded populations, such as children, elderly people, and people of different sizes, whose needs were often treated as "special" or "exceptional" rather than as integral to the design of built space.[27] This early framing of Universal Design reveals attention to the dimensions of power and privilege that determine belonging in built environments. In addition to their design expertise, both Mace and Lusher were wheelchair users, the category of user on which the majority of barrier-free design standards focused. They used their relatively privileged positions as disabled designers who *were* included in accessibility codes to affiliate with those who were not. Their attention to the collective stakes of access implied that disability advocates must seek inclusive design not only for themselves but also for other marginalized populations.

Mace and Lusher's approach matched a cultural model of disability, not as pure impairment but rather as an intra-active phenomenon. This cultural model approached disability as simultaneously defined by medical diagnostic categories, biocertification, and standardization on the one hand, and disability culture, allyship, and affiliation on the other. Their framing thus disclosed a *critical* disposition toward disability, which David Mitchell and Sharon Snyder describe as "a political act of renaming that designates disability as a site of cultural resistance and a source of cultural agency previously suppressed."[28] Affiliating disability with other categories of social discrimination enabled Mace and Lusher to identify resonances between challenges to the normate template. Interaction designer Graham Pullin would later refer to this sense of collective affiliation as "resonant design," which begins by including the most marginalized and then explores the benefits of those inclusions for other populations.[29] Mace and Lusher's framing also captured disabled peoples' resourcefulness in fostering interdependence and relationality: an ethos that Alison Kafer calls the "political/relational" dimensions of disability.[30] These capacious political, relational, and resonant dimensions characterized disability-focused Universal Design in the late 1980s.

From these experimental, intra-acting variables, it becomes clear that Mace and Lusher were introducing Universal Design as an intervention into the normate template, rehabilitation-centered barrier-free design, and compliance codes. Their objective was not to promote a neutral concept of the universal or assimilate disabled people into mainstream white, middle-class values but to torque design culture from within. But these interventions were subtle, requiring close reading and attentiveness to context. They were more akin to the muted vibrations that one feels on the street level while a subway car plunges through a tunnel below than the sudden, shattering force of sledgehammers on sidewalks. No less effective or politicized, these subtle interventions took effect over time, producing a heterogeneous landscape of Universal Design discourses, products, and spaces. As Universal Design entered into circulation, questions of Universal Design's users, relationship to disability politics, and attitudes toward rehabilitation remained subject to experiment.

Cripping the Accessible Home

Mace and Lusher's theory of Universal Design was as much about reconfiguring disabled peoples' access to public space as it was about the private sphere in which the racialized, economized, and gendered lives of disabled people took place. In the 1980s the meaning and materiality of home shifted through encounters with access-knowledge. Disability activists used accessibility codes and design discourses to challenge the middle-class, able-bodied norms of domestic space. Many, including Mace, argued that for those forcibly institutionalized, housing was a place of confinement;

for those with the economic privileges to consume accessible products and modify homes, home was a place of private dwelling and possibly certain forms of productive labor (Figure 6.5).[31] Others, such as activist Eleanor Smith, agitated for "visitability." This design philosophy centered on the notion that disabled people should be able to visit others' homes, even if they do not live in them. Because most private homes were beyond the scope of state or federal laws, however, Smith used local building codes to mandate zero-step entrances, accessible restrooms, and similar features.[32] Her organization, Concrete Change, successfully lobbied for visitability requirements in the building codes of Atlanta, Georgia, and raised awareness about visitability at state and federal levels.[33]

Although technical guidance for accessibility codes appeared mundane and bureaucratic, opportunities to illustrate and clarify accessibility standards for domestic space provided opportunities for epistemic activism. Mace's firm Barrier Free Environments (BFE) provided technical assistance and consulting on issues of architectural accessibility at the state and federal levels. Starting in 1984, Mace collaborated with Lusher, who had studied with gerontologist Leon Pastalan and developed the concept of

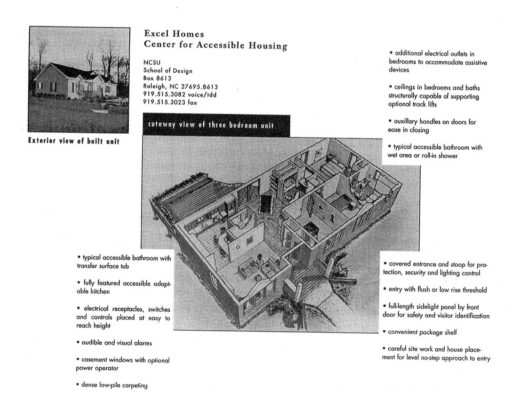

Figure 6.5. Center for Accessible Housing, "Excel Home" (ca. early 1990s). Courtesy of Joy Weeber.

"design for the lifespan," to develop accessible housing standards for the American Association of Retired Persons (AARP) and the U.S. Department of Housing and Urban Development (HUD).[34] Through this work, Mace joined DREDF in a coalition that included mental health and HIV/AIDS activists to address "gender and age discrimination and kids' issues" through an amendment to the Fair Housing Act of 1968.[35] This groundbreaking civil rights law was one of many geared toward enforcing racial desegregation in the 1960s and prohibited housing discrimination on the basis of race, religion, national origin, or sex. Because barrier-free design largely remained within the domain of white, middle-class citizenship, however, there was little consideration of disability as an oppressed minority category. In 1988 activists working in legal and policy advocacy successfully expanded the law to prohibit discrimination on the basis of disability and family status (including pregnancy and the age of children). The Fair Housing Amendments Act drew national attention and served as the basis for a more substantial civil rights law: the ADA.[36]

Simultaneously, Mace worked to inject a Universal Design consciousness into barrier-free design. In 1988 the HUD hired BFE to develop guidance for Universal Design in housing. Mace collaborated with Lusher to produce *Universal Design: Housing for the Lifespan of All People*, a booklet describing accessible design's wide-ranging benefits for housing. The most striking feature of this publication was its illustrations, which were replicated in many other BFE guides over the next decade and materialized the legibility of an ever-expanding array of users.

In the 1980s and '90s, Universal Design proponents experimented with describing a broad user group for Universal Design. Eventually, design handbooks would show figures with diverse racial backgrounds, ages, and disabilities (Figure 6.6a, b, c, and d). Rather than rely upon terms such as "all" or "everyone," proponents would represent specific types of users. Some of these representations, such as an older white man using a cane in the bathroom, a middle-aged white woman using a wheelchair, and a young boy standing before a closet, reflected earlier barrier-free design tropes. *Universal Design: Housing for the Lifespan of All People* added complexity to these depictions. For example, one illustration showed a front door with a lever-style handle, used by an apparently young, nondisabled, African American woman dressed in a suit and holding a briefcase (suggesting her professional status and employment in nondomestic labor) (Figure 6.7). The woman carried a bag of groceries, indicating that she possibly lived alone or was a single parent. While the woman was not depicted with any visible sign of physical disability, the illustration suggested that she was a marginalized user, encumbered by what she carried, and therefore benefited from the added leverage of the door handle, which she pressed down with her elbow.

While representations of people of color, particularly women of color, in architectural documents depicting users are rare, there are also limitations to these types of representation. In *Universal Design: Housing for the Lifespan of All People*, the apparently young, nondisabled African American woman's image becomes legible as part

of "all" users by serving as an emblem of racial difference itself. The illustration recalls A. A. Marks's depictions of prosthetics wearers in a variety of occupations,
class positions, and styles of dress, which used stereotyped markers of difference to
promote assistive technologies as tools for rehabilitation and liberal citizenship (see
chapter 2).

Nevertheless, *Universal Design: Housing for the Lifespan of All People* provides an
example of BFE's work to decenter and reconfigure seemingly neutral representations
of architectural inhabitants that circulated in the *Architectural Graphic Standards*.

a

site furniture should not
intrude on accessible route
and block the clear path

US MAIL

Elements on Accessible Routes

Figure 6.6a, b, c, and d. Barrier Free Environments revolutionized the depiction of the
disabled user in the 1980s and '90s, representing multiple types of disabilities, depicting
disabled people of many races, illustrating children, and even including Mace himself. Barrier
Free Environments, *Accessibility in Georgia: A Technical and Policy Guide to Access in
Georgia* (Raleigh, N.C.: Barrier Free Environments, 1996), 39, 65, 67, 84. Text by Leslie
Young and Ronald Mace. Illustrations by Rex Pace.

BUILDING PRODUCTS

Building products such as telephones, plumbing fixtures, drinking fountains, and alarms are more or less permanently installed in a building. To be accessible, a building product must be located on an accessible route and have a clear floor space that allows a person to get close enough to use the item. However, items that protrude from walls or posts must be located in the clear floor space in such a way that they are not a hazard for a person with a visual impairment, see page 56 of this manual. Any controls should be within easy reach of seated and standing people, and should be easy to use even for someone with little or no use of his/her hands.

CLEAR FLOOR SPACE AND REACH RANGES
ANSI 4.2 ♦ ADAAG 4.2

When people in wheelchairs wish to use a fixture or item such as a vending machine or a drinking fountain, they need sufficient space to maneuver their wheelchairs close to the object. They may pull up either alongside it (parallel approach) or in front of it (front approach).

The orientation of the clear floor space affects how high the person can reach. With a parallel

approach, many wheelchair users can reach as high as 54 inches. With a front approach, they only can reach 48 inches. Sometimes the clear floor space can extend under an object such as a table; this works only if there is enough room for the front of the wheelchair and the person's legs to fit beneath the edge of the table.

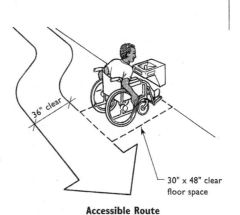

36" clear

30" x 48" clear floor space

Accessible Route

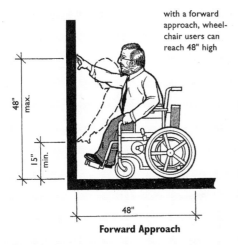

with a forward approach, wheelchair users can reach 48" high

48" max.

15" min.

48"

Forward Approach

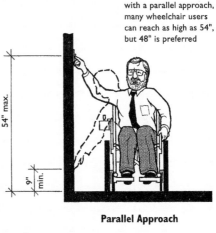

with a parallel approach, many wheelchair users can reach as high as 54", but 48" is preferred

54" max.

9" min.

Parallel Approach

65

C

AUTOMATED TELLER MACHINES (ATMS)
ADAAG 4.34

The ANSI Standard gives no specifications for ATMs, a relatively new building product. However, related human factors and performance specifications such as the previously discussed "Clear Floor Space and Reach Ranges" and "Controls and Operating Mechanisms" can be applied to achieve accessibility.

The ADAAG, on the other hand, gives specifications for ATMs that address clear floor space, reach ranges, and controls, as well as instructions for use by people who are blind or have low vision. These include Braille and raised letters and/or audio handsets, along with tactile keys.

Where two or more ATMs are provided in the same location, only one must comply with the ADAAG. Drive-up installations are not required to comply with regard to clear floor space and reach range requirements. However, specifications for controls and use by people with vision impairments still must be met.

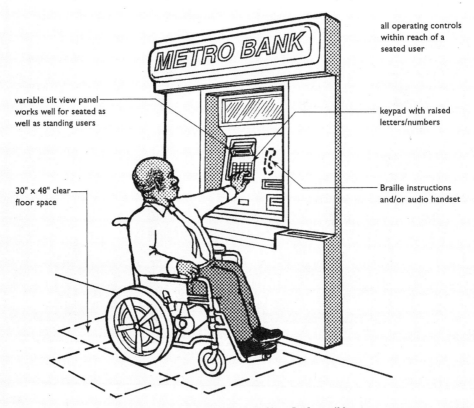

variable tilt view panel works well for seated as well as standing users

30" x 48" clear floor space

all operating controls within reach of a seated user

keypad with raised letters/numbers

Braille instructions and/or audio handset

Automated Teller Machines Must Be Accessible

67

full-length mirrors
work well for
everyone

d

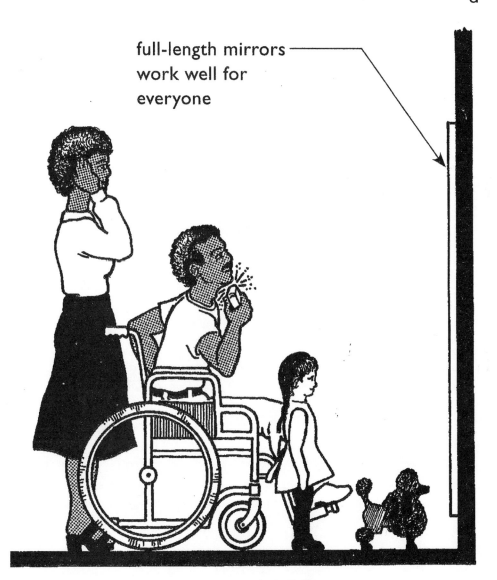

Full-Length Mirrors

Figure 6.7. An African American woman is depicted carrying bags and groceries into her home using her elbow to turn the lever handle. Center for Universal Design, *Universal Design: Housing for the Lifespan of All People* (Raleigh, N.C.: Center for Universal Design, 2000), 5.

Earlier versions of the illustrations appeared in another BFE publication, *Accessible Housing: A Manual on North Carolina's Building Code Requirements for Accessible Housing* (1980), which also included drawings of apparently African American wheelchair users and photographs of a young white man in his wheelchair, casually dressed, trying to access a restroom or an apartment rental office.[37] The copious illustrations and photographs put the state building code in sociospatial context. They were contextual, referencing the human uses of space as well as human variations on the basis of race, gender, and disability. These illustrations expanded the visual and material rhetorics of the user beyond white disabled housewives, veterans, or normate figures such as Joe and Josephine.

Whereas barrier-free design guidelines for buildings had existed for decades, product design was a new dimension of housing accessibility with potential for mass-marketability. Experiments with product designs that could benefit multiple types of users, including disabled users, became testing grounds for Universal Design's internal theories. The lever handle, for instance, had been the focus of much experimentation in the twentieth century.[38] For Mace, the lever handle became a conceptual tool for expanding the definition of the user.

> The front door to the house is made easier for everyone to open by one simple change—a lever handle in place of the traditional knob. This is appreciated by anyone returning home with hands and arms full of parcels, a briefcase, grocery bags, a baby and a diaper bag, or a cane. Small children can manipulate a lever more easily than a knob, as can those with arthritis or other physical disabilities that limit a full range of movement.[39]

Mace's description of the lever handle appeared to parallel liberal curb cut theories, which insist that curb cuts create an ease of use. But the description equally recalls the crip curb cut, which used leverage as a source of friction and movement. Here, the lever handle challenges the primacy of the doorknob and its presumption of fully fingered, gripping hands. The lever handle's potential for multiple uses became clear in Mace's own experiments as a disabled maker. For years, he had worked with technologies of manual grasp, even designing a folding, accessible tub seat with an "internal grab bar" on its backrest, a "molded plastic armrest," and "adjustable legs."[40] To produce the final grab bar, Mace worked through iterations of knob-variety and handle-variety armrests.

Another technology of the home that became an experimental site for Universal Design in the late 1980s was the adjustable thermostat. Since the mid-twentieth century, industrial designer Henry Dreyfuss's Honeywell "Round" thermostat had been ubiquitous in U.S. suburban homes (Figure 6.8). Dreyfuss determined that the Round's streamlined design was universally usable by drawing on ergonomics data and diagrams of the hand to determine the best size and shape for gripping and turning the

Figure 6.8. Honeywell thermostat advertisement, "Choose your room temperature" (1959), featuring two women's hands interacting with thermostat interfaces. Cooper Hewitt, Smithsonian Design Museum / Art Resource, NY.

thermostat. But the Round materialized knowledge and assumptions about its users. Using the device required a user to grip with a hand, turn a wrist, and read small numbers on a dial. As Figure 6.8 illustrates, Honeywell's advertisements for the Round presumed a white, middle-class, suburbanite woman with normate hands as its user. Consequently, Honeywell redesigned variations of the Round several times to include raised lettering and a larger dial for blind and visually impaired people.[41]

Mace's product development and housing guidelines work translated into major grant funding and institutional recognition. In 1989 the National Institutes on Disability and Rehabilitation Research (NIDRR) granted Mace a Rehabilitation Research Training Center (RRTC) grant to establish the Center for Accessible Housing (CAH) at NC State.[42] The CAH addressed accessible housing research, product testing, and design education for undergraduate and graduate students and became an important testing ground for Universal Design (see Figure 6.5).[43] In the coming years, Universal Design theory developed through the network of experts surrounding the CAH.[44] Beyond producing and disseminating knowledge about accessible housing, the CAH became the primary public face of Universal Design geared toward private markets, while BFE remained a technical consultancy promoting Universal Design in subtle ways within the sphere of compliance-knowledge.

In the late 1980s, Mace and the CAH designed an alternative thermostat interface, the Universal Thermostat, which abandoned the Round's streamlined design in favor of a multisensory approach (Figure 6.9).[45] The Universal Thermostat incorporated large buttons, auditory feedback, and multiple options for input, including a remote control device. These features reflected a trend of incorporating disability-specific accessibility features into mass consumer products.[46] Experts asked to comment on the device offered encouraging feedback.[47] Although far less streamlined than the Honeywell Round, the Universal Thermostat interrogated human factors assumptions about normate hands. Its multimodal design revealed the Round's unmarked requirements for particular sensory and physical abilities, such as sight and wrist flexion, as well as cognitive abilities, such as the ability to read and interpret numbers.[48] Its functions and materiality, in other words, were direct interventions into the historical regimes of knowledge-construction presupposing normate users.

If the Universal Thermostat had been an assistive technology, its likely user would have remained a middle-class, home-owning, and perhaps white consumer with disposable income. In public or rented housing, such a device would likely only appear as an accommodation, replacing existing thermostats such as the Round (if any kind of personalized temperature adjustment was available at all). It would appear that even in the absence of a white woman's hands to display it, the Universal Thermostat merely repackaged and redesigned consumer control over the thermal environment. Yet Mace's analysis of product design in his 1985 article suggests that accessibility standards were creating a market for Universal Design products, which could, in turn, appear in new construction.[49] BFE publications would integrate products such as wall

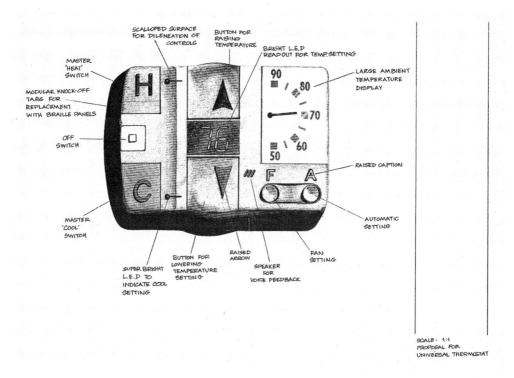

Figure 6.9. Center for Accessible Housing, Universal Thermostat with buttons, sound, and a remote control (ca. late 1980s). Courtesy of Joy Weeber.

interfaces and thermostats into illustrations of how to create accessibility as a total system rather than as component parts of buildings or products (Figure 6.10).

Depoliticizing Universal Design

By the late 1980s the CAH's work on the Fair Housing Amendments Act entered Universal Design into circulation in newspapers, architecture and building publications, and magazines. But how it circulated depended on journalists' familiarity with the discourse of barrier-free design. Some emphasized Universal Design's public face as commonsense, good design. For instance, refrains such as "accessibility for all is simply good design" sought to make the concepts of accessibility and Universal Design more palatable for mainstream designers.[50] Others adopted the language of technological progress, framing Universal Design as science fiction that had become reality.

> Universal Design is coming. It may creep into your life as a tiltable mixing bowl or scream at you from the monitor of the newest computer-driven model "smart" house, but it will appear in your own home. While it addresses the special needs of the elderly,

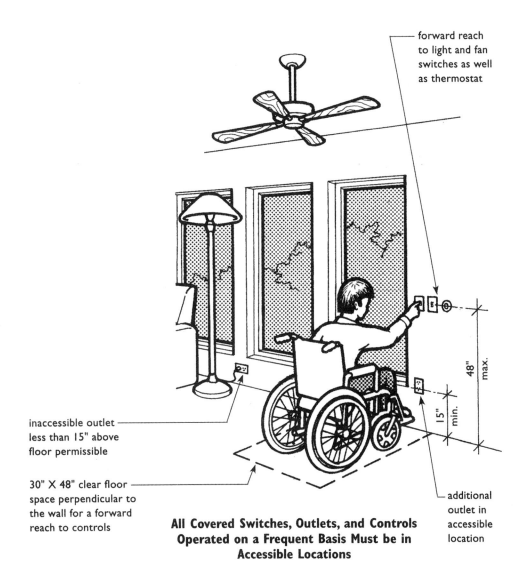

forward reach
to light and fan
switches as well
as thermostat

48" max.

15" min.

inaccessible outlet
less than 15" above
floor permissible

30" X 48" clear floor
space perpendicular to
the wall for a forward
reach to controls

additional
outlet in
accessible
location

**All Covered Switches, Outlets, and Controls
Operated on a Frequent Basis Must be in
Accessible Locations**

Figure 6.10. Design guidelines to make wall controls such as switches and thermostats accessible for wheelchair users. Barrier Free Environments, *Accessibility in Georgia: A Technical and Policy Guide to Access in Georgia* (Raleigh, N.C.: Barrier Free Environments, 1996), 130. Text by Leslie Young and Ronald Mace. Illustrations by Rex Pace.

physically challenged and young, it provides a new approach to design that goes beyond the accessibility and barrier-free schemes of the past. Universal design doesn't impose solutions for only the fittest over the needs of the less able. It transcends ability with innovation. It's design that works for everyone.[51]

While these rhetorics were a way of modeling accessibility, using plain language to describe complex practices, the discourse of simplicity, common sense, and good design was not substantive or specific enough to encourage accessibility. Nor did it depart in any significant way from the discourse of barrier-free design or the emphasis on the accessible home as a site of consumerism.[52] The "you" to whom the article spoke, however, was not the disabled person who had fought and waited for spatial justice to arrive. It was, rather, a mainstream consumer unmarked by any supposedly "special" needs. What role disabled people played in this technological future remained uncertain, even written out. By the end of 1989, Universal Design's depoliticized, largely consumerist public face increasingly contrasted with its internal theories, which foregrounded disabled people and activism, understood disability capaciously, addressed issues of race and class, and challenged core cultural assumptions about disability as tragedy or disqualification.

UNIVERSAL DESIGN IN THE POST-ADA ERA

It was all about the connections. Disabled architect Yoshihiko Kawauchi, a wheelchair user, traveled from Japan to the United States in 1989 to gather interviews for a comparative study of international accessibility approaches.[53] Beginning on the west coast and moving through the southeast, Kawauchi's travels mapped the evolution of access-knowledge expertise, particularly among disabled people, in spatial form. His primary contact, Michael Winter, a Berkeley-based activist and the president of the National Council on Independent Living, introduced him to Berkeley architecture professor Raymond Lifchez, Atlanta-based activist Eleanor Smith (to whom he supplied the European term "visitability"), and (through his DREDF connections) Mace, whom Kawauchi visited in his accessible Raleigh, North Carolina, home.[54]

The following year, Winter participated in a major, highly publicized public protest for disability rights. Concurrently, accessibility experts worked behind the scenes to materialize their strategies. On March 12, 1990, hundreds of disability activists left behind wheelchairs, scooters, canes, and crutches to climb the steps of the U.S. Capitol Building in Washington, D.C. Their demand—passing the Americans with Disabilities Act of 1990 (ADA)—encompassed rights to employment and legible, public citizenship for which disability activists and advocates had fought since the early twentieth century. Direct action and epistemic activism were mutually woven. Whereas the Capitol Crawl and the ADA materialized disability politics through legible, public means, Universal Design served as a more subtle, opaque strategic resource

for enacting politics "by other means"—through epistemic activism, theory forma- ·
tion, design reiteration, and other processes of access-making.[55]

The ADA promised disabled people civil rights to employment, government services such as public transportation, and access to restaurants, movie theaters, and
other spaces of public accommodation. These legal mandates propelled Universal
Design into broad circulation. Although the ADA promised to address discrimination
against over fifty million U.S. citizens with disabilities, Universal Design's relationship
to the law was uncertain. In the pre-ADA era, Mace, Lusher, and other Universal
Design advocates had foregrounded disabled users and other people marginalized
by built environments. The public face of Universal Design in the post-ADA era
shifted away from a focus on disabled users. The primary reason for this shift was
that architects and designers resisted compliance by insisting (as had generations of
architects before them) that accessible design would hamper their creative processes
and increase costs.[56] As the term "Universal Design" entered the mainstream vocabulary, it appeared in design newspapers, magazines, and handbooks as a signifier for a
shifting array of meanings, from "barrier-free design for everyone" to design that
eschews the category of disability.[57] While this malleability had consequences, Universal Design's versatility afforded opportunities for experimental propagation, which
had an impact on its internal theory and public face.

Code-Switching and Other Strategic Proliferations

In 1990 the American Institute of Architects' Colorado Chapter hosted a Universal
Design competition, for which Mace served on the jury.[58] Echoing the AIA's 1967
report, which suggested research on the "true physical characteristics of the population which constitutes the real market for barrier-free design" and "designing and
building for the real rather than the assumed average physical and mental characteristics of the population," eligible projects were to "address actual user characteristics,
rather than 'average' characteristics."[59] A list of possible examples included improved
signage, the development of new building materials or fixtures, the design of storage
areas for people of different heights, and improved ramps. The only commonality
between these examples (and what qualified them as Universal Design), however,
was that they were supposedly accessible to more than one user group. As the competition call demonstrated, Universal Design's meaning, scope, and practices were
not yet formalized, despite plentiful examples of design addressing non-average users.

From 1990 and 1995, Universal Design entered a highly experimental phase. The
movement's critical potential found tension with the ways that its versatility afforded
opportunities for appropriation and remaking. The term proliferated as journalists,
manufacturers, and consumers adopted the language of Universal Design to describe
myriad late twentieth-century user-centered concepts and practices.[60]

Proliferation is a way that things materialize when their meaning becomes unstable. The concept of proliferation offers a way of thinking about the work of Universal

Design—whether as broadening barrier-free design, replicating the past, or pushing into new terrain—that captures the dizzying sense of how confusing the term itself became in the early 1990s. "Proliferation" was also a term that Mace used in the 1970s to describe the pre-ADA world of federal, state, and local accessibility codes, which often conflicted.[61] The ADA had resolved some of these issues by adopting the Uniform Federal Accessibility Standards (UFAS), which used the voluntary ANSI A117.1 standard of 1980 as a template for federal code. But the problem was not simply the number of laws—it was also the quality of access. With Universal Design, Mace sought another kind of proliferation, which would restart barrier-free design not as a code compliance strategy but as a tactical approach for encouraging subtle cultural shifts and infusing strategic sites of power.

More than just a mark of instability, the broad proliferation of Universal Design's meanings enabled potent yet subtle work. One strategy entailed what linguists describe as "code-switching," or vacillations between two or more languages as required by social context.[62] For Universal Design advocates, code-switching manifested in the language they used to persuade designers and manufacturers and in the ways they interacted with, condoned, or rejected accessibility codes. As Mace and others framed it publicly, Universal Design was a complementary but superior approach to the ADA's minimum guidelines.[63] But the ADA invited Universal Design's proliferation by expanding potential markets and opening new funding streams geared toward access-knowledge experts. A growing epistemic community tapped into these resources to develop Universal Design's internal theories, as well as the translational means of their dissemination. In 1990 the National Endowment for the Arts funded the Universal Design Leadership Initiatives Meeting. Raymond Lifchez, Elaine Ostroff, Ruth Lusher, John Salmen, James Mueller, and industrial designer Patricia Moore met with Mace at the CAH to discuss Universal Design's future. "There is a pressing, short-term need in 1990–1991," they decided, "to provide some type of training on ADA and Universal Design practices. It should involve disabled individuals."[64] But regarding the promise of codes for social change, Mace, erstwhile code compliance expert, was candid.

> As long as we design a few special things and places for a few special categories of people, we will always fail at introducing the concept and practice of Universal Design. Current codes and standards are framed this way. After 15 years of working to change federal standards and state codes, I know that codes alone are not the best vehicle for influencing change. They are an important and necessary tool, but alone, they can too easily perpetuate a minimalist, segregated approach.[65]

The conceptual apparatus of barrier-free design at this point was reduced entirely to code, and Universal Design became the new philosophical term for broad accessibility. As the language shifted, however, it became necessary to define precisely what

Universal Design could be and how it differed from the ADA guidelines. But while disabled designers led Universal Design's development and while they emphasized that disabled peoples' knowledge was crucial to training architects in the ADA era, the mention of disability began disappearing from updated definitions of Universal Design written for outsider audiences.[66] For instance, the CAH's 1991 definition of Universal Design, published in an edited collection on design innovation, read:

> Universal Design means simply designing all products, buildings and exterior spaces to be usable by all people to the greatest extent possible. It is advanced here as a sensible and economical way to reconcile the artistic integrity of a design with human needs in the environment.[67]

Unlike the two earlier definitions, which had specified categories of disabled users, children, aging people, and people of non-average size, this definition embraced the rhetorics of "all people" and "everyone" that had for so long dominated barrier-free design. But this new definition was so general that a designer unaware of the need for disability access could miss the imperative for spatial inclusion entirely. At the same time, in its supporting examples, the CAH explained barrier-free designs almost exclusively through disability access, as if to suggest that what was ostensibly disability design could pass undetected as a more general form of "good design." Although the new definition was exceedingly general, then, the document as a whole epitomized code-switching.

A major challenge for barrier-free design was to make disabled users legible for designers through research, public policy, and participatory design, with the goal of built-in or anticipatory access in future design. Whether through the International Symbol of Access (ISA), better accessibility research, or more accessible buildings, making disability legible would save disabled people from the stigmas of visible misfit. Legibility, in other words, worked in the service of illegibility and mainstreaming. But in the 1990s illegibility—the illusion of smooth, frictionless design created by enhanced usability—became an aesthetic strategy for Universal Design. The post-ADA perception that disability had become more legible, albeit misunderstood, led Universal Design advocates to argue that the best accessible designs were so materially "subtle" and "so well integrated that they become indistinguishable" from mainstream design.[68] Anything else was segregation and separated disabled people from the rest of the population through separate features marked by accessibility signs.[69] But while promoting "indistinguishable" or frictionless design when speaking to those outside their epistemic community, conversations between proponents emphasized a different use of subtlety: shifting the burden of access from the misfit user to the environment. Regarding the ISA, for instance, Mace argued at the Universal Design Leadership Initiatives meeting,

If a parking lot were designed according to Universal Design principals [sic], there would be no need to differentiate certain spaces for use by people with wheelchairs. . . . Rather than have a symbol for places and buildings that are accessible, why not a symbol for those that aren't. This might force non-disabled people to realize how unaccommodating the environment is.[70]

These criticisms of mainstream design suggest that the internal theory of Universal Design retained an understanding of disability as marginalized embodiment for which society was responsible. When Universal Design proponents discussed the concept among themselves, their ideas and discussions highlighted various forms of human difference and particularity and were much more capacious in their understanding of disability injustice than when they promoted their ideas to outsiders such as journalists.

Writing the Book

Despite their reservations about code compliance, Mace and his colleagues did not abandon the compliance regime outright. Given that code-making had been a contested political realm in the 1980s, and given that the ADA had expanded resources and opportunities for accessibility experts, ceding the space of compliance-knowledge would have hindered proponents' goals of creating a more accessible world. Mace and his colleagues channeled their status as compliance experts to plant seeds of Universal Design in the unexpected, mundane, technical spaces of accessibility standards, compliance manuals, handbooks, and research. By building Universal Design ideas into code compliance and technical guidance, these experts materialized the strategy of built-in rather than retrofit accessibility.

In 1990 the Access Board hired BFE to develop an implementation manual for the UFAS codes, which the Access Board would use to enforce the ADA Accessibility Guidelines (ADAAG).[71] Mace enlisted the help of his Universal Design colleagues, including Elaine Ostroff, Edward Steinfeld, Eric Dibner, and John Salmen, to complete the project. From its typewriter font to its technical diagrams and illustrations, the 1991 *UFAS Retrofit Manual* typified the aesthetics of bureaucratic code compliance. It did not contain a single glossy photo of an accessible kitchen, product, or home. Its cover bore the stigmatized term "retrofit," a word that, like "code," connoted rigidity and poor design.

If one flipped through it, the 334-page tome would appear (at first glance) as any other guide to accessibility, detailing disability as a functional limitation, explaining regulatory issues, and providing technical diagrams of the space requirements for wheelchair users—everything that an architect would need to produce UFAS-compliant retrofits. Nothing would appear out of the ordinary, conspicuous, or radical. But read more closely, this was not a code compliance manual. It was a manifesto for Universal Design.

The first clue was that not a single checklist was to be found. The second was that the manual problematized historical patterns of accessibility that took shape as barrier-free design—including the same practices of code-mandated retrofit that it purported to explain.[72] Through reflexive friction, the manual emphasized the limitations of "minimal" guidelines and standards (particularly checklist-style standards).[73] Not only were checklists inadequate, according to the manual, but retrofits themselves—the very type of design that the manual was supposed to explain—also failed to "integrat[e] [access] into the fabric of the building or site."[74] But if one thought more capaciously about the underlying meaning of the code, it clarified, access would reveal itself as a universal good.

> Even very specific requirements that appear to benefit only a small portion of society make the environment safer and easier to use for everyone.... In recent years, the experience gained from designing facilities and products to meet mandated access requirements has established a direction toward the new era of a universally usable environment.[75]

The test of accessible design, furthermore, was whether a space could be "used by anyone," as *inaccessible* design features such as stairs and uneven sidewalks are hazardous and dangerous to "all users," a category that the manual defined as including normates alongside a wide range of impairments including mobility, sensory, and neurological disabilities, temporary disabilities, heart conditions, and types of misfit related to being smaller or larger than the average population size.[76] Here, the universality was not a normate fantasy but a requirement for keeping misfits in mind.

To summarize: the Access Board hired Mace to quite literally *write the book* on retrofit and code compliance, perhaps the most important and wide-ranging in the scope of its application. Instead, he wrote a covert manifesto for Universal Design.

Mace's strategic appropriation of the retrofit manual suggests a tactical sensibility that played with available resources, as well as habits of perception. By replicating the values and discourses of earlier accessibility proponents but problematizing the regime of code compliance governmentality, the manual delivered more than facts about user populations or guidelines about best practices. Rather, it trained architects how to think critically about the public face of barrier-free design (i.e., codes and standards) and the underlying theory that meaningful, broad accessibility requires design for the full range of human variation without resort to averages or intuitive assumptions.

Experiments in Access-Knowledge

As Universal Design entered a phase of experimentation with methods of public dissemination, proponents also created forums for experimentation around its internal theory. These forums responded to the globalization of Universal Design's epistemic community, which soon encompassed experts in Europe and Asia.[77] While legal contexts and disability rights histories differed across national borders, this international epistemic community invoked terms such as "Universal Design," "barrier-free design," "accessibility," and "design for all" in reference to the project of access-knowledge. Disabled architects Selwyn Goldsmith (UK) and Yoshihiko Kawauchi (Japan) began corresponding and meeting with U.S. experts, particularly Mace, Ostroff, and Lifchez.[78] Beyond cultivating practices of access, both Goldsmith and Kawauchi consulted extensively with Mace, among others, as they pieced together the histories of barrier-free and Universal Design in their books, *Designing for the Disabled: The New Paradigm* and *Universal Design: A Reconsideration of Barrier-Free.*[79] The archive of Universal Design, so to speak, is in many ways a product of conversations between U.S. designers and their non-U.S. colleagues, whose concerns with translation across national contexts both forced greater conceptual clarity and mapped the tensions between the public face and internal theories of accessibility.

Universal Design's internal theory took shape through conversations between an epistemic community that first connected in the 1980s and continued to grow. In 1982 a number of accessibility experts had met at a series of conferences, including "Designed Environments for All People" at the United Nations and "Teaching Design for All People," a gathering devoted to infusing accessibility principles into the design curriculum. A decade later, the Pratt Institute in New York hosted "Universal Design: Access to Daily Living," the "first national multidisciplinary conference to explore Universal Design."[80] This event showed that Universal Design's own practitioners understood it as a contested practice taking valid form across disciplines and approaches. Conference attendees included Lusher, now a member of the Access Board, industrial designer Bruce Hannah, Diane Pilgrim (director of the Cooper Hewitt, Smithsonian Design Museum, and a wheelchair user), and blind photographer George Covington, who served on the event's executive board. Mace, Mueller, Moore, Ostroff, Salmen, and Steinfeld were also all in attendance, as were designers representing new areas, such as Greg Vanderheiden (a telecommunications accessibility expert), Satoshi Kose (a Japanese Universal Design expert), Jim Sandhu (an advocate of "design for all" from the United Kingdom), and Susan Behar (an interior designer). Vice President Dan Quayle delivered the opening address, and renowned Israeli disabled concert violinist Itzhak Perlman, a close friend of Mace's, delivered a keynote talk. What these continuities reveal is that Universal Design's epistemic community was both consolidating and expanding. "Exploring" Universal Design required advocates to treat the concept as an experiment rather than an enduring truth. Consequently, new hybrids of design concepts and practices were becoming possible.

Two experimental access-knowledge products emerged from the meeting. One was the *Universal Design Newsletter,* spearheaded by Salmen's firm Universal Designers and Consultants, in conversation with Barrier Free Environments.[81] The newsletter, which circulated from 1993 until 2014, first in print and later via e-mail, provided basic

knowledge to designers about emerging accessibility regulations, upcoming conferences, best practices, and accessible products. Each issue published designers' questions to the editor (Salmen himself) and provided contact information for relevant
experts. Without the *Newsletter,* Universal Design may never have come to appear as
a cohesive, innovative, and growing field. Experts used its pages to invent new language for describing and promoting Universal Design as a distinct and more flexible
alternative to barrier-free design.[82] Although its purpose was education, the *Newsletter*
provided a space to share knowledge about disability rights, international disability
culture, and new access technologies and products.[83] Historic preservation, safety, and
access to recreation were all frequent topics.[84] Internet and telecommunications accessibility, a new domain of accessible design, was also an emerging topic of discussion.[85]

The *Newsletter* equally revealed Universal Design's ambiguous relationship to the
ADA by reporting the news on code expansions and clarifications. But what appeared
as simply reporting the news about tedious code expansions was in fact an opportunity for building new concepts. When the Access Board expanded the kinds of spaces
that the ADAAG would regulate, the *Newsletter* not only reported on these expansions but also developed over time a conception of which new design features would
support or hinder the expanding scope of Universal Design. Take, for example, the
now-ubiquitous unisex, accessible "family restroom," a type of restroom that typically
provides enough space for a wheelchair user, includes grab bars, a locking door,
and sometimes even a changing table.[86] In their current iterations, such restrooms
also often feature lever-style door handles, and their toilets, sinks, and other fixtures
are lower to the ground than those in inaccessible multi-user restrooms. Similar to the
curb cut, the accessible, single-user restroom has become a symbol of broad accessibility for disabled, queer, trans, and gender nonconforming people, whose needs for
safe and accessible space such restrooms purportedly afford.[87]

Whether an object of disability or queer advocacy, the accessible, single-stall
restroom is, for the most part, an invention of the post-ADA era. Even in the early
1990s, such "family restrooms" were voluntary, ad hoc fixtures of public spaces such
as shopping malls and restaurants. Many were not yet wheelchair accessible. But the
Access Board began to consider whether such restrooms, if properly designed and
outfitted with locking doors, would also benefit disabled users. As this shift occurred,
the *Newsletter* became a testing ground for framing accessible restrooms as possible
Universal Design sites, which could address the intersecting needs of families and
wheelchair users. If required by law, the *Newsletter* insisted, their widespread adoption would benefit parents who could not take their children into standard gender-
segregated restrooms, as well as disabled people who traveled with attendants.[88] But
many ad hoc family restrooms were still gender segregated. In 1995 the Access Board
began deliberating about whether to require in code that single-stall family restrooms
also be wheelchair accessible and "unisex," introducing a shift in the focus of bathroom politics from family structures to the gender of even individual users.[89] In other

words, if families could use it, and disabled people could use it, people of any gender could use the restroom, too. While an awareness of trans issues would not enter discussions of Universal Design until much later, this unfolding process provides some insight into how Universal Design advocates were subtly broadening accessibility to include the landscape of gender norms and identities in the late twentieth century.

A second product of Universal Design's epistemic community was new attention to design pedagogy. Questions of Universal Design's scope and users reached beyond the *Newsletter* to the structure of architectural education itself. Under the leadership of Elaine Ostroff and Polly Welch, proponents turned to design education at the university level as an experimental site.[90] In 1993 Adaptive Environments initiated the Universal Design Education Project (UDEP) at twenty-one universities in the United States, with funding from an ADA Voluntary Compliance grant from the Public Access Office of the U.S. Department of Justice, the National Endowment for the Arts (NEA), and several private foundations.[91] UDEP's objective, as advocate Polly Welch put it, was to approach the ADA with "greater creativity and a challenge for designers to think beyond the minimum requirements . . . [to] understand the needs of users well enough to make informed judgments and to effectively use the input of users with disabilities."[92] Design research and education continued to serve as loci for these types of user-informed interventions.

UDEP was an extension of 1982 "Teaching Design for All" and 1990 Universal Design Leadership Initiative meetings. While it began as an attempt to infuse accessibility concerns into design education, the project was structured to allow a high level of experimentation. At each university, faculty worked with students on a project over the course of the year and recorded their strategies for a later edited volume. Recalling that the ADA had only been in effect for three years, and that in prior decades, accessibility codes only applied to a small number of buildings housing federally funded projects, UDEP was the first attempt to seriously integrate accessibility into the design curriculum.

UDEP's pedagogical model reflected proponents' critiques of standardization. The program tasked faculty with training architecture students to understand the "rationale behind an access feature" rather than simply compliance.[93] Whereas compliance-based learning would have adopted a model of education in which faculty deposit standardized, objective information into students' minds, UDEP encouraged a high level of ideological questioning, critical theory, and social justice concepts to encourage "creative approach[es] to inclusive design" beyond minimal standards.[94] Critical perspectives from disability studies, feminist theory, and other fields provided an adjunct theoretical resource for discouraging students from "typecasting" users and faculty from adopting "ableist, gendered, classist, and eurocentric course content" that was typical to architectural education.[95] Modeling alternative pedagogies, Adaptive Environments offered essays such as "Unhandicapping Our Language," written by disability studies pioneer Paul Longmore, to challenge ableist language in the classroom.[96]

These perspectives challenged the dominance of rehabilitation models in accessibility and created new opportunities for interdisciplinary exchanges between humanities scholars and architects, much as environmental design research had done for architects and social scientists in the 1970s.

UDEP was also an experimental site for new concepts and methods. Methodologically, the goal was to "make universal design thinking an automatic part of the design process."[97] UDEP thus initiated a new generation of designers and experts into access-knowledge (Figure 6.11). Students, in turn, asked difficult political questions such as, "Can a design be universal if it excludes people who are homeless or economically disabled or if it fails to take into account future generations and other species with whom we share this earth?"[98] Design school faculty similarly asked, "What are the limits to 'Universality?' . . . Is Universal Design being used to simply maintain a status quo (despite its claims) or can it be a force for significant social change? Is there underlying conflict between an association of Universal Design with Modernism's claim to universality and its failure to create a socially just world?"[99] These lines of questioning opened a new scholarly and humanistic space within Universal Design, particularly given that many of its experts had been trained in more technical milieus of architectural design, rehabilitation engineering, and scientific research.

UDEP's conceptual experiments influenced the practice and dissemination of access-knowledge. Reflecting on the critical questions that students and faculty posed regarding the philosophy and scope of the universal, Mace, Ostroff, Mueller, Salmen, and others crafted a *Universal Design Newsletter* editorial in which they conveyed these questions to their audience of architects and builders. They characterized these lines of questioning as "broadening" thought to "include expanded environmental, historical, and social consciousness as part of Universal Design," expanding the "function of the designer in the design process," and transforming designers' "understanding of function."[100] Where barrier-free design had narrowly addressed issues at the interface of body and environment, UDEP led to experimental developments of the Universal Design concept that included a scholarly or social justice understanding of structural context and milieu, which in turn shaped strategies for disseminating knowledge.

As Lifchez and Winslow had done in decades prior, many UDEP design studios included figures whom Ostroff would later term "user-experts" to establish a sense of designerly humility and expose the limits of designers' intuition about inhabitants.[101] But rather than treating disabled people as accessories to the design process, some UDEP schools put user-experts into teaching roles. California Polytechnic State University's UDEP teaching assistant, for example, was a disabled student who reflected that in the UDEP setting his assistive technologies ("wheelchair, braces, crutches [and] hearing aids") were considered an asset and a resource, even providing "a dash of validity to some of the dialogue" around accessibility rather than "pity and avoidance."[102] The key was to incorporate "multiple constituencies" rather than to generalize from the needs of a single user to the needs of all.[103]

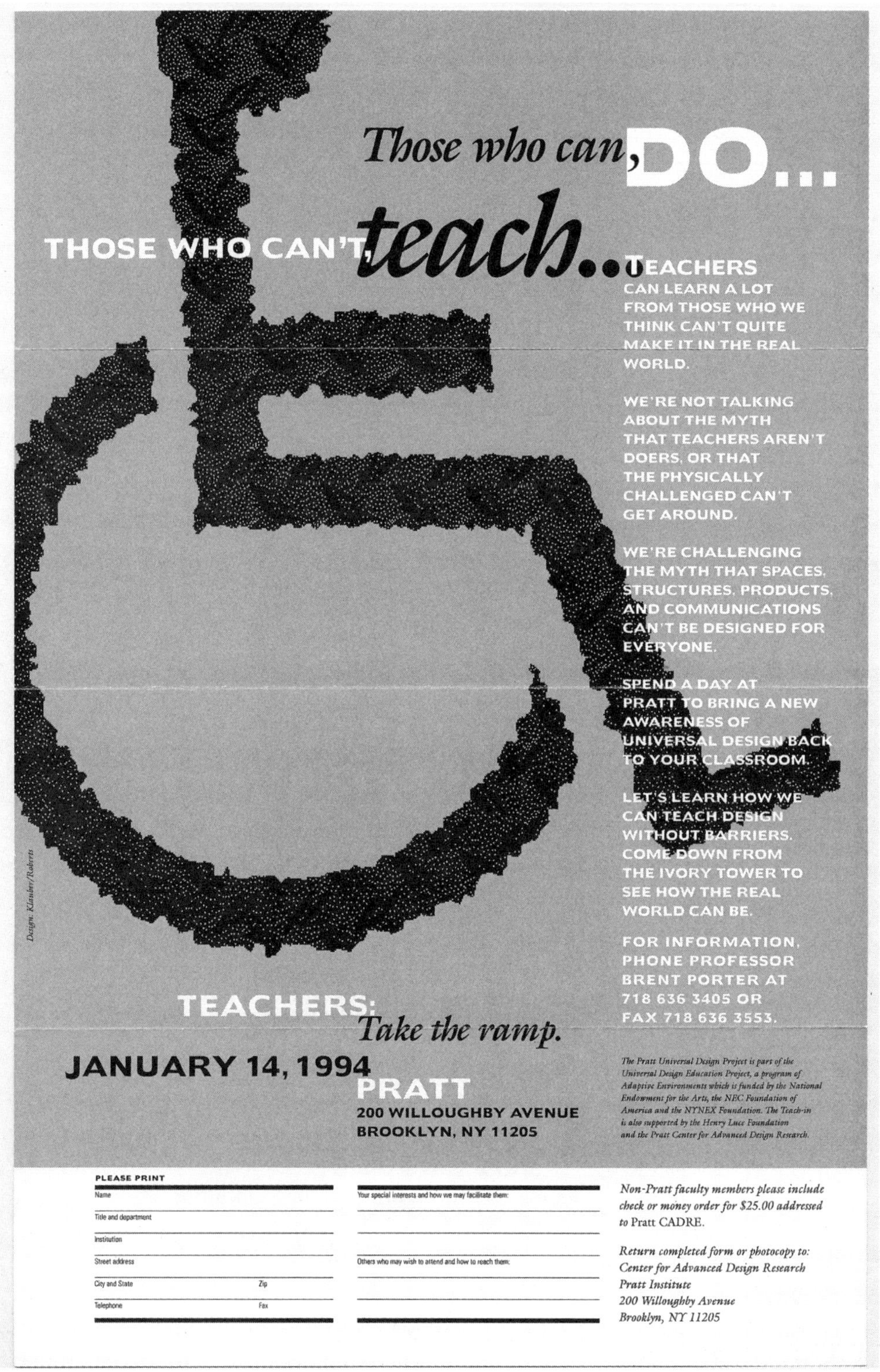

Figure 6.11. A poster advertising a 1994 "teach-in" on Universal Design at the Pratt Institute, featuring a large wheelchair symbol. Courtesy of Bruce Hannah, professor emeritus, Pratt Institute, School of Art and Design.

Accordingly, UDEP offered Universal Design as a method of challenging prevailing modes of design authority. Participants in UDEP's program at the State University of New York at Buffalo, organized by Steinfeld, contended that working against the concept of expert knowledge was crucial to conveying Universal Design as a sensibility and ethos of inclusion. They noted that disability-inclusive design "demonstrates how cultural forces can redefine the object and social context of design, often in resistance to the established professional position. We used universal design to challenge traditional and emerging professional perspectives and examine the limits of expert knowledge."[104] In place of designer-experts, user-experts could convey both functional needs and a sense of the diversity within the broader population. Likewise, designing for diversity required the input of a diversity of experts. As Abir Mullick, an industrial designer participating in the project argued, "If universal design is about diversity, then it should be represented in the selection of consultants. They could have been artists, scientists, sociologists, and politicians—some who were disabled and others who were not."[105] A diversity of user-experts, in other words, made situated expertise central to design practice.[106]

Because UDEP was in many ways inventing architectural education for disability design, it drew upon and critiqued existing strategies for educating nondisabled students about disabled users, particularly strategies employed in rehabilitation education. For instance, some schools used empathic simulation exercises, activities in which nondisabled students spend a day wearing blindfolds, using wheelchairs, or in gloves that simulate the functional limitations of arthritis.[107] As many disability activists have pointed out, simulation exercises are reductive, ineffective, and depoliticizing. While their purpose is to create disability awareness among nondisabled people, simulations misrepresent and trivialize the learned resourcefulness of disabled people who adapt to and change their environments. As a result, they also fail to account for privilege and structural oppression.[108] For the nondisabled people who engage in these exercises, they serve to impart pity and communicate a notion of disability as lack or excess.

As pedagogical and research tools, such "awareness activities" have been acknowledged to be inaccurate and dangerous—a point that Lifchez and Mueller both emphasized in UDEP's planning stages.[109] When UDEP schools *did* use disability simulations, professors discovered that these were failed experiments, particularly compared to direct conversations with disabled user-experts. Faculty at Purdue University, for instance, found that despite the use of simulation exercises, "the human element of universal design was, for the most part, lacking."[110] They hypothesized that this was because students did not receive adequate time with user-experts, who only appeared briefly as speakers rather than consultants. As a result, student work suffered, was less innovative, and proved inaccessible. Other faculty at the Pratt Institute adopted a different approach, encouraging students to "take a walk with a person with disabilities" and discuss their experiences rather than simulating the disability itself.[111] Faculty and project leaders reflected on the usefulness and efficacy of these activities, noting that they encouraged greater respect for disabled people and turned critical attention to the built environment as a site of intervention. Through these experiments in design education, UDEP provided faculty and students opportunities to witness the pitfalls of simulation activities and the value of user-expertise as a resource for knowing and making Universal Design.

Ultimately, UDEP's experiments in design pedagogy influenced the dissemination of access-knowledge about Universal Design more broadly. For instance, Salmen emphasized in a 1996 editorial based on the UDEP experience that "to improve our environments and products we must include the perspective that people with disabilities have to offer, and we must learn to value their input in the process."[112] This claim echoed the 1990s disability rights motto, "Nothing About Us Without Us," translating it into language that would more directly appeal to designers.

What also emerged from UDEP was a theory of Universal Design as a process or sensibility rather than a definable or standardizable practice.[113] This awareness continued to challenge dominant cultural, professional, and marketing definitions of "good design" and in many cases even drew attention to the privileges and particularities of majority-white, nondisabled, male, middle-class designers. Drawing connections between the marginalized experiences of disabled people and those of racial minorities, women, and queer people, UDEP faculty represented the Universal Design process as epistemological and political.[114]

The results of the project appeared in *Strategies for Teaching Universal Design,* a volume that Adaptive Environments published in 1994. UDEP faculty also translated their experiences into continuing education for architects. For instance, in November 1994 Adaptive Environments hosted a two-day symposium called "Designing the Future: Toward Universal Design" as an extension of UDEP.[115] The symposium had 375 attendees and occurred as part of the larger "Build Boston" architectural expo held at the Boston World Trade Center—a massive turnout that suggested that Universal Design had effectively harnessed the post-ADA injunction for designers to learn and practice better accessibility.[116]

The conference served as a forum for barrier work, distinguishing Universal Design's internal theory from its public face. Building on UDEP students' inquiries into the expansiveness of Universal Design, some participants raised issues of what Universal Design discourse had omitted. A glaring issue was race. Although the racial representation of users had diversified in BFE and CAH materials, Universal Design advocates had not taken up racial desegregation as an issue that intersected with disability exclusions. A panel on "Design for Diversity: An Issue of Sustainability" raised this issue. Brad Grant, an African American architect and educator, pointed out that while black and Latino people of color constituted a large proportion of the disabled population, white, middle-class users often remained at the center of conversations about Universal Design.[117] Responding to Grant's comment, Salmen drew parallels between concerns about the built environment's effects vis-à-vis race, gender, and homelessness, which other panelists had raised.[118] The depth of theorization appeared to stop there, however, as the conversation turned to strategies for convincing designers and consumers of Universal Design's necessity. Describing Universal Design as a "marketing concept," Mace clarified that the term was a strategy for overcoming architects' boredom and resistance to compliance by working within the market as a site of power with value and prestige for designers.[119] This strategy, he acknowledged, had not been successful because of what he identified as architects' "attitudes": so long as architects understood accessible products as only necessary on projects with disabled clients or explicitly for disabled users, the market for such products would not exist.[120] If accessible products and spaces appear in spaces of "mainstream commerce," such as corporate headquarters and government buildings, Mace proposed, "Then we're winning."[121]

UNIVERSAL DESIGN IN NEOLIBERAL TIMES

Mace's comments suggest a shift in his thinking and in the broader Universal Design discourse. Where his earlier concerns had been with marginalized users, the swift transition from discussing race, gender, and homelessness to marketing discourses suggests the pressures that advocates felt to access the privileged domain of neoliberal manufacturing and marketing, which they perceived as governing Universal Design's success in the architectural realm.[122] Regardless of how nuanced and critical Universal Design's internal theory became, the public face of Universal Design marketing obscured these nuances, often in the very ways that proponents sought to avoid. In the post-ADA era, journalists and manufacturers appropriated the term "Universal Design" to brand any form of user-centered design as good design, ranging from disability designs to mere ergonomics.[123] For instance, they used slick and insubstantial language, characterizing accessibility as "one of the hottest markets for the immediate future."[124] Disability marketing firms, such as Evan Kemp and Associates, similarly emphasized the "buying power" of millions of disabled consumers. Advertisements and marketing discourses such as these extended the associations between citizenship, gainful employment, and the right to consume.

Marketing justifications for Universal Design also left behind the politicized claims of disability rights advocates for inclusion in public life in favor of appealing to more normate, mainstream consumers' desire for freedom or more usable consumer products. "After all," one magazine claimed, "America was founded on freedom, and universal design sets people free."[125] While this media attention appeared to be a product of successful branding, many designers and journalists seemed unaware that advocates of Universal Design claimed that it was a different approach than barrier-free design. As one commentator in *Kitchen and Bath Business* wrote, "While universal design makes sense everywhere, the government has made it law in certain circumstances."[126] The law did not go quite this far, but these impressions are unsurprising given that many of the most influential barrier-free design experts were also promoting Universal Design as a strategy for ADA enforcement.

While the ADAAG regulated access at the scale of public buildings and cities, it did not concern itself with most products, leaving the consumer product market's accessibility unregulated and unstandardized. Where in earlier decades barrier-free design had circulated through the language of productive spatial citizenship, Universal Design identified disabled people as a "rapidly growing" niche market, a base of "diverse and hard-to-reach" consumers to whom businesses could market products.[127] A 1991 Access Expo in Washington, D.C., identified awareness of accessible products as a significant source of "knowledge" for "those people who are responsible that their facility, products and services are barrier-free."[128] "Many of the recent advances in assistive and access technology," the expo's announcement claimed, "had been developed and brought to market by entrepreneurs with disabilities."[129] The same year, BFE collaborated with DREDF on "Main Street," a video project geared toward promoting "cooperation between the business and disability communities" by asking businesses to recognize disabled peoples' expertise and encouraging them to comply with the ADA (Figure 6.12).[130]

A number of manufacturers, including OXO Good Grips and Herman Miller, claimed the term "Universal Design" as their own.[131] Product magazines made similar errors. "Universal Design, a term coined by Whirlpool Corp.," wrote *Appliance Manufacturer* magazine, "is described by the Benton Harbor, Mich.-based appliance maker as 'a configuration that is usable to all people.' The features to achieve universal design are merely components assembled in a way to provide access and use for a broad range of people."[132] Although contributing the greater visibility of Universal Design as a concept, these proliferations were also eroding its meaning. To the uninformed consumer, for instance, generalized language about usability for all simply would have implied that Whirlpool's products were of high quality, not that they equalized access between disabled and nondisabled people.

The language of Universal Design itself became flexible in the post-ADA world as it grew to capitalize on rights discourses, market trends, and new legal landscapes. An inevitable outcome of this flexibility was that the *language* of accessibility became a neoliberal commodity.[133] Like the Universal Design advocates who used the ADA's momentum to fund their research and conceptual developments, product manufacturers trained their attention on emerging markets: home and building products aligned with federal codes. They borrowed the language of accessibility and Universal Design, synthesizing this language through what their market research revealed about changing consumer habits and understandings of "home." Whirlpool Corp., for instance, invited Mace, in addition to other architects and social scientists, to consult on new market research regarding the shifting demographics, affordability, and functionality of the "American home" in the twenty-first century.[134] The impetus for this

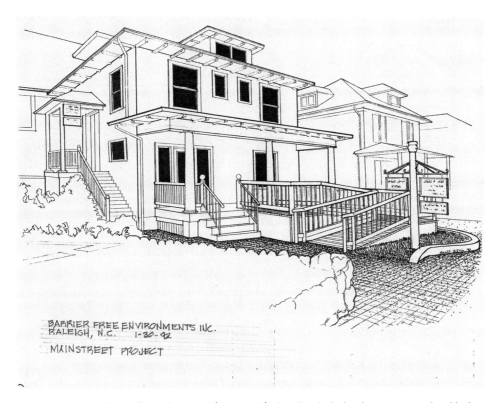

BARRIER FREE ENVIRONMENTS INC.
RALEIGH, N.C.   1-30-92

MAINSTREET PROJECT

Figure 6.12. The "Main Street" project (1991–92) aimed to help businesses comply with the ADA. This drawing offers a potential design for a ramp. Ronald L. Mace Papers, MC 00260, Special Collections Research Center, North Carolina State University Libraries, Raleigh, N.C.

research came from demographic shifts and new human uses of space. Whirlpool reassessed the product manufacturer's role: manufacturers were now called to provide consumer services in the form of more usable environments, extending rehabilitation engineering to broader consumer markets.

In marketing, the decision to prioritize accessibility in private homes placed the language of Universal Design into the matrix of neoliberal economics. Mace's response to Whirlpool's report detailed the cultural influence of social movements, including independent living, deinstitutionalization, the black civil rights movement, feminism, and the American Indian movement, on shifting experiences of the American home, education, and employment.[135] He concluded, however, that the result of greater disability inclusion via barrier-free design was that there was now a larger market for accessible products. Marginalized users thus became new niche markets for neoliberal marketing campaigns. In addition to benefiting privileged white, middle-class housewives, accessible home products could provide corporations such as Whirlpool with opportunities for catching up to shifting cultural norms. Alongside green, smart, flexible, and adaptive homes, Universal Design became interwoven with neoliberal marketing strategies: not a niche exception trained on "special" needs but a concept whose time had arrived in late capitalism. Where barrier-free design had upheld white, middle-class productive citizenship, the increasingly diverse household demanded adaptability, similar to the way that neoliberalism required "human capital" to adapt to new conditions of labor.[136] Universal Design, in this case, was both the worker (in the sense that it performed material and conceptual labor) and the apparatus for producing flexible labor.

Mace and others had hoped that Universal Design would operate as an extralegal phenomenon alongside the ADA, with the latter encouraging a market for accessible projects and the former devising strategies for accessible design. But as Universal Design entered circulation as a product description among other neoliberal forms, it became increasingly depoliticized and divorced from disability justice—within certain discourses. Design magazines characterized Universal Design as simply a form of good design or quickly dismissed its potential for promoting justice for disabled people by remarking on its added value for nondisabled people.[137] Even when journalists mistakenly conflated Universal Design with barrier-free design and retrofit, their focus was marketing to consumers, not the rights that the ADA afforded.[138] In other words, the public face of Universal Design did not appear to have a politicized commitment to disability rights or an understanding of access as valuable on its own terms. The primary emphasis was added value for the normate consumer.

Corporations such as Whirlpool, Leviton, General Electric, and Bobrick Washroom Equipment also consulted with Mace directly, incorporating the language and claims of Universal Design into their catalogs and market research (Figures 6.13 and 6.14).[139] Yet these materials rarely, if ever, credited Mace, Lusher, or the CAH, reproducing the apparently disinterested objectivity of accessibility guidelines that BFE's manuals had contested. Nor did they replicate Mace's insights about the disability rights movement, economic privilege, or other dimensions of power.

Epistemic activism within marketing discourses took shape in several ways. Industrial designer Jim Mueller used his position and expertise in vocational rehabilitation, ergonomics, and barrier-free design to develop a new marketing vocabulary for Universal Design that put disability at its center. To do this, he published in product design, marketing, and rehabilitation journals and magazines, intervening into industrial design discourses in much the same way that Mace was intervening into architecture. Mueller's strategy was to challenge the idea of the average or normal consumer by interjecting the philosophy of Universal Design.[140] But rather than blatantly characterize disabled people as a niche market on which manufacturers should capitalize, Mueller carefully argued for the social value of design for forgotten consumers.[141] Disability, Mueller explained to manufacturers, is not a discrete category. It intersects with race, class, age, and geographic identities, and represents within it a broad range of impairment types, all of which are forms of variation for which designers must account.[142] While his primary objective was more meaningful access, Mueller also

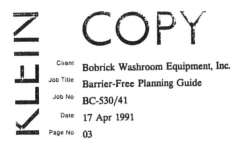

COPY

Client Bobrick Washroom Equipment, Inc.

Job Title Barrier-Free Planning Guide

Job No BC-530/41

Date 17 Apr 1991

Page No 03

Furthermore, with the advancement in washroom equipment, barrier-free compliance need not be at odds with clean, architectural design and durable, vandal-resistant operation for both ~~handicapped and non-handicapped~~ patrons.

↳ PATRONS WITH DISABILITIES & OTHERS

OR

ALL USERS

THIS IS DESCRIBING THE CONCEPT WE CALL UNIVERSAL DESIGN WHICH MEANS MAKING ALL COMMON PRODUCTS & SPACES USABLE BY EVERYONE TO THE GREATEST EXTENT POSSIBLE SO THE RESULT IS NOT SPECIAL, DIFFERENT & NEED NOT BE LABELED OR OTHERWISE DESIGNATED AS FOR "HANDICAPPED" PEOPLE.

YOU MAY WANT TO USE TERMS LIKE MORE UNIVERSALLY USABLE.

Figure 6.13. As a consultant to manufacturers, Mace offered framing and terminology. His notes on a Bobrick Washroom Equipment's draft "Barrier-Free Planning Guide" (1991) suggest nonstigmatizing language and introduce the idea of Universal Design. Ronald L. Mace Papers, MC 00260, Special Collections Research Center, North Carolina State University Libraries, Raleigh, N.C.

Some people call it Universal Design. Others call it Lifespan

Design. We think a better, more accurate description is

REAL LIFE

DESIGN, BY GE

Figure 6.14. Companies such as General Electric advertised Universal Design products as "Real Life Design" (1991).

foregrounded the cultural and political work of disability activism, identity, and knowledge production; debunked popular assumptions about disability as passivity; and criticized the normalizing emphasis of barrier-free and rehabilitation design on boosting productivity and devaluing some users based on their perceived labor value—all direct responses to the ways that barrier-free design and rehabilitation had promoted white ablenationalism in the civil rights era.[143] He also challenged product designers' and manufacturers' focus on aesthetics over usability and used the ergonomics of Universal Design to argue the need for both.[144] Making these claims in a milieu dictated by economic calculations rather than social justice would very likely have been impossible if not for Mueller's established expertise in vocational rehabilitation and workplace ergonomics. But by using the language of markets, Mueller succeeded in challenging ideologies of compulsory productivity, ablenationalism, and even (to a limited extent) whiteness that dominated marketing discourses. Ultimately, what this suggested was that it was possible to speak the language of product marketing and persuade designers and manufacturers in a way that retained a politicized sense of disability.

Marketing Usability and the Rise of Post-disability Discourse

Epistemic experiments with promoting Universal Design met with both failure and success. In 1993 Mueller began focus groups with disabled user-experts to evaluate interfaces such as light switches, door handles, and toilet flushes through the CAH's "Disability Advisory Network," composed of 1,400 disabled and elderly people.[145] After publishing its findings on consumer preferences, the CAH contacted manufacturers to promote Universal Design as an approach for reaching broader markets and to offer the center's services in shaping promotional materials.

One strategy was to shape marketing materials in a way that made clear to disabled consumers that their needs were being met. Mike Jones, a psychologist who directed the CAH through its transition to the Center for Universal Design (CUD), connected in particular with one electrical manufacturing company, Leviton, which produced automatic and sliding electrical switches.[146] Jones convinced Leviton to share their marketing materials with the CUD and provided feedback that "emphasized the importance of a marketing approach appropriate to elders and people with disabilities."[147] The center saw the connection as an opportunity to emphasize that "good design recognizes the needs of the elderly and people with disabilities, without stigmatizing them."[148] The company's marketing manager, unsure at first of how to proceed, began her own investigations of widespread inaccessibility in the housing industry through site visits and conversations with builders. This research inquired into builders' and developers' "awareness of design for elders and people with disabilities" and found that many were uninformed or usually came to her for information.[149] Ultimately, the company used the CUD's services to formulate a Universal Design marketing strategy that would address disabled consumers and educate the development community.

Leviton integrated advertisements for Universal Design products into its existing product pamphlets in an attempt to avoid singling out (and therefore stigmatizing) disabled and elderly users. Yet the pamphlets did so by displaying privileged normate users benefiting from Universal Design products. In a move that ran counter to the CUD's project of diversifying representations of the user, Leviton's marketing materials depicted users and spaces that more closely resembled the white, middle-class suburbia of (coincidentally named) Levittown, New York, than the range of racial, economic, gender, and disability diversity that the CUD's educational materials sought to reach. None of these users were identifiable as disabled.

One pamphlet (Figure 6.15) displayed two seemingly unrelated product lines ("Security Lighting" and "Universal Design"), normalizing the latter by integrating it into the former. Placed together, the products recalled the early marketing of barrier-free design as an improvement on public safety and the planning of white communities, such as Levittown, New York, in the postwar era to supposedly protect white suburban residents from the perceived racialized dangers of cities, a trend that resulted

Informed homebuyers concerned about safety should consider installing security lighting and Universal Design products. The installation of these product options is becoming increasingly popular in new homes.

It is impossible to put a monetary value on making your home a "safe haven." Now is your opportunity to check out what Leviton has to offer to give you "peace of mind" and help make your family and home more safe and secure.

SECURITY LIGHTING AND CONTROLS

What is it?
Lighting that is designed to illuminate darkened areas of your home's interior and exterior, such as a foyer, driveway, pathway, front entry, side yard, backyard and pool.

What does it do?
It is lighting that provides an additional level of security to protect your home from intruders and help you and your family see clearly around your home in the dark or in an exit path during an emergency.

Create a "lived-in" look by programming your lights to automatically turn on at dusk. It will beautify your property and make walkways and pool areas safe to navigate at night.

What does it do for me?
Security experts agree that the first line of defense against intruders is a home that looks "lived in" – and lighting is a powerful deterrent. Exterior lighting can enhance the beauty of your property while at the same time give you a feeling of confidence and well-being.

Because exterior and interior lights can be controlled to turn on and off at specific times, they are a precautionary measure taken to provide protection as well as cost savings. Leviton offers a variety of lighting control options that will make your life easier and your home more secure and comfortable.

Keep an eye on them while they are inside or outside

· SCENE CONTROL DIMMERS · REMOTE CONTROLS · TIMERS · OUTDOOR MOTION SENSORS · INDOOR/OUTDOOR CAM
· ILLUMINATED RECEPTACLES AND WALL SWITCHES · 911 FLASHER SWITCHES · DECORA® ROCKER SWITCHES

Figure 6.15. Leviton Manufacturing Company, "Security Lighting and Universal Design" (2005).

Security lighting and control options

PRODUCT	DESCRIPTION	APPLICATION
SCENE CONTROL DIMMER	Control the intensity of light using a scene controller that allows for the creation and selection of preset lighting scenes throughout a room, or a group of rooms or your home's exterior.	Make your home look occupied at all times. Program times to turn on and off lights automatically. Select a security mode that randomly turns lights on and off. Can be programmed to automatically turn lights on at dusk and off at dawn.
REMOTE CONTROL	Exterior and entry lights can be turned on and off by pressing a button on the remote.	Turn on your interior and exterior lights from within your car when you pull into the driveway.
TIMER	Wall-mounted timers activate lighting and other products at a pre-selected time and then shut the power off when the time period has expired.	Ideal for turning interior and exterior lights on when home is unoccupied. Great for turning on and shutting off pool filters and hot tubs.
OUTDOOR MOTION SENSOR	This light monitors a specific area and automatically turns on lights when presence is detected and turns off lights when the area is unoccupied.	Warns you when anyone or anything is approaching. Ideal for driveways, entranceways, porches, side yards, back-yards and pool areas.
INDOOR/ OUTDOOR CAMERA	Cameras that allow you to watch on a dedicated security channel from any TV in your home.	Monitor your child's room, playroom, back yard, front door or any area an extra eye is desirable.
ALL LIGHTS ON SWITCH OR TABLE TOP CONTROLLER	Controls multiple light switches – able to turn on all lights.	Can be installed near the bed for use in emergency situations.

Note: *You can tie in your home's lighting system into a third party security system which will flash the lights on and off while the alarm is sounding.*

UNIVERSAL DESIGN

What is it?
Universal Design is a concept that is becoming more and more important to homeowners. It incorporates special products or design elements that are useable by everyone regardless of their age or level of physical ability.

What does it do?
Universal Design products are easy to install... user-friendly... and intended to adapt to a home-owner's temporary or permanent life-changing needs. A typical example is a touch dimmer switch that requires very little physical pressure to turn a light on and off. These products should not be confused with those used in "Accessible Design" (a group of products created for people with physical disabilities). However, Universal Design products and systems often complement Accessible Design schemes.

The Center for Universal Design routinely recommends Leviton's Decora® Rocker Style Switches. Their large surface and low-effort rocker action make them easier to use than a common toggle switch.

OR CAMERAS · ALL LIGHTS ON SWITCHES · OCCUPANCY SENSORS · TOUCH DIMMERS · RF UNIVERSAL REMOTES ·
TCHES · ANYWHERE SWITCHES · TAMPER-RESISTANT ELECTRICAL OUTLETS · ELECTRICAL OUTLET COVERS

in racial segregation. Given these histories, it may not be surprising that Leviton promoted Universal Design features alongside technologies intended to protect palatial suburban, single-family homes. With their lush landscaping lit by Leviton products, these homes appeared adjacent to photos of smiling white and light-skinned families in well-lit living rooms. The pamphlet emphasized Universal Design as "good design" for all users, arguing that Leviton products such as light switches "should not be confused with those used in 'Accessible Design' (a group of products created for people with physical disabilities)." The pamphlet's only apparently disabled user, an elderly man using a walker (not pictured in Figure 6.15), appeared next to the image of a young white woman holding a bag of groceries, with the light switch placed between them in the layout as if to suggest an equal sign. This technology, the pamphlet implied, is accessible to "everyone" (here encompassing young white nondisabled women and older white disabled men). Finally, by grouping the two types of lighting technologies together, the pamphlet suggested that Universal Design features could make "your home a 'safe haven'" and offer "peace of mind," rhetorics that distinguished well-lit suburbias from the presumed darkness (of skin or environment) in dangerous, urban locales. Universal access, in other words, made unseen threats visible: the pamphlet promised legibility, securitization, and racialized geographies even while trying to recuperate a destigmatized depiction of disability inclusion.

It is often in spaces of unmarked whiteness that broad accessibility fails. Earlier tropes of barrier-free design for "everyone" emphasized access to home as a rehabilitation tool for enabling disabled people to become productive spatial citizens. The post-ADA era of product design reconfigured the private sphere as a privileged domain of white, middle-class consumerism through a neoliberal "post-disability" discourse.[150] This discourse encompassed a series of claims, ranging from disability universalism (e.g., "we are all disabled") to disability neutrality (e.g., "design for everyone" rather than "design for disability") to antidisability (e.g., design focused on "eliminating" disability), all of which enabled the barrier work of differentiating Universal Design from barrier-free design. One post-disability logic was that even mentioning disability would produce stigma. Resembling the post-racial notion that talking about racial difference or oppression is racist, this logic purported that disability is a negative, stigmatizing quality, lending an automatic institutional appearance to a product. This logic often led to the erasure of disability from Universal Design discourse. Indeed, the pamphlets described above could have marketed anything related to home or safety without disability inclusion being their goal. But the post-disability notion that mere mention of disability is stigmatizing also misunderstood Mace's original position in 1985, which challenged architects' erroneous beliefs about disability by emphasizing disabled peoples' critical mass, political practices, and design expertise. Mace imagined a world in which disabled peoples' value was recognized at all stages of the design process, not one in which designers avoided discussing disability or resorted to euphemizing marginalization. His arguments against the *institutionalized* appearance of disability-focused design, for instance, reflected his experiences living in a rehabilitation hospital and nearly experiencing long-term institutionalization. In response, Mace challenged the apolitical, medicalized, and static representation of disability in marketing materials for products such as shower seats or bed lifts. But he did not adopt a disability-neutral position, which would omit mention of disability. Rather, Mace used epistemic activism to challenge normalizing misconceptions and disseminate new knowledge about disabled people.

Similar to the post-racial sense in which Leviton unironically marketed white, suburban securitization as good design for "everyone," the company's marketing materials represented a post-disability trend toward redesigning the language through which accessible products were marketed without challenging the ideological conditions through which disability had come to be viewed as a stigmatizing quality. Leviton characterized Universal Design as a usability enhancement for built environments (particularly for nondisabled people) that disavowed the milieus of disability activism, culture, and shared experiences of oppression that had produced inclusive design in the first place. While I am not suggesting that an overtly political disability rights advertisement would have been a more profitable marketing strategy, my concern here is with the ethical, political, and material-epistemic work of representation in shaping and challenging norms. It mattered that these framings and the distinctions they engendered were a kind of barrier work, distinguishing Universal Design from earlier approaches to accessibility. It mattered for disabled users that post-disability ideology shifted Universal Design away from disability-explicit design.

Missed or disregarded subtleties can fail to shape new ways of knowing disability or making access. While Universal Design proponents calculated that market-driven approaches would offer architects incentives for inclusive design, their strategies (at best) came into conflict with engrained beliefs about disability and (at worst) reproduced the false neutrality they sought to avoid. Epistemic activism carried risks, to be sure. For as proponents continually defined and redefined Universal Design, the concept's meaning materialized, shifted, and often dematerialized, often in unexpected ways. But the instability of Universal Design's meaning also enabled proponents to reconfigure their future tactics. Public confusions regarding Universal Design's relationship to accessibility soon made it necessary to move beyond the experimental phase of boundary work into a more formalized set of principles and guidelines for Universal Design, much as codes had provided coherence for barrier-free design. What remained to be seen in the mid-1990s was how proponents would negotiate architects' resistance and the appropriating effects of branding discourses as they answered the question of who benefits from a more accessible world.

Chapter 7

Entangled Principles

Crafting a Universal Design Methodology

How do designers know when they have achieved Universal Design?
—MOLLY F. STORY, "Principles of Universal Design"

Knowing what defines a more accessible world depends, in one sense, on how *much* we know, and in another, on the *politics* of knowing-making. Since the late 1990s, post-disability discourses have dominated the narrative of what counts as Universal Design. Proponents distinguish between *Universal Design,* framed as a "market driven concept . . . reflect[ing] the realities of contemporary societies with their diverse populations" and "an inclusive approach that benefits the entire population," and *accessibility for disabled users,* described in terms of "legal mandates" and "a civil rights issue focused on eliminating discrimination against one minority group."[1] These distinctions dovetail with disability universalist positions, which insist that "we all experience variations in our abilities," making Universal Design a universal need.[2] Some proponents have even gone as far as insisting that barrier-free design approaches themselves are a "'barrier' to a richer understanding of Universal Design," arguing that Universal Design instead functions as a "facilitator of human experience and performance."[3] Consequently, a depoliticized approach now dominates the Universal Design narrative. This depoliticized approach to Universal Design pivots around scientific constructs of function and usability proclaiming that "through the design of thoughtful environments—ones which anticipate and celebrate the diversity of human ability, age, and culture—we have the capacity to eliminate a person's disability."[4] Critical disability scholars, however, challenge this post-disability position, which is reminiscent of the rehabilitation-informed design practices that Universal Design sought to unsettle.

"To eliminate disability," argues Alison Kafer, "is to eliminate the possibility of discovering alternative ways of being in the world, to foreclose the possibility of recognizing and valuing our interdependence."[5] Put another way, post-disability discourses

223

THE PRINCIPLES OF

1 EQUITABLE USE

The design is useful and marketable to people with diverse abilities.

GUIDELINES **1a.** Provide the same means of use for all users: identical whenever possible; equivalent when not.

1b. Avoid segregating or stigmatizing any users.

1c. Make provisions for privacy, security, and safety equally available to all users.

1d. Make the design appealing to all users.

EXAMPLES ■ Power doors with sensors at entrances that are convenient for all users

■ Integrated, dispersed, and adaptable seating in assembly areas such as sports arenas and theaters

2 FLEXIBILITY IN USE

The design accommodates a wide range of individual preferences and abilities.

GUIDELINES **2a.** Provide choice in methods of use.

2b. Accommodate right-or left-handed access and use.

2c. Facilitate the user's accuracy and precision.

2d. Provide adaptability to the user's pace.

EXAMPLES ■ Scissors designed for right-or left-handed users

■ An automated teller machine (ATM) that has visual, tactile, and audible feedback, a tapered card opening, and a palm rest

5 TOLERANCE FOR ERROR

The design minimizes hazards and the adverse consequences of accidental or unintended actions.

ile	**Edit**	View	Label	Special
	Undo		⌘Z	
	Cut		⌘X	
	Copy		⌘C	
	Paste		⌘V	
	Clear			
	Select All		⌘A	

GUIDELINES **5a.** Arrange elements to minimize hazards and errors: most used elements, most accessible; hazardous elements eliminated, isolated, or shielded.

5b. Provide warnings of hazards and errors.

5c. Provide fail safe features.

5d. Discourage unconscious action in tasks that require vigilance.

EXAMPLES ■ A double-cut car key easily inserted into a recessed keyhole in either of two ways

■ An "undo" feature in computer software that allows the user to correct mistakes without penalty

6 LOW PHYSICAL EFFORT

The design can be used efficiently and comfortably and with a minimum of fatigue.

GUIDELINES **6a.** Allow user to maintain a neutral body position.

6b. Use reasonable operating forces.

6c. Minimize repetitive actions.

6d. Minimize sustained physical effort.

EXAMPLES ■ Lever or loop handles on doors and faucets

■ Touch lamps operated without a switch

Figure 7.1. "The Principles of Universal Design," Version 2.0 (4/1/97). Courtesy of the Center for Universal Design, North Carolina State University.

UNIVERSAL DESIGN
Version 2.0 (4/1/97)

3 SIMPLE AND INTUITIVE USE

Use of the design is easy to understand, regardless of the user's experience, knowledge, language skills, or current concentration level.

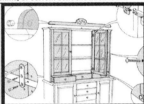

GUIDELINES   **3a.** Eliminate unnecessary complexity.

         3b. Be consistent with user expectations and intuition.

         3c. Accommodate a wide range of literacy and language skills.

         3d. Arrange information consistent with its importance.

         3e. Provide effective prompting and feedback during and after task completion.

EXAMPLES   ■ A moving sidewalk or escalator in a public space

         ■ An instruction manual with drawings and no text

7 SIZE AND SPACE FOR APPROACH AND USE

Appropriate size and space is provided for approach, reach, manipulation, and use regardless of user's body size, posture, or mobility.

GUIDELINES   **7a.** Provide a clear line of sight to important elements for any seated or standing user.

         7b. Make reach to all components comfortable for any seated or standing user.

         7c. Accommodate variations in hand and grip size.

         7d. Provide adequate space for the use of assistive devices or personal assistance.

EXAMPLES   ■ Controls on the front and clear floor space around appliances, mailboxes, dumpsters, and other elements

         ■ Wide gates at subway stations that accommodate all users

4 PERCEPTIBLE INFORMATION

The design communicates necessary information effectively to the user, regardless of ambient conditions or the user's sensory abilities.

GUIDELINES   **4a.** Use different modes (pictorial, verbal, tactile) for redundant presentation of essential information.

         4b. Maximize "legibility" of essential information.

         4c. Differentiate elements in ways that can be described (i.e., make it easy to give instructions or directions).

         4d. Provide compatibility with a variety of techniques or devices used by people with sensory limitations.

EXAMPLES   ■ Tactile, visual, and audible cues and instructions on a thermostat

         ■ Redundant cueing (e.g., voice communications and signage) in airports, train stations, and subway cars

THE PRINCIPLES WERE COMPILED BY ADVOCATES OF UNIVERSAL DESIGN, IN ALPHABETICAL ORDER:

Bettye Rose Connell, Mike Jones,
Ron Mace, Jim Mueller,
Abir Mullick, Elaine Ostroff,
Jon Sanford,
Ed Steinfeld, Molly Story,
and Gregg Vanderheiden.

NOTE:
The Principles of Universal Design are not intended to constitute all criteria for good design, only universally usable design. Certainly, other factors are important, such as aesthetics, cost, safety, gender and cultural appropriateness, and these aspects must also be taken into consideration when designing.

of Universal Design dictate that disability is a measurable impediment to human performance, a functional limitation in need of elimination. Despite Universal Design's origins in the work of disabled designers and the growth of its popularity in the aftermath of the ADA, contemporary post-disability narratives misunderstand the histories of epistemic activism, crip technoscience, and early Universal Design. These narratives (and their disavowal of disability oppression frameworks in favor of function and human performance) are not neutral, accidental, or inevitable ways of approaching Universal Design, however. As *Building Access* has argued, post-disability narratives are but one trajectory in the broader arc of access-knowledge.

If the first decade of Universal Design was an experimental phase concerned with defining the user and disseminating new access-knowledge, its second decade and beyond centered on questions of method and assessment, or how designers can know when Universal Design has been achieved. This shift in emphasis was attributed to a sense that, as John Salmen put it, "people everywhere are now using the term [Universal Design], though often in slightly different ways. In the growing number of conferences on universal design, people often have to define the particular realm of universal design, or the range of users that have been involved and/or considered in the design."[6] Universal Design's epistemic community responded to the seeming boundlessness of the concept in 1997 by introducing a set of guidelines, known as "The Principles of Universal Design," and disseminating them widely.[7] How these "Principles" materialized and whether they upheld or challenged dominant forms of access-knowledge are the subjects of this chapter.

Seeking to contain (rather than expand) the universe of users and design approaches, the "Principles" enabled a new type of barrier work. It became possible to discuss Universal Design without reference to disability, while maintaining a focus on functionality and usability. Likewise, the public reception of the "Principles" consolidated the post-disability narrative, its concerns with human performance, and its apparent disavowal of disability. But the wide circulation of the "Principles" in recent years has made it easy to forget that Universal Design's theory and practice are both nominally recent and still-in-formation. The project of defining Universal Design's methods and values has also involved critical epistemic activism, which intervened in dominant practices of twentieth-century access-knowledge, as well as in Universal Design discourse itself. Reaching into Universal Design's recent history, I unpack the "Principles" as a material, epistemic, and discursive object, using its history, text, design, and circulation to reveal the frictions, materializations, and critical boundary work through which this document sought to translate internal theory into design practice. At stake in this unpacking is an understanding of the shifting stakes of Universal Design theory and practice in our present moment. The "Principles," I argue, were an ambitious intervention, which simultaneously targeted architecture, product manufacturing, and the structures of access-knowledge itself.

READING MATERIAL DISCOURSE

Readers familiar with the "Principles of Universal Design" may not have considered that as users of this document, they, too, are part of its history. If objects and users are engaged in ongoing patterns of mutual configuration, then our engagements with objects also reproduce them. With a textual object, such as the "Principles," engagements often take the form of citation. When scholars, designers, and advocates cite the "Principles" as a universal referent for Universal Design, they often reproduce the appearance of a stable, coherent phenomenon from a contested and sedimented patchwork of ideas. Like design, then, citation is a practice of knowing-making.

We have observed similar intra-actions in previous chapters. For instance, citations of "barrier-free design" as accessibility codes, standards, and retrofits produced the phenomenon as such in the late twentieth century by placing the underlying philosophy of disability access into conversation with the governance of disability rights. Likewise, designers, scholars, and activists working within architecture and product design, and in fields such as education, the arts, museum studies, and the critical fields of disability, feminist, and queer theories, have applied Universal Design to their domains by citing the "Principles," as well as arguments about Universal Design as "good design" for "everyone."[8] These and other citations are often taken to signify the project of Universal Design writ large.

Given the interdisciplinary depth of access-knowledge and the spheres in which access has become legibly enactable in the post-ADA world, these citation practices are unsurprising. But because the "Principles" circulate through quick citations, much like the marketing sound bites and promotional claims that Universal Design is "good design," there has not yet been a greater depth of conceptual, historical, and ideological engagement with the principles, their consequences, and their critical work.

For many of the fields in which Universal Design has spread—disciplines positioned as external to but drawing inspiration from Universal Design's origins in architecture and product design—Universal Design's internal theories have been lost in translation. But the methodologies of these disciplines—particularly the critical humanities and social sciences—provide necessary tools for excavating the gritty sedimentations and evolving textures of Universal Design discourse, its circulation, and its dispersal. My objective, then, is to sharpen our ability to discern Universal Design's strategies, theories, and interventions from the marketing and promotional discourses deployed in its name.

Throughout the history of design, templates have provided tools for communicating and stabilizing a particular approach. Da Vinci's Vitruvian Man, Dreyfuss's folio of Joe and Josephine, and the "Principles of Universal Design" poster (Figure 7.1) share this propensity for stabilization. Although each template was designed to appear objective and impartial, each also bears traces of its own history. But compared to the Vitruvian Man, or Joe and Josephine, the "Principles" appear abstract, disembodied, and heavy on text, with the exception of a few utilitarian illustrations. The poster's minimalist aesthetics reflect the apparently technical nature of its content, aligning it more closely with accessibility codes than glossy design handbooks or advertisements.

Optics can be deceiving, however. The poster and the "Principles" displayed therein leave clues about their own tenuousness and partiality. Reading the "Principles" and their entanglements with particular historical arrangements of knowing-making shows that they were not composed as a final directive regarding universal usability. Rather, they were designed as one small part of the ongoing project of access-knowledge, similar to what Barad calls an "agential cut," or a distinction enacted through "particular practices that are perpetually open to rearrangements, rearticulations, and other reworkings."[9] In their many iterations, the "Principles" were an unfinished, stabilizing tool for animating tensions central to access-knowledge, and thus reiterating the project of Universal Design. Here, I adopt what Barad considers a "diffractive" method of reading the "Principles." This method pays close attention to intra-actions, reiterations, and the making-legible of distinctions, both in terms of barrier work *between* Universal Design and other approaches and *within* the "Principles" themselves.[10] Although the "Principles" appeared to provide an apparently coherent set of guidelines for designing more usable built environments, they were instead unsettling and remaking the concepts of usability, performance, and function.

The "Principles of Universal Design," Version 2.0, appears to have been one product in a series of revisions and reiterations. But the iterative nature of the "Principles" also made it one experimental tool among many. I track these iterations, the intra-actions between them, and their relationships to other models of access-knowledge. To highlight the seemingly unmarked but iterative history of the principles, I use a notation system that refers to each iteration using the authors' numerical assignments, except when additional, unnumbered drafts require further distinctions. Figure 7.2 provides a map of these reiterations. For instance, "Principles 2.0" refers to "Principles of Universal Design," Version 2.0 (4/1/97). The history that follows is impossible without these and other markings.[11]

KNOWING-MAKING THE PRINCIPLES OF UNIVERSAL DESIGN

In 1996 Paralyzed Veterans of America (PVA) sued Ellerbe Becket Architects and Engineers under ADA Title III.[12] PVA argued that Ellerbe's proposed design for a Washington, D.C., stadium failed to provide meaningful accessibility. By concentrating wheelchair-accessible seating in only one area, the design did not provide adequate "lines of sight" for wheelchair users, and (according to PVA) set a precedent for repeating these denials of access in future stadiums.[13] In response, Ellerbe claimed that the firm was exempt from compliance with the ADA because the law only held parties liable if they both "design and construct facilities."[14] In other words, architects should not be held liable because they only design facilities and rarely construct them. This loophole in the law's language threatened to weaken the ADA regime. The American Institute of Architects (AIA) submitted an amicus brief in Ellerbe's defense, arguing that while architects support the spirit of the law and design in good faith, they should not be held liable to it.[15] While the high-profile case was never heard by the U.S. Supreme Court, it received the attention of U.S. Attorney General Janet Reno. The Department of Justice, with help from disability activists including Liz Savage, a compliance expert and counsel to the assistant U.S. Attorney, and Ronald Mace, who had also served as a consultant for PVA, submitted an amicus brief explaining that if architects were not liable under the ADA, as Ellerbe alleged, then few

Principles of Universal Design V.1.0 4/1995	Principles of Universal Design V.1.0.2 7/1995	Principles of Universal Design V.1.0.3 8/31/1995	Principles of Universal Design V.1.1 12/7/1995	Principles of Universal Design V.2.0 4/1/1997
		7. Equitable Use	1. Equitable Use	1. Equitable Use
9. Alternative Methods of Use	5. Accommodate a Range of Methods of Use	5. Accommodate a Range of Methods of Use	2. Flexibility in Use (formerly Accommodation of Preferences and Abilities)	2 Flexibility in Use
1. Simple Operation 2. Intuitive Operation	1. Make It Easy to Understand 2. Make It Easy to Operate	1. Make it Easy to Understand 2. Make it Easy to Operate	3. Simple and Intuitive Use	3. Simple and Intuitive Use
3. Redundant Feedback 10. Perceptible Information	3. Communicate with the User	3. Communicate with the User	4. Perceptible Information	4. Perceptible Information
8. Minimization of and Tolerance for Error	4. Design for User Error	4. Design for User Error	5. Tolerance for Error	5. Tolerance for Error
6. Low Physical Demand			6. Low Physical Effort	6. Low Physical Effort
4. Gradual Level Changes 5. Space for Approach and Movement 7. Comfortable Reach Range	6. Allow Space for Access	6. Allow Space for Access	7. Size and Space for Approach and Use	7. Size and Space for Approach and Use

Figure 7.2. Iterations of the "Principles of Universal Design."

parties would be.[16] Ultimately, the U.S. District of Columbia Court ruled in favor of PVA, with the DOJ's amicus brief figuring heavily in the decision.[17]

At stake in *PVA v. Ellerbe* were several issues at the heart of Universal Design debates: whether compliance with minimal accessibility standards was enough to ensure broad, anticipatory access and substantive justice under the law; what constitutes good, accessible design when the metric is meaningful, substantive equality; and how designers can both become aware of and take responsibility for producing such design in good faith. The shifting ADA landscape had a profound influence on Universal Design's public face and internal theory. In the post-ADA era, many access-knowledge experts worked in both barrier-free design and Universal Design, using their knowledge of these approaches to inform and transform the other. Proponents increasingly framed Universal Design as an extralegal, innovative, creative, and market-based approach to distinguish it from what was apparently the main source of architects' resistance to accessible design: the frustrating proliferation of codes and standards, and their unpredictable interpretation in the courts. But if Universal Design was to be considered distinct from (rather than a "euphemism" for) code compliance, then advocates were charged with finding another way to define the practice while maintaining its open-ended, creative promise.[18]

In the midst of architects' backlash to the ADA and post-disability marketing discourses (such as those discussed in the previous chapter), the impetus for more specific Universal Design guidelines grew. Framing Universal Design as good design for everyone was fairly simple and straightforward. *Producing* good design for everyone, and knowing when this had been achieved, was another matter. In 1997, the same year that the DOJ issued its brief holding architects legally responsible for compliance with the ADA, the Center for Universal Design (formerly the CAH) at NC State released "Principles of Universal Design 2.0" as a parallel strategy framed in terms of usability guidelines. In its language, authorship, and resource stream, "Principles 2.0" materialized from the epistemic community that had grown around Universal Design and barrier-free compliance since the 1970s. When Mace established the CAH in 1989, its primary funding had come from the Department of Education's National Institute on Disability and Rehabilitation Research (NIDRR), which provided a five-year Rehabilitation Research and Training Center (RRTC) grant.[19] By 1994 the center's priorities had broadened and it sought new funding from NIDRR to support Universal Design research and development.

It may seem odd that Universal Design's development relied on rehabilitation research funding. After all, disability activists had proposed the social model in opposition to rehabilitation experts and Mace had initially reiterated this position by offering Universal Design as an alternative to stigmatizing medicalized views of disability. But in the mid-1990s, the funding landscape for rehabilitation research had shifted, like the profession itself, toward person-environment models of disability, which were informed by social gerontology, environment-behavior research, and other interdisciplinary fields. Funding agencies such as NIDRR began to prioritize research supporting social models of disability. This shift in priorities was, in part, a type of epistemic activism. As disabled people increasingly occupied positions of power in the governance of rehabilitation research, the funding landscape and areas of research shifted in response. Beginning in 1994, Katherine Seelman, a hard-of-hearing scholar of disability studies, rehabilitation, accessibility, and participatory action research, became NIDRR's director. Seelman had great interest in Universal Design, and under her leadership, NIDRR funded several projects related to expanding the range of users typically considered as part of accessibility.[20] In the 1994 funding cycle, the CAH received NIDRR funding as a Rehabilitation Engineering Research Center (RERC) geared toward Universal Design development, and in 1996 it renamed itself the Center for Universal Design (CUD).[21] With support from NIDRR, Universal Design research became possible on a larger scale but also remained tethered to the realms of federally funded technoscience and rehabilitation research, which brought with them old and new ideas about access-knowledge.

The "Principles" were one facet of a larger RERC-funded research project. "Studies to Further the Development of Universal Design" involved product and building evaluations, focus groups, interviews, and site visits to determine the "optimal performance characteristics and use features that make products and environments usable by the greatest diversity of people."[22] On its face, the project experimented with Universal Design methods that would approximate the rehabilitative engineering of assistive technologies, wherein usability, performance, and function served as primary metrics. The apparent strategy was to portray Universal Design as a method for creative but focused innovation. Using this approach, proponents could encourage slow social change from within architectural and design practices, which would result in a more substantively accessible built environment regardless of architects' attitudes toward codes or manufacturers' marketing strategies. As part of this strategy, the "Principles" embodied a subtle and ambitious tactic of epistemic activism, trained on unsettling the mainstream constructs of usability research and, more broadly, of access-knowledge.

Reading the "Principles"

If readers are users who intra-act with, interpret, and reshape the meanings of a design, it may be helpful to take a moment and engage more closely with Figure 7.1, a poster displaying the seven "Principles of Universal Design." If it is available to you, take a look at the text and images. You may notice that beneath the title, a line of fine print reads "Version 2.0 (4/1/97)." If this is the second version, what was the first, and how do the two relate?

Visually, the original poster's columned layout and beige background feature navy blue and white text (reproduced here in black and white). The poster lists each principle in numbered order. Some of the principles contain terms such as "equitable," "flexible," and "simple" that may appear more familiar to nondesigners. Some, such as "tolerance for error," "perceptible information," "low physical effort," and "size and space for approach and use" may feel more technical in nature. Each bolded principle appears above a definition, an illustrated or photographed example, a list of guidelines, and a few examples. For instance, "Perceptible Information" is defined as "the design communicates necessary information effectively to the user, regardless of ambient conditions or the user's sensory abilities." The accompanying image depicts a light-skinned person turning the dial of a large thermostat, which appears to provide raised, tactile numbering as well as visually perceptible information. We will return to these terms and images later, but for now, take a moment to think about any associations they bring up.

Finally, a highlighted box on the right indicates, "The Principles were compiled by advocates of Universal Design, in alphabetical order: "Bettye Rose Connell, Mike Jones, Ron Mace, Jim Mueller, Abir Mullick, Elaine Ostroff, Jon Sanford, Ed Steinfeld, Molly Story, and Greg Vanderheiden." To unpack the "Principles," and the context from which they emerged, let us begin here.

Knowing-making "Principles 2.0" was a collective endeavor aimed at producing a more useful toolbox for Universal Design. Although credited to the Center for Universal Design and an alphabetically ordered list of ten authors, the broader project of which it was one small part required input from a specific cohort of knowers and makers, whose relationships had coalesced over at least two decades. A broad network of experts, with whom Mace had formed professional ties since the 1970s, met and defined the new performance principles for Universal Design.[23] Mace, Elaine Ostroff, Edward Steinfeld, Mike Jones, and Jim Mueller worked on the project. But with Universal Design's proliferating meanings, new experts became involved. Several environment-behavior researchers and human factors specialists, including Bettye Rose Connell, Molly Follette Story, and Jon Sanford, had joined the CUD. Like many of the other authors, they had been involved in the environmental design research field for several years. Abir Mullick, an industrial designer and colleague of Steinfeld's, was relatively new to the group. Greg Vanderheiden, director of the NIDRR-funded Trace Research & Development Center at the University of Wisconsin and outgoing president of the Rehabilitation Engineering Society of North America, was an experienced researcher in the assistive technology field.[24] Other experts, including Ruth Lusher, Polly Welch, and John Salmen, provided feedback on drafts.

It is important to underscore that the authors were a particular cohort of experts, representative of social and professional relationships, epistemic communities, and advocacy projects that had sedimented for decades. Most of the authors knew one another through EDRA, UDEP, or the compliance industry. They cited one another's work, collaborated on design handbooks and research projects, and were both colleagues and friends. Most were geographically situated in the midwestern and southeastern United States, unlike West Coast–based activist organizations such as the Center for Independent Living or the Disability Rights and Education Defense Fund. Many of the authors were experts in the same code compliance regime they sought to unsettle. Their fields—architecture, industrial design, gerontology, computing, rehabilitation, education, and environmental design research—represented the broad interdisciplinary and historical reach of access-knowledge itself. This interdisciplinarity mattered for the "Principles." While architects, industrial designers, rehabilitation engineers, and social scientists may not generally work closely with one another, for many of the authors, interdisciplinary collaborations were part of their training and professional experiences. The "Principles" arranged the authors' broad collective expertise into apparent coherence. By introducing disciplinary knowledge and negotiating disciplinary boundaries, the project generated productive uncertainty surrounding the "Principles," which the authors understood not as a concrete end point but as a starting place for rearranging, rearticulating, and reworking Universal Design methods, similar to the work of revising accessibility codes.[25]

It is equally important to emphasize that this cohort of authors were particular and embodied, with the "Principles" reflecting the discourses, norms, and demographics of their professions. The majority of the authors were (apparently) white, nondisabled adult men.[26] Only one of the ten was (apparently) disabled. Only one was (apparently) a person of color. Two out of the ten were (apparently) women. Most were employed professionals at universities or nonprofit research centers. The "Principles" materialized from these authors' intra-actions and expertise. These connections become more apparent as we follow the path to "Principles 2.0."

Iterating the "Principles"

"Principles 2.0" were *working principles,* by which I mean that they performed particular types of conceptual and material labor. At their most basic, they appeared to describe or even prescribe aspirations for Universal Design. But the document's provenance also simultaneously belonged to early human factors research, disability activism, barrier-free design, and environmental design research. It grew from U.S.-centric constructs of usability, flexibility, and equity and was rooted in particular research practices, such as disability anthropometry. Its guidelines drew upon specific terms of art, referred to existing knowledge bases, and, despite all this, challenged the disciplinary configurations from which access-knowledge had evolved. The labor of "Principles 2.0," I will demonstrate, was to introduce torsion into the norms of standard embodiment, the dominant ways of knowing the human body, and the values of equity, flexibility, physical and cognitive ability, and, fundamentally, what it meant to take up space. Like any designed product or building, the design of "Principles 2.0" materialized from a series of iterations, in the course of which Universal Design remained open to rearrangements, rearticulations, and reworkings.

Each new version required an agential cut. To craft "Principles 1.0," the first iteration, the advocates traveled to the CUD in Raleigh, North Carolina, for a two-day meeting in April 1995. Their objective was to produce guidelines that designers could "apply to all design disciplines and all people and are useful for design, evaluation, and instruction."[27] The authors collected the "substantial collective knowledge of universal design," as well as the "maxims, guidelines, and concepts" that had thus far configured Universal Design discourse.[28] Essentially, they mapped the field of access-knowledge and chose from it strategically. One cut took place when the authors chose to develop usability guidelines, which appeared to limit the "Principles" to functional questions by default. This narrowed emphasis was strategic, however. Rather than develop guidelines claiming to inform all aspects of design, the authors clarified the vague notion of "good design." During the "Principles" drafting process, Mueller wrote:

> How do you define "good design"? Design that considers the needs of as many people as possible should be the accepted, rather than the exceptional, approach.... And the practice of design involves more than consideration for usability. Successful designers must incorporate cultural, economic, engineering, environmental, and gender considerations. With that in mind, the following Principles of Universal Design offer designers guidance to better integrate features that meet the needs of as many users as possible.[29]

The phrase "as many" here was used reflexively, acknowledging the limits of Universal Design even while reorienting its approach to knowing-making usability. But Mueller's statement, more generally, suggests the barrier work of distinguishing Universal Design from other established approaches and philosophies, such as feminist or green design. In direct contrast to classical and modernist design platforms emphasizing the universality of human needs in built environments, the authors marked the particularity of the "Principles," announced their limitations, and pursued them as the starting point of a certain kind of usable world.

After the initial two-day meeting, the CUD gathered and culled "Principles 1.0" from the authors' brainstorming session. This first iteration consisted of ten principles: Simple Operation, Intuitive Operation, Redundant Feedback, Gradual Level Changes, Space for Approach and Movement, Low Physical Demand, Comfortable Reach Range, Minimization of and Tolerance for Error, Alternate Methods of Use, and Perceptible Information.[30] Each principle reflected a particular term of art or knowledge base that the authors brought to the meeting. Many invoked human factors, industrial design, and rehabilitation constructs, while others appeared more relevant to the architectural scale. Still others referenced design considerations in computing and telecommunications design.

As working principles, version 1.0 set in motion a series of reiterations, each of which produced new meanings and approaches. Following the April 1995 meeting, the CUD sent "Principles 1.0" to external experts gathered from the interdisciplinary epistemic community surrounding access-knowledge.

A second version of "Principles 1.0," which the authors considered to be part of the same iteration, appeared in July 1995. This six-principle document (which I refer to here as "Principles 1.0.2") replaced technical language with simple directives: Make It Easy to Understand, Make It Easy to Operate, Communicate with the User, Design for User Error, Accommodate a Range of Methods of Use, and Allow Space for Access.[31] Each command synthesized previous suggestions, such as Simple Operation, Intuitive Operation, and Redundant Feedback, into singular principles, such as Make It Easy to Understand, suggesting both a synthesis and a cut.

"Principles 1.0.3," a third iteration, appeared in August 1995. This version retained the language of its predecessor but added one additional principle: "Equitable Use."[32] Although it was the last to surface, it went to the beginning of the list.

Although "Principles 1.0.3" described what designers should do, they did not measure successful Universal Design. The fourth iteration, "The Principles of Universal Design," Version 1.1 (12/7/95), consisted of seven principles. This version retained the content of the previous seven principles but reverted back to the technical language of "Principles 1.0." The "Simple and Intuitive Use" principle, for instance, took shape from "Make It Easy to Understand" and "Make It Easy to Operate." Once again, the CUD sent out the "Principles" for review.

The authors made very clear that the guidelines were a "work in progress and [that] efforts are ongoing to make them easier to apply."[33] Although in contemporary citations, the "Principles" have been applied to many forms of design practice, the authors insisted from the outset that "all guidelines may not be relevant to all designs" and that they "in no way comprise all criteria for good design, only universally usable design. Certainly, other factors are important, such as aesthetics, cost, safety, gender and cultural appropriateness, and these aspects should be taken into consideration as well when designing."[34] These evolving caveats were traces of theory-building and boundary-cutting debates regarding the scope of Universal Design, its responsibilities for "aesthetics, cost, safety, gender and cultural appropriateness," and the need to address functionality.

External reviewers responded, once again, to the scope, efficacy, and clarity of "Principles 1.1." Some objected that the "Principles" were concretizing an open-ended concept into a set of guidelines.[35] Salmen, for instance, noted the similarities between code requirements and the attempt to "define a creative process" via static guidelines, a project he characterized as "difficult and dangerous."[36] Others insisted that it was impossible to develop design criteria for both individual products and larger-scale buildings.[37] Indeed, most of the "Principles" apparently referenced individual-scale products and technologies. Most drew terms of art from fields such as rehabilitation, human factors, and ergonomics, all central to access-knowledge but not necessarily legible to the mainstream of architectural design.

If the "Principles" were primarily responding to constructs in these scientific fields rather than to architectural practice, it may seem odd that the CUD would publish

"The Principles of Universal Design," Version 2.0 (4/1/97), in the midst of architects' legal challenges to the responsibilities of ADA compliance. Version 2.0, in reality the fifth iteration, replicated "Principles 1.1." Seven principles—Equitable Use, Flexibility in Use, Simple and Intuitive Use, Perceptible Information, Tolerance for Error, Low Physical Effort, and Size and Space for Approach and Use—appeared on posters, in pamphlets, and in publications and began to circulate widely.

UNPACKING THE PRINCIPLES

A closer examination of "Principles 2.0" provides clues about the strategy surrounding their production and release in 1997. Consider Figure 7.1 once again. Each "Principle" is accompanied by a definition, a list of guidelines, and an illustrative example of a product. Unlike the definition of Universal Design, which emphasizes both products and spaces, "Principles 2.0" almost exclusively addresses individual-scale devices, offering questions such as, "Can the device be used with a closed fist or open palm, either left or right hand?," "Can the device be used from a seated or standing position?," and "Are built-in adjustments easy to make?"[38] In a literal sense, these questions suggest functionality at the individual scale of user interfaces rather than the mass scale of buildings or cities. Read differently, these questions provide clues about the critical function of the "Principles" as a question-generating device designed with a particular user—an uninformed or even resistant designer—in mind.

Equitable Use

In "Principles 2.0," "Equitable Use" appears first, its prominent display suggesting its role as a guiding principle. Yet, this principle was the last to appear in the list. Molly Story, who organized the "Principles" initiative, later recalled:

> The authors . . . struggled with the concept of *equitable use,* which first appeared in the third draft, dated August 31, 1995. Its initial definition was "The Design does not disadvantage or stigmatize any group of users." Some on the team thought that because this issue was so fundamental to the concept, it should not be a principle, but, rather, part of the definition of universal design. It was the only principle that did not address usability, but, rather, egalitarianism. In the end, though, because it was so essential, the team decided that this aspect of universal design needed to be articulated just as much as and, in some ways, maybe even more than the others. From this version on, "Equitable Use" was included among the Principles of Universal Design, prominently placed first on the list.[39]

At this point, the authors were contending with the post-disability presumption that usability is ethically or politically neutral and can be produced without reference to considerations of the user population's privileges. They apparently realized that by centering on usability alone, the "Principles" risked omitting nonnormate users. "Equitable Use" was added as an additional metric, which would filter usability through its social impacts. In this sense, "Equitable Use" is the inverse of modern human factors design. Narrating the birth of his approach to "human engineering," U.S. industrial designer Henry Dreyfuss recalled discovering, while drawing a human user for the interior of an army tank, that he had "been putting together a dimensional chart of the average adult American male," a figure that recalled da Vinci's Vitruvian Man.[40] If Dreyfuss's epiphany was a founding moment for normate user-centered design, premised upon narrow ranges of usability and performance, the "Principles" authors appeared to position themselves in this history by inserting a critical question, centered on social equity: who benefits from a more accessible world? As a critical principle, "Equitable Use" operated on a higher order, guiding the remaining usability principles with an ethics- or rights-based metric. In this sense, it was an agential cut, a challenge to the remaining principles' neutrality. Put differently, "Equitable Use" was the key that would decode and perhaps deneutralize the remaining "Principles."

As part of "Studies to Further the Development of Universal Design," the "Principles" project took place at the same time that the CUD was experimenting with the notion of broad accessibility through product design, under the rationale that small-scale interventions into inaccessible buildings could make them more accessible, even when architects were reluctant to abide by codes.[41] One experimental design was the Universal Thermostat, a multimodal device that integrated several sensory and input features and thus addressed accessibility for people with cognitive, sensory, and motor disabilities. The CUD had also been working to raise manufacturers' awareness of disability and aging through marketing consultations, with varying degrees of success. These experiments were both expanding the universe of users beyond the prototypical wheelchair user *and* raising questions about how to convey a complex notion of broad accessibility to manufacturers and designers who did not have relationships to disability or prioritize access in their work. The marketing narrative of Universal Design's added value to nondisabled consumers contrasted, however, with the "Equitable Use" principle, which insisted upon equal benefits for disabled and nondisabled people.

Despite these interventions, the "Principles" reinforced other norms and values. For instance, "Equitable Use" was identity-neutral: it did not preclude addressing race, class, or gender equity, but it also did not *include* such a focus. Nor did it name disability explicitly. In several ways, "Equitable Use" and the narratives surrounding it appeared to reproduce post-disability ideologies and cultural norms related to the rehabilitation regime. For instance, the term "equitable" and its description as "egalitarian" recalled the emphasis on "design for all Americans" in barrier-free design. As explained in chapter 3, these terms reference formal equality regimes, which mandate equal access. As we have learned, however, such regimes provide the impression that systematic inequality is no longer a material reality, while often failing to produce substantive justice and even rendering ongoing oppression illegible. The ADA, following formal equality approaches of earlier civil rights laws, defined "the Nation's proper goals regarding individuals with disabilities" as promoting "equality of opportunity, full participation, independent living, and economic self-sufficiency"—responsibilities that reflected earlier barrier-free design discourses of productive citizenship.[42]

Universal Design advocates who were also compliance experts in the pre-ADA era were aware that formal equality failed to produce broad, meaningful accessibility. For Mace, Ostroff, Steinfeld, and others, this awareness shaped ongoing strategies for change within and beyond the code. Many had a notion that unlike barrier-free design, Universal Design could produce more substantive inclusion. Yet the "Equitable Use" principle's egalitarianism and equity mirrored formal rights propositions, which assume that general promises of inclusion (such as "design for all") ensure meaningful access. Under formal rights regimes, equal rights protection becomes a matter of compliance with standards. Given the ties between "equity" and formal equality, the "Equitable Use" principle appears to contradict Universal Design's oppositional framing against codes and standards by aligning with the principle of egalitarianism that compliance was meant to enforce. Read another way, however, "Equitable Use" suggests that the "Principles" were an attempt to eventuate the accessible future that the ADA imagined *through* epistemic activism and cultural change rather than legal compliance.

Without denying the ingenuity of this strategy, however, it is important to consider that the "Principles" also provided a tangible public face for post-disability ideologies. Earlier in the process, a decision to concentrate the "Principles" on usability and leave philosophical questions for a new definition of Universal Design contributed to this problem. Universal Design, according to "Principles 2.0," was "the design of all products and environments to be usable by all people, to the greatest extent possible, without the need for adaptation or specialized design."[43] Like midcentury barrier-free design discourses, this definition presumed an even playing field of consumers in a market untouched by marginalization. Similarly, "Equitable Use" sought accountability toward human diversity, but its vague, neutral, and depoliticized language obscured an understanding of power and privilege, notably the gradients of entangled marginalization that disability, race, gender, class, and age produce.

Moreover, "Equitable Use" adopted post-disability logics by endorsing design that is "useful and marketable to people with diverse abilities." Here, "abilities" serves as a euphemism for "disabilities," suggesting that disability is a stigmatizing quality from which design should distance itself. As disability scholar Simi Linton argued just a year later, "ability" and similar euphemisms, including "physically challenged, the able disabled, handicapable, and special people/children," appear to "refute common stereotypes of incompetence" but are "defensive and reactive terms rather than terms that advance a new agenda" (such as correcting stereotypes and misconceptions about disability, as Mace had done in 1985).[44] Likewise, disability theorist Tobin Siebers explained that the "ideology of ability" affirms ability as a positive value, which societies have an imperative to reproduce, and disavows disability as a condition of disqualifi-cation in need of elimination.[45] The affirmation of "diverse abilities" thus obscures discrimination on the basis of marginalized *disability*. To understand how post-disability discourses came to dominate the Universal Design narrative after 1997, however, we also have to consider the other "Principles."

Flexibility in Use

Perhaps the most frequently invoked of all the "Principles" is the second, "Flexibility in Use." "Principles 2.0" defines "Flexibility in Use" as design that "accommodates a wide range of individual preferences and abilities." The disability-neutral language of this principle and its emphasis on a "wide range" recalled the "Equitable Use" prin-ciple and its language of "diverse abilities," as well as the barrier-free design discourse of design for "all" users. While these goals appear neutral in each case, they align the "Principles" with the twentieth-century biopolitical imperatives for productive citi-zenship and normalization discussed in chapters 2 and 3. Flexibility, I argued in those chapters, was a concept born from early twentieth-century industrial management, rehabilitation, and human factors research, which sought citizens to make themselves amenable to performance-enhancing built arrangements that would decrease fatigue and enable more productive labor.

Although flexibility apparently encouraged design for a range of embodiments, this value also aligned with expectations for productivity and normalization in ex-change for spatial belonging. Military and industrial human factors research, for instance, produced knowledge about the range of users to produce better-fitting mil-itary and industrial tools, uniforms, and machines. Similarly, the rehabilitation regime produced adaptive tools for injured veterans and polio survivors to qualify them for citizenship. Flexibility, then, was not a value derived from acceptance for radical or marginal difference but an ideology premised upon folding the margins into the cen-ter of productivity-driven liberal democracy. In turn, the imperative to normalize dis-ability rendered unthinkable other ways of approaching accessibility, such as default access to housing, health insurance, voting, and education regardless of a disabled person's productivity, race, gender, or class status.

Reflecting their funding source and the authors' areas of expertise, the "Principles" refer to disability only in reference to rehabilitative devices. "The goal of Universal Design," Story explained, "is to maximize the normalcy of disability, but assistive technology will always be needed."[46] The imperative to maximize the normalcy of disability, I argued previously, is rooted in the ideology of ability, which understands disability as a problem in need of correction. But "Flexibility in Use" also mirrors these ideologies in their contemporary manifestation: neoliberal marketing logics. Since the 1970s, David Harvey has argued, flexibility has become a core neoliberal value; in the shift away from more standardized modes of factory production, for instance, increasingly diverse methods of production have accompanied the rise of niche marketing toward particular consumers.[47] These processes have been central to global financial conditions, as well as the structures of urban and architectural spaces in which consumerism increasingly defines belonging.[48] "Flexibility in Use" references the niche marketization of disability in the post-ADA era by suggesting that design should accommodate consumers' "individual preferences and abilities." This phrasing also alludes to the ADA, a law forged from extensive concessions to private businesses, which protects "qualified individuals with a disability" on an individual basis.[49] Where the ADA protects such individuals in places of employment, publicly funded facilities (such as mass transit), and places of public accommodation and consumption (including restaurants and stadiums), "Flexibility in Use" proposes accessibility for individual consumers according to their preferences.

The trope of the individual consumer similarly relegates responsibility for access to isolated purchasing choices rather than systemic changes. "The most significant benefit to the proliferation of universal design practice," Story wrote of the principles in 1998, "is that all consumers will have more products to choose from that are more usable, more readily available, and more affordable."[50] Demonstrating a consumer-focused orientation, the authors illustrated "Flexibility in Use" with the example of an ATM with an adjustable screen position, large buttons and graphics, and auditory feedback—an individual-use, multimodal cash dispensary for the new neoliberal citizen.[51] Combined with its emphasis on design for a wide range of "abilities," "Flexibility in Use" dovetails with the notion that disability is inevitable and universal. If flexibility improves usability for all consumers, then there is no need to distinguish between those who need access because they have been excluded and those who merely consume and benefit from the enhanced usability. Citations of "Flexibility in Use" often reproduce these ideological valences by presenting multifeature and flexible designs as commonsense, good design while rarely considering their implications for who appears to count as a user and how designers can know.

As with "Equitable Use," however, "Flexibility in Use" offers clues about the other, more critical work of the "Principles." Here, I want to pinpoint the specific disciplinary discourses through which "Flexibility in Use" developed and what these discourses reveal about Universal Design's approach to users. It has become a truism of Universal Design citations that "Principles 2.0" emerged from architecture and was then applied to other fields. But prior to "Principles 2.0," proponents rarely used the term "flexibility" to describe Universal Design. They were far more likely to use terms such as "good design," "adaptability," or design for "all" or "everyone." "Flexibility in Use" was a product of interdisciplinary intra-actions between architects, industrial designers, human factors researchers, and, most significantly, telecommunications designers, who imported the language of flexibility into the "Principles."

Although most references to the ADA concentrate on Titles I, II, and III, which correspond to employment rights, government-funded facilities, and public facilities, few include Title IV, which requires an accessible national telecommunications service.

Throughout the history of barrier-free design, wheelchair users had been the pro-totypical disabled inhabitant. Title IV, however, expanded civil rights protections for D/deaf and hard-of-hearing people and people with speech-related disabilities through text and video relay services. Concurrent to the CUD's "Principles" project, the Berkeley-based World Institute on Disability's (WID) Universal Access Project (UAP) defined guidelines for "building accessibility for disabled persons into the information superhighway."[52] Vanderheiden, an author of "Principles 2.0" and direc-tor of the Trace Center, worked with WID on the UAP, which received funding from the National Telecommunications and Information Administration (NTIA). In the 1980s Vanderheiden had drawn inspiration from architectural accessibility and the curb cut to inform his work on accessible information technologies. He used the curb cut as a metaphor for system-wide accessibility in information systems and com-puting hardware—not as a liberal theory based on the curb cut's multiple users but as a justice-oriented theory of how the curb cut's built-in nature signaled anticipa-tory access. Just as a city with only periodic curb cuts was not truly beneficial and accessible to wheelchair users, Vanderheiden explained in his 1983 keynote speech at a "Computers for the Disabled" conference, information systems without built-in accessibility exclude disabled computer users.[53]

With the rise of home computers and consumer Internet access in the mid-1990s, the electronic curb cut metaphor broadcasted widely. The Internet and the personal computer offered opportunities to build accessibility into the digital world still-in-formation. Telecommunications accessibility advocates turned their attention to im-plementing Section 255 of the Telecommunications Act of 1996.[54] In 1995 Deborah Kaplan, WID's vice president, proclaimed,

> We have come to the "curb-pouring" stage in building the information superhighway; now is the time to place electronic "curb ramps" in place. Implementing the concept of Universal Design means that accessibility for all users will be designed in at the blueprint stage, avoiding costly retrofits.[55]

Architecture and electronic information thus exchanged metaphors and language (such as "accessibility for all users" and "avoiding costly retrofits"). In one sense, it appeared that the electronic curb cut metaphor was part of a post-ADA narrative, which dictated that the law had addressed accessibility issues in built environments and that the time had come to address information environments. But the concept was equally a continuation of earlier frictions between physically disabled and blind or visually impaired people over the design of the physical curb cut: it drew upon the curb cut's capacious intervention but also gave prominence to those whose access needs the curb cut on the street may or may not have served.

Universal Design discourses clearly informed telecommunications and informa-tion accessibility, but the UAP also intra-acted with the Universal Design "Principles."

Similar to the "Principles" project, UAP participants met between 1994 and 1996 to define design criteria. Notably, the UAP used the term "flexibility" before it became a Universal Design principle, dictating in its 1994 report, "Systems should be flexible enough that one can have one or more of the following capabilities missing and still use the device or system: vision; hearing; speech; fine motor control; reach; average cognitive skills; ability to concentrate."[56] The term "flexible" here reflects the human factors sense of accounting for the unpredictability that human variation introduces, as well as the rehabilitation sense of defining capabilities through sensory and physical functions (and their limitations). Despite this focus on function and performance, however, the UAP offered an alternative conception of flexibility, which addressed excluded populations rather than solely emphasizing added value for nondisabled consumers.

The intra-actions between the UAP and the CUD's "Principles" project reflect interdisciplinary syntheses of meanings and language. The UAP consulted a September 1995 working draft of "Principles 1.1," perhaps provided by Vanderheiden or Mace, which lists the principle of "Accommodation of Preferences and Abilities" rather than "Flexibility in Use."[57] When it exported the language of a "broad range" of users and the value of flexibility into "Principles 2.0," the UAP also transferred its attention to customization and individual choice, hallmarks of personal computing, into Universal Design methods. "The goal of Universal Design," UAP's directors noted, "is to build broad flexibility into systems that allow users with specific needs to customize the product for their use."[58] This explanation of Universal Design as customization to individual preferences suggests that the "Flexibility in Use" principle was likely an extension of industrial design, computing, and engineering constructs regarding interfaces. It reflected the ways that designers in these fields facilitated accessibility through attention to the specific interactions between individual users, machines, and systems. Rather than portray disabled users as error-prone liabilities for the system as a whole, the UAP adopted the social model philosophy of placing the burden of change and inclusion on the system.

Ideas from working drafts of the "Principles" also appear in the UAP's guidelines (Figure 7.3).[59] Far more specific than "Principles 2.0," the UAP principles reflected WID's history and political connections to the independent living movement. They were more explicit about their relationship to disability. Pinpointing interfaces such as buttons, controls, voice and visual interfaces, and Braille type, these guidelines made Universal Design in telecommunications a strategy centering disabled access needs, broadly conceived. Particular attention to blind users, a population often illegible in conversations about physical accessibility, suggests the UAP (and WID more generally) had continued the work of crip technoscience and its interventions into rehabilitation knowledge. Accordingly, the UAP principles were less concerned than "Principles 2.0" with dimensions of user cognition and environmental behavior, which experts trained in environmental design research brought to the latter.

Principles of Universal Design V.2.0 4/1997	Universal Access Project 6/6/1995	Donald Norman, The Design of Everyday Things, 1988
1. Equitable Use	1. A product should be fully usable by anyone regardless of physical and/or sensory disabilities.	1. *Use both knowledge in the world and knowledge in the head.*
2. Flexibility in Use	2. A product should give the user a choice of interface—e.g., graphics, speed, or text options. 6. Whatever is mouse-controlled should also be able to be fully controlled by keyboard use.	7. *When all else fails, standardize*
3. Simple and Intuitive Use		2. Simplify the structure of tasks.
4. Perceptible Information	3. Raised buttons or tactile controls and labels are usable by both sighted and nonsighted users. 4. Whatever is accessible by visual interface should also be accessible by audio interface. 5. Whatever is accessible by voice, voice recognition, synthesized speech, or any other audio interface should be accessible by visual interface, Baudot (TDD) tones, and/or captioned.	3. Make things visible: bridge the gulfs of Execution and Evaluation 4. Get the mappings right
	7. Braille is an option for some, but not for the majority, of blind users.	
5. Tolerance for Error		6. Design for error
6. Low Physical Effort	8. Systems requiring user response/ input need to allow enough response time by motor-impaired users—or the option to customize this feature.	5. *Exploit the power of constraints, both natural and artificial.*
7. Size and Space for Approach and Use		

Figure 7.3. Intra-actions with other principles.

Intratextuality between the two sets of guidelines, which were developed in the same years, reveals the logics of several Universal Design "Principles." "Tolerance for Error" resembles the UAP guideline of providing adequate response time and customization. "Flexibility in Use," "Simple and Intuitive Use," and "Perceptible Information" resemble the suggestions that designs should provide a choice of interface with various options for sensory and physical interactions. Guidelines for "Perceptible Information" thus suggest that designs should "use different modes (pictorial, verbal, tactile) for redundant display of essential information."[60] As an example, the "Principles" offer computer software designed with text, photos, and audio; screen enlargement; and screen reader software (to render text audible), materially and discursively grounding the principle in computing. These iterative exchanges do not undo the other ideological work of flexibility, but they do provide a sense of the disciplinary knowledges, frictions, and torsions through which the "Principles" formed.

Simple and Intuitive Use, Perceptible Information, Tolerance for Error, and Low Physical Effort

The third, fourth, fifth, and sixth principles, "Simple and Intuitive Use," "Perceptible Information," "Tolerance for Error," and "Low Physical Effort," sought to decrease the cognitive, sensory, and physical requirements of users' interactions with the designed environment. These principles drew upon language from the field of human-machine interface design, adjacent to human factors and ergonomics, which sought to simplify users' interactions with increasingly complex technologies.[61] Three of the principles also directly referenced cognitive scientist and researcher Donald Norman's "Seven Principles for Transforming Difficult Tasks into Simple Ones," listed in Figure 7.3.[62] In *The Design of Everyday Things* (1988), Norman wrote about frustrating user experiences in a world of poor design decisions. He was critical, for instance, of doors because their varied designs and functions do not notify users about how to operate them, which way to push or pull handles, and with what amounts of dexterity and force.[63] For Norman, poorly designed doors failed to communicate through simple, intuitive, and perceptible material language to their users. Borrowing from Norman, Mace created his own hierarchy of Universal Design, expressed through the metaphor of doors.[64] In Mace's hierarchy, the worst doors are heavy and require gripping round handles—two types of interaction that require a great deal of physical effort, as well as the ability to grasp and turn a handle. The best doors are automatic and work with sensors, requiring little direct interaction between the user and the machine.

Mace's door hierarchy referenced, but also cripped, Norman's ideas of good design in ways that also translated into the "Principles."[65] Indeed, the "Principles" drew upon some of Norman's principles and shifted others. Where they found productive resonances, we can find their allegiances to particular ways of knowing-making. Where they shifted, we can trace their interventions, frictions, and torsions. As Figures 7.2 and 7.3 show, "Principles 1.0.2" and Norman's "Seven Principles" shared simple, prescriptive language: each delivered a set of commands, such as "Make It Easy to Understand" or "Simplify the structure of tasks." Norman's sixth principle, "Design for error," appears nearly verbatim in "Design for User Error" ("1.0.2" and "1.0.3") and "Tolerance for Error" ("1.0," "1.1," "2.0"). Another near-replication is Norman's second principle, "Simplify the structure of tasks," which resembles "Simple and Intuitive Use" in "Principles 2.0." Apparently, "Simple and Intuitive Use" evolved from "Simple Operation" and "Intuitive Operation" ("Principles 1.0") to "Make It Easy to Understand" and "Make It Easy to Operate" ("Principles 1.0.2") to its 2.0 form. At every step, the language reflects either Norman's word choices or ways of framing principles as commands.

"Principles 2.0," by contrast, enacted agential cuts separating Universal Design from mainstream conceptions of good design. In Figure 7.3, Norman's first, fifth, and seventh principles (in italics) reflect these mainstream conceptions. Norman's first directive, to "use both knowledge in the world and knowledge in the head," speaks to a general philosophy of design as a relation of knowing-making. While many of the authors shared this philosophy, however, there is no parallel in "Principles 1.0.2." At this point the authors were concerned with function and usability and had decided to relegate philosophical questions to the definition of Universal Design. A turning point came with version "1.0.3," which added "Equitable Use." This addition may have occurred in recognition that a pure focus on functionality is depoliticized and fails to take differences between users seriously. But if understood as in conversation with Norman's first principle, "Equitable Use" appears to mandate equitable *knowing* and not just equitable making.

Each cut made a strategic intervention. Where the "Principles" sought design for a diversity of users, Norman's principles endorsed standardization: "When all else fails," his seventh principle dictated, "standardize." As a rejoinder, "Principles 2.0" invoked "Flexibility in Use," the evolving iterations of which referenced "alternative" and "range" instead of "standardize." In their treatments of human perception, cognition, and behavior, the "Principles" also drew upon the environmental design research field to challenge Norman's third principle, "Make things visible." Rejecting the primacy of visual perception, the fourth Universal Design principle, "Perceptible Information," reflected this point in all its iterations, from "Redundant Feedback" ("1.0") to "Communicate with the User" ("1.0.2" and "1.0.3") to "Perceptible Information" ("1.0," "1.1," "2.0").

Where Norman's fifth principle advocated for "us[ing] constraints so that the user feels as if there is only one possible thing to do—the right thing, of course,"[66] "Principles 2.0" offered "Flexibility in Use," "Tolerance for Error," and "Low Physical Effort" in tandem as approaches that reject the "One Best Way" or "right thing" of industrial management and human factors engineering. The sixth Universal Design principle, "Low Physical Effort," appeared to reference nineteenth- and twentieth-century notions of human energy, fatigue, and performance central to human factors research. As chapter 2 explains, the study of human fatigue in industrial, military, and domestic settings has been central to engineering more efficient systems of labor. The "Low Physical Effort" principles' guidelines—"Allow user to maintain a neutral body position," "Use reasonable operating forces," "Minimize repetitive actions," and "Minimize sustained physical effort"—could have appeared in a mid-twentieth-century ergonomics or rehabilitation handbook. Along with the three principles preceding it, however, "Low Physical Effort" tasked designers with evaluating the costly physical, sensory, and cognitive labor of misfitting in a world designed with average bodies in mind. Unlike rehabilitation practices aimed at building strength to relieve fatigue, the principle made low effort the measure of good design, thus unraveling standards of average (or above-average) strength and productivity.

To be sure, the Universal Design "Principles" and their rejoinders to standardization cohered with neoliberal trends toward flexible production and niche marketization. Yet their intra-actions with accessibility for often-excluded disabled people, including people who identify as D/deaf, hard-of-hearing people, speech-impaired, blind, or visually impaired, suggests that the authors were experimenting with access-knowledge, using subtle shifts in language and frame to address the evidence base of mainstream usability research. "Principles 2.0," then, was a targeted intervention, which responded to mainstream discourses of "good design," framed as neutral common sense, by appropriating, unsettling, and torqueing them.[67]

Size and Space for Approach and Use

"Size and Space for Approach and Use," the seventh principle of Universal Design, was a curious addition. The only principle apparently addressing architectural space, it used obscure, technical, and scientific language. Despite these obscurities, this principle referenced a half century of epistemic activism in the field of anthropometry, or the large-scale measurement of human bodies for the purpose of statistical calculation. In the late nineteenth and early twentieth centuries, anthropometry had been a tool for eugenicists, physical anthropologists, military human factors researchers, and rehabilitation experts, whose aims ranged from hierarchical racial differentiation to normalization.[68] Designers of fashion, products, and (much later) buildings referenced anthropometric data and methods to understand how users' bodies take up space. But while most design applications addressed population averages or standardized deviations, proponents of barrier-free design since the 1950s adopted anthropometric research for another purpose: to build an evidence base around typically excluded users and apply this evidence toward better design standards.[69]

Epistemic activism in the realm of anthropometry has received little attention in histories of science or disability, however, because the practice is so often associated with its early origins in eugenics. Similarly, some critics have characterized Universal Design's adherence to evidence-based design as an uncritical acceptance of Enlightenment epistemologies and techno-empirical solutions.[70] But the history of this practice and its role in access-knowledge suggest that anthropometric measurement is an

arrangement of disparate concepts, practices, and objects deployed for strategic purposes: not a stable material practice but politics by other means.

Although highly technical in its language, "Size and Space for Approach and Use"
refers to decades of experimentation with core questions of Universal Design: Who
counts as a user in a population? How can designers know? Rather than measure
bodies with calipers and rulers, early disability anthropometry research used instruments such as an adjustable ramp, plywood boxes marked with sizing specifications,
and mock kitchens to document how wheelchair users take up space. This research,
in part, yielded the ANSI A117.1 standard and its subsequent revision in 1980. Even
further, however, wheelchair anthropometrics resulted in material-epistemic experiments concerned with what it meant to produce evidence of environmental exclusion.
Because they were closely involved with this research, some of the "Principles" authors
were aware of the epistemological and political stakes of knowing how bodies take
up space. In the 1970s Steinfeld had conducted wheelchair anthropometry studies
with elderly women in public housing, paying close attention to population outliers
often excluded from other studies.[71] Just a few years following the 1997 "Principles,"
Steinfeld and his colleagues at the State University of New York at Buffalo would
begin a decade-long experiment in disability anthropometrics that would reframe
the "science" of statistically calculating bodies through new material practices, methods of modeling data, and standards of measurement.[72] This research would recon-
ceptualize anthropometry as a measure of bodies, technologies, and environments
in intra-action. Building upon previous efforts to measure bodies in "movement envelopes," such as gridded rooms or adjustable ramps, this research would employ three-
dimensional imaging technology to capture aspects of movement that were not
detectable in static, "structural" anthropometry.

Unlike disability-neutral or post-disability discourses of Universal Design, the
Anthropometry of Wheeled Mobility project would engage with large samples of
users at the far ends of the bell curve, particularly those considered extreme outliers
in general population statistics.[73] "Most people with severe disabilities," Steinfeld
and his colleague Jordana Maisel write, are excluded or "underrepresented in conventional anthropometric studies," which "exclude people with disabilities and older
people to keep the results unaffected by 'outlying cases' or people who have widely
divergent abilities and characteristics."[74] Unlike conventional anthropometry, which
requires that users stand upright and erect, and have predictable bodily landmarks
from which to measure, new anthropometric methods and sampling practices would
seek to make a greater range of users legible. In the process, they would reinvent the
science of anthropometry, not as a practice enabling objective, neutral, statistical
generalization but as a way of studying the surfaces at which particular bodies, technologies, and built forms touch.[75]

Extending Steinfeld's previous work and resuming not long after the "Principles
2.0" were released, the new anthropometric research would seek to make "Size and

Space for Approach and Use" more apparent as a reference to questions of embodied spatial belonging and legibility, which disability anthropometrics were reconfiguring. What is significant here is that new anthropometric modes of legibility would not be involved in regimes of compulsory bodily productivity, surveillance, or governance, as in barrier-free design. Instead, these new methods of measurement would create evidence of disabled ways of moving through the world.

The "Size and Space for Approach and Use" principle torqued the relationships between disability and anthropometry in the late twentieth century. Recalling Mace and Lusher's 1989 discussion of Universal Design, this principle imagined built environments in which many marginalized bodies, including wheelchair and power chair users, people of above or below average size and weight, or people who communicate through sign language, can take up space.[76] Admittedly, there are limitations to an approach that concentrates on space requirements alone. Although wheelchair and power chair users are becoming legible to anthropometric measurement, there are many types of misfitting that occur outside conventional architectural space— in digital spaces or through technological interfaces. While other technoscientific domains have developed to make sensory or cognitive disabilities legible to designers, there are many ways of taking up space that remain illegible to usability research and consequently to the "Principles of Universal Design." Considerations of user preferences, for example, do not account for the financial accessibility of a design. Designs oriented toward consumption in domestic space, such as accessible kitchen gear, do not address the historically gendered division of domestic labor, nor do they account for the overrepresentation of white, elderly women in accessibility research. None of the "Principles" could be conceived as promoting attention to the racialized nature of domestic consumption or public belonging.

I want to underscore, too, that the "Principles of Universal Design," their critical labor and their omissions, were not late 1990s phenomena. Coalescing from historical processes of knowing-making, the "Principles" offer a key for deciphering the historical map of access-knowledge. If the first two principles invoke twentieth-century regimes of normalization through user-centered design, the third and fourth resemble the independent living movement and crip technoscience, which challenged normate design, rehabilitation, human factors research, and barrier-free design to widen their conception of the disabled user in acknowledgement of sensory and cognitive disabilities. Blind peoples' challenges to curb cuts as universal "good design," for instance, produced frictions *within* disability cultures that materialized new curb cut designs in the broader built environment. While these historical tensions are imperceptible to many curb cut users, the curb cut itself bears traces of crip friction in its tactile paving. Continuing the metaphor, if "Equitable Use" and "Flexibility in Use" typically represent the well-established streetscape of hegemonic values, the last four principles— "Simple and Intuitive Use," "Perceptible Information," "Tolerance for Error," "Low Physical Effort," and "Size and Space for Approach and Use"—are the textured surface of a curb ramp that both passes through and rematerializes the sidewalk above.

A REFLEXIVE METHODOLOGY?

How do designers know when they have achieved Universal Design? In 1996 Mace compiled an extensive list of examples illustrating each of the Universal Design principles, organized under a series of headings. The space beneath a final heading, "Designs Using All of These Principles," remained blank.[77] The principles may not have succeeded at creating a usable checklist for inclusive user-centered design, as the authors had hoped. But if we understand the principles as a historical artifact of Universal Design's material culture, rather than an objective metric of good design, it becomes possible to decipher the authors' subtle strategies, experiments, and negotiations.

Although the "Principles of Universal Design" appeared to reproduce the history of access-knowledge, their release triggered Universal Design's proliferation beyond architectural discourses, reaching into new fields of study, areas of application, and across international borders.[78] One significant product of these experiments with Universal Design in the 1990s, whether through the principles, product design, or UDEP, was an emerging discourse of good design as a *process,* a beginning point, rather than a measurable end. This methodological discourse was closely tied to Universal Design's interdisciplinarity. The authors and other proponents increasingly recognized the limits of their own expertise, even as they challenged the expert cultures surrounding Universal Design.[79] In 1997 Steinfeld and his colleague Beth Tauke proposed that the phenomenon was best understood as "Universal Design*ing,*" a process through which to "eliminate discrimination by design and support full social participation for all members of society," as opposed to the "therapeutic" and "purely functional goals of accessible design."[80] Referencing disability theory and feminist methodologies, they argued for a reflexive theory of Universal Design, in both its public face and internal theory: "We must develop a reflective pedagogy that not only retains the original critical focus of universal design as a philosophy but also involves self-criticism to uncover the significant intellectual foundation behind the ideology and also the limitations in the ideology itself."[81] The promise of a critical Universal Design theory contrasted with the presumably nonreflexive realm of compliance, marking the experimental, iterative nature of knowing-making. This iterativity extended beyond the design of products and buildings to the structure of knowledge production itself. As John Salmen later explained,

> There is a profound difference between universal design and accessibility. Accessibility is a function of compliance with regulations or criteria that establish a minimum level of design necessary to accommodate people with disabilities. Universal Design, however, is the art and practice of design to accommodate the widest variety and number of people throughout their lifespans. It can be thought of as the process of embedding choice for all people into the things we create. As more is learned about human needs and abilities, and as technologies develop, the practice of universal design improves, evolves, and changes. In truth, it might be better to think of this field

as "universal designing," so as to focus on the decision-making process rather than on some end product that may be improved in the future. . . .

The more designers know about users, the better they can design. But no person can ever "know it all." This reality demands collaborative efforts among designers, environmental decision makers, and users as the diversity and complexity of our global society increase. In this fluid context, it is necessary to establish flexible criteria for what constitutes a universal design, allowing universal design to lead the march toward an ever-receding goal of increasingly good design that modifies the environment to fit the needs of its users.[82]

In other words, access-knowledge is an accountability-producing mechanism *and* an open-ended commitment to reflexive, value-explicit design. Scientific facts, while useful, are subject to revision with ongoing research, but the aspirational project of access is open-ended, never completed by checking boxes or gaining building permits. These powerful statements carried the hope of a forward march toward optimized good design.

DESIGN FOR THE TWENTY-FIRST CENTURY

"Of course, the whole point of Universal Design," said Donald Norman in his opening address at the "Designing for the 21st Century" conference at Hofstra University in 1998, "is that it's nothing special. It's common sense. Of course, what I'm here to tell you about is why common sense is so rare."[83] "The problem with good design principles," he continued, "is that they don't necessarily translate into economics. They don't translate into increased sales or increased profit.[84]" Billed as the first international Universal Design conference, Designing for the 21st Century brought together most members of a well-established epistemic community, as well as disability organizations, rehabilitation experts, and representatives of professional design societies, to imagine the future of Universal Design discourses and practice.[85] The event took place in June 1998, just a year after the "Principles of Universal Design" were released and only thirteen years after the publication of Mace's seminal article, "Universal Design: Barrier-Free Design for Everyone." Nearly one thousand "world experts in the universal design of products, information, and environments" met with designers, educators, and manufacturers to explore Universal Design's future.[86]

If "Principles 2.0" mapped access-knowledge in the twentieth century, Designing for the 21st Century embodied the broad disciplinary, geographic, and scholarly reach of Universal Design in the most recent thirteen years. Reflecting upon Universal Design's growth in the previous decade, the conference organizers recognized experts such as Ruth Lusher and Katherine Seelman for their service and leadership. Mace recognized the winners of a student design competition, who would represent a new generation of Universal Design expertise.[87] International inclusive design experts, such as Yoshihiko Kawauchi from Japan and Roger Coleman from the UK, offered non-U.S. perspectives on Universal Design. High-profile speakers, such as Donald Norman, consolidated Universal Design's public image as a persuasive marketing argument, premised upon commonsense, good design.

Legibility, methodology, and ideology, in addition to marketing and common sense, dominated many of the discussions. Story and Mueller showcased the newly minted "Principles of Universal Design" as an instrument for "measuring usability."[88] Steinfeld emphasized the creative qualities of market-based Universal Design, which he compared to "foster[ing] the development of innovation like a gardener [rather] than audit[ing] compliance with laws like the police."[89] Others challenged the post-disability marketing narrative and its treatment of accessibility laws. Ruth Lusher, who had developed Universal Design with Mace in the 1980s, addressed the concept from her position as technical assistance manager at the Department of Justice, reminding the audience that the ADA had provided the momentum for Universal Design's success and that the two were entwined.[90] In a more overtly political vein, feminist architectural theorist Leslie Kanes Weisman, described by one conference attendee as the "Ralph Nader of architecture," addressed Universal Design's theoretical and ideological connections to the environmental inclusion of disabled people, women, people of color, and poor people.[91]

Once Universal Design became legible as a methodology, rather than a quality of architectural spaces or designed products, it also became a useful discourse for exploring critical approaches to disability. Notions of Universal Design as a critical methodology interfaced with emerging humanistic and social scientific theories in the field of critical disability Studies. At Designing for the 21st Century, two feminist disability scholars—Simi Linton and Rosemarie Garland-Thomson—offered a historical and humanistic view of Universal Design, which connected the concept to the broader contexts of disability knowing-making.

> Universal design cannot be an appendage to the academic curriculum, any more than a "universal design" plan can be appended to an existing blueprint.... [Universal Design] is more than a method, it is more than a solution to "problems," it is an interwoven set of ideas and applications owing as much to social and political imperatives as to intellectual ones.... We intend to explore these intersections . . . and map out a more universal knowledge base, the epistemological foundation of universal design.[92]

"Appendage" here refers to an emerging notion of retrofit as an afterthought, a quality of poorly conceived, add-on design. Appendages and retrofits, they implied, reflect social and political values, which require unpacking. Criticisms of "retrofit" would be central to humanistic studies of Universal Design in the coming decades, but Linton and Garland-Thomson's reference to the "epistemological foundation" of Universal Design, which appears to correspond with their scholarship on disability identity, knowledge, and culture in the mid- and late 1990s, has remained largely unexplored.[93] For Universal Design theory, however, epistemological questions had been (and continued to be) central to the project of defining a more capacious and inclusive approach to knowing-making.

Bookending Norman's comments regarding good design, and synthesizing perspectives offered throughout the conference, Mace's keynote, "A Perspective on Universal Design," concluded the event. His subject was an issue at the center of Universal Design theory: its relationship to the ADA and assistive technologies.[94] Everyone needs access, Mace impressed, referencing a claim he had made for decades (Figure 7.4). The primary difference between Universal Design, the ADA, and assistive technologies, he argued, was epistemological, resting on how designers know and understand users. By debunking the myth of the average user, he emphasized, "Universal Design *broadly defines the user.*" While his speech was not overtly political, it

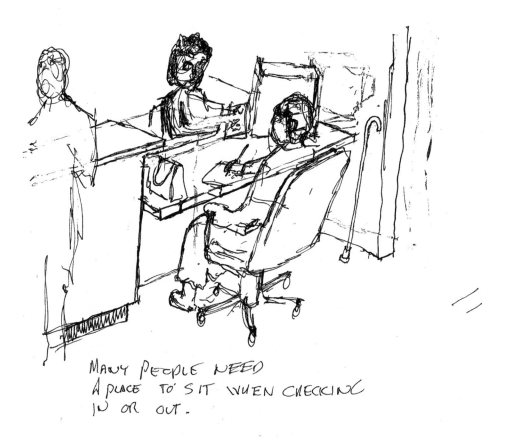

Figure 7.4. Mace experimented with claims about the user. This hand-drawn sketch (ca. 1998) speculates that "many people need a place to sit when checking in or out." Courtesy of Joy Weeber.

captured Mace's strategy of subtle epistemic activism. He explained that Universal Design was a "consumer market driven issue," addressing (what he believed to be) the universal experience of disability. He refused the post-disability narrative, however, by drawing upon his own experiences as a disabled user and designer to examine how "barrier-free, universal, and assistive technology blend and move." Noting that the ADA intra-acts with and "facilitates the promotion of Universal Design," Mace made clear that Universal Design, like the normate template, is an elusive aspiration: "I have never seen a building or facility that I would say is universally usable. I don't know that it's possible to create one. . . . It's not a weakness in the term. We use that term because it's the most description of what the goal is, something people can live with and afford." Mace concluded by emphasizing, as he had done for over three decades, that the key to working toward this goal was broad, interdisciplinary collaboration. In this respect, the successful convergence had "exceeded [his] expectations."

With great momentum toward the future of Universal Design, Designing for the 21st Century culminated twentieth-century efforts to produce, rework, and disseminate access-knowledge.

On June 29, 1998, only a week after the conference, Mace unexpectedly passed away in his Raleigh, North Carolina, home.[95]

The shock of his death launched immediate action among his colleagues and friends. Salmen declared Mace's death to be the "end of the first generation" of Universal Design and the beginning of the second.[96] A memorial in his honor was held at the National Building Museum in Washington, D.C., later that year. In dedication to Mace, Ostroff and Lusher began "Access to the Design Professions," a new mentorship initiative for disabled designers.[97] The Cooper Hewitt, Smithsonian Design Museum, in New York City, whose director was Diane Pilgrim, a disabled woman, debuted "Unlimited by Design," an exhibit of Universal Design products, in 1999.[98] As Salmen predicted, Universal Design—the concept, its "Principles," and its epistemic community—would continue to grow and change in the new century, particularly through international conferences, books, cross-disciplinary initiatives, competitions, and citations. Although these sites of knowing-making may appear neutral, distant, or irrelevant to overt struggles for spatial justice, our paths to the present insist that they are also the material, epistemic, and social laboratories in which our built world is contested, negotiated, and remade.

So, how do we make and share a more accessible world? Well, that depends on how we know.

Conclusion

Disability Justice

Disability is not monolithic. Ableism plays out very differently for wheelchair users, deaf people or people who have mental, psychiatric and cognitive disabilities. None of these are mutually exclusive, and are all complicated by race, class, gender, immigration, sexuality, welfare status, incarceration, age and geographic location.

—MIA MINGUS, "Changing the Framework"

Let's conclude as we began: by traveling.

If you are sighted, you can see it from the outside, but the building does not require you to see. Textured concrete sidewalks along Adeline Street signal its arrival. Even so, you may not know what it is, if you belong there, or if it was designed with you in mind. Regardless, the Ed Roberts Campus, a "universally designed, transit-oriented campus located at the Ashby BART Station in Berkeley, California," and its glass and steel structure may catch your attention (Figure C.1).[1]

The building's street-level window overlooks an interior ramp, a winding red spiral suspended from cables beneath a large, circular skylight. According to architect William Leddy, the building "expresses the idea that good design is fundamentally a social justice issue. Everyone has a right to inspiring, supportive places in which to live and work."[2] Making disability explicit, the building is far removed from rehabilitation models of disability as a deficit to overcome and from post-disability approaches to Universal Design. Against a long, rounded wall behind the ramp, photos from the Paul Longmore Institute's exhibit *Patient No More* commemorate the historic 504 sit-in, showing disability activists engaged in acts of protest that led to the enforcement of major civil rights legislation. Although the ramp appears to be a central feature, the building's wayfinding signage, textured concrete, automatic sensors and doors, accessible restrooms, sound-producing fountain, natural light, open spaces, and raised-bed rooftop gardens work together, materializing in built form the legacy of Ed Roberts, as well as the Bay Area disability organizations housed inside.

While the Ed Roberts Campus opened to the public in 2011, its placement and symbolism invoke decades of local disability history.[3] Nearly as old as Berkeley's disability communities, Bay Area Rapid Transit (BART) was the first U.S. public transportation system built in the midst of a shifting federal disability rights landscape,

Figure C.1. Interior of the Ed Roberts Campus, Berkeley, California (2016). Courtesy of Anthony Tusler.

including the 1968 Architectural Barriers Act and the 1972 Federal Rehabilitation Act. The same year that Berkeley adopted its mandate for city-funded curb cuts, 1973, the Ashby station opened to the public, its construction having been delayed by disability activists' frictioned demands for integrated features, such as elevator access.[4] Together, the curb cuts and BART's transit system are often attributed to the rise of the area's large disabled population and the independent living movement's success.

There is another history surrounding the site, however, one that is rarely discussed: a history of race, architecture, knowledge, and their political economies. In the 1960s, as part of urban renewal efforts that displaced many poor and elderly African Americans in Oakland and Berkeley, BART broke ground on the Ashby station, using eminent domain to clear a rail corridor along Adeline Street.[5] Many homes and businesses were displaced. Justified in the name of solving urban poverty, these events were built into a regime of productive white, spatial citizenship, which buttressed legal efforts toward barrier-free design and simultaneously intensified the surveillance and displacement of urban communities of color.

History does not just repeat itself; it doubles back and proliferates. In 2014 San Francisco's most recent "tech boom" increased the population of young, white, male workers in the technology industries, displacing African American, Latino, Asian, and middle-class white populations that had occupied the inner city for decades.[6] Along with speculative investments and evictions that decreased the rental housing stock, companies such as Google created neoliberal micro-structures of transit and housing, offering private buses and other amenities to arriving tech workers.[7] Concerns about dislocation rippled into the Bay Area's surrounding cities and suburbs, including Oakland and South Berkeley, as populations shifted outward. In the five years since the Ed Roberts Campus was built, development proposals along the Adeline Street corridor have intensified, leading nearby residents to express concerns about gentrification and displacement.[8] With new amenities, many fear, will come higher rent prices in a metropolitan area already experiencing an affordable housing crisis, evictions, and the country's largest population of unsheltered homeless people, many of whom are disabled.[9]

Fears of displacement dovetail with ever-present (but for some, only newly legible) struggles of communities of color in U.S. cities. At the downtown West Oakland station, four miles from Ashby, police arrested Black Lives Matter activists, who protested the police shootings of Oscar Grant at nearby Fruitvale station and Michael Brown in Ferguson, Missouri, in 2014. Activists planned to inhabit the station for the four and a half hours that Brown's body was left in the street after his death. Juxtaposing bodies and built forms, they created a chain spanning from a rail car's interior out onto the platform. Outside the station, commuters gathered, waiting to use this key gateway point in the transit system between the east and west sides of the Bay.[10] In the public discourse surrounding Black Lives Matter, some have challenged protesters' emphasis on some, rather than "all," lives, while others have derided their tactics as illegal, unsanctioned transgressions. Still others have considered these protests to be politics by embodied, spatial, and epistemic means, holding space within the transit system and its nodes of power to make legible the lives of those hidden, erased, and eliminated. Given reports that approximately 50 percent of unarmed civilians killed by law enforcement, including Eric Garner, Sandra Bland, Tanisha Anderson, Freddie Gray, Kajieme Powell, and Keith Lamott Scott, were disabled, the protests appear to both trouble and answer the questions of who counts as "all," how those who make and dwell in the world purport to know, and for what purposes.[11]

Another way of saying that history repeats itself is to point out that struggles for access, belonging, and citizenship are not contained in a linear march toward progress. The consumer-centric post-ADA narrative that dominates much of Universal Design marketing tells us little about the sociopolitical economy of design or what purpose profitability serves, who benefits, and toward what ends. Buttressing this narrative, rehabilitation experts continue to raise alarm about the aging white, suburban baby boomer population and its unique vulnerabilities in single-family homes and spatially dispersed, car-centric communities.[12] Emphasizing the added value of Universal Design for this population, designers and manufacturers introduce new products into private consumer markets and attest to their commonsense, good design. It is easy to forget, however, that concerns about population aging have been raised for nearly a century, since even before today's baby boomers were born, and that access to aging is a marker of privilege in a dominant culture that does not antic-ipate or value all lives. The baby boom's current status as a crisis of suburban con-sumer life bears the intersecting imprints of racial injustice, poverty, ableism, and gender discrimination that materialized in twentieth-century patterns of urban, sub-urban, and even rural and international development. As the trope of the productive citizen endures in our twenty-first-century conversations about aging, disability, class, race, gender, and immigration status in built space, and as cities expand and rebuild, questions of who belongs and how we know remain urgent.

A triumph for disability movements, the Ed Roberts Campus embodies Universal Design's spirit and function and simultaneously symbolizes potent histories of crip noncompliance and disruption. But the building is also a single, vulnerable node in the contentious politics of systematic change. The Ashby station on which the build-ing sits was one of the independent living movement's accessibility victories, but spaces and technologies change, and with them, the social conditions of inhabitation.

In 2014 BART announced plans to replace its dated, 1970s-era rail cars in anticipa-tion of population growth due to the Bay Area's "tech boom." Borrowing the language of deficit models of disability, the agency explained that the old cars had been "reha-bilitated in the 1990s to extend their use, but are now near the end of their useful lives and need to be replaced."[13] A new "Fleet for the Future" would provide a rare oppor-tunity to adopt cutting-edge technology and redesign the user experience of public transit. Designing the "Fleet for the Future" entailed a "data-rich," evidence-based de-sign strategy, propelled by user feedback and iteration to "mak[e] sure the new designs will actually benefit the people who use BART." Rider surveys and, in some stations, "seat labs" enrolled users to "test out different seat spacing arrangements—a matter of inches and centimeters that determines, to a large degree, the entire spatial design of the car interior." And like product designers since Henry Dreyfuss and Alexander Kira, BART "considered how population growth rates would affect the demand for trains, and how the aging Baby Boomer population would affect the need for seats designed for seniors and people with disabilities."[14] Based on this data, a prototype was designed and members of the public were invited to visit.

The initial design sought to accommodate a greater number of riders more effi-ciently—at least those who could stand and grip floor-to-ceiling rails for the dura-tion of their ride.[15] Increased standing space was provided in the middle of the car. Although the designers consulted demographic data on aging and disability, however, the new cars were inaccessible to chair users. The middle of the car, with its increased standing space, featured new railings and bicycle racks, "while wheelchair users [were] directed to use the doors at the end of the car."[16] A coalition of disabled riders pro-tested the new design, arguing that additional handrails blocked entry for chair users and introduced unpredictable obstructions for blind people.[17] The prototype, in other words, threatened to disassemble hard-won access gains in anticipation of normate, upright, and standing users.

User feedback yielded a compromise: entries would have more clearance and the center of the car would gain two new spaces dedicated to wheelchair users.[18] Rather than remove the floor-to-ceiling poles blocking wheelchair users from entering, each pole would be moved a few feet away, leaving material evidence of the frictioned design process, much like the curb cut's textured surface. But as with the curb cut, a narrative of compromise followed. An official BART press release quoted representatives of its Accessibility Task Force hailing the new fleet as providing "diverse amenities to meet diverse needs within the disability community."[19] A local disability organization cited the compromise as a "victory" of grassroots mobilization, quoting a "BART rider who uses a wheelchair and also has a daughter in a stroller" as endorsing the new design.[20] Media reports depicted the new seats and their arrangement as ergonomic enhancements of the previous cars, which "feature a mix of light-blue and neon-green seats, with brighter colored upholstery marking spots for seniors and the disabled. The seats are thinner but feel sturdier, with lumbar supports, and they sit higher above the floor, providing more room for luggage."[21] As accessibility blends into ergonomics and aesthetics, one gets the impression that the seats, the cars, and their design had been this way all along.

Contrary to post-disability and post-racial narratives, physical structures and the stories that we tell about them matter for how we understand who gets to be in the world and under what conditions. *Building Access* has challenged the idea that Universal Design is merely commonsense, good design for all. Accepting this idea on its face elides the frictioned struggles and strategic interventions that accessible design produces and therefore tells us little about the critical work of negotiating, contesting, and remaking access-knowledge.

Where do we go from here? What kind of future will Universal Design produce? The "future," Alison Kafer argues, is often a place of disability disavowal: "the value of a future that includes disabled people goes unrecognized, while the value of a disability-free future is seen as self-evident," often because "the political nature of disability, namely its position as a category to be contested and debated, goes unacknowledged."[22] Rather than imagining futures in which disability is eliminated or overcome, this book has argued that a critical Universal Design, which plays close attention to theory, rhetoric, discourse, representation, history, and ideology, is crucial to addressing the gaps in commonsense understandings of access. As Universal Design spreads into the future, finds international endorsement, is reproduced in marketing materials and through new performance standards, and is applied to design at the urban scale, there remains an urgent need to remember that struggle and inequality are not historical artifacts displayed in museums as a reminder of the way that things used to be. Even if eclipsed temporarily by civil rights legislation, exclusions in the built environment rematerialize in the banal conditions of neoliberal

urban restructuring, development, and displacement, in everyday marketing discourses and their imagined populations, and in the ways that we imagine who gets to
be part of our collective futures.

The history of access-knowledge is a history of how disability has been defined,
studied, and deployed as a concept, whether in the academy, industry, law, or activism. Studies of disability, design, and user research are also part of access-knowledge.
As Universal Design extends into classrooms, education technologies, campus wayfinding projects, and academic publishing, our ways of reproducing claims about
Universal Design matter. How we study, teach, and claim knowledge about disability
matters for the material arrangements we pursue. How we approach the intersections
of disability with race, gender, class, and aging *matter* for questions of belonging and
justice in contemporary conditions.

The framework of critical access studies draws attention to knowledge production
as a site in which the structures of everyday life are redesigned. Scholars such as Jay
Dolmage, Margaret Price, Melanie Yargeau, and many others have shown that the
ways in which we produce and transmit knowledge, whether in the classroom, on
the World Wide Web, or in everyday negotiations of access, are design practices, and
for this reason, philosophies such as Universal Design can inform broader perspectives on knowing-making. But experiments in access-knowledge do not belong solely
to the university, nor should they. If Universal Design is only developed in the domains
of the university and the consumer market, the movement is unlikely to shake the
vestiges of rehabilitation models and military-industrial norms of the user.

A framework guided by accountability can take us much further. The contemporary disability justice movement challenges disability rights frameworks that
concentrate on individual rights, legal change, compromise, productive citizenship,
and technical aspects of accessibility. Emphasizing material justice over nominal formal equality, disability justice organizers such as Mia Mingus, Patty Berne, Leroy
Moore, Alice Wong, Stacy Milbern, collectives such as Sins Invalid and the Silicon
Valley Independent Living Center, and many others are reshaping access-knowledge.[23]
Berne's "working draft" of disability justice principles explains the movement's philosophy as encompassing "Intersectionality," "Leadership of the Most Impacted,"
"Anti-Capitalist Politic," "Commitment to Cross-Movement Organizing," "Recognizing Wholeness," "Sustainability," "Commitment to Cross-Disability Solidarity," "Interdependence," "Collective Access," and "Collective Liberation."[24] In some respects,
disability justice resembles Universal Design's early theory, which stressed broad,
anticipatory accessibility for the most marginalized, challenged class hierarchies and
recognized the limits of formal rights regimes. But where the mainstream discourse
of Universal Design has turned away from addressing oppression and often centers
rehabilitation concepts, practices such as disability simulations, and consumer marketing, disability justice contends that the response to liberalism's failures is, instead,
collective liberation.[25]

Reorienting Universal Design toward disability justice lets us imagine futures in which the legacies of racial segregation, mass incarceration, homelessness, immigration systems, and environmental injustice, alongside aging, disability, and gender, are issues that shape who counts as "everyone" and how designers can know. But these futures will require realigning Universal Design's relationship to disability. If the stories we tell about bodies and users matter for questions of justice, then it is with more accountable, historical knowing-making that we must begin. How we take up space depends upon it.

Acknowledgments

My deepest gratitude goes to those who held space for this project, in all of its iterations. Rosemarie Garland-Thomson recognized the kernel and planted the seed. David Serlin, Deboleena Roy, and Sander Gilman helped it to grow. This book would have been impossible without Joy Weeber, who generously opened her home to me, along with Ron Mace's papers, materials, and ephemera, and gave me my first taste of access activism in March 2012, when we rode her accessible van through Raleigh and documented ADA violations with my camera. Katherine Ott's wisdom, encouragement, and office full of (then-unsorted) Universal Design ephemera at the Smithsonian were crucial. Disabled artists Sunaura Taylor, Anthony Tusler, and Tom Olin graciously allowed their work to be reproduced. Thank you for capturing disability history and theory in action. I was fortunate to speak to Universal Design's leaders and advocates, who were generous with their ideas and time. Thank you to Elaine Ostroff, Leslie Kanes Weisman, Valerie Fletcher, Edward Steinfeld, Jim Mueller, Abir Mullick, Jon Sanford, Mike Jones, Richard Duncan, Robert Shibley, Jordana Maisel, Eric Dibner, and many others for taking time away from world-building for conversation and reflection.

My fabulous colleagues in the Center for Medicine, Health, and Society supported me through this process. Thank you to my friends, mentors, and writing groups at Vanderbilt. Ken, Laura, Rebecca, Vanessa, Claire, Lisa, and Brooke kept me accountable to my craft. My Society for Disability Studies colleagues, thank you for modeling access in everyday life.

I am grateful to everyone who supported this project, whether as a mentor, interlocutor, or reader of drafts: Rosemarie, David, Sander, Deboleena, Eunjung Kim, Beth Reingold, Berky Abreu, Lynne Huffer, Elizabeth Wilson, Bess Williamson, Anson Koch-Rein, Sara Hendren, Tanya Titchkosky, Rob Imrie, Margaret Price, Corbette O'Toole, Jos Boys, Melanie Yargeau, Jay Dolmage, Alison Kafer, Johnna Keller, Sami Schalk, Wanda Liebermann, Nirmala Erevelles, Sandie Yi, Maria Town, Louise Hickman, Kevin Gotkin, Ally Day, Liat Ben-Moshe, Ryan Perry-Munger, Kim Q. Hall, Rebecca Garden, Elizabeth Guffey, Amanda Cachia, Kelly Fritsch, Shelley Tremain,

Michael Leo Owens, David Pena-Guzman, Nikki Karalekas, Harold Braswell, and so many others.

Michelle Murphy and Rob Imrie were brilliant readers. I am grateful for their thoughtful comments, which improved the book tremendously. Thank you to the University of Minnesota Press. Thorough and accountable advice from my editor Pieter Martin, editorial assistant Anne Carter, and copyeditor Sheila McMahon were essential in turning this assemblage of words and images into a book.

Early funding for this project came from the Social Science Research Council's Dissertation Proposal Development Fellowship, but my "Spaces of Inquiry" colleagues were really the best gift. Thank you to Carla Yanni, Bill Leslie, Jenna Tonn, Casey Oberlin, Chris Heaney, James Skee, Sara Witty, Brittney Shields, Karen Robbins, Jennifer Kosmin, Phil Clements, and Roberto Chauca for everything that you have taught me about knowing and making.

Generous support from Vanderbilt's Research Scholar sabbatical grant; the Smithsonian Lemelson Center for the Study of Invention and Innovation; the Robert Penn Warren Center for the Humanities; the Curb Center for Art, Enterprise, and Public Policy; and Emory's Laney Graduate School also made research and completion of this book possible. The Graham Foundation for Advanced Studies in the Fine Arts generously funded the book's production. Thank you to the Cooper Hewitt, Smithsonian Design Museum; the National Museum of American History; the University of California, San Diego; Goldsmiths; the University of Toronto (and the Feminist Technoscience Salon); and the Ohio State University for generative visits, talks, and discussions.

My utmost gratitude goes to Melanie Adley, whose tireless labor made completing this book (including its visual materials and index) possible. Traces of her support, encouragement, and attention to detail appear on every page. I am grateful for your practices of accountability, feminist interdependence, and collective access.

Moonbow, Penumbra, Firlefanz, and Sosi have been patient nonhuman companions.

Finally, thank you to my parents, Abdolhamid and Farivash Hamraie, each knowers and makers in their own way, and to my brother, James, for encouragement and support.

Notes

Preface

1. Tanya Titchkosky, *The Question of Access: Disability, Space, Meaning* (Toronto: University of Toronto Press, 2011).

2. "Bodymind" is a term I borrow from Margaret Price, "The Bodymind Problem and the Possibilities of Pain," *Hypatia* 30, no. 1 (2015): 268–84.

Introduction

1. As a critical concept, "misfit" is elaborated by Rosemarie Garland-Thomson, "Misfits: A Feminist Disability Materialist Concept," *Hypatia* 26, no. 3 (2011): 591–609. Along with Garland-Thomson's neologism "normate," misfit offers a useful reference to bodies for whom the world was not designed. I elaborate my theory of normate and misfit as users of built environments in Aimi Hamraie, "Designing Collective Access: A Feminist Disability Theory of Universal Design," *Disability Studies Quarterly* 33, no. 4 (2013), http://dsq-sds.org/article/view/3871/3411.

2. I use the term "disabled people," and occasionally "people with disabilities," throughout this book. "Disabled people" is the preferred usage for many disability activists, who argue that they are disabled by society and claim disability as an identity. "Person-first language," such as "people with disabilities," is often associated with medical and rehabilitative models, which identify personhood as separate from disabled embodiment and experience. With the exception of historical quotations, I avoid outdated terms such as "handicapped" and the myriad derogatory terms used to refer to cognitively and physically disabled people. When describing disabled people, I have used terms with which they appear to identify in public. Ronald Mace, for instance, used the term "disabled person." There are also generational differences in term preferences and meanings. Although "crip" emerged as an identity term in the 1970s, it has more recently gained popularity within academic discourse, personal identification, and group affiliation.

3. Disability social movement scholars often identify direct action as a key tactic for disability activists, who use their bodies as evidence that disability is a socially produced, rather than medical, phenomenon. See Tom Shakespeare, "Disabled People's Self-organisation: A New Social Movement?," *Disability, Handicap and Society* 8, no. 3 (1993): 251–52.

4. On the politics of disability in post-ADA narratives of design, see Aimi Hamraie, "Universal Design and the Problem of 'Post-Disability' Ideology," *Design and Culture* 8, no. 3 (2016): 285–309.

5. As disability scholars such as Georgina Kleege (*Sight Unseen* [New Haven, Conn.: Yale University Press, 1999]) have argued, optical metaphors for knowledge (such as "plain view") are part of the culture of disability discrimination, elevating the primacy of vision as a way of knowing. My use of these metaphors here is deliberate, however, as this book is concerned with the primacy afforded to legibility and illegibility, whether scientific or political, as a form of power.

6. Most analyses focus on the ADA's failures to achieve labor inequality, despite mandating accessible built environments and services. See Michelle Maroto and David Pettinicchio, "Twenty-Five Years after the ADA: Situating Disability in America's System of Stratification," *Disability Studies Quarterly* 35, no. 3 (2015), http://dsq-sds.org/article/view/4927/4024. Data from the U.S. Department of Labor shows that eight out of ten disabled people lack access to employment, compared to three out of ten in the nondisabled population. See Department of Labor, "Persons with a Disability: Labor Force Characteristics," Department of Labor Statistics News Release, June 21, 2016, 1–11. Disability law expert and former Department of Justice attorney Sam Bagenstos attributes the ADA's failures to the "inherent limitations of antidiscrimination laws," which do not provide the "social welfare" necessary to overcome barriers. See Sam Bagenstos, "Disability Laws Are Not Enough to Combat Discrimination," *New York Times*, July 26, 2015. The failures of ADA Title III to achieve accessible public accommodations is attributed to a "fragile compromise" between advocates and businesses, argues one disability law scholar. See Ruth Colker, "ADA Title III: A Fragile Compromise," *Berkeley Journal of Employment & Labor Law* 21, no. 1 (2000): 378.

7. An earlier version of this analysis appears in Hamraie, "Universal Design and the Problem of 'Post-Disability' Ideology."

8. Ronald Mace, "Universal Design: Barrier-Free Environments for Everyone," *Designer's West* 33, no. 1 (1985): 148.

9. My concept of access-knowledge references Foucault's "power-knowledge." See Michel Foucault, *Discipline and Punish: Birth of the Prison,* trans. Alan Sheridan (New York: Vintage Books, 1975), 26–28. Access-knowledge is a regime of intelligibility, or what Foucault calls a "dispositif," a "thoroughly heterogeneous ensemble consisting of discourses, institutions, architectural forms, regulatory decisions, laws, administrative measures, scientific statements, philosophical, moral and philanthropic propositions—in short, the said as much as the unsaid. Such are the elements of the apparatus. The apparatus itself is the system of relations that can be established between these elements." Michel Foucault, "The Confession of the Flesh" (1977), in *Power/Knowledge: Selected Interviews and Other Writings,* ed. Colin Gordon (New York: Pantheon Books, 1980), 194. Although access-knowledge fits Foucault's description of a biopolitical arrangement, I avoid using terms such as "biopower" and "governmentality" because their overuse often obscures meaning. Disability scholars adopting Foucault's notion of power-knowledge have often treated knowledge as a mere instrument of power relations, rather than taking the politics of knowledge seriously. My approach to entangled knowing-making is more epistemological. Closely affiliated with Foucault's archaeological method, I locate knowledge-production as itself an exercise of power. See Aimi Hamraie, "Historical Epistemology as Disability Studies Methodology: From the Models Framework to Foucault's Archaeology of Cure," *Foucault Studies,* no. 19 (June 2015): 108–34. This approach builds on feminist technoscience scholarship, which has deployed archaeological methods (often referred to as "historical ontology" or "historical epistemology") to study the relationships between buildings and bodies. The most elegant use of such analysis, in my estimation, is Michelle Murphy, *Sick Building Syndrome and the Problem of Uncertainty: Environmental Politics, Technoscience, and Women Workers* (Durham, N.C.: Duke University Press, 2006).

10. Molly Follette Story, James L. Mueller, and Ronald L. Mace, *The Universal Design File: Designing for People of All Ages and Abilities* (Raleigh, N.C.: Center for Universal Design, North Carolina State University, 1998), 6.

11. Mace, "Universal Design," 147–52.

12. The barrier work of this debate is explored in the last half of the book. For examples of these debates, see John Salmen, "The Differences between Accessibility and Universal Design," *Universal Design Newsletter* 1, no. 7 (1994): 2; Abir Mullick and Edward Steinfeld, "Universal Design: What It Is and What It Isn't," *Innovation* 16, no. 1 (1997): 14–24; S. Iwarsson and A. Ståhl, "Accessibility, Usability and Universal Design—Positioning and Definition of Concepts Describing Person-Environment Relationships," *Disability and Rehabilitation* 25, no. 2 (2003): 57–66; Denise Levine, *Universal Design New York* (Buffalo, N.Y.: Center for Inclusive Design and Environmental Access, 2003), 8; Josh Safdie, quoted in Susan Szenasy, "Accessibility Watch: Q&A with Josh Safdie," *Metropolis* magazine, February 2011; Daniel McAdams and Vincent Kostovich, "A Framework and Representation for Universal Product Design," *International Journal of Design* 5, no. 1 (2011): 29–42, http://www.ijdesign.org/ojs/index.php/IJDesign/article/view/602/327.

13. On "good design" as a commonsense discourse, see Stephen Hayward, "'Good Design Is Largely a Matter of Common Sense': Questioning the Meaning and Ownership of a Twentieth-Century Orthodoxy," *Journal of Design History* 11, no. 3 (1998): 217–33.

14. John Hockenberry, "Design Is Universal," *Metropolis* magazine, December 2004.

15. Center for Universal Design, North Carolina State University, "The Principles of Universal Design," Version 2.0, April 1, 1997, http://www.ncsu.edu/ncsu/design/cud/about_ud/udprinci plestext.htm.

16. Center for Universal Design, North Carolina State University, "Principles of Universal Design in Languages Other than English," 2008, https://www.ncsu.edu/ncsu/design/cud/about_ ud/udnonenglishprinciples.html.

17. Science and technology studies (STS), particularly feminist STS, as well as the histories and sociologies of science and technology, grew from these postpositivist approaches, often working as activists within academic discourse by referencing or working in concert with activists outside the academy. These relations and their challenges to knowing and making are explored productively in Michelle Murphy, *Seizing the Means of Reproduction: Entanglements of Feminism, Health, and Technoscience* (Durham, N.C.: Duke University Press, 2012).

18. Disability and design scholars, including myself, have made similar arguments about Universal Design's disability-neutralizing approaches. See Hamraie, "Designing Collective Access"; Bess Williamson, "Electric Moms and Quad Drivers: People with Disabilities Buying, Making, and Using Technology in Postwar America," *American Studies* 52, no. 1 (2012): 232–33; Elizabeth Ellcessor, "Blurred Lines: Accessibility, Disability, and Definitional Limitations," *First Monday* 20, no. 9 (2015), http://firstmonday.org/ojs/index.php/fm/rt/printerFriendly/6169/4904.

19. The Society for Disability Studies was founded in 1986, just a year after Mace named Universal Design. Society for Disability Studies, "Mission and History," https://disstudies.org/index .php/about-sds/mission-and-history/.

20. Union of Physically Impaired Against Segregation, "Policy Statement," 1972, http://dis ability-studies.leeds.ac.uk/files/library/UPIASUPIAS.pdf; Simon Brisendon, "Independent Living and the Medical Model of Disability," *Disability, Handicap and Society* 1, no. 2 (1986): 173–78; Michael Oliver, *The Politics of Disablement: A Sociological Approach* (Basingstoke, UK: Palgrave Macmillan, 1990).

21. Also in the mid-1960s, medical sociologist Saad Nagi introduced a matrix distinguishing pathology, impairment, functional limitation, and disability in relation to built environments, defining (as the social model does) disability as oppression and functional limitation as person-environment misfit. Saad Nagi, "Disability Concepts Revisited," in *Disability in America: Toward a National Agenda for Prevention*, ed. Andrew Pope and Andrew Tarlov (Washington, D.C.: National Academy Press, 1991), 309–27.

22. Shelley Tremain, "On the Subject of Impairment," in *Disability/Postmodernity: Embodying Disability Theory*, ed. Mairian Corker and Tom Shakespeare (London: Continuum Press, 2002), 32–47; Isabel Dyck, "Geographies of Disability: Reflecting on New Body Knowledges," in *Toward Enabling Geographies: "Disabled" Bodies and Minds in Society and Space*, ed. Vera Chouinard, Edward Hall, and Robert Wilton (Burlington: Ashgate, 2010), 254–55.

23. Crip theory originated in disability activism of the civil rights era and continues to be developed outside the academy in the disability justice movement. However, scholars drawing on crip theory since 2003 have offered it as a method of analysis, similar to critical race, feminist, or queer frameworks. See Carrie Sandahl, "Queering the Crip or Cripping the Queer? Intersections of Queer and Crip Identities in Solo Autobiographical Performance," *GLQ: A Journal of Lesbian and Gay Studies* 9, nos. 1–2 (2003): 25–56; Robert McRuer and Abby Wilkerson, "Introduction," *GLQ: A Journal of Lesbian and Gay Studies* 9, nos. 1–2 (2003): 1–23; Robert McRuer, *Crip Theory: Cultural Signs of Queerness and Disability*, Cultural Front (New York: New York University Press, 2006). The reclamation of "crip" for radical theorizing has been criticized for centralizing physical disability. This critique is important for my analysis of Universal Design, as well. In this book, I show that physically disabled people, particularly those with postpolio disabilities, were most often the objects of barrier-free design research in the mid-twentieth century and later served in leadership roles when it came to redefining standards. This is not to grant primacy to physical disability but to show why access-knowledge focused on physical disability through most of the century. While I use "crip" to describe a political orientation, I have been careful to note when disabilities that are considered sensory or cognitive appear in relation to these practices.

24. Deaf culture offers an example of a cultural model of disability, wherein disability is the basis of shared language and culture and not understood in purely medical terms. See H-Dirksen L. Bauman and Joseph J. Murray, eds., *Deaf Gain: Raising the Stakes for Human Diversity* (Minneapolis: University of Minnesota Press, 2014). The coalitional, cultural, epistemic, and relational aspects of crip theory are explored in Alison Kafer, *Feminist, Queer, Crip* (Bloomington: Indiana University Press, 2013).

25. David Mitchell and Sharon Snyder, *Cultural Locations of Disability* (Chicago: University of Chicago Press, 2006), 125.

26. Kafer, *Feminist, Queer, Crip*, 8–10.

27. Feminist disability scholars have shown that the liberal project of disability elimination was pervasive in twentieth-century culture. This project had more overt manifestations, such as sterilization and killing, but also circulated through the logics of devalued dependency, the foil of the productive citizen. See Rosemarie Garland-Thomson, "Disability and Representation," *PMLA* 120, no. 2 (2005): 522–27; Martha Fineman, *The Autonomy Myth: A Theory of Dependency* (New York: New Press, 2005).

28. Sandahl, "Queering the Crip or Cripping the Queer?," 30.

29. Jay Dolmage, "Mapping Composition," in *Disability and the Teaching of Writing: A Critical Sourcebook*, ed. Brenda Brueggeman and Cindy Lewiecki-Wilson (Boston: Bedford/St. Martin's, 2006), 14–27.

30. Mia Mingus, "Changing the Framework: Disability Justice," *Leaving Evidence,* February 12, 2012, https://leavingevidence.wordpress.com/2011/02/12/changing-the-framework-disability-jus tice; Hamraie, "Designing Collective Access."

31. Kelly Fritsch, "Accessible," in *Keywords for Radicals,* ed. Kelly Fritsch, Clare O'Connor, and AK Thompson (Chico, Calif.: AK Press, 2016), 23–28.

32. Ibid., 25. Access studies emerged from the historical materialist and political economic traditions of the social model, particularly in British disability studies. Much of this work was devoted to making a case for access. Critical access studies does not displace the former, per se, but its objects of inquiry are often the discourses surrounding access (i.e., first wave access stud ies). A few texts and projects that I consider to be central to critical access studies include Rob Imrie and Peter Hall, *Inclusive Design: Designing and Developing Accessible Environments* (New York: Spon Press, 2001), 14–18; Rob Imrie, "Universalism, Universal Design and Equitable Access to the Built Environment," *Disability and Rehabilitation* 34, no. 10 (2012): 873–82; N. D'Souza, "Is Universal Design a Critical Theory?," in *Designing a More Inclusive World,* ed. S. Keates and J. Clarkson (London: Springer, 2004), 3–9; Graham Pullin, *Design Meets Disability* (Cambridge, Mass.: MIT Press, 2009); Jos Boys, *Doing Dis/Ability Differently: An Alternative Handbook on Architecture, Dis/Ability, and Designing for Everyday Life* (London: Routledge, 2014); Titchkosky, *The Question of Access;* Margaret Price, *Mad at School: Rhetorics of Mental Illness and Academic Life* (Ann Arbor: University of Michigan Press, 2011); Jay Dolmage, "Universal Design: Places to Start," *Disability Studies Quarterly* 35, no. 2 (2015), http://dsq-sds.org/issue/view/144; Melanie Yargeau, Elizabeth Brewer, Stephanie Kershbaum, Sushil Oswal, Margaret Price, Cynthia Selfe, Michael Salvo, and Franny Howes, *Multimodality in Motion: Disability & Kairotic Spaces,* http://kairos. technorhetoric.net/18.1/coverweb/yergeau-et-al/pages/access.html; Inger Marie Lid, "Universal Design and Disability: An Interdisciplinary Perspective," *Disability & Rehabilitation* 36, no. 16 (2014): 1344–49; Elizabeth Ellcessor, *Restricted Access: Media, Disability, and the Politics of Partici pation* (New York: New York University Press, 2016).

33. Chris Bell, "Introducing White Disability Studies: A Modest Proposal," in *The Disability Studies Reader,* 2nd ed., ed. Lennard J. Davis (New York: Routledge, 2006), 275. The generative con tributions of black disability studies to the field, though often unrecognized, should not be dis counted. See Chris Bell, ed., *Blackness and Disability: Critical Examinations and Cultural Interventions* (East Lansing: Michigan State University Press, 2011); Jane Dunham, Jerome Harris, Shancia Jarrett, Leroy Moore, Akemi Nishida, Margaret Price, Britney Robinson, and Sami Schalk, "Developing and Reflecting on a Black Disability Studies Pedagogy: Work from the National Black Disability Coali tion," *Disability Studies Quarterly* 35, no. 2 (2015), http://www.dsq-sds.org/article/view/4637/3933.

34. In architectural history and theory, see Lance Hosey, "Hidden Lines: Gender, Race, and the Body in Graphic Standards," *Journal of Architectural Education* 55, no. 2 (2006): 101–12; Paul Emmons and Andreea Mihalache, "Architectural Handbooks and the User Experience," in *Use Matters: An Alternative History of Architecture,* ed. Kenny Cuppers (New York: Routledge, 2013), 35–50; Kenny Cupers, *The Social Project* (Minneapolis: University of Minnesota Press, 2014). In science and technology studies, see Michelle Murphy, *Sick Building Syndrome;* Ruth Schwartz Cowan, "Consumption Junction: A Proposal for Research Strategies in the Sociology of Technol ogy," in *The Social Construction of Technological Systems: New Directions in the Sociology and History of Technology,* ed. Wiebe E. Bijker, Thomas P. Hughes, and Trevor Pinch (Cambridge, Mass.: MIT Press, 1987); Nelly Oudshoorn and Trevor Pinch, eds., *How Users Matter: The Co-Construction of Users and Technologies,* Inside Technology (Cambridge, Mass.: MIT Press, 2003), 8.

35. Susan M. Schweik, *The Ugly Laws: Disability in Public* (New York: New York University Press, 2010).

36. Anna Carden-Coyne, *Reconstructing the Body: Classicism, Modernism, and the First World War* (Oxford: Oxford University Press, 2009), 22; David Serlin, *Replaceable You: Engineering the Body in Postwar America* (Chicago: University of Chicago Press, 2004), 12; Beth Linker, *War's Waste: Rehabilitation in World War I America* (Chicago: University of Chicago Press, 2011).

37. I appropriate the terms "entanglement" and "sedimentation" from Karen Barad, *Meeting the Universe Halfway* (Durham, N.C.: Duke University Press, 2007).

38. Sandra Harding, *Whose Science? Whose Knowledge? Thinking from Women's Lives* (Ithaca, N.Y.: Cornell University Press, 1991), 10.

39. My concept of crip technoscience was first introduced in Aimi Hamraie, "Cripping Feminist Technoscience," *Hypatia* 30, no. 1 (2014): 307–13. This concept references and builds on feminist STS. See, for example, Beatriz da Costa and Kavita Phillip, eds., *Tactical Biopolitics: Art, Activism, and Technoscience* (Cambridge, Mass.: MIT Press, 2008), xvii–xxii; Michelle Murphy, *Seizing the Means of Reproduction;* Elizabeth A. Wilson, *Psychosomatic: Feminism and the Neurological Body* (Durham, N.C.: Duke University Press, 2004); Barad, *Meeting the Universe Halfway.*

40. On material culture as an approach to the history of disability, see Katherine Ott, "Disability Things," in *Disability Histories,* ed. Susan Burch and Michael Rembis (Urbana: University of Illinois Press, 2014), 119–35.

1. Normate Template

1. Leslie Kanes Weisman, "Women's Environmental Rights: A Manifesto," in *Gender Space Architecture: An Interdisciplinary Introduction,* ed. Iain Borden, Barbara Penner, and Jane Rendell (London: Routledge, 2000), 1–5.

2. Elaine Ostroff, "Universal Design: The New Paradigm," in *Universal Design Handbook,* ed. Wolfgang F. E. Preiser and Elaine Ostroff (New York: McGraw-Hill, 2001), 1.9.

3. Stephen M. Stigler, "Francis Galton's Account of the Invention of Correlation," *Statistical Science* 4, no. 2 (1989): 73–79; Michel Foucault, *Security, Territory, Population: Lectures at the Collège de France, 1977–1978* (New York: Picador, 2009), 29–49, 55–86.

4. Lennard J. Davis, "Constructing Normalcy: The Bell Curve, the Novel, and the Invention of the Disabled Body in the Nineteenth Century," in *The Disability Studies Reader,* 2nd ed., ed. Lennard J. Davis (New York: Routledge, 2006), 3–16.

5. Genealogies of normate templates in architecture include (sans analysis of disability) Hosey, "Hidden Lines"; Emmons and Mihalache, "Architectural Handbooks and the User Experience"; Georges Teyssot, "Norm and Type: Variations on a Theme," in *Architecture and the Sciences: Exchanging Metaphors,* ed. Antoine Picon and Alessandra Ponte (Princeton, N.J.: Princeton Architectural Press, 2003), 140–73.

6. Vitruvius, *Ten Books on Architecture* (New York: Cambridge University Press, 2001), 72, 14. On the influence of Greek mathematics on Vitruvius, see Richard Padovan, *Proportion: Science, Philosophy, Architecture* (New York: Taylor and Francis, 2002), 305–6; Alexander Tzonis, *Towards a Non-Oppressive Architecture* (Cambridge, Mass.: MIT Press, 1972), 20, 27; Henry Guerlac, "Copernicus and Aristotle's Cosmos," *Journal of the History of Ideas* 29, no. 1 (1968): 109–13.

7. Vitruvius, *Ten Books on Architecture,* 73.

8. Rob Imrie, "Architects' Conceptions of the Human Body," *Environment and Planning D: Society and Space* 21, no. 1 (2003): 47–65; Rudolph Wittkower, *Architectural Principles in the Age of Humanism* (New York: W. W. Norton, 1971), 7; Padovan, *Proportion,* 82, 106.

9. Vitruvius, *Ten Books on Architecture*, 3.

10. In the Renaissance revival of architecture as an aesthetic (rather than functional) discipline, da Vinci renewed interest in Vitruvius by retaining epistemological associations of the body with nature and nature with the cosmos. See Dennis Cosgrove, "Ptolemy and Vitruvius: Spatial Representation in the Sixteenth-Century Texts and Commentaries," in *Architecture and the Sciences: Exchanging Metaphors*, ed. Antoine Picon and Alessandra Ponte (Princeton, N.J.: Princeton Architectural Press, 2003), 22–24.

11. Toby Lester, *Da Vinci's Ghost: Genius, Obsession, and How Leonardo Created the World in His Own Image* (New York: Free Press, 2012), 40.

12. On the professionalization of drafting as distinct from architects' work, see George Johnston, *Drafting Culture: A Social History of Architectural Graphic Standards* (Cambridge, Mass.: MIT Press, 2008); David Brain, "Practical Knowledge and Occupational Control: The Professionalization of Architecture in the United States," *Sociological Forum* 6, no. 2 (1991): 239–68.

13. Indra Kagis McEwen, *Vitruvius: Writing the Body of Architecture* (Cambridge, Mass.: MIT Press, 2003), 2; William Wetmore Story, *Proportions of the Human Figure, According to the Canon, for Practical Use* (London: Chapman and Hall, 1864), 21–23, 25.

14. Michel Foucault, "The Ethics of the Concern of the Self as a Practice of Freedom," in *Ethics, Subjectivity, and Truth,* ed. Paul Rabinow (New York: New Press, 1997), 281.

15. Evelyn Hammonds and Rebecca Herzig, *The Nature of Difference: Sciences of Race in the United States from Jefferson to Genomics* (Cambridge, Mass.: MIT Press, 2008), 148; Daniel Kevles, *In the Name of Eugenics: Genetics and the Uses of Human Heredity* (Berkeley: University of California Press, 1985), 14–15; Stephen Jay Gould, *The Mismeasure of Man* (New York: W. W. Norton, 1981), 108, 116, 171; Allan Sekula, "The Body and the Archive," *October* 39 (Winter 1986): 20.

16. Stephen Stigler, *The History of Statistics: The Measurement of Uncertainty before 1900* (Cambridge, Mass.: Harvard University Press, 2000), 170; Gould, *The Mismeasure of Man,* 108, 116, 171.

17. Ian Hacking, *The Taming of Chance* (Cambridge: Cambridge University Press, 1990), 180–88.

18. Adolphe Quetelet, *Sur l'homme et le développement de ses facultés, ou essai de physique sociale* (Paris: Bachelier, 1835). Quetelet charted data of Scottish soldiers' chest measurements, discovering that they fell along what mathematicians refer to as a "Gaussian curve."

19. As Ian Hacking explains, Quetelet's rendering of human statistics on the bell curve "transformed the theory of measuring unknown physical quantities, with a definite probable error, into the theory of measuring ideal or abstract properties of a population. Because these could be subjected to the same formal techniques they became real quantities. This is a crucial step in the taming of chance. It began to turn statistical laws that were merely descriptive of large-scale regularities into laws of nature and society that dealt in underlying truths and causes" (*Taming of Chance,* 107–8).

20. Tobin Siebers, *Disability Theory* (Ann Arbor: University of Michigan Press, 2008), 8.

21. Hayward, "'Good Design Is Largely a Matter of Common Sense.'"

22. "Boundary work" is a term that sociologists of science use to describe the ways that differences and boundaries are drawn between interests, concepts, and other phenomena. See Thomas Gieryn, "Boundary-Work and the Demarcation of Science from Non-Science: Strains and Interests in Professional Ideologies of Scientists," *American Sociological Review* 48, no. 6 (1983): 781–95.

23. Le Corbusier, "Eyes Which Do Not See: Automobiles," in *The Industrial Design Reader,* ed. Carma Gorman (New York: Allworth Press, 2003), 107.

24. Le Corbusier, *The Modulor: A Harmonious Measure to the Human Scale, Universally Applicable to Architecture and Mechanics* (1954; repr., Boston: Birkhäuser, 2004).

25. On the "view from nowhere," see Donna J. Haraway, "Situated Knowledges," in *Simians, Cyborgs, and Women: The Reinvention of Nature* (New York: Routledge, 1991), 183–202.

26. Michel Foucault, *Archaeology of Knowledge and the Discourse on Language*, trans. A. M. Sheridan Smith (New York: Vintage Books, 2010), 198.

27. Buckminster Fuller, "Universal Architecture" (1932), in *Programs and Manifestoes on 20th-Century Architecture*, ed. Ulrich Conrads (Cambridge, Mass.: MIT Press, 1975), 128–36.

28. Congrès internationaux d'architecture moderne (CIAM), "Charter of Athens," in *Programs and Manifestoes on 20th-Century Architecture*, ed. Ulrich Conrads (Cambridge, Mass.: MIT Press, 1975), 142.

29. Rob Imrie, "The Interrelationships between Building Regulations and Architects' Practices," in *Papers in "The Codification and Regulation of Architects' Practices,"* ed. Rob Imrie and Emma Street (London: King's College, 2007).

30. Chris Chapman, Allison Carey, and Liat Ben-Moshe, "Reconsidering Confinement: Interlocking Locations and Logics of Incarceration," in *Disability Incarcerated*, ed. Chris Chapman, Allison Carey, and Liat Ben-Moshe (New York: Palgrave Macmillan, 2014), 6–7; Mitchell and Snyder, *Cultural Locations of Disability*, 84–85.

31. On the "ugly laws" and public space in the United States, see Schweik, *The Ugly Laws*. On urban public space and feeble-mindedness, see Mitchell and Snyder, *Cultural Locations of Disability*, 84–85. On streamlining and eugenics, see Christina Cogdell, *Eugenic Design: Streamlining America in the 1930s* (Philadelphia: University of Pennsylvania Press, 2010). See also Adolf Loos, "Ornament and Crime," in *Programs and Manifestoes on 20th-Century Architecture*, ed. Ulrich Conrads (Cambridge, Mass.: MIT Press, 1975), 19–24.

32. Ernst Neufert, *Bauentwurfslehre [Architects' Data]* (Berlin: Bauwelt Verlag, 1936); Charles Ramsey and Harold Sleeper, *Architectural Graphic Standards* (New York: John Wiley and Sons, 1932).

33. On the Latin prefix "ortho-" and its relation to norms, see Hacking, *The Taming of Chance*, 162–63.

34. Emmons and Mihalache, "Architectural Handbooks and the User Experience," 40.

35. Ernest Irving Freese, *The Geometry of the Human Figure, American Architect and Architecture*, July 1934, 57–60. For several editions, the figures appear under "General Information" near the back of the book. See, for example, Charles Ramsey and Harold Sleeper, *Architectural Graphic Standards*, 5th ed. (New York: Wiley, 1962), 669. See also Hosey, "Hidden Lines," 109.

36. Hyungmin Pai, *The Portfolio and the Diagram: Architecture, Discourse, and Modernity in America* (Cambridge, Mass.: MIT Press, 2002), 348.

37. Anna G. Creadick, *Perfectly Average: The Pursuit of Normality in Postwar America* (Amherst: University of Massachusetts Press, 2010), 15.

38. Ibid., 28–32.

39. Rosemarie Garland-Thomson, "Eugenic World Building and Disability: The Strange World of Kazuo Ishiguro's *Never Let Me Go*," *Journal of Medical Humanities* (December 2015): 1–13.

40. On neutrality and the unmarked architectural inhabitant, see Imrie, "Architects' Conceptions of the Human Body," 47–65; Leslie Kanes Weisman, *Discrimination by Design: A Feminist Critique of the Man-Made Environment* (Urbana: University of Illinois Press, 1992); Jos Boys, "Neutral Gazes and Knowable Objects," in *Desiring Practices: Architecture, Gender, and the Interdisciplinary,*

ed. Katerina Rüedi, Sarah Wigglesworth, and Duncan McCorquodale (London: Black Dog Publishing, 1996), 32–45.

41. Hosey, "Hidden Lines," 105.

42. American Institute of Architects, *Architectural Graphic Standards,* 7th ed. (New York: Wiley, 1981), 2–8.

43. By the 1980s, Henry Dreyfuss Associates had acquired anthropometric data from the general population. However, earlier figures relied on military human factors data from World Wars I and II. Henry Dreyfuss, *The Measure of Man: Human Factors in Design,* 2nd ed. (New York: Whitney Library of Design, 1967), 5.

44. Henry Dreyfuss, *Designing for People* (1955; repr., New York: Allworth Press, 2003). On Dreyfuss's career, see Russell Flinchum, *Henry Dreyfuss, Industrial Designer: The Man in the Brown Suit* (New York: Rizzoli, 1997). Dreyfuss had been a theater designer for Norman Bell Geddes, a designer and eugenics proponent. See Cogdell, *Eugenic Design,* 3.

45. "Configuration" is a term I borrow from Nelly Oudshoorn and Trevor Pinch, *How Users Matter: The Co-Construction of Users and Technologies,* Inside Technology (Cambridge, Mass.: MIT Press, 2003), 8.

46. Dreyfuss, *The Measure of Man,* 4.

47. Ibid. On this passage as a reflection of ergonomics as an emerging science, see John Harwood, "The Interface: Ergonomics and the Aesthetics of Survival," in *Governing by Design: Architecture, Economy, and the Politics of the Twentieth Century* (Pittsburgh: University of Pittsburgh Press, 2012), 78–80.

48. Michel Foucault, *Abnormal: Lectures at the Collège de France, 1974–1975,* trans. Graham Burchell (New York: Picador, 2003), 33.

49. Dreyfuss, *The Measure of Man,* 4.

50. Henry Dreyfuss, "Tailoring the Product to Fit," *Industrial Design* 7, no. 6 (1960): 68–81.

51. Ibid.; Henry Dreyfuss Associates, "Background Data: Joe & Josie Portfolio," July 26, 1960, Whitney Publications, Dreyfuss Collection, Cooper Hewitt, Smithsonian Design Museum. This portfolio was published as the book *The Measure of Man* in 1960 and the drawings were included as loose pages in an attached folder.

52. William Wilson Atkin, letter to Dick Stinette (Henry Dreyfuss Associates), May 9, 1961, Henry Dreyfuss Collection, Cooper Hewitt, Smithsonian Design Museum.

53. Henry Dreyfuss Associates, "Bibliography," 1973, folder 5.9, Henry Dreyfuss Collection, Cooper Hewitt, Smithsonian Design Museum.

54. Dreyfuss, *The Measure of Man* (1967), 3.

55. Ibid., 4.

56. Ibid., 27.

57. On the genealogy of autism symptoms and diagnosis, see Steve Silberman, *Neurotribes: The Legacy of Autism and the Future of Neurodiversity* (New York: Penguin Random House, 2015), 261–334.

58. Dreyfuss, *The Measure of Man* (1967), page R.

59. Alvin Tilley notes that the majority of the firm's data was derived from military sources, which depicted "90% of the adult males acceptable for certain segments of military service," and that even in the 1960s when the U.S. Department of Health, Education, and Welfare made civilian data available, it was still not as "comprehensive as the military data." See Alvin Tilley, *The Measure of Man and Woman: Human Factors in Design* (New York: Whitney Design Library, 1993), 9.

60. Niels Diffrient, Alvin R. Tilley, and Joan C. Bardagjy, *Humanscale 1/2/3: A Portfolio of Information* (Cambridge, Mass.: MIT Press, 1974).

61. The rise of "barrier-free design" and its legal enforcement is detailed in chapters 3–6.

62. Ronald Mace, *An Illustrated Handbook of the Handicapped Section of the North Carolina State Building Code* (Raleigh: North Carolina Building Code Council, 1974).

63. Niels Diffrient, Alvin R. Tilley, and Joan C. Bardagjy, *Humanscale 4/5/6: A Portfolio of Information* (Cambridge, Mass.: MIT Press, 1981).

2. Flexible Users

Chapter epigraph: Krystyna Golonka, "Ronald Mace and His Philosophy of Universal Design," *Ergonomia: An International Journal of Ergonomics and Human Factors* 28, no. 3 (2006): 189.

1. See, for example, Karen A. Franck, "A Feminist Approach to Architecture: Acknowledging Women's Ways of Knowing," in *Gender Space Architecture: An Interdisciplinary Introduction*, ed. Iain Borden, Barbara Penner, and Jane Rendell (London: Routledge, 2000), 300.

2. Center for Universal Design, "Principles of Universal Design." For examples of discourses of flexibility within Universal Design, see Jim Weiker, "Universal Design Lab—A Dream Home for User of Wheelchair—To Open for Public Tours," *Columbus Dispatch,* October 19, 2014; Melissa Stanton, "5 Questions for Richard Duncan," *AARP Livable Communities,* July 2014, http://www .aarp.org/livable-communities/info-2014/interview-richard-duncan-better-living-design.html; Martin C. Petersen, "Total Access," *Metropolis* magazine, March 2007.

3. David Meister, *The History of Human Factors and Ergonomics* (Mahwah, N.J.: Lawrence Erlbaum Associates, 1999), 25; Avigail Sachs, "Architects, Users, and the Social Sciences in Postwar America," in *Use Matters: An Alternative History of Architecture*, ed. Kenny Cupers (London: Routledge, 2013), 72. On flexibility and Cold War–era spatial planning, see William J. Rankin, "The Epistemology of the Suburbs: Knowledge, Production, and Corporate Laboratory Design," *Critical Inquiry* 36 (Summer 2010): 777–80. Accounts of the "user" and "flexibility" in relation to architecture are found in Adrian Forty, *Words and Buildings: A Vocabulary of Modern Architecture* (London: Thames & Hudson, 2000), 312–15, 142–48. In contrast to Adrian Forty, who argues that the user "was always a person unknown" (312), this chapter is concerned with how specific types of users and knowledge about them materialized. Accounts of twentieth-century ergonomics attribute the first use of the term to British operations researcher K. F. H. Murrell in the late 1940s. See W. T. Singleton, *The Body at Work: Biological Ergonomics* (Cambridge: Cambridge University Press, 1982), 1–2; John Harwood, "The Interface: Ergonomics and the Aesthetics of Survival," in *Governing by Design: Architecture, Economy, and the Politics of the Twentieth Century* (Pittsburgh: University of Pittsburgh Press, 2012), 74. Murrell's work focused on introducing data on human variation to industrial engineers. K. F. H. Murrell, *Data on Human Performance for Engineering Designers* (London: Engineering, 1957); K. F. H. Murrell, *Fitting the Job to the Worker: A Study of American and European Research into Working Conditions in Industry* (Paris: Organization for European Economic Cooperation, 1958); K. F. H. Murrell, *Human Performance in Industry* (New York: Reinhold, 1965).

4. Singleton, *The Body at Work,* 1.

5. Few historians have considered the role that disability has played in the development of user-centered design. One exception is Bess Williamson, "Getting a Grip: Disability in American Industrial Design of the Late Twentieth Century," *Winterthur Portfolio* 46, no. 4 (2012): 214–15.

6. Arthur Williams, quoted in "'Labor Turnover,' an Amazing Industrial Waste," *International Steam Engineer* 34 (January 1818): 51.

7. For example, the adoption of "user" in reference to the operation of guns and weapons. See William Greener, *The Science of Gunnery, as Applied to the Use and Construction of Fire Arms* (London: E. Churton, 1846), vii.

8. Anson Rabinbach, *The Human Motor: Energy, Fatigue, and the Origins of Modernity* (Berkeley: University of California Press, 1990), 45, 90.

9. Wojciech Jastrzębowski, "An Outline of Ergonomics: I.e. Science of Work, Based on Truths Taken from the Natural Science" (1857), in *International Encyclopedia of Ergonomics and Human Factors*, 2nd ed., vol. 1., ed. Waldemar Karkowski (Boca Raton: CRC Press, 2006), 161–75.

10. Ibid., 163.

11. Ibid.

12. Ibid., 168.

13. Near the end of the first Industrial Revolution, American sculptor Horatio Greenough articulated an early version of the doctrine of architectural functionalism. See Horatio Greenough, "The Law of Adaptation" (1852), in *The Industrial Design Reader*, ed. Carma Gorman (New York: Allworth Press, 2003), 11–18. See also Forty, *Words and Buildings*, 175–77.

14. Robert Scott Burn, *The Grammar of House Planning: Hints on Arranging and Modifying Plans of Cottages, Street-Houses, Farm-Houses, Villas, Mansions, and Out-Buildings* (Edinburgh: A. Fullarton, 1864), 3.

15. Rabinbach, *The Human Motor*, 52.

16. Robert Scott Burn, *Practical Ventilation as Applied to Public, Domestic, and Agricultural Structures* (Edinburgh: William Blackwood and Sons, 1850); Robert Scott Burn, *The Illustrated London Practical Geometry: And Its Application to Architectural Drawing; For the Use of Schools and Students* (London: Ingram, Cooke, 1853); Robert Scott Burn, *The Steam Engine: Its History and Mechanism; Being Descriptions and Illustrations of the Stationary, Locomotive, and Marine Engine; For the Use of Schools and Students* (London: H. Ingram, 1854).

17. Cliff White, *The Steam User: A Book of Instruction for Engineers and Steam Users* (New York: C. A. White, 1890); Robert Scott Burn, ed., *The Steam Engine User, Being Practical Descriptions and Illustrations of the Stationary Steam Engine in Its Various Forms* (London: Ward, Lock, and Bowden, 1894). See also David Meister and Thomas G. O'Brien, "The History of Human Factors Testing and Evaluation," in *Handbook of Human Factors Testing and Evaluation*, ed. S. Charlton and T. G. O'Brien (Mahwah, N.J.: Lawrence Erlbaum Associates, 1996), 6–8, on human performance testing of weapons; Rabinbach, *The Human Motor*, 117.

18. George Stocking, ed., *Bones, Bodies, Behavior: Essays on Biological Anthropology* (Madison: University of Wisconsin Press, 1988), 5; S. S. Adebisi, "Medical Impacts of Anthropometric Records," *Annals of African Medicine* 7, no. 1 (2008): 42–47; Kavita Philip, *Civilizing Natures: Race, Resources, and Modernity in Colonial South India* (New Brunswick, N.J.: Rutgers University Press, 2004), 99; Claude Blanckaert, "On the Origins of French Ethnology: William Edwards and the Doctrine of Race," in *Bones, Bodies, Behavior: Essays on Biological Anthropology*, ed. George W. Stocking Jr. (Madison: University of Wisconsin Press, 1988), 49.

19. The history of the Sanitary Commission appears in Charles J. Stillé, *History of the United States Sanitary Commission, Being the General Report of Its Work during the War of the Rebellion* (Philadelphia: J. B. Lippincott, 1866). The commission led efforts on behalf of civilians to support the war effort, in both fundraising and providing care. Among its notable leaders was landscape architect Frederick Law Olmstead, who left his post in New York to serve as executive secretary. See Ianthe Jeanne Dugan, "Civil War Letters Shed Light on Pain of Troops' Families," *Wall Street*

Journal, June 22, 2007. For chronicles of Olmstead's work at the commission, see *The Papers of Frederick Law Olmsted,* vol. 4, *Defending the Union: The Civil War and the U.S. Sanitary Commission, 1861–1863* (Baltimore: Johns Hopkins University Press, 1986).

20. Stillé, *History of the United States Sanitary Commission,* 453.

21. Ibid., 453, 459. Olmstead was responsible for expanding the emphasis on anthropometrics to include "social statistics." See Olmstead, *The Papers of Frederick Law Olmsted,* 4:51. This is around the time that Francis Galton began publishing about statistics and eugenics. See Kevles, *In the Name of Eugenics,* 3–4, 13–14.

22. Stillé, *History of the United States Sanitary Commission,* 460.

23. Ibid.

24. Benjamin Apthorp Gould, *Investigations in the Military and Anthropological Statistics of American Soldiers* (New York: Arno Press, 1869).

25. Ibid., 107.

26. See Lundy Braun, "Black Lungs and White Lungs," in *Breathing Race into the Machine: The Surprising Career of the Spirometer from Plantation to Genetics* (Minneapolis: University of Minnesota Press, 2014), 27–54.

27. Gould, *Investigations in the Military and Anthropological Statistics of American Soldiers,* 464.

28. Ibid., 153.

29. Ibid., 115.

30. Ibid., 244.

31. Statisticians such as Francis Galton, a eugenicist, used statistical calculations of the average to determine standard deviations, which they used to make claims about racial difference. See Ruth Schwartz Cowan, "Francis Galton's Statistical Ideas: The Influence of Eugenics," *Isis* 63, no. 4 (1972): 509–28; Hacking, *The Taming of Chance,* 183–84.

32. Gould, *Investigations in the Military and Anthropological Statistics of American Soldiers,* v.

33. On a similar paradox in biomedical research, see Steven Epstein, *Inclusion: The Politics of Difference in Medical Research* (Chicago: University of Chicago Press, 2007).

34. Edward Hartwell, "A Preliminary Report on Anthropometry in the United States," *Publications of the American Statistical Association* 3, no. 24 (1893): 557; Noël Cameron and Laura L. Jones, "History, Methods, and General Application of Anthropometry in Human Biology," in *Human Evolutionary Biology,* ed. Michael P. Muehlenbein (New York: Cambridge University Press, 2010), 94.

35. See Cameron and Jones, "History, Methods, and General Application of Anthropometry in Human Biology," 91 and 94–99, for detailed descriptions of anthropometric instruments in historical perspective.

36. Frank Spencer, "Anthropometry," in *History of Physical Anthropology: An Encyclopedia,* vol. 1, ed. Frank Spencer (New York: Garland, 1997), 80–88.

37. Cameron and Jones, "History, Methods, and General Application of Anthropometry in Human Biology," 94.

38. The term "epistemic object," which describes objects of scientific study once they are deemed knowable, is attributed to Hans-Jörg Rheinberger, *Toward a History of Epistemic Things: Synthesizing Proteins in the Test Tube* (Stanford: Stanford University Press, 1997), 29.

39. Kevles, *In the Name of Eugenics,* 82.

40. Harris Wilder, *A Laboratory Manual of Anthropometry* (Philadelphia: Blakiston, 1920), 151. Foucault describes the work of a similar position in bodily discipline, particularly in prisons, schools, and the military. Foucault, *Discipline and Punish,* 15.

41. Charles Davenport and Albert Love, *Army Anthropology: The Medical Department of the United States Army in the World War* (Washington, D.C.: Government Printing Office, 1921).

42. Charles Davenport and Albert Love, *Defects Found in Drafted Men: Statistical Information Compiled from the United States Surgeon General's Office* (Washington, D.C.: Government Printing Office, 1920), 25, 51; Davenport and Love, *Army Anthropology*.

43. Davenport and Love, *Defects Found in Drafted Men*, 19–24.

44. Ibid., 25. This occurs throughout the text, which examines "defect" in relation to state-based locations. The authors frequently comment on the distribution of immigrants and their dominant physical features or illness experiences as explanations for morphological phenomena. For instance, they correlate small chest size to inherited congenital conditions, as well as to hookworm infestations, which they characterize as prevalent in "French-Canadian immigrants" and the "agricultural Negroes of the South and agricultural Whites of the South" but not in the urban citizens of the northeastern United States (34).

45. H. T. Hertzberg, G. S. Daniels, and E. Churchill, *Anthropometry of Flying Personnel—1950*, WADC Technical Report 52-321 (Wright-Patterson Air Force Base, Ohio: Wright Air Development Center, 1953), 1.

46. Aleš Hrdlička, *Anthropometry* (Philadelphia: Wistar Institute of Anatomy and Biology, 1920), 46.

47. Meister, *The History of Human Factors and Ergonomics*, 147; Meister and O'Brien, "The History of Human Factors Testing and Evaluation," 6.

48. Sekula, "The Body and the Archive."

49. Georges Canguilhem, *The Normal and the Pathological* (1966; repr., New York: Zone Books, 1991), 42, 110–11, 122–23.

50. Horace Wells, *A History of the Discovery of the Application of Nitrous Oxide Gas, Ether, and Other Vapors to Surgical Operations* (Hartford: J. Gaylord Wells, 1847); Joseph Lister, "On the Antiseptic Principle in the Practice of Surgery," *British Medical Journal* 2, no. 351 (1867): 246–48; Henri Jacques Garrigues, *Practical Guide in Antiseptic Midwifery in Hospital and Private Practice* (Detroit: G. S. Davis, 1886).

51. Stephen Mihm, "A Limb Which Shall Be Presentable in Polite Society," in *Artificial Parts, Practical Lives: Modern Histories of Prosthetics*, ed. Katherine Ott, David Serlin, and Stephen Mihm (New York: New York University Press, 2002), 284.

52. Rabinbach, *The Human Motor*, 86–87.

53. U.S. Orthopedic Institute, "Pamphlet for the Application of Improved Anatomical Machinery to the Treatment of Every Variety of Deformity," ca. 1851, Warshaw Collection of Business Americana, Archives Center, National Museum of American History, Smithsonian Institution.

54. Ibid., 5.

55. Beth Linker, *War's Waste: Rehabilitation in World War I America* (Chicago: University of Chicago Press, 2011), 2; Mihm, "A Limb Which Shall Be Presentable in Polite Society," 283.

56. Mihm, "A Limb Which Shall Be Presentable in Polite Society," 290.

57. A. A. Marks, *Artificial Limbs with India Rubber Hands and Feet* (New York: William B. Smyth, 1867), 37.

58. James Foster, "Illustrated Circular," ca. 1868, Warshaw Collection of Business Americana, Archives Center, National Museum of American History, Smithsonian Institution.

59. A. A. Marks, *Manual of Artificial Limbs: Copiously Illustrated* (New York: A. A. Marks, 1905).

60. Mihm, "A Limb Which Shall Be Presentable in Polite Society," 290.

61. Mary Ellen Zuckerman and Mary L. Carsky, "Contribution of Women to U.S. Marketing Thought: The Consumers' Perspective, 1900–1940," *Journal of the Academy of Marketing Science* 18, no. 4 (1990): 313–18.

62. Marks, *Manual of Artificial Limbs,* 226–29.

63. Ibid., 290.

64. Heather Perry, "Re-Arming the Disabled Veteran: Artificially Rebuilding State and Society in World War One Germany," in *Artificial Lives, Practical Parts,* ed. Katherine Ott, David Serlin, and Stephen Mihm (New York: New York University Press, 2002), 93.

65. Frederick Winslow Taylor, *Principles of Scientific Management* (Minneapolis: Filiquarian, 1911), 8.

66. Ibid., 11, 32–33.

67. James Hartness, *The Human Factor in Works Engineering* (London: McGraw-Hill, 1912), 24–25.

68. Ibid., v.

69. James Hartness, *Hartness Flat Turret Lathe Manual: A Hand Book for Operators* (London: Jones and Lamson Machine, 1910), 5.

70. Hartness, *The Human Factor in Works Engineering,* 32–35.

71. Ibid., 112–13.

72. Lillian Gilbreth, *The Psychology of Management: The Function of the Mind in Determining, Teaching and Installing Methods of Least Waste* (New York: Sturgis and Walton, 1914), 223.

73. Ibid., 24.

74. Ibid., 27.

75. Ibid., 49–50.

76. Frank B. Gilbreth, "Measurement and Standardization," in *The Human Factor in Industrial Preparedness: Complete Proceedings of the National Conference* (Chicago: Western Efficiency Society, 1917), 178–86. On the rise of rehabilitation as a medical and vocational corrective in relation to scientific management, see Glenn Grittier and Arnold Arluke, *The Making of Rehabilitation: A Political Economy of Medical Specialization, 1890–1980* (Berkeley: University of California Press, 1985), 38–60.

77. Gilbreth, "Measurement and Standardization," 179.

78. Elspeth Brown, "The Prosthetics of Management: Time Motion Study, Photography, and the Industrialized Body in World War I America," in *Artificial Parts, Practical Lives: Modern Histories of Prosthetics,* ed. Katherine Ott, David Serlin, and Stephen Mihm (New York: New York University Press, 2002), 249–81.

79. Henri-Jacques Stiker, *A History of Disability,* trans. William Sayers (Ann Arbor: University of Michigan Press, 2000), 125.

80. Williamson, "Getting a Grip," 213–36.

81. Gilbreth, "Measurement and Standardization," 179.

82. Rabinbach, *The Human Motor,* 269.

83. Gilbreth, "Measurement and Standardization," 186.

84. Lillian Gilbreth and Frank Gilbreth, *Motion Study for the Handicapped* (London: Routledge, 1920), 68.

85. Ibid., xi.

86. Gilbreth, "Measurement and Standardization," 179.

87. Ibid., xiv.

88. Ibid., 182–83.

89. Stiker, *A History of Disability*, 124; Serlin, *Replaceable You*, 115, 124.

90. Gilbreth and Gilbreth, *Motion Study for the Handicapped*, xv.

91. Ibid.

92. Garland-Thomson, "Disability and Representation."

93. Edna Yost, in collaboration with Lillian Gilbreth, *Normal Lives for the Disabled* (New York: Macmillan, 1944), vii.

94. Howard Rusk and Eugene Taylor, *New Hope for the Handicapped* (New York: Harper and Brothers, 1949), quoted in Book Reviews, *Journal of Bone and Joint Surgery* 32, no. 2 (April 1950): 472.

95. Serlin, *Replaceable You*, 12–13; Carden-Coyne, *Reconstructing the Body*, 22. On the cultural influence of rehabilitation, see also Jennifer James, "'On Such Legs Are Left Me': Gwendolyn Brooks, World War II, and the Politics of Rehabilitation," in *Feminist Disability Studies*, ed. Kim Q. Hall (Bloomington: Indiana University Press, 2011), 136–58.

96. Michael C. Wood and John C. Wood, eds., *Frank and Lillian Gilbreth: Critical Evaluations in Business and Management*, vol. 1 (New York: Routledge, 2003), 128; Jane Lancaste, *Making Time: Lillian Moller Gilbreth—A Life beyond "Cheaper by the Dozen."* (Lebanon, N.H.: University Press of New England, 2004), 315. See also Charles R. Shrader, *History of Operations Research in the United States*, vol. 2, *1961–1973* (Washington, D.C.: Government Printing Office, 2008), 7–12.

97. Meister, *The History of Human Factors and Ergonomics*, 148.

98. Morley Gray Whillans, *Anthropometry and Human Engineering: A Symposium on Anthropometry, Human Engineering and Related Subjects* (London: Butterworths Scientific, 1955), 113.

99. David Meister and Valerie Gawron, "Measurement in Aviation Systems," in *Handbook of Aviation Human Factors*, ed. John A. Wise, V. David Hopkin, and Daniel J. Garland (Boca Raton: CRC Press, 2010), 3-1.

100. Cogdell, *Eugenic Design*, 5.

101. M. W. Ireland, Charles Davenport, and Albert Love, *Army Anthropology: The Medical Department of the United States Army in the World War* (Washington, D.C.: Government Printing Office, 1921); Hertzberg, Daniels, and Churchill, *Anthropometry of Flying Personnel—1950*, 1.

102. The collection of anthropometric data for uniforms after World War I was one of the first human factors studies conducted by trained scientists using the scientific method (which, in this case, included the eugenicist and statistician Charles Davenport, among others). See Ruth O'Brien, *An Annotated List of Literature References on Garment Sizes and Body Measurements*, U.S. Department of Agriculture, Miscellaneous Publication no. 78 (Washington, D.C.: U.S. Department of Agriculture, 1930), 3.

103. Meister and Gawron, "Measurement in Aviation Systems," 3-1–3-2.

104. Robert Procter and Trisha Van Zandt, *Human Factors in Simple and Complex Systems* (Boca Raton: CRC Press, 1993), 12–13; Meister and Gawron, "Measurement in Aviation Systems," 3-1–3-2. Some of these programs were formally established in the late twentieth century, but human factors preceded them within the military on the whole.

105. Whillans, *Anthropometry and Human Engineering*, 113.

106. Marcy Babbit, "As a Woman Sees Design: An Interview with Belle Kogan" (1935), in *The Industrial Design Reader*, ed. Carma Gorman (New York: Allworth Press, 2003), 138–39.

107. H. H. Manchester, "Recent Investigations of Average Proportions," *Clothing Trade Journal* 27 (1926): 18–20; O'Brien, "An Annotated List of Literature References on Garment Sizes and Body Measurements," 3.

108. Meister, *The History of Human Factors and Ergonomics*, 152–53.

109. See chapter 1.

110. Murrell, *Human Performance in Industry*, 146.

111. Ibid., 160.

112. Ibid.

3. All Americans

1. Bernard McNulty, *Strength for the Fight: A History of Black Americans in the Military* (New York: Free Press, 1986), 204–5.

2. Raymond Frey, "Truman's Speech to the NAACP, 29 June 1947," in *The Civil Rights Legacy of Harry S. Truman,* ed. Raymond H. Geselbracht (Kirskville, Mo.: Truman State University Press, 2007), 97. Regarding the line "When I say all Americans I mean all Americans," Frey notes that Truman had "penciled [it] in himself during the writing process" (97).

3. Timothy J. Nugent, "Founder of the University of Illinois Disabled Students' Program and the National Wheelchair Basketball Association, Pioneer in Architectural Access," conducted by Fred Pelka, 2004–5, Oral History Center, Bancroft Library, University of California, Berkeley, 2009, xiii (Fred Pelka, "Interview History").

4. Keith Roberts and Ray Crigger, "Wheelchair Vets Trek to Springfield in Vain Effort to Keep Division Open," *Galesburg Illini* 3, no. 20 (1949), 1; "Disabled Vets Protest Closing of U. of I. Unit," *Chicago Tribune*, April 2, 1949, 10; Nugent, "Founder," 17. Asked whether any black students were part of the group, Nugent reported that there were none until the second year (29).

5. Nugent, "Founder," 46.

6. Ibid.

7. Ibid., 49.

8. The University of Michigan's Institute for Human Adjustment extended the rehabilitation frame to gerontology and the concerns of aging citizens in 1948 by holding several well-attended annual national conferences on topics such as the "Rehabilitation of the Handicapped Worker over Forty." In 1952 the conference focused on "Housing the Aging" and included panels on housing and architecture for both disabled and nondisabled elderly people.

9. My approach here draws from rhetorical histories of disability. See, for example, Jay Dolmage, *Disability Rhetoric* (Syracuse: Syracuse University Press, 2014), 63–92; Allison Hitt, "Dis/Identification with Disability Advocacy: Fraternity Brothers Fight against Architectural Barriers, 1967–1975," *Rhetoric Review* 34, no. 3 (2015): 336–56. My analysis of race focuses on the racialization of blackness and whiteness in the mid-twentieth-century United States. This focus reflects my primary sources, but future research should consider the racialized construction of barrier-free design in relation to other racial categories. Likewise, my focus on the figure of the white, middle-class disabled woman arises from the prevalence of this figure in primary source documents. Further investigation on more legible queer gender and sexual identities in relation to barrier-free design is encouraged.

10. Ostroff, "Universal Design," 1.3. These types of claims are further contextualized in chapters 6 and 7.

11. Elizabeth Grace Hale, *Making Whiteness: The Culture of Segregation in the South, 1890–1940* (New York: Vintage Books, 1999), xi, 151–67. On Jim Crow–era built environments, see Elizabeth Guffey, "Knowing Their Space: Signs of Jim Crow in the Segregated South," *Design Issues* 28, no. 2 (2012): 41–60.

12. On whiteness in disability studies, see Bell, "Introducing White Disability Studies."

13. Daniel Bernardi, *The Birth of Whiteness: Race and the Emergence of U.S. Cinema* (New Brunswick, N.J.: Rutgers University Press, 1996), 1; Tracy Teslow, *Constructing Race: The Science of Bodies and Cultures in American Anthropology* (Cambridge: Cambridge University Press, 2014), 246–49.

14. Michelle Alexander, *The New Jim Crow: Mass Incarceration in the Age of Colorblindness* (New York: New Press, 2011), 2–3; Bernardi, *The Birth of Whiteness*, 1–2. While race-neutral ideology is typically associated with the post–Jim Crow era, the discourse of "all" performed similar work in eliding the realities of racial oppression in the midst of state-mandated segregation, essentially reinforcing the doctrine of "separate but equal."

15. Teresa Guess, "The Social Construction of Whiteness: Racism by Intent, Racism by Consequence," *Critical Sociology* 32, no. 4 (2006): 660–62.

16. Charles Mills, *The Racial Contract* (Ithaca, N.Y.: Cornell University Press, 1997), 97.

17. Sarah E. Chinn, *Technology and the Logic of American Racism: A Cultural History of the Body as Evidence* (New York: Continuum, 2000), 93–140.

18. Ibid., 103–6.

19. Ibid., 122, 126.

20. I borrow the term "redesigned" from Alexander, *The New Jim Crow*, 2.

21. Nirmala Erevelles, *Disability and Difference in Global Contexts: Enabling a Transformative Body Politic* (New York: Palgrave Macmillan, 2011), 165.

22. Ibid., 165–66. Ethnic studies scholar Lisa Lowe makes a similar, useful point about racialized "economies of affirmation and forgetting," wherein freedom becomes a celebrated affordance of Western democratic cultures in the majority world, while non-Western cultures are cast as "backward, uncivilized, and unfree." Lisa Lowe, *The Intimacies of Four Continents* (Durham, N.C.: Duke University Press, 2015), 3.

23. David Mitchell and Sharon Snyder frame this figure as an embodiment of "ablenationalism." See David Mitchell and Sharon Snyder, *The Biopolitics of Disability: Neoliberalism, Ablenationalism, and Peripheral Embodiment* (Ann Arbor: University of Michigan Press, 2015).

24. Gilbreth, "Measurement and Standardization."

25. Timothy Nugent, "Design of Buildings to Permit Their Use by the Physically Handicapped," in *New Building Research: Proceedings of the Conference of the Building Research Institute* (Washington, D.C.: National Academy of Sciences, 1960), 52. The notion of disabled people as "burdens" to society came from U.S. eugenicists, whose ideas informed Nazi efforts to eliminate disabled people. Henry Friedlander, *The Origins of Nazi Genocide: From Euthanasia to the Final Solution* (Chapel Hill: University of North Carolina Press, 2000), 7–9.

26. Leon Chatelain, "Architectural Barriers—A Blueprint for Action," in *A National Attack on Architectural Barriers* (Chicago: National Society for Crippled Children and Adults, 1965), 2.

27. Ibid., 4.

28. Mills, *The Racial Contract*, 83–89; Ally Day, "Resisting Disability, Claiming HIV: Introducing the Ability Contract and Conceptualizations of Liberal Citizenship," *Canadian Journal of Disability Studies* 3, no. 3 (2014): 113.

29. Mitchell and Snyder, *Cultural Locations of Disability*, 28, 71–72.

30. Harriet McBryde Johnson, "The Disability Gulag," *New York Times Magazine*, November 23, 2003, 1–6; Chapman, Carey, and Ben-Moshe, "Reconsidering Confinement," 8–9. On the institutionalization of nonwhite disabled, elderly, and low-income people in the early and mid-twentieth

centuries, see Richard Frank and Sherry Glied, *Better but Not Well: Mental Health Policy in the United States* (Baltimore: Johns Hopkins University Press, 2008), 8–20.

31. For instance, in 1944 the U.S. Supreme Court upheld the constitutionality of Japanese internment in *Korematsu v. United States*.

32. Douglas C. Baynton, "Disability and the Justification of Inequality in American History," in *The New Disability History: American Perspectives,* ed. Paul Longmore and Lauri Umanski (New York: New York University Press, 2011), 33–57.

33. Barry Trevelyan, Matthew Smallman-Raynor, and Andrew D. Cliff, "The Spatial Dynamics of Poliomyelitis in the United States: From Epidemic Emergence to Vaccine-Induced Retreat, 1910–1971," *Annals of the Association of American Geographers* 95, no. 2 (2005): 269–93.

34. Naomi Rogers, "Race and the Politics of Polio: Warm Springs, Tuskegee, and the March of Dimes," *American Journal of Public Health* 97, no. 5 (2007): 784–95.

35. On racial disparities to accessing the benefits of the G.I. Bill, see Ira Katznelson, *When Affirmative Action Was White* (New York: W. W. Norton, 2005), 111–39; Melissa Murray, "When War Is Work: The G.I. Bill, Citizenship, and the Civic Generation," *California Law Review* 96, no. 4 (2008): 967–98; Sarah H. Rose, "The Right to a College Education? The G.I. Bill, Public Law 16, and Disabled Veterans," *Journal of Policy History* 24, no. 1 (2012): 26–52.

36. Physically disabled people, particularly wheelchair users, gained access to public spaces with the availability of accessible built environments in some cities in the 1960s, but deinstitutionalization for intellectually and cognitively disabled people became a major point of disability struggle in the 1970s. See Fred Pelka, *What Have We Done: An Oral History of the Disability Rights Movement* (Amherst: University of Massachusetts Press, 2012), 312–23.

37. W. M. L. Wilkoff, *Practicing Universal Design: An Interpretation of the ADA* (New York: John Wiley & Sons, 1994), 14.

38. Dierdre L. Cobb, "Segregated Students at the University of Illinois, 1945–1955," *Journal of the Midwest History of Education Society* 24 (1997): 46–51; Carrie Franke, "Injustice Sheltered: Race Relations at the University of Illinois and Champaign-Urbana, 1945–1962" (PhD diss., University of Illinois at Urbana-Champaign, 1990), 61.

39. Franke, "Injustice Sheltered," 26–27. See also Natalie Prochaska, "'Old' Urban Renewal in Champaign-Urbana, 1960–1969," *The Public,* March 2016, http://publici.ucimc.org/old-urban -renewal-in-champaign-urbana-1960-1969/.

40. In his 2009 oral history, Nugent reports that there were black players on the wheelchair basketball team and black students at the university. When the team traveled to southern states, for instance, Nugent and other coaches apparently stayed in black hotels with the black players. See Nugent, "Founder," 102–3.

41. The American National Standards Institute was called the American Standards Association in 1961 and underwent several name changes in later years. For consistency, I use the contemporary abbreviation ANSI (rather than ANS). Nugent, "Founder," 126, describes this research. See also Nugent, "Design of Buildings."

42. Chatelain, "Architectural Barriers," 3.

43. "Minutes of the Sectional Committee Meeting," A.S.A. Project A-117, June 19, 1961, Box 1, Accessibility Standards Project File, 1955–74, University of Illinois Archives.

44. "Minutes of the Steering Committee," A.S.A. Project A-117, May 8, 1961, Box 1, Accessibility Standards Project File, 1955–74, University of Illinois Archives.

45. "Minutes: Organization Meeting, Sectional Committee on Facilities in Public Buildings for Persons with Physical Handicaps, A117," September 2, 1959, Box 1, Accessibility Standards Project File, 1955–74, University of Illinois Archives, 11.

46. Chatelain, "Architectural Barriers," 2.

47. "Minutes of the Steering Committee Meeting," A.S.A. Project A-117, June 12, 1961, Box 1, Accessibility Standards Project File, 1955–74, University of Illinois Archives.

48. "Minutes of the Steering Committee Meeting," A.S.A. Project A-117, May 18, 1961, Box 1, Accessibility Standards Project File, 1955–74, University of Illinois Archives.

49. "Minutes: Organization Meeting, Sectional Committee on Facilities in Public Buildings for Persons with Physical Handicaps, A117," 9.

50. Nugent, "Design of Buildings," 59.

51. Ibid., 56.

52. William Lotz, "Let's Stop Constructing Inaccessible Buildings," *The Constructor,* May 1962, 1–2.

53. Nugent, "Design of Buildings," 59.

54. Ibid.

55. Ibid., 52.

56. Chatelain, "Architectural Barriers," 2–3.

57. Nugent, "Design of Buildings," 52.

58. Ibid.

59. Barbara Penner, *Bathroom* (London: Reaktion Books, 2013), 200.

60. Selwyn Goldsmith, *Universal Design: A Manual of Practical Guidance for Architects* (New York: Routledge Architectural Press, 2000), 16. See also Selwyn Goldsmith, *Designing for the Disabled: The New Paradigm* (New York: Routledge Architectural Press, 1963).

61. For a concise overview of these policies and effects, see Martha R. Mahoney, "Residential Segregation and White Privilege," in *Critical White Studies: Looking behind the Mirror,* ed. Richard Delgado and Jean Stefancic (Philadelphia: Temple University Press, 1997), 273–75.

62. Robert Sickels, *The 1940s* (Westport, Conn.: Greenwood Press, 2004), 69–70.

63. Leon Chatelain and Donald Fearn, "That All May Enter," *Your Church,* October 1963, 1–2. On the segregation of U.S. churches in relation to housing and other factors, see Michael L. Owens, *God and Government in the Ghetto: The Politics of Church-State Collaboration in Black America* (Chicago: University of Chicago Press, 2007), 49, 68–69.

64. Chatelain and Fearn, "That All May Enter," 1–2. See also J. J. Gilbert, "Keep Handicapped in Mind, Group Urges Church Planners," *Catholic Standard,* March 31, 1966, 1, reprinted by the President's Committee on Employment of the Handicapped, Elaine Ostroff Collection, Archives Center, National Museum of American History, Smithsonian Institution.

65. Chatelain and Fearn, "That All May Enter," 1–2.

66. Ibid., 2.

67. Ronald Junius, "Twenty Million," 1966, 1–3, reprinted by the President's Committee on Employment of the Handicapped, Elaine Ostroff Collection, Archives Center, National Museum of American History, Smithsonian Institution.

68. "Banning Those Barriers," *Journal of American Insurance* 40, no. 9 (1964): 1–4.

69. Jayne Shover, "Architectural Barriers," *Home Safety Program Guide,* Summer 1962, 6–7.

70. Ibid.

71. Dolores Hayden, *The Grand Domestic Revolution: A History of Feminist Designs for American Homes, Neighborhoods, and Cities* (Cambridge, Mass.: MIT Press, 1982): 285–86; Ruth Schwartz Cowan, *More Work for Mother: The Ironies of Household Technology from the Open Hearth to the Microwave* (New York: Basic Books, 1983) 211–14.

72. Hayden, *The Grand Domestic Revolution*, 28.

73. Serlin, *Replaceable You*, 56.

74. Howard A. Rusk, *A Manual for Training the Disabled Homemaker* (New York: Bellevue Medical Center, 1955).

75. Gordon H. Hughes, "Review of *Planning Homes for the Aged*, ed. Geneva Mathiasen and Edward Noakes," *Psychiatric Services* 1 (April 1960): 53.

76. Rusk, *A Manual for Training the Disabled Homemaker*; Howard Rusk, *A Functional Home for Easier Living, Designed for the Physically Disabled, the Cardiac, and the Elderly* (New York: NYU Medical Center, Institute of Physical Medicine and Rehabilitation, 1959); Helen E. McCullough and Mary B. Farnham, *Space and Design Requirements for Wheelchair Kitchens*, Bulletin no. 661 (Urbana, Ill.: College of Agriculture Extension Service, 1960); Helen E. McCullough and Mary B. Farnham, *Kitchens for Women in Wheelchairs*, Circular 841 (Urbana, Ill.: College of Agriculture Extension Service, 1961).

77. Alexander Kira, *The Bathroom* (Ithaca, N.Y.: Center for Housing and Environmental Studies, Cornell University, 1966); Alexander Kira, "Housing Needs of the Aged, with a Guide to Functional Planning for the Elderly and Handicapped," *Rehabilitation Literature* 21, no. 12 (1960): 370–77. See also Penner, *Bathroom*.

78. This trope of the white, elderly disabled woman appears throughout representations of the user in rehabilitation manuals of the 1950s–70s. See, for example, Figure 3.2.

79. Nancy Krieger, Jarvis Chen, Brent Coull, Jason Beckfield, Mathew Kiang, and Pamela Waterman, "Jim Crow and Premature Mortality among the US Black and White Population, 1960–2009: An Age–Period–Cohort Analysis," *Epidemiology* 25, no. 4 (2014): 494–504.

80. On racism in rehabilitation practices, see Beth Linker, *War's Waste: Rehabilitation in World War I America* (Chicago: University of Chicago Press, 2011), 115, 136–38. On whiteness in the rehabilitation profession, see Paul Leung, "National Association of Multicultural Rehabilitation Concerns," in *Encyclopedia of American Disability History*, ed. Susan Burch (New York: Facts on File, 2009), 641–42. For a history of whiteness and black resistance in the architecture profession, see Victoria Kaplan, "Architecture: A White Gentleman's Profession?," in *Structural Inequality: Black Architects in the United States* (Lanham, Md.: Rowman & Littlefield, 2006), 19–52, 205.

81. On the black feminist critique of the figure of the white suburban housewife, see bell hooks, "Rethinking the Nature of Work," in *Feminist Theory: From Margin to Center* (Cambridge: South End Press, 2000), 96–107.

82. William Henry Chafe, *Civilities and Civil Rights: Greensboro, North Carolina, and the Black Struggle for Freedom* (New York: Oxford University Press, 1981), 71.

83. Ibid., 122.

84. I draw these biographical details from a range of sources, including oral histories, published biographies, and my own archival research in Mace's private home. Mace's entry to the hospital was reported in "Forsyth County Reports Sixth Polio Case; Four Transferred," *Greensboro Daily News*, August 29, 1950, 7; Charles Sasser, "Report of 10 More Polio Cases Made," *Greensboro Daily News*, August 30, 1950, 15.

85. Chafe, *Civilities and Civil Rights*, 29; "Polio Patient Total Holds at 105," *Greensboro Daily News*, August 31, 1950, 1.

86. "Polio Patient Total Holds at 105," 1.

87. Arthur Johnsey, "Law Schools Case Rested for Negroes," *Greensboro Daily News*, August 31, 1950, 1.

88. J. S. Stevenson, "Everybody's Hospital: A Brief History of the Central Carolina Convalescent Hospital," *North Carolina Medical Journal* 27, no. 1 (1966): 23–28.

89. Tom Turner, "Blind Persons Are Operating the Largest Broom Plant between Richmond and Atlanta," *Greensboro Record*, August 30, 1950, 15.

90. Rixie Hunter, "'51 Polio Seen Relatively Low," *Winston-Salem Journal Sentinel*, July 29, 1951.

91. Alexander, *The New Jim Crow*. See also Jonathan Metzl, *The Protest Psychosis: How Schizophrenia Became a Black Disease* (Boston: Beacon Press, 1999).

92. Civil Rights Congress, *We Charge Genocide: The Historic Petition to the United Nations for Relief from a Crime of the United States Government against the Negro People* (New York: International Publishers, 1951).

93. "Three Discharged at Polio Hospital," *Greensboro Record*, August 8, 1951, 10; Steven Litt, "Breaking Down Barriers, Stubbornly, by Design," *News and Observer*, August 7, 1988, 3D.

94. Jim Southerland, "Polio Victim Invited to Model Plane Meet," *Winston-Salem Journal*, August 6, 1953, 16.

95. Mace's high school yearbooks confirm that his school remained white even after mandated desegregation.

96. On such signage in the Jim Crow South, see Guffey, "Knowing Their Space."

97. Patricia Leigh Brown, "House Plans Begin to Meet Needs of Disabled," *Springfield Union*, September 4, 1988, D6.

98. Vic Garcia, "Disabled Architect Dreams of World Accessible to All," *Salt Lake Tribune*, December 16, 1991.

99. Litt, "Breaking Down Barriers."

100. William Doggett, Ronald Mace, William Marchant, Fred Tolson, and L. Rockett Thompson, "Housing Environmental Research" (fifth year architecture thesis, North Carolina State University, Raleigh, 1966), 77.

101. Litt, "Breaking Down Barriers."

102. James Jeffers, "Barrier-Free Design: A Legislative Response," in *Barrier-Free Environments*, ed. Michael J. Bednar (Stroudsburg, Pa.: Dowden, Hutchinson & Ross, 1977), 46.

103. Litt, "Breaking Down Barriers."

104. Even today, nonwhite architects in the United States comprise less than 2 percent of the population. Lekan Oguntoyinbo, "In Architecture, African-Americans Stuck on Ground Floor in Terms of Numbers," *Diverse: Issues in Higher Education* (August 5, 2013), http://diverseeducation.com/article/55050/.

105. Black civil rights activists engaged in direct action to demand desegregation. See Henry Hampton and Steve Fayer, *Voices of Freedom: An Oral History of the Civil Rights Movement from the 1950s through the 1980s* (New York: Bantam Books, 1991), 18; Metzl, *The Protest Psychosis*, xi. On the historical relationship between disability and incarceration, see Liat Ben-Moshe, "Disabling Incarceration: Connecting Disability to Divergent Confinements in the USA," *Critical Sociology* 39, no. 3 (December 2011): 385–403. Feminist activists also demanded desegregation and spatial access, drawing connections to disability rights demands. See Dolores Hayden, "What Would a

Non-Sexist City Be Like? Speculations on Housing, Urban Design, and Human Work," *Signs* 5, no. 3 (1980): 170–87; Weisman, "Women's Environmental Rights," 4. On disability rights protests in intersection with race, see Susan M. Schweik, "Lomax's Matrix: Disability, Solidarity, and the Black Power of 504," *Disability Studies Quarterly* 31, no. 1 (2011), dsq-sds.org/article/view/1371/1539.

106. On individual versus systemic racism, see Stokely Carmichael and Charles V. Hamilton, *Black Power: The Politics of Liberation in America* (New York: Vintage Books, 1967), 2–3. On the mundane, everyday aspects of racism, see Clair Drake and Horace R. Clayton, *Black Metropolis: A Study of Negro Life in a Northern City* (Chicago: University of Chicago Press, 1945).

107. Disability theorists have drawn similar parallels. See Phil Smith, "Whiteness, Normal Theory, and Disability Studies," *Disability Studies Quarterly* 24, no. 2 (2004), http://dsq-sds.org/article/view/491/668.

108. Chatelain, "Architectural Barriers," 4.

109. Ibid.

110. Elizabeth Hinton, "'A War within Our Own Boundaries': Lyndon Johnson's Great Society and the Rise of the Carceral State," *Journal of American History* 102, no. 1 (2015): 100–112.

111. On the role of experts in the Kerner Report, see Ellen Herman, "The Kerner Commission and the Experts," in *The Romance of American Psychology: Political Culture in the Age of Experts* (Berkeley: University of California Press, 1995), 208–37.

112. See National Advisory Commission on Civil Disorders, "Kerner Report," 1968, https://www.ncjrs.gov/pdffiles1/Digitization/8073NCJRS.pdf. On the Kerner Report and the politics of integration (versus nonsegregation and material spatial equality), see John O. Calmore, "Spatial Equality and the Kerner Commission Report: A Back-to-the-Future Essay," in *Race, Poverty, and American Cities,* ed. John Boger and Judith Wegner (Chapel Hill: University of North Carolina Press, 1996), 309–42.

113. National Advisory Commission on Civil Disorders, "Kerner Report," 1.

114. On the co-construction of race and disability, see Baynton, "Disability and the Justification of Inequality in American History," 33; Leroy Moore Jr. and Pamela S. Fadem, "Race," in *Encyclopedia of American Disability History,* ed. Susan Burch (New York: Facts on File, 2009), 757–59; Dea H. Boster, *African American Slavery and Disability: Bodies, Property, and Power in the Antebellum South, 1800–1860* (New York: Routledge, 2013); Ellen Samuels, *Fantasies of Identification: Disability, Gender, Race* (New York: New York University Press, 2014).

115. Herman, "The Kerner Commission and the Experts," 212.

116. Ibid., 223–34.

117. National Advisory Commission on Civil Disorders, "Kerner Report," 1.

118. Ibid.

119. Metzl, *The Protest Psychosis.*

120. Hinton, "'A War within Our Own Boundaries.'"

121. Edmond Leonard, "Lives Are Salvaged" (speech delivered to the Seventh International Conference of the Federation Internationale des Mutiles et Invalides du Travail et des Invalides Civils, Italy, 1965), 3–5, Elaine Ostroff Collection, Archives Center, National Museum of American History, Smithsonian Institution.

122. Wilkoff, *Practicing Universal Design,* 15.

123. Ibid.

124. Ibid., 16.

125. National Commission on Architectural Barriers to Rehabilitation of the Handicapped,

Design for All Americans: A Report of the National Commission on Architectural Barriers to Rehabilitation of the Handicapped (Washington, D.C.: Rehabilitation Services Administration, 1967), 2. See also Jeffers, "Barrier-Free Design," 46.

126. Jeffers, "Barrier-Free Design," 46–47.

127. Ibid., 47.

128. See U.S Congress, Senate, *A Barrier-Free Environment for the Elderly and the Handicapped: Hearings before the Special Committee on Aging, United States Senate, 92nd Congress, First Session* (October 18–20, 1971) (Washington, D.C.: Government Printing Office, 1972).

129. National Commission on Architectural Barriers to Rehabilitation of the Handicapped, *Design for All Americans*, 2.

130. Ibid., 4.

131. On the gendering of disabled soldiers, see Rose, "The Right to a College Education?"

132. National Commission on Architectural Barriers to Rehabilitation of the Handicapped, *Design for All Americans*, 2.

133. For a historical overview of the intersections of race, poverty, aging, and disability in healthcare disparities of the 1960s, including a focus on nursing homes and institutions, see Rosemary A. Stevens, "Health Care in the Early 1960s," *Health Care Financing Review* 18, no. 2 (1996): 11–22.

134. National Commission on Architectural Barriers to Rehabilitation of the Handicapped, *Design for All Americans*, 19.

135. U.S. Department of Justice, Civil Rights Division, "A Guide to Disability Rights Laws," July 2009, http://www.ada.gov/cguide.htm. Mace's firm, Barrier Free Environments, took the lead on publishing guides for accessible housing. See Barrier Free Environments, *Fair Housing Act Design Manual* (Raleigh, N.C.: Barrier Free Environments, 1996). Mace justified the inclusion of disability alongside racial, gender, and religious protections by invoking disability as a unique type of vulnerability. "As a protected class," Mace argued, "people with disabilities are unique in at least one respect because they are the only minority that can be discriminated against solely by the built environment." Barrier Free Environments, *Fair Housing Act Design Manual*, 1.

136. Peter Lassen, quoting a New York State law, "Statement of Peter L. Lassen, Executive Director, Paralyzed Veterans of America, Washington, D.C.," in *Design and Construction of Federal Facilities to Be Accessible to the Physically Handicapped: Hearings before the United States House Committee on Public Works, Subcommittee on Public Buildings and Grounds, Ninety-First Congress, First Session, on December 9, 1969* (Washington, D.C.: Government Printing Office, 1970), 20.

137. Jack H. McDonald, quoted in *Design and Construction of Federal Facilities to Be Accessible to the Physically Handicapped*, 6.

4. Sloped Technoscience

Chapter epigraph: Karen Barad, "Intra-actions (Interview of Karen Barad by Adam Kleinman)," *Mousse* 34 (Summer 2012): 81.

1. As an origin story for the disability rights movement, the guerrilla curb cut narrative circulates widely. Joseph Shapiro discusses it briefly in *No Pity: People with Disabilities Forging a New Civil Rights Movement* (New York: Times Books, 1994), 126. Those alleged to have been involved, particularly Hale Zukas and Eric Dibner, deny involvement in heroic, unsanctioned, guerrilla curb cutting but have acknowledged engaging in do-it-yourself curb cutting at other times of the day and often for less explicitly confrontational purposes. See Hale Zukas, "National Disability

Activist: Architectural and Transit Accessibility, Personal Assistance Services," an oral history conducted in 1998 by Sharon Bonney and published in *Builders and Sustainers of the Independent Living Movement in Berkeley*, vol. 3, (Berkeley: Oral History Center, Bancroft Library, University of California, 2000), 122; Eric Dibner, "Advocate and Specialist in Architectural Accessibility," an oral history conducted in 1998 by Kathy Cowan and published in *Builders and Sustainers of the Independent Living Movement in Berkeley*, 3:24–25; Eric Dibner, e-mail message to author, August 18, 2016. In 2015 Dibner, now a national accessibility expert, reframed the story at an event celebrating the twenty-fifth anniversary of the ADA: "Myth is rampant, however, and it is retrospective. There is a story that we had a guerrilla group building curb ramps in the middle of the night. The city had begun to replace curbs at the busy corners, but there were several thousand corners without ramps, yet to be built. Ed, who traveled about a dozen blocks to get to CIL, could manage his wheelchair on quiet residential streets, where some corners only had very low curbs or there were driveways that sometimes let him on or off the sidewalk. So, we decided to save the city some effort and mixed up a bag of concrete and smoothed out a half dozen low curbs along his route, troweling a wedge of cement at the gutter. Now, the story is told that the first curb ramp was put in by a gang of midnight revolutionaries." Eric Dibner, "Disability and Learning" (presentation at Willing and Able ADA Slam Event, Portland, Maine, July 2, 2015). This chapter is concerned not with whether these events occurred at night but with the political work of crip design cultures.

2. "Critical making," a more recent concept, resembles the sensibility that I describe in this chapter as "crip technoscience." Matt Ratto and Robert Ree, "Materializing Information: 3D Printing and Social Change," *First Monday* 17, no. 7 (2012), http://firstmonday.org/ojs/index.php/fm/article/view/3968/3273.

3. Jane Jacobs, *The Death and Life of Great American Cities* (1961; repr., New York: Vintage Books, 1992), 55.

4. Jack Fisher, quoted in Steven Brown, "The Curb Ramps of Kalamazoo: Discovering Our Unrecorded History," *Disability Studies Quarterly* 19, no. 3 (1999): 205, https://www.independentliving.org/docs3/brown99a.html.

5. Ibid.

6. In 1973 Section 504 of the federal Rehabilitation Act established a right to federally funded programs and activities for disabled people and Section 228 of the Federal-Aid Highway Act allocated funds for building curb cuts at crosswalks.

7. Bess Williamson, "The People's Sidewalks: Designing Berkeley's Wheelchair Route," *Boom California* 2, no. 1 (2012), http://www.boomcalifornia.com/2012/06/the-peoples-sidewalks/.

8. Ed Roberts, quoted in Doris Zames Fleisher and Frieda Zames, *The Disability Rights Movement: From Charity to Confrontation*, 40. Zames and Fleisher do not note the date of the speech, but judging by its content and language, it was most likely from the early 1990s, between the ADA's passage in 1990 and Roberts's death in 1995.

9. On the work of disability as multivalent and complex, see Susan Schweik, "Homer's Odyssey: Multiple Disabilities and the *Best Years of Our Lives*," in *Civil Disabilities: Citizenship, Membership, and Belonging*, ed. Nancy Hirschmann and Beth Linker (Philadelphia: University of Pennsylvania Press, 2015), 22.

10. "Crip technoscience" is a term I coined in "Cripping Feminist Technoscience." While historical studies of crip technoscience are so far rare, scholars have studied disabled makers in the recent past. See Elizabeth Petrick, *Making Computers Accessible* (Baltimore: Johns Hopkins University Press, 2015); Bess Williamson, "Electric Moms and Quad Drivers: People with Disabilities

Buying, Making, and Using Technology in Postwar America," *American Studies* 52, no. 1 (2012): 5–29; Melanie Yargeau, "Disability Hacktivism," in "Hacking the Classroom: Eight Perspectives," curated by Jentery Sayers and Mary Hocks, special issue of *Computers and Composition Online* (Spring 2014).

11. My term "politically adaptive" here references Chikako Takeshita's study of the intrauterine device as a "politically versatile technology," which materializes new arrangements of knowing-making. Chikako Takeshita, *The Global Biopolitics of the IUD: How Science Constructs Contraceptive Users and Women's Bodies,* Inside Technology (Cambridge, Mass.: MIT Press, 2012), 3.

12. Institute of Medicine, *Enabling America: Assessing the Role of Rehabilitation Science and Engineering* (Washington, D.C.: National Academies Press, 1997), 148; Nagi, "Disability Concepts Revisited."

13. This movement is narrated later in this chapter. Politicized disability activism began as early as the 1930s. See Paul Longmore and David Goldberger, "The League of the Physically Handicapped and the Great Depression: A Case Study," *Journal of American History* 87, no. 3 (2000): 888–92. I use the term "D/deaf" here to signify a recognition of deaf culture, as well as people who identify as hearing impaired but not as culturally deaf.

14. These terms emerged from UK disability activism and theory. See Union of Physically Impaired Against Segregation (UPIAS), "Policy Statement," 1972, http://disability-studies.leeds .ac.uk/files/library/UPIAS-UPIAS.pdf; Oliver, *The Politics of Disablement;* Carmelo Masala and Donatella Rita Petretto, "Models of Disability," in *International Encyclopedia of Rehabilitation,* ed. Maurice Blouin and John Stone (New York: Center for International Rehabilitation Research Information and Exchange, 2012), http://cirrie.buffalo.edu/encyclopedia/en/article/135/. On critiques of the social model, see Tom Shakespeare and Nicholas Watson, "The Social Model of Disability: An Outdated Ideology?," *Research in Social Science and Disability* 2 (2002): 9–28.

15. UPIAS, "Policy Statement."

16. Here my argument is in conversation with Rosemarie Garland-Thomson's notion of the "misfit," articulated in her article "Misfits." Whereas Garland-Thomson is concerned with disability as an epistemic position, however, my aim is to historicize crip practices of knowing-making across the periods in which the social model was articulated.

17. Iris Marion Young, "Foreword," in *Disability/Postmodernity: Embodying Disability Theory,* ed. Marion Corker and Tom Shakespeare (London: Continuum, 2002), xii. For further examples of this association between ramps and Universal Design, see Rosemarie Garland-Thomson, *Extraordinary Bodies: Figuring Physical Disability in American Culture and Literature* (New York: Columbia University Press, 1997), 7; Kafer, *Feminist, Queer, Crip,* 175; Katherine Seelman, "Universal Design and Orphan Technology: Do We Need Both?," *Disability Studies Quarterly* 25, no. 3 (2005), http:// www.dsq-sds.org/article/view/584/761.

18. Product designer George Covington has claimed that "the first barrier to universal design is the human mind. If we could put a ramp into the mind, the first thing down the ramp would be the understanding that all barriers are the result of narrow thinking." George Covington, quoted in Susan Szenasy, "Twenty Years and Counting," *Metropolis* magazine, September 2010.

19. Steve Jacobs, "Section 255 of the Telecommunications Act of 1996: Fueling the Creation of New Electronic Curbcuts," 1999, http://www.accessiblesociety.org/topics/technology/eleccurb cut.htm; Brooke A. Ackerly, *Universal Human Rights in a World of Difference* (Cambridge: Cambridge University Press, 1998), 35.

20. Steve Jacobs, "The Electronic Curb Cut Effect," 2002, http://www.icdri.org/technology/ ecceff.htm.

21. McRuer, *Crip Theory*, 35.

22. Dibner, "Advocate and Specialist in Architectural Accessibility," 26.

23. Galileo understood simple machines as instruments that magnify force by creating mechanical advantage. Terry S. Reynolds, *Stronger Than a Hundred Men: A History of the Vertical Water Wheel* (Baltimore: Johns Hopkins University Press, 1983), 200.

24. Ibid.

25. See Carl DiSalvo, *Adversarial Design* (Cambridge, Mass.: MIT Press, 2012). This "agonistic" approach to design draws on radical democratic theory, which locates politics in antagonism, divergence, and contention. See Ernesto Laclau and Chantal Mouffe, *Hegemony and Socialist Strategy: Toward a Radical Democratic Politics* (New York: Verso, 2001).

26. Sara Hendren, *Slope:Intercept*, http://slopeintercept.org/.

27. I borrow "disorientation" from feminist theorist Sara Ahmed, *Queer Phenomenology: Orientations, Objects, Others* (Durham, N.C.: Duke University Press, 2006), 166. If disorientation works queerly to disrupt normative orders, crip operates in a similar capacity here.

28. Anthony Dunne, *Hertzian Tales: Electronic Products, Aesthetic Experience, and Critical Design* (Cambridge, Mass.: MIT Press, 2008). See also Anthony Dunne and Fiona Raby, *Speculative Everything: Design, Fiction, and Social Dreaming* (Cambridge, Mass.: MIT Press, 2013).

29. Critical disability scholars have critiqued simulation exercises conducted in the name of "disability awareness." These exercises appear to have been part of rehabilitation education throughout the twentieth century. Critiques of such activities emerged with the independent living movement and entered scholarly debates in the 1980s. See Daniel Pfeiffer, "Disability Simulations Using a Wheelchair Exercise," *Journal of Post-Secondary Education and Disability* 7, no. 2 (1989): 53–60; Sally French, "Simulation Exercises in Disability Awareness Training: A Critique," *Disability and Society* 7, no. 3 (1992): 257–66.

30. Dunne, *Hertzian Tales*, 42.

31. Murphy, *Seizing the Means of Reproduction*; Barad, *Meeting the Universe Halfway*. On design and feminist technoscience, see Maja van der Velden, "Design for a Common World: On Ethical Agency and Cognitive Justice," *Ethics and Information Technology* 11, no. 1 (2009): 37–47; Jutta Weber, "Making Worlds: Epistemological, Ontological, and Political Dimensions of Technoscience," *Poiesis & Praxis* 7, no. 1 (2010): 17–36. On technoscience and environmental design, see John Law and Annemarie Mol, "Situating Technoscience: An Inquiry into Spatialities," *Environment and Planning D: Society & Space* 19, no. 5 (2001): 609; Thomas F. Gieryn, "What Buildings Do," *Theory and Society* 31, no. 1 (2002): 53. On the critique of technology as inherently enframing, see Andrew Feenberg, *Questioning Technology* (London: Routledge, 1999).

32. Ahmed, *Queer Phenomenology*, 166. "Disorientation" is also a phenomenological experience related to disability. Practices of orienteering and wayfinding, for instance, focus on providing people with sensory or cognitive disabilities access to the spatial layouts of built environments. My intention is not to valorize disorientation but to use this concept to point out where tensions arise within the category of disability, as well as between disabled and nondisabled ways of accessing built space.

33. Kafer, *Feminist, Queer, Crip*, 107.

34. Ibid., 119–20.

35. Williamson, "Electric Moms and Quad Drivers."

36. Young, white, middle-class polio survivors and their families were disproportionately represented in the *Toomey Gazette*, while people of color only appeared as representations of institutionalized populations. Williamson, "Electric Moms and Quad Drivers," 9.

37. Ibid.

38. Ibid., 24.

39. Ibid.

40. Alice Loomer, "Hanging onto the Coattails of Science," *Rehabilitation Gazette* 25 (1982): 30–31.

41. Ibid.

42. Ibid.

43. On crip critiques of the disabled cyborg figure, see Kafer, *Feminist, Queer, Crip*, 103–28.

44. Dolmage, "Universal Design."

45. "Disabled Vets Protest Closing of U. of I. Unit." Accounts of the University of Illinois Rehabilitation Education Center also appear in chapters 3 and 5.

46. Roberts and Crigger, "Wheelchair Vets Trek to Springfield in Vain Effort to Keep Division Open," 1.

47. Ibid.

48. Nugent, "Founder," 49. My narrative here draws in large part from Nugent's oral history, which has some limitations in terms of historical accuracy that are addressed in other chapters. For my purposes, however, Nugent's perceptions of the strategies and material practices taking place at the University of Illinois are both far more detailed than other accounts and provide evidence of the ways in which narratives about curb cuts and ramps form.

49. Ibid.

50. Fleischer and Zames, *The Disability Rights Movement*, 36–37.

51. Nugent, "Design of Buildings to Permit Their Use by the Physically Handicapped," 56.

52. Nugent, "Founder," 54–59.

53. "The University Picture," *Toomey Gazette* 5, no. 1 (1962): 22.

54. In the early 1950s, vocational rehabilitation counselor Emerson Dexter, the city's mayor, mobilized to install curb cuts even before the university itself became accessible (Nugent, "Founder," 112–13). In some cases, such as when existing narrow sidewalks would not allow space for a ramp, the city completely repaved entire sidewalks, elevating them at a slight incline to be level with doorways (118–19).

55. Ibid., 135–36.

56. Ibid.

57. Ibid.

58. Ibid., 68–69.

59. "Higher Education," *Toomey Gazette* 10, no. 1 (1967): 42–43.

60. The term "crip," though experiencing recent repopularization with crip theory, was used in the movement to distinguish between rehabilitation and anti-assimilation positions. Raymond Lifchez and Barbara Winslow, *Design for Independent Living: The Environment and Physically Disabled People* (Berkeley: University of California Press, 1979), 9.

61. James Donald, "University of California's Cowell Hospital Residence Program for Physically Disabled Students, 1962–1975: Catalyst for Berkeley's Independent Living Movement," an oral history conducted in 1998 by Kathryn Cowan and published in *University of California's Cowell Hospital Residence Program for Physically Disabled Students, 1962–1975: Catalyst for Berkeley's Independent Living Movement* (Berkeley: Oral History Center, Bancroft Library, University of California, 2000), 93–94.

62. As Corbett O'Toole notes, the majority of disability rights movement leaders and activists memorialized in the movement's primary archive at the Bancroft library at the University of

California at Berkeley are white (as well as cisgender and heterosexual). Corbett O'Toole, *Fading Scars: My Queer Disability History* (Fort Worth, Tex.: Autonomous Press, 2015), 48. Major histories of the movement barely mention race. These histories typically draw parallels between racism and ableism rather than analyzing the dynamics of race within the movement. See, for example, Fleisher and Zames, *The Disability Rights Movement*, 38–39.

63. Michael Fuss and John Hessler, "Proposal for the Physically Disabled Students' Program—First Draft—1969," Michael Fuss Papers, BANC MSS 99/146 c, Bancroft Library, University of California, Berkeley; Michael Fuss and John Hessler, "Draft Proposal to Expand Cowell Program—1969," Michael Fuss Papers; John Hessler, "Grant Proposal for the Physically Disabled Students' Program, Proposed to Assistant Secretary/Commissioner of Education for Support Through the Special Services for Disabled Students in Institutions of Higher Education," 1970, Michael Fuss Papers.

64. Billy Charles Barner, "First African American Student in Cowell Program, 1969–1973," an oral history conducted in 1999 by Kathryn Cowan and published in *University of California's Cowell Hospital Residence Program for Physically Disabled Students, 1962–1975*, 253, 278; Catherine Caulfield, "First Woman Student in the Cowell Program," an oral history conducted in 1996 by Susan O'Hara and published in *University of California's Cowell Hospital Residence Program for Physically Disabled Students, 1962–1975*, 139.

65. In vocational rehabilitation, the term "independent living" had, prior to the disability rights movement, meant to benefit people "for whom a vocational goal is thought to be impossible. Independent living is seen as an alternative to the vocational goal—thus, the term 'independent living rehabilitation' as distinct from 'vocational rehabilitation.'" Gerben DeJong, "Independent Living: From Social Movement to Analytic Paradigm," *Archives of Physical Medicine and Rehabilitation* 60, no. 10 (1979): 438.

66. Michael Fuss, "A Proposal for Berkeley Disabled and Blind Supportive Services Program Center for Independent Living, Inc.," March 1972, Michael Fuss Papers, BANC MSS 99/146 c, Bancroft Library, University of California, Berkeley.

67. See chapter 3.

68. Martinez and Duncan, "The Road to Independent Living in the USA: An Historical Perspective and Contemporary Challenges," *Disability World* 20 (2003): 3; Rosemarie Garland-Thomson, "Integrating Disability, Transforming Feminist Theory," *NWSA Journal* 14, no. 3 (2002): 14. See also Paul Longmore, *Telethons: Spectacle, Disability, and the Business of Charity* (New York: Oxford University Press, 2016).

69. I borrow the concept of "epistemic cultures," or "amalgrams of arrangements and mechanisms—bonded from affinity, necessity, and historical coincidence," from Karin Knorr-Cetina, *Epistemic Cultures* (Cambridge, Mass.: Harvard University Press, 1989), 1.

70. Boston Women's Health Collective, *Our Bodies, Ourselves*, 2nd ed. (New York: Simon & Schuster, 1971). On the politics of knowledge in the feminist women's health movement in California, see Murphy, *Seizing the Means of Reproduction*.

71. Herbert R. Willsmore, "Student Resident at Cowell, 1969–1970," an oral history conducted in 1996 and 1999 by Susan O'Hara and published in *University of California's Cowell Hospital Residence Program for Physically Disabled Students, 1962–1975*, 168–88; Fleisher and Zames, *The Disability Rights Movement*, 39; Gerald Belchick, "Department of Rehabilitation Counselor, Liaison to the Cowell Program, 1970s," an interview conducted by Sharon Bonney and published in *UC Berkeley's Cowell Hospital Residence Program: Key Administrators and California Department of*

Rehabilitation Counselors (Berkeley: Oral History Center, Bancroft Library, University of California, 1998), 187–90.

72. Dibner, "Advocate and Specialist," 26; Willsmore, "Student Resident at Cowell," 190–91.

73. Willsmore, "Student Resident at Cowell,"168.

74. James Charlton, *Nothing about Us without Us: Disability Oppression and Empowerment* (Berkeley: University of California Press, 2004), 3–4.

75. Sandra G. Harding, "Rethinking Standpoint Epistemology: What Is 'Strong Objectivity'?," in *Feminist Theory: A Philosophical Anthology,* ed. Ann E. Cudd and Robin O. Andreasen (Oxford: Blackwell, 2005), 218–36.

76. Fuss and Hessler, "Draft Proposal to Expand Cowell Program," 5.

77. On the influence of the self-help movement on disability activism, see Irving Zola, "Helping One Another: A Speculative History of the Self-Help Movement," 1979, http://www.indepen dentliving.org/docs4/zola1979.html; Dejong, "Independent Living," 438–39.

78. Fuss and Hessler, "Draft Proposal to Expand Cowell Program," 1–2.

79. Ibid.

80. DeJong, "Independent Living," 440.

81. Hessler, "Grant Proposal for the Physically Disabled Students' Program," 7.

82. Fuss, "A Proposal for Berkeley Disabled and Blind Supportive Services Program," 7.

83. On independent living as a paradigm shift within rehabilitation, see DeJong, "Independent Living," 435–78.

84. "Disabled People Help Run Herrick's New Clinic," *HMH Hospitaler,* Herrick Memorial Hospital, Berkeley, California, February 1974, 3–9, Hale Zukas Papers, BANC MSS 99/150 c, courtesy of the Bancroft Library, University of California, Berkeley.

85. "Disabled People Help Run Herrick's New Clinic," 4.

86. Hessler, "Grant Proposal for the Physically Disabled Students' Program," 16.

87. Corbett O'Toole, "Advocate for Disabled Women's Rights and Health Issues," an oral history conducted in 1998 by Denise Sherer Jacobson (Oral History Center, Bancroft Library, University of California, Berkeley, 2000), 38; Catherine Caulfield, "First Woman Student in the Cowell Program," an oral history conducted in 1996 by Susan O'Hara and published in *University of California's Cowell Hospital Residence Program for Physically Disabled Students, 1962–1975,* 32–33.

88. O'Toole, "Advocate for Disable Women's Rights," 39; Barner, "First African American Student in Cowell Program," 264; Center for Independent Living, "Wheelchair Design Innovation," *CIL Newsletter* (1975), Hale Zukas Papers, BANC MSS 99/150 c, courtesy of the Bancroft Library, University of California, Berkeley.

89. "Computer Training Project 1975," pamphlet, Eric Dibner Papers, BANC MSS 99/186 c, courtesy of the Bancroft Library, University of California, Berkeley. In the 1980s computing would once again become a frontier of disability technoscience when the CIL helped to establish the Disabled Children's Computer Group, an organization in which parents hacked and tinkered computer technologies to create access for disabled children. See Elizabeth Petrick, "Fulfilling the Promise of the Personal Computer: The Development of Accessible Computer Technologies, 1970–1998" (PhD diss., University of California, San Diego, 2012). As Petrick notes, "This was an environment of problem solving, reminiscent of the kinds of hobbyist tinkering with personal computers that had helped start the personal computer industry roughly a decade earlier" (125).

90. My concept of "epistemic activism," further explored in subsequent chapters, points to strategies and tactics carried out within the domain of knowledge to change material arrangements.

This dimension of knowing-making encompasses the materialization of knowledge production and dissemination and not simply acts of design themselves. Epistemic activism relates to "tactical politics" (da Costa and Phillip, *Tactical Biopolitics*, xix) and practices that sociologists of technoscience refer to as "evidence-based activism." See Vololona Rabeharisoa, Tiago Moreira, and Madelein Akrich, "Evidence-Based Activism: Patients', Users' and Activists' Groups in Knowledge Society," *BioSocieties* 9, no. 2 (2014): 111–28.

91. "Disabled People Help Run Herrick's New Clinic," 9.

92. DeJong, "Independent Living," 437.

93. Willsmore, "Student Resident at Cowell," 221.

94. Zukas, "National Disability Activist," 119–20. When Ed Roberts joined the CIL after its founding, he began entering the organization into federal rehabilitation grant competitions for rehabilitation engineering and design. A grant in 1975 from the California Department of Rehabilitation allowed the CIL to expand its maker activities into "an exhaustive study of the state of the art of wheelchair design" (Center for Independent Living, "Wheelchair Design Innovation"). Through that program, the CIL offered more trainings in wheelchair repair, taught by its "augmented engineering and machine staff" (ibid.). These trainings constituted a form of citizen rehabilitation engineering, using the technological expertise of disabled people trained in repairs at the CIL to carry out research and design with rehabilitation funding. Note that Roberts is often misattributed as the founder of the CIL and the Rolling Quads. Reportedly, he joined the CIL in 1973 or 1974. See Zukas, "National Disability Activist," 174. See also O'Toole, *Fading Scars*, 125.

95. "CIL Facts—August 1979," brochure listing CIL activities, Eric Dibner Papers, BANC MSS 99/186 c, courtesy of the Bancroft Library, University of California, Berkeley.

96. Jean A. Cole, "What's New about Independent Living?," *Archives of Physical Medicine and Rehabilitation on Independent Living* 60, no. 10 (1979): 458.

97. Williamson, "The People's Sidewalks," 4; Zukas, "National Disability Activist," 139; Hessler, "Grant Proposal for the Physically Disabled Students' Program," 25.

98. Dibner, e-mail to author, August 18, 2016.

99. Ibid.

100. Dibner, "Advocate and Specialist in Architectural Accessibility," 3.

101. Ibid., 24.

102. Ibid., 25.

103. Ibid.

104. One of the other services that Dibner performed was DIY wheelchair maintenance. Ibid., 12.

105. Ibid., 140; Charles A. Grimes, "Attendant in the Cowell Residence Program, Wheelchair Technologist, and Participant/Observer of Berkeley's Disability Community, 1967–1990s," an oral history conducted in 1998 by David Landes (Oral History Center, Bancroft Library, University of California, Berkeley, 2000), 117–18.

106. Zukas, "National Disability Activist," 140.

107. Ibid., 141.

108. Ibid.

109. Dibner, "Advocate and Specialist in Architectural Accessibility," 85–86.

110. Grimes, "Attendant in the Cowell Residence Program," 79–80.

111. Ibid., 80.

112. Hale Zukas, letter to Edwin Shomate, June 14, 1976, Eric Dibner Papers, BANC MSS 99/186 c, courtesy of the Bancroft Library, University of California, Berkeley.

113. Ibid.

114. Ibid.

115. Ibid.

116. One model, which used terminology of the time, positioned disabled people as "consumers" with significant power and knowledge (in apparent reference to Ralph Nader's consumer protection movement). See Lex Frieden, "Independent Living Models," *Rehabilitation Literature* 41, nos. 7–8 (1980): 169–73. The term is not just an unfortunate coincidence, however. While activists challenged dominant rehabilitation norms, they did not always unsettle the values associated with white, middle-class citizenship. O'Toole argues that while histories of the early disability rights movement give the impression that "all disabled people who came into their circles were welcomed and included" and that, simultaneously, few disabled people of color were present, movement leadership did not reflect the diversity of disabled people of color at the time. O'Toole, *Fading Scars*, 125–26.

117. CIL, "Public Education," Eric Dibner Papers, BANC MSS 99/186 c, courtesy of the Bancroft Library, University of California, Berkeley.

118. Edmond Leonard, "National Center for a Barrier-Free Environment Report," December 11, 1975, Eric Dibner Papers, BANC MSS 99/186 c, courtesy of the Bancroft Library, University of California, Berkeley; "Architecture 198: Barrier-Free Design community design course," flier, Eric Dibner Papers; letter from Friedner D. Wittman to Richard Bender on CIL and UC–Berkeley Architecture department collaborations, February 20, 1975, Eric Dibner Papers; letter from Eric Dibner to Raymond Lifchez, ca. 1975, Eric Dibner Papers.

119. Leonard, "National Center for a Barrier-Free Environment Report."

120. Ibid.; "Bibliography for Barrier-Free Design," Eric Dibner Papers, BANC MSS 99/186 c, Bancroft Library, University of California, Berkeley; letter from Eric Dibner to Edwin Shomate, June 14, 1976, Eric Dibner Papers. The ANSI A117.1–1961 standard did mention the need to make curb cuts accessible to blind people, noting that curbs, "particularly if they occur at regular intersections, are a distinct safety feature for all of the handicapped, particularly the blind." American Standards Association, *American Standard Specifications for Making Buildings and Facilities Accessible to, and Usable by, the Physically Handicapped* (ANSI A117.1–1961, approved October 31, 1961) (New York: American Standards Association, 1961), 8.

121. Raymond Lifchez, "Educator in Architectural Access, University of California, Berkeley," an oral history conducted by Susan O'Hara in 2000 and published in *Architectural Accessibility and Disability Rights in Berkeley and Japan* (Berkeley: Oral History Center, Bancroft Library, University of California, 2004), 75. Some of these efforts were carried out by a Campus Committee for Removal of Architectural Barriers. Dibner, "Advocate and Specialist in Architectural Accessibility," 34.

122. Lifchez, "Educator in Architectural Access," 75–76.

123. Ibid., 76.

124. Lifchez and Winslow, *Design for Independent Living*, 140–41.

125. Lifchez, "Educator in Architectural Access," 76.

126. Lifchez and Winslow, *Design for Independent Living*; Raymond Lifchez, *Rethinking Architecture: Design Students and Physically Disabled People* (Berkeley: University of California Press, 1987); Lifchez, "Educator in Architectural Access," 89–90. Elaine Ostroff later coined the term

"user-expert." Elaine Ostroff, "Mining Our Natural Resources: The User as Expert," *Innovation* 16, no. 1 (1997): 33–35.

127. Phil Draper, Jerry Wolf, and Eric Dibner, letter to Ray Lifchez and Barbara Winslow, December 29, 1976, Eric Dibner Papers, BANC MSS 99/186 c, courtesy of the Bancroft Library, University of California, Berkeley.

128. Dibner, "Advocate and Specialist in Architectural Accessibility," 54–55; Eric Dibner, e-mail to author, August 18, 2016.

129. Lifchez and Winslow, *Design for Independent Living,* 150.

130. Ibid., 153.

131. Williamson, "The People's Sidewalks."

132. Grimes, "Attendant in the Cowell Residence Program," 23; Michael Fuss, "Attendant for Cowell Residents, Assistant Director of the Physically Disabled Students' Program, 1966–1972," an oral history conducted in 1997 by Sharon Bonney and published in *Builders and Sustainers of the Independent Living Movement in Berkeley,* 2:67–68; Charles Grimes, "Attendant in the Cowell Residence Program," 117–18; Board of Directors Meeting, September 30, 1974, BANC MSS 99/150 c, courtesy of the Bancroft Library, University of California, Berkeley; Dibner, e-mail to author, August 18, 2016.

133. Dibner, "Advocate and Specialist in Architectural Accessibility," 36–37.

134. Invoice from CIL to the Center for Feminist Therapy and Education, January 3, 1978, Eric Dibner Papers, BANC MSS 99/186 c, courtesy of the Bancroft Library, University of California, Berkeley.

135. Ibid.

136. Eric Dibner, letter to Aileen Frankel, March 5, 1979, Eric Dibner papers, BANC MSS 99/186 c, courtesy of the Bancroft Library, University of California, Berkeley.

137. Alison Kafer pointed out this detail in a personal communication, February 7, 2015.

138. Dibner, e-mail to author, August 18, 2016.

139. John Curl and Ishmael Reed, *For All the People: Uncovering the Hidden History of Cooperation, Cooperative Movements, and Communalism in America* (Oakland: PM Press, 2012), 379, 428. Eventually Ma Revolution was shut down in 1977 when it became the site of a shooting arising over conflicts in the movement (ibid., 217).

140. Dibner, "Advocate and Specialist in Architectural Accessibility," 65; Eric Dibner, report in preparation for *Less Than the Minimum* (videotape), June 6, 1982, Eric Dibner Papers, BANC MSS 99/186 c, courtesy of the Bancroft Library, University of California, Berkeley.

141. For an in-depth sociological and historical analysis of the cross-disability coalitions engendered by the occupation, see Sharon Barnartt and Richard Scotch, *Disability Protests: Contentious Politics, 1970–1999* (Washington, D.C.: Gallaudet University Press, 2001); Michael Ervin, "The 25 Day Siege That Brought Us 504," *Mainstream,* April 18, 1986, http:www.independentliving.org/docs4/ervin1986.html; O'Toole, "Advocate for Disabled Women's Rights and Health Issues," 48.

142. O'Toole, "Advocate for Disabled Women's Rights and Health Issues," 47.

143. Ibid., 48.

144. Kitty Cone, quoted in Fred Pelka, *What Have We Done,* 267. Frank Bowe, a deaf activist, organized the nationwide protest in ten cities. Fred Pelka attributes the occupation strategy to Saul Alinsky's *Rules for Radicals,* which Franke Bowe, executive director of the National Coalition of Citizens with Disabilities in 1977, reportedly consulted to organize the sit-ins. Pelka, *What Have*

We Done, 262–63; Saul Alinsky, *Rules for Radicals: A Practical Primer for Realistic Radicals* (New York: Vintage Books, 1989).

145. Kitty Cone, "Short History of the 504 Sit In," 1996, http://dredf.org/504site/histover .html. See also Alice Wong, "Disability Justice and Social Justice: Entwined Histories and Futures," *BK Nation*, January 16, 2014, http://bknation.org/2014/01/disability-justice-social-justice-en twined-histories-futures/.

146. On incarceration, disability, and whiteness, see Ben-Moshe, "Disabling Incarceration." Some disability scholars, such as Nirmala Erevelles, focus on "how race and disability are imbricated in their collective formation of the black disabled body that now becomes a commodity that has economic, social, cultural, and linguistic implications for transnational subjectivities." Erevelles, *Disability and Difference in Global Contexts*, 39. I am concerned with how drawing parallels elides this imbrication.

147. Richard E. Allen, "Legal Rights of the Disabled," *Braille Monitor*, December 1970. For contemporary examples of advocates drawing parallels between race and disability, see Korydon H. Smith, Jennifer Webb, and Brent T. Williams, *Just below the Line: Disability, Housing, and Equity in the South* (Fayetteville: University of Arkansas Press, 2010), 51–52.

148. Joseph Shapiro, "Disability Rights as Civil Rights," in *The Disabled, the Media, and the Information Age*, ed. Jack A. Nelson (Westport, Conn.: Greenwood Press, 1994), 62.

149. On the disappearance of racial segregation from activist and policy rhetorics in the 1970s and '80s, see Douglas Massey and Nancy Denton, *American Apartheid: Segregation and the Making of the Underclass* (Cambridge, Mass.: Harvard University Press, 2003), 1–3.

150. As Massey and Denton note in *American Apartheid*, "Despite the provisions of the Fair Housing Act, segregation continued; . . . the decade [of the 1970s] ended in record unemployment, inflation, falling wages, increasing income inequality, and rising rates of black poverty. Not only did the ghetto fail to disappear; in many ways its problems multiplied. As segregation persisted, black isolation deepened, and the social and economic problems that had long plagued African American communities worsened. During the 1970s, the ghetto gave birth to the underclass." Massey and Denton, *American Apartheid*, 61–64.

151. Ibid., 81. On the persistence of residential segregation in the early twenty-first century, see John R. Logan, "The Persistence of Segregation in the 21st Century Metropolis," *City & Community* 12, no. 2 (2013): 160–68. On contemporary residential segregation and its effects on environmental injustice, see Dorceta E. Taylor, *Toxic Communities: Environmental Racism, Industrial Pollution, and Residential Mobility* (New York: New York University Press, 2014), 147–90.

152. Massey and Denton, *American Apartheid*, 66–67.

153. Combahee River Collective, "Combahee River Collective Statement," April 1977, http:// circuitous.org/scraps/combahee.html; Kimberlé Crenshaw, "Mapping the Margins: Intersectionality, Identity Politics, and Violence against Women of Color," *Stanford Law Review* 43, no. 6 (1993): 1241–99.

154. On intersectionality and disability history, see Susan Burch and Lindsey Patterson, "Not Just Any Body: Disability, Gender, and History," *Journal of Women's History* 25, no. 4 (2013): 122–37.

155. Disability historiography has turned attention to disabled people of color and their omission from official histories and narratives. As Susan Schweik argues in "Lomax's Matrix," "We come to a better understanding of the fluid and intricate dynamics of alliance that comprised the 'power of 504' when we place a disabled Black Panther and a Black Panther caregiver at the center both of Panther and of American disability history." On the contributions of the Black Panther

Party to the 504 protests, see O'Toole, "Advocate for Disabled Women's Rights and Health Issues," 48. Few narratives from disabled women of color appear in the archives of the independent living movement. One exception is Johnnie Lacy, "Director, Community Resources for Independent Living: An African-American Woman's Perspective on the Independent Living Movement in the Bay Area, 1960s–1980s," an oral history conducted in 1998 by David Landes (Oral History Center, Bancroft Library, University of California, Berkeley, 2000). O'Toole discusses Lacy in *Fading Scars*, 118–33.

156. Josh Lukin, "The Black Panther Party," in *Encyclopedia of American Disability History*, ed. Susan Burch (New York: Facts on File, 2009), 113–14.

157. "Interest convergence" is a term that critical race scholars use to describe the overlapping interests of seemingly disparate groups (such as black civil rights activists and white residents of suburbs) that result in consensus about shared outcomes. See Derrick Bell Jr., "*Brown v. Board of Education* and the Interest Convergence Dilemma," *Harvard Law Review* 93, no. 3 (1980): 518–33. On accessible design as an "interest convergence," see Jay Dolmage, "Disability Studies Pedagogy, Usability and Universal Design," *Disability Studies Quarterly* 25, no. 4 (2005), http://dsq-sds.org/article/view/627/804.

158. Leroy Moore, "Black History of 504 Sit-In for Disability Rights: More Than Serving Food—When Will the Healing Begin?," *San Francisco Bay View National Black Newspaper*, February 11, 2014, http://sfbayview.com/2014/02/black-history-of-504-sit-in-for-disability-rights-more-than-serving-food-when-will-the-healing-begin/.

159. Schweik, "Lomax's Matrix."

160. Ibid.

161. Zukas, "National Disability Activist," 169–70; Dibner, "Advocate and Specialist in Architectural Accessibility," 52–53. Dibner began officially consulting for the Oakland Housing Authority on accessibility on May 17, 1978, and served as an accessibility expert for museums and hospitals in the area, as well. See letter from Eric Dibner to Robert R. Raber, Modernization Projects Manager, Housing Authority of the City of Oakland, June 7, 1978, Eric Dibner Papers, BANC MSS 99/186 c, Bancroft Library, University of California, Berkeley; letter from Eric Dibner to Tish Brown, Document Council at the De Young museum, January 9, 1979, Eric Dibner Papers; Eric Dibner, "Comments on plans for additions to Children's Hospital Medical Center," February 13, 1979, Eric Dibner Papers; letter from Eric Dibner to Aileen Frankel, Office of Community Development, Oakland, March 5, 1979, Eric Dibner Papers.

5. Epistemic Activism

1. F. W. Rees Jr. and E. Burch, "Barrier-Free Design Reflects the Spirit of the Law," *Hospitals* 52, no. 4 (1978): 121–26. See also Edward Steinfeld, "Barrier-Free Design Begins to React to Legislation, Research," *Architectural Record* 165, no. 3 (1979): 69–71.

2. Shakespeare, "Disabled People's Self-Organization," 251–52; Barnartt and Scotch, *Disability Protests*, 62.

3. James Donald, "University of California's Cowell Hospital Residence Program for Physically Disabled Students, 1962–1975: Catalyst for Berkeley's Independent Living Movement," an oral history conducted in 1998 by Kathryn Cowan and published in *University of California's Cowell Hospital Residence Program for Physically Disabled Students*, 93–94.

4. See chapter 3.

5. See chapter 1.

6. On architectural expertise and modernism, see Sachs, "Architects, Users, and the Social Sciences in Postwar America." On the "research economy" within which architectural research circulated, see Avigail Sachs, "The Postwar Legacy of Architectural Research," *Journal of Architectural Education* 62, no. 3 (2009): 53–64.

7. American Institute of Architects, "Barrier-Free Architecture: A Report to the Rehabilitation Services Administration," in National Commission on Architectural Barriers to Rehabilitation of the Handicapped, *Design for All Americans,* 42–43, 48.

8. Ibid., 43.

9. Ibid., 46.

10. Ibid., 45.

11. Ibid., 44.

12. Mace, quoted in Elaine Ostroff, Mark Limont, and Daniel G. Hunter, *Building a World Fit for People: Designers with Disabilities at Work* (Boston: Adaptive Environments, 2002), 15. See also Litt, "Breaking Down barriers," 3D.

13. Vic Garcia, "Disabled Architect Dreams of World Accessible to All," *Salt Lake Tribune,* December 16, 1991. St. Andrews University, ninety-six miles from Raleigh, built its barrier-free campus in 1961. Whether Mace was aware of its existence or would have attended a Catholic university is unknown.

14. Ibid.; Golonka, "Ronald Mace and His Philosophy of Universal Design," 184–90.

15. Doggett, Mace, Marchant, Tolson, and Thompson, "Housing Environmental Research."

16. Ibid., 183. Although the thesis is coauthored, several aspects of the texts lead me to conclude that these sections were written by Mace. The ethnographic portion took place at two public housing communities where, according to photos, the buildings had stairs to their entrances and would not have been accessible to him. The interview instruments and solicitation letters suggest that the other students played a more active role in collecting ethnographic data. Given Mace's accounts of his social isolation during this time, it is likely that he conducted and wrote the bulk of the literature review. The most important clue, however, is that much of the language quoted here also continues to appear later in Mace's work on barrier-free design and Universal Design, indicating the influence of the thesis on his later work.

17. Ibid., 76.

18. Ibid.

19. On an earlier exploration of this argument, see Aimi Hamraie, "Universal Design Research as a New Materialist Practice," *Disability Studies Quarterly* 32, no. 4 (2012), http://dsq-sds.org/article/view/3246/3185. The multidisciplinary scholarly field of environmental design research (often alternately referred to as the study of environment-behavior, environmental psychology, human-centered design, evidence-based design, or person-environment relations) emerged to study the relationships between people, their bodies and minds, and built environments. Although these fields are in some ways discrete, I will refer to them collectively as "environmental design research," naming them individually when appropriate to differentiate them historically or functionally. Gary T. Moore, D. Paul Tuttle, and Sandra C. Howell, *Environmental Design Research Directions: Process and Prospects* (New York: Wiley, 1985), ix. A classic of the field is John Zeisel, *Inquiry by Design: Tools for Environment-Behavior Research* (Cambridge: Cambridge University Press, 1984). For a more recent review of knowledge circulating in environmental design research, see Keith Diaz Moore and Lyn Geboy, "The Question of Evidence: Current Worldviews in Environmental Design Research and Practice," *Architectural Research Quarterly* 14, no. 2 (2010): 105–14.

20. Sachs, "Architects, Users, and the Social Sciences in Postwar America," 71–73, 76.

21. Joy R. Knoblauch, "Going Soft: Architecture and the Human Sciences in Search of New Institutional Forms (1963–1974)" (PhD diss., Princeton University, 2012).

22. Moore, Tuttle, and Howell, *Environmental Design Research Directions*, xvi–xvii, 21. See also John Burgess, *Human Factors in Built Environments* (Newtonville, Mass.: Environmental Design and Research Center, 1981), 1.

23. Sachs, "Architects, Users, and the Social Sciences in Postwar America," 71.

24. Jon Lang, *Design for Human Behavior: Architecture and the Behavioral Sciences* (Strouds-burg, Pa.: Dowden, Hutchinson & Ross, 1974), 3. See also Edward Steinfeld, Steven Schroeder, James Duncan, Rolf Paste, Deborah Chollet, Marilyn Bishop, Peter Wirth, and Paul Cardell, *Access to the Built Environment: A Review of Literature* (Washington, D.C.: U.S. Department of Housing and Urban Development, Office of Policy Development and Research, 1979).

25. On epistemologies of ignorance in relation to design, see the introduction.

26. On "epistemic community" in relation to access-knowledge, see Hamraie, "Universal Design Research as a New Materialist Practice"; Imrie, "Universalism, Universal Design and Equitable Access to the Built Environment."

27. EDRA's precursor was the Design Methods Group at MIT. Henry Sanoff, "The Roots of EDRA," in *The Ethical Design of Places: Proceedings of the 40th Annual Environmental Design Research Association Conference* (Edmond, Okla.: Environmental Design Research Association, 2009) 9-12. See also Sachs, "Architects, Users, and the Social Sciences in Postwar America," 78; Knoblauch, "Going Soft."

28. Henry Sanoff and Sidney Cohn, *Proceedings of the 1st Annual Environmental Design Research Association Conference* (Stroudsburg, Pa.: Dowden, Hutchinson & Ross, 1970), 29.

29. Doggett, Mace, Marchant, Tolson, and Thompson, "Housing Environmental Research," 13–15.

30. Ibid., 20.

31. Moore, Tuttle, and Howell, *Environmental Design Research Directions*, xvi–xvii.

32. Moore and Geboy, "The Question of Evidence," 105.

33. Moore, Tuttle, and Howell, *Environmental Design Research Directions*, 45; Gary T. Moore, "Environment-Behavior Studies," in *Introduction to Architecture*, ed. J. C. Snyder and A. J. Catanese (New York: McGraw-Hill, 1979), 53–56.

34. Moore, "Environment-Behavior Studies"; Clovis Heimsath, *Behavioral Architecture: Toward an Accountable Design Process* (New York: McGraw-Hill, 1977).

35. Gary T. Moore and Reginald Gollege, *Environmental Knowing: Theories, Research, and Methods* (Stroudsburg, Pa.: Dowden, Hutchinson & Ross, 1976); Moore, "Environment-Behavior Studies," 53–56. On the history of architectural phenomenology, see Jorge Otero-Pailos, *Architecture's Historical Turn: Phenomenology and the Rise of the Postmodern* (Minneapolis: University of Minnesota Press, 2010). On function as "environmental competence," see Steinfeld et al., *Access to the Built Environment*, 138–39. See also Leon Pastalan, Robert K. Mautz II, and John Merrill, "The Simulation of Age-Related Sensory Loss," in *Environmental Design Research: Fourth International EDRA Conference*, vol. 1, *Selected Papers*, ed. Wolfgang Preiser (Stroudsburg, Pa.: Dowden, Hutchinson & Ross, 1973), 383–93.

36. Doggett, Mace, Marchant, Tolson, and Thompson, "Housing Environmental Research," 13–15.

37. See chapter 3. These dynamics are also explored in Knoblauch, "Going Soft," 64–103.

38. "The Interface between Behavior and the Milieu in the Total Institution" (panel presentation, Proceedings of EDRA3/AR8 conference, University of California at Los Angeles, January 1972), 2.

39. Charles H. Burnette, "Design Languages as Design Methods," in *Environmental Design Research: Fourth International EDRA Conference*, vol. 2, *Symposia and Workshops*, ed. Wolfgang Preiser (Stroudsburg, Pa.: Dowden, Hutchinson & Ross, 1973), 309.

40. Charles Burnette, Donald Lyndon, Kent Bloomer, Michael Benedict, Ray Lifchez, Thomas Hubka, Jay Farbstein, W. Mike Martin, Uriel Cohen, David Gaarder, Linda Johnson, Tim Ginty, and Gary Moore, "The Role of Environmental Psychology in Basic Design Education," Section 4: Teaching and Learning, in *EDRA7 Proceedings*, vol. 2 (Stroudsburg, Pa.: Dowden, Hutchinson & Ross, 1976), 166–72.

41. Gary T. Moore, *Designing Environments for Handicapped Children* (New York: Educational Facilities Laboratories, 1979).

42. As early as 1972, scholarship on "Discrimination by Design: Mobility Barriers" and "Environments for the Aged" had made their way into this epistemic community, albeit represented as "Special Group Needs." Carolyn Vash, "Discrimination by Design: Mobility Barriers" (panel presentation, Proceedings of EDRA3/AR8 conference, University of California at Los Angeles, January 1972), 1–5.

43. Ibid., 4.

44. See Henry Sanoff, *Community Participation Methods in Design and Planning* (New York: John Wiley and Sons, 2000). For a discussion of this method and its relation to standards of good design, see Sachs, "Architects, Users, and the Social Sciences in Postwar America," 78–79.

45. Edward Steinfeld, "Action Research in Man-Environment Relations," in *Environmental Design Research*, 2:396.

46. Elaine Ostroff, "Reflections after Having Begun to Loosen Up a Very Tight Bureaucratic System" (panel presentation, Proceedings of EDRA6 conference, Lawrence, Kans., January 1975), 1–2, Elaine Ostroff Universal Design Papers, Archives Center, National Museum of American History, Smithsonian Institution. Ostroff's many projects included repurposing a casino in Providence, Rhode Island, as the Looking Glass Theater, a participatory community theater project that enlisted design researchers in its construction. In 1968 Ostroff was awarded a Radcliffe fellowship for her work with the Research and Design Institute on interdisciplinary, research-driven design. Ronald Beckman, letter to Constance Smith, Radcliffe Institute for Independent Study, October 29, 1968, Elaine Ostroff Universal Design Papers.

47. Elaine Ostroff, "Understanding the Physical Environment in the Education of Children with Special Needs," unpublished manuscript, July 1972, 1–4, Elaine Ostroff Universal Design Papers, Archives Center, National Museum of American History, Smithsonian Institution. At this time, mentally disabled children were described as "mentally retarded," a label implying so-called degeneracy or atavism.

48. Elaine Ostroff, "Do-It-Yourself Kits for the Handicapped," pamphlet, 119–24, Elaine Ostroff Universal Design Papers, Archives Center, National Museum of American History, Smithsonian Institution; Elaine Ostroff, "Enriching the Learning Environment: Doing It Ourselves, with Recycled Materials," flier, Fernald State School, 1972, Elaine Ostroff Universal Design Papers; Elaine Ostroff, "Fact Sheet on the Fernald Associate Instructional Material Center," ca. 1972, Elaine Ostroff Universal Design Papers; Benjamin Taylor, "New Center Opens at Fernald," *Boston Evening*

Globe, November 16, 1972, 40; Lynda Morgenroth, "People with Special Needs Need Special Places," *Boston Globe,* July 17, 1983.

49. Ostroff, "Understanding the Physical Environment in the Education of Children with Special Needs," 1.

50. Ibid.

51. Later, Ostroff would coin the term "user-expert" to describe the focus of her work. Ostroff, "Mining Our Natural Resources," 33–35.

52. Elaine Ostroff, *Humanizing Environments: A Primer* (Cambridge, Mass.: Word Guild, on behalf of the Massachusetts Department of Mental Health, 1978).

53. EDRA later awarded Ostroff with two achievement awards, for both her accessibility work and her publication of the *Universal Design Handbook* with Wolfgang Preiser, another EDRA leader.

54. Lifchez, "Educator in Architectural Access," 74–75.

55. Lifchez and Winslow, *Design for Independent Living,* 20. See also Steinfeld et al., "Impact of Accessibility," in Steinfeld et al., *Access to the Built Environment,* 129–43.

56. Mayer Spivack, back cover blurb, in Lifchez and Winslow, *Design for Independent Living.*

57. Lifchez and Winslow, *Design for Independent Living,* 150.

58. Ibid., 20.

59. Ostroff, Limont, and Hunter, *Building a World Fit for People,* 15; Litt "Breaking Down Barriers," 3D.

60. Litt, "Breaking Down Barriers," 3D.

61. Ibid.

62. Ostroff, Limont, and Hunter, *Building a World Fit for People,* 15.

63. Mace, *An Illustrated Handbook of the Handicapped Section of the North Carolina State Building Code.* On the process of developing the standards, see Ronald Mace, "Architectural Accessibility in North Carolina—The Quest for Barrier-Free Design," *N.C. Insight,* October 1983, 40–47.

64. Theresa J. Rosenberg Raper, "Regulations and Communication in the Implementation of a Building Code for Accessibility to the Physically Handicapped," in *Research and Innovation in the Building Regulatory Process,* ed. Patrick Cooke (Washington, D.C.: National Bureau of Standards, 1977), 243.

65. On the process of developing and implementing the North Carolina accessibility code, see ibid., 241–51.

66. Ibid., 242.

67. Ibid.

68. Ibid., 244.

69. Ibid.

70. Barrier Free Environments, "Capsule History of the Firm," 1991, Ronald L. Mace Papers, MC 00260, Special Collections Research Center, North Carolina State University Libraries, Raleigh, N.C.; Barrier-Free Environments, pamphlet produced for the North Carolina Department of Insurance on state laws for persons with disabilities, ca. mid-1970s, Elaine Ostroff Universal Design Papers, Archives Center, National Museum of American History, Smithsonian Institution.

71. Barrier Free Environments, "Design for Disability," pamphlet, ca. 1989, Ronald L. Mace Papers, MC 00260, Special Collections Research Center, North Carolina State University Libraries, Raleigh, N.C.

72. Barrier Free Environments, "Mobile Homes: Alternate Housing for the Handicapped," pamphlet produced for the HUD Office of Policy Development and Research, 1976, Ronald L. Mace Papers, MC 00260, Special Collections Research Center, North Carolina State University Libraries, Raleigh, N.C.; Barrier Free Environments, *Group Homes: The Design of Accessible HUD 202 Small Group Homes* (Washington, D.C.: Department of Housing and Urban Development, 1990).

73. Elizabeth Geimer, "A Top Job for Lockhart Mace," *Fayetteville Observer,* September 19, 1977, I8; Rebecca Angell, "Her Goal: Helping the Handicapped Live as Others Do," *Winston-Salem Journal,* September 27, 1977, 8.

74. "Lockhart Follin-Mace, Advocate for Disabled," *Raleigh News & Observer,* November 28, 1991.

75. Barrier Free Environments, "Mobile Homes: 504 Technical Assistance," pamphlet, Elaine Ostroff Universal Design Papers, Archives Center, National Museum of American History, Smithsonian Institution.

76. National Commission on Architectural Barriers to Rehabilitation of the Handicapped, *Design for All Americans,* 9.

77. On the spatial contexts of scientific knowledge production, see David Livingstone, *Putting Science in Its Place: Geographies of Scientific Knowledge* (Chicago: University of Chicago Press, 2003). On the "spatial turn" in the history of science, and the humanities more generally, see Beat Kümin and Cornelie Usborne, "At Home and in the Workplace: A Historical Introduction to the 'Spatial Turn,'" *History and Theory* 52, no. 3 (2013): 305–18. On science as shared and coproduced knowledge, see Helen Longino, *Science as Social Knowledge: Values and Objectivity in Scientific Inquiry* (Princeton, N.J.: Princeton University Press, 1990).

78. American Institute of Architects, "Barrier-Free Architecture," 48.

79. Jeffers, "Barrier-Free Design," 46–47; Frank Laski, "Civil Rights Victories for the Handicapped, Part I," *Social and Rehabilitation Record* 1, no. 6 (1975): 25–32; Mary E. Osman, "Barrier-Free Architecture: Yesterday's Special Design Becomes Tomorrow's Standard," *AIA Journal* 63, no. 3 (1975): 40–44; Michelle Morgan, "Beyond Disability: A Broader Definition of Architectural Barriers," *AIA Journal* 65, no. 5 (1976): 50–53.

80. Jeffers, "Barrier-Free Design," 53–55.

81. Ibid., 62.

82. Ibid., 55, 60–62.

83. The legal literature on the Americans with Disabilities Act has made a similar argument that the narrow definition of disability (as a legally knowable object) limited the efficacy of the ADA's protections, particularly in the courts. See Ani Satz, "Disability, Vulnerability, and the Limits of Anti-Discrimination," *Washington Law Review* 83, no. 4 (2008): 513–68; Samuel Bagenstos, "The Future of Disability Law," *Yale Law Journal* 114, no. 1 (2004): 1–84.

84. Lifchez, *Rethinking Architecture,* 39.

85. U.S. Architectural and Transportation Barriers Compliance Board, *UFAS Retrofit Manual* (Raleigh, N.C.: Barrier Free Environments, 1991), 8.

86. The center was established as a nonprofit organization in 1974 and was to serve as a clearing house for information by eleven "major design, rehabilitation, and disability organizations." See National Center for a Barrier Free Environment, *Technical Assistance Network Newsletter* 9 (1981), Eric Dibner papers, BANC MSS 99/186 c, Bancroft Library, University of California, Berkeley; National Center for a Barrier Free Environment, *Opening Doors: A Handbook on Making*

Facilities Accessible to Handicapped People (Washington, D.C.: National Center for a Barrier Free Environment, 1978). Ruth Hall Lusher, a disabled architect and gerontologist whose work on compliance issues was groundbreaking and who worked closely with Mace, began working at the NCBFE in 1982. Elaine Ostroff, Mark Limont, and Daniel G. Hunter, "Ruth Lusher," in Elaine Ostroff, Mark Limont, and Daniel G. Hunter, *Building a World Fit for People: Designers with Disabilities at Work* (Boston: Adaptive Environments Center, 2002), 77–80.

87. Selwyn Goldsmith, "The Ideology of Designing for the Disabled" (panel presentation, Proceedings of EDRA14 conference, Lincoln, Neb., January 1983), 198–214.

88. Susan Hammerman and Barbara Duncan, eds., "Report of the United Nations Expert Group Meeting on Barrier-Free Design, June 3–8, 1974, United Nations Secretariat, New York," in *Access to the Environment,* vol. 3 (London: Forgotten Books, 2013), 396.

89. Ibid., 389–90.

90. Ibid., 390.

91. Ibid., 412.

92. Ibid.

93. Ibid., 419.

94. Ibid. On histories of the ISA, see Liat Ben-Moshe and Justin Powell, "Sign of Our Times: Revis(it)ing the International Symbol of Access," *Disability and Society* 22, no. 5 (2007): 489–505; Guffey, "The Scandinavian Roots of the International Symbol of Access," *Design and Culture* 7, no. 3 (2015): 357–76.

95. Ronald Mace, "Architectural Accessibility," in *White House Conference on Handicapped Individuals,* vol. 1, *Awareness Papers* (Washington, D.C.: Government Printing Office, 1977), 160–61.

96. Dean Phillips, "Opening Plenary Session," in *Proceedings of National Conference on Housing and the Handicapped,* ed. Eileen Lavine (Houston, Tex.: Goodwill Industries of America, 1974), 14.

97. Paraphrased in "Summary and Recommendations," in Lavine, *Proceedings of National Conference on Housing and the Handicapped,* 11. See also Edward Noakes, "What Is the Problem? Whose Problem Is It? How Widespread Is It?," in Lavine, *Proceedings of National Conference on Housing and the Handicapped,* 15–17.

98. "Summary and Recommendations," 11.

99. Ibid., 12.

100. Ibid., 11–12.

101. "Discussion Groups," in Lavine, *Proceedings of National Conference on Housing and the Handicapped,* 10.

102. Edward Steinfeld, "Developing Standards for Accessibility," in *Barrier-Free Environments,* ed. Michael Bednar (Stroudsburg, Pa.: Dowden, Hutchinson & Ross, 1977), 81.

103. Donna Shalala, "Foreword," in Edward Steinfeld, Steven Schroeder, and Marilyn Bishop, *Accessible Buildings for People with Walking and Reaching Limitations* (Washington, D.C.: U.S. Department of Housing and Urban Development, Office of Policy and Development Research, 1979), i.

104. Steinfeld, Schroeder, and Bishop, *Accessible Buildings.*

105. Edward Steinfeld, Jonathan White, and Danise R. Levine, *Inclusive Housing: A Pattern Book; Design for Diversity and Equality* (New York: W. W. Norton, 2010), 17–18.

106. John T. McConville, "Anthropometry in Sizing and Design," in *Anthropometric Source Book,* vol. 3 (Washington, D.C.: National Aeronautics and Space Administration, Scientific and Technical Information Office, 1978), 3.

107. Ibid., 5.

108. Steinfeld, Schroeder, and Bishop, *Accessible Buildings,* 9.

109. Steinfeld, Schroeder, and Bishop, *Accessible Buildings,* 23.

110. Steinfeld, White, and Levine, *Inclusive Housing,* 17–18.

111. Wilder, *A Laboratory Manual of Anthropometry,* 8–9.

112. Steinfeld et al., *Access to the Built Environment,* 3.

113. Ibid.

114. For instance, see its role in an overview of the practice and theory of evidence-based design in Moore and Geboy, "The Question of Evidence."

115. Steinfeld, "Developing Standards for Accessibility," 86.

116. Steinfeld wrote in 1977 that the lack of evidence-based standards was a "significant issue" determining the "validity of technical criteria" for accessibility. Steinfeld, "Developing Standards for Accessibility," 85.

117. Steinfeld et al., *Access to the Built Environment.*

118. Ibid., 140.

119. Ibid., 11.

120. Steinfeld, "Developing Standards for Accessibility," 85. See chapter 1 for a discussion of Freese's drawings.

121. Edmund Leonard, "The Handicapped Building," *Rehabilitation Literature* 39, no. 9 (1978): 266.

122. Ibid., 267.

123. Lynn Catanese, "Thomas Lamb, Marc Harrison, Richard Hollerith and the Origins of Universal Design," *Journal of Design History* 25, no. 2 (2012): 206–17.

124. Williamson, "Getting a Grip," 223.

125. James Mueller, *Designing for Functional Limitations* (Washington, D.C.: George Washington University Rehabilitation Research and Training Center, Job Development Laboratory, 1979); K. Mallik, S. Yuspeh, and J. Mueller, eds., *Comprehensive Vocational Rehabilitation for Severely Disabled Persons* (Washington, D.C.: George Washington University Medical Center, Job Development Laboratory, 1975).

126. James Mueller, "Design Criteria and Functional Aids," in Mallik, Yuspeh, and Mueller, *Comprehensive Vocational Rehabilitation for Severely Disabled Persons,* 117.

127. James Mueller, "Letters: Experience Proves Designers Can Aid the Handicapped," *Industrial Design* 24, no. 3 (1977): 1.

128. Ibid.

129. See, for example, Lifchez and Winslow, *Design for Independent Living,* 150; see also chapter 3.

130. Jeffers, "Barrier-Free Design," 44.

131. Ibid.

132. Lifchez and Winslow, *Design for Independent Living,* 150.

133. Bednar, *Barrier-Free Environments,* 3.

134. Gerben DeJong and Raymond Lifchez, "Physical Disability and Public Policy," *Scientific American* 248, no. 6 (1983): 40–49.

135. Nugent, "Founder," 156–57; Ostroff, Limont, and Hunter, *Building a World Fit for People,* 15.

136. Ostroff, Limont, and Hunter, *Building a World Fit for People,* 15. See also Nora Richter Greer, "The State of the Art of Design for Accessibility," *Architecture* 76, no. 1 (1987): 58.

137. Mace, "Architectural Accessibility," 147–64.

138. Steinfeld, "Developing Standards for Accessibility," 81–82. See also Edward Steinfeld, James Duncan, and Paul Cardell, "Toward a Responsive Environment: The Psychosocial Effects of Inaccessibility," in *Barrier-Free Environments,* ed. Michael Bednar (Stroudsburg, Pa.: Dowden, Hutchinson & Ross, 1977), 7–16.

139. Ronald Mace, quoted in Don Bedwell, "New Buildings Must Consider the Handicapped," *Charlotte Observer,* June 3, 1977, 7B.

140. Mace, "Architectural Accessibility," 153.

141. Ibid., 154.

142. Ibid., 156.

143. Ibid., 156.

144. Federal Highway Administration, *Designing Sidewalks and Trails for Access* (Washington, D.C.: U.S. Department of Transportation, 1999), 1–2.

145. Ronald Mace, letter to Hale Zukas, September 9, 1980, Eric Dibner Papers, BANC MSS 99/186 c, Bancroft Library, University of California, Berkeley.

146. Ibid.

147. Steinfeld was commissioned to study how people with multiple disabilities experience design. Researchers at the Georgia Institute of Technology gathered data about surface treatments and textures on curb cuts. Access American, information from the United States Architectural Barriers Compliance Board, Washington, D.C., Sept./Oct. 1982, 1–2, Eric Dibner Papers, BANC MSS 99/186 c, Bancroft Library, University of California, Berkeley.

148. United States Architectural and Transportation Barriers Compliance Board, *UFAS Retrofit Manual,* 9.

149. My narrative here draws from Mace, "Architectural Accessibility," 40–47.

150. Ibid., 40.

151. Mace, quoted in Yoshihiko Kawauchi, *Universal Design: A Reconsideration of Barrier-Free* (Boston: Institute for Human Centered Design, 2010), 6.

152. Barrier Free Environments, "Technical Proposal: Provide Section 504 Training and Technical Assistance to Handicapped Persons and Their Parents in the Northeastern United States," submitted to the Department of Education, December 30, 1980, Ronald L. Mace Papers, MC 00260, Special Collections Research Center, North Carolina State University Libraries, Raleigh, N.C.; Joseph Hafery, letter to Ronald Mace, March 28, 1991, Ronald L. Mace Papers. On the involvement of disabled people in the 504 training process, see O'Toole, *Faded Scars,* 68–73.

153. Mary Lou Breslin, "Cofounder and Director of the Disability Rights Education and Defense Fund, Movement Strategist," an oral history conducted in 1996–98 by Susan O'Hara (Oral History Center, Bancroft Library, University of California, Berkeley, 2000), 259–60, 304.

154. National Center for a Barrier Free Environment, "Cooperative Future in Barrier Free Design," November 6–7, 1980, Eric Dibner Papers, BANC MSS 99/186 c, Carton 1, Bancroft Library, University of California, Berkeley.

155. Ibid.

156. Ibid.

157. Conference Proceedings, "Designed Environments for All People," United Nations Headquarters, New York City, January 22–24, 192, Eric Dibner papers, BANC MSS 99/186 c, Carton 1, Bancroft Library, University of California, Berkeley.

158. *Pennhurst State School v. Halderman* (1981).

159. Elaine Ostroff and Daniel Iacofano, "Teaching Design for All People: The State of the Art," Design Faculty Seminar, Adaptive Environments Center, Boston, Mass., April 1–3, 1982, Elaine Ostroff Universal Design Papers, Archives Center, National Museum of American History, Smithsonian Institution.

160. Ibid., 11.

161. Ibid.

162. Ibid.

6. Barrier Work

1. Mace, "Universal Design," 147.

2. Thomas Gieryn, "Boundary Work and the Demarcation of Science from Non-Science: Strains and Interests in Professional Ideologies of Scientists," *American Sociological Review* 48, no. 6 (1983): 781–95.

3. Karen Barad, "Posthumanist Performativity: Toward an Understanding of How Matter Comes to Matter," *Signs: Journal of Women in Culture and Society* 28, no. 3 (2003): 815.

4. Mace and Perlman met at a benefit concert hosted by DREDF in 1984. Invitation to "An Evening with Itzhak Perlman," October 1, 1984, courtesy of Joy Weeber. Like Mace, Perlman was also disabled due to childhood polio, and used crutches and a wheelchair to navigate his environment. See Carol Vogel, "Adapting a House for Itzhak Perlman," *New York Times,* February 25, 1982, C8.

5. Based on his conversations with Charles Goldman, general counsel of the Access Board, in 1982, it appears that Pei understood that meaningful access required going beyond the codes. Meeting the minimal standards, however, was still difficult to navigate. See Charles Goldman, "Architectural Barriers: A Perspective in Progress," *Western New England Law Review* 5, no. 3 (1983): 465.

6. What Perlman or Pei meant by "accessible escalator" is unclear. Curiously, the Javits Center's building rules note, "All large and heavy equipment should be transported using the freight elevator. No equipment may be transported on escalators. This includes items such as easels, chairs, tables, wheelchairs, baby carriages, and other similar devices." Javits Center, "Building Rules," http://www.javitscenter.com/exhibit/building-rules/.

7. Mace's strategy is described in Elaine Ostroff, letter to John Cary, September 9, 2005, Elaine Ostroff Universal Design Papers, Archives Center, National Museum of American History, Smithsonian Institution.

8. Lifchez and Winslow, *Design for Independent Living,* 150.

9. Hayward, "'Good Design Is Largely a Matter of Common Sense,'" 222.

10. Doggett, Mace, Marchant, Tolson, and Thompson, "Housing Environmental Research," 183.

11. Mace, "Universal Design," 152.

12. During this period, Mace was married to Lockhart Follin-Mace, a disabled woman and wheelchair user who was involved in antiracist, feminist, and disability activism. Steven Litt, "Breaking Down Barriers," 3D. Although neither discussed it, Follin-Mace's influence on the article and on Mace's broader work (at least until her death in 1991) is more than likely.

13. Mace, "Universal Design," 152.

14. Ibid., 148.

15. Ibid.

16. Ibid.

17. Ibid., 147.

18. Ellen Samuels, *Fantasies of Identification: Disability, Gender, and Race* (New York: New York University Press, 2014), 9.

19. Ronald Mace, "Universal Design," 148, 150.

20. Ibid., 148–49.

21. Ibid., 150.

22. Ibid., 151, emphasis added.

23. Ibid., 148.

24. Ibid., 150.

25. Bednar, *Barrier-Free Environments,* 3.

26. Ruth Lusher and Ronald Mace, "Design for Physical and Mental Disabilities," in *Encyclopedia of Architecture: Design Engineering and Construction,* ed. Joseph A. Wilkes and Robert T. Packard (New York: John Wiley and Sons, 1989), 755.

27. Lynn Nesmith, "Designing for 'Special Populations,'" *Architecture* 76, no. 1 (1987): 62; James J. Pirkl, "Transgenerational Design: An Instructional Project to Prepare Designers," *Innovation: The Journal of the Industrial Designers Society of America* (Summer 1987): 4–5.

28. Mitchell and Snyder, *Cultural Locations of Disability,* 10.

29. Pullin, *Design Meets Disability,* 93

30. Kafer, *Feminist, Queer, Crip,* 4.

31. Mace, "Universal Design," 147.

32. "Visitability: Becoming a National Trend?," *Ragged Edge Online,* January/February 2003, http://www.raggededgemagazine.com/0103/visitability.html; "Concrete Change: An Advocate for Visitability," *Universal Design Newsletter* 5, no. 3 (2000): 9–10.

33. Eleanor Smith, "Advocate for Accessible Housing," oral history conducted by Laura Hershey in 2008 (Oral History Center, Bancroft Library, University of California, Berkeley, 2011), 88–89.

34. Katherine Ott, "Ruth Lusher," in *Encyclopedia of American Disability History,* ed. Susan Burch (New York: Facts on File, 2009), 581; Department of Housing and Urban Development, *Universal Design: Housing for the Lifespan of All People* (Washington, D.C.: U.S. Department of Housing and Urban Development, 1988), reprinted in 2000 with updates by the Center for Universal Design (citations are to the 2000 reprint); Ostroff, Limont, and Hunter, "Ruth Lusher." Mace and Lusher also coauthored housing standards together a year before the publication of Mace's "Universal Design." See Ronald Mace and Ruth Hall Phillips, *ECHO Housing: Recommended Construction and Installation Standards* (Washington, D.C.: American Association of Retired Persons, 1984); Ruth Lusher, letter to Ron Mace, June 5, 1987, courtesy of Joy Weeber.

35. Breslin, "Cofounder and Director of the Disability Rights Education and Defense Fund," 237.

36. Ibid., 236–37.

37. Barrier Free Environments, *Accessible Housing: A Manual on North Carolina's Building Code Requirements for Accessible Housing* (Raleigh: North Carolina Department of Insurance, 1980).

38. Williamson, "Getting a Grip," 221.

39. Center for Universal Design, *Universal Design,* 6.

40. Ronald Mace, Tub Seat Design, 1982, Ronald L. Mace Papers, MC 00260, Special Collections Research Center, North Carolina State University Libraries, Raleigh, N.C.

41. The Honeywell "Easy-to-See" model is a product of these redesigns.

42. Center for Universal Design, "CUD Show and Tell," ca. July 1994, courtesy of Joy Weeber.

43. Center for Accessible Housing, "Center for Accessible Housing Thermostat Project," 1993, from the private collection of Joy Weeber; Center for Accessible Housing, "CAH Management Meeting Minutes," 1995, from the private collection of Joy Weeber.

44. The historical details I present here are arranged from my archival research from Mace's personal files in Joy Weeber's private collection, as well as from communications with many of the people I mention here. The CAH's collaborators included James Mueller, Elaine Ostroff, John Salmen, Bettye Rose Connell, Mike Jones, Jon Sanford, Leslie Young, and Richard Duncan. See also James Mueller, "Toward Universal Design: An Ongoing Project on the Ergonomics of Disability," *American Rehabilitation* 16, no. 2 (1990); Center for Affordable Housing, "CAH Meeting Minutes," 1995, from the private collection of Joy Weeber; Lucy Harber, letter to Catherine Shaw of the American Institute of Architects Professional Development Department, 1991, Ronald L. Mace Papers, MC 00260, Special Collections Research Center, North Carolina State University Libraries, Raleigh, N.C.

45. James Leahy, "Supply Push Program: Transferring New, Useful, and Innovative Products to the Marketplace through a Supply Push Approach," *Tech Transfer RERC* 6, no. 2 (2004): 11–12.

46. Arthur Jampolsky, letter to Ronald Mace, January 20, 1994, from the private collection of Joy Weeber.

47. Ibid.

48. Although unbuilt in his lifetime, the Universal Thermostat marks Mace's experiments with more conspicuously showing access features, a strategy that would later manifest in "Principles 2.0."

49. Mace, "Universal Design," 152.

50. Michael Cala, "House Retrofits That Make It Easier for the Handicapped," *Home Mechanix*, March 1985, 90, 86.

51. Elizabeth Schmidt Ringwald, "On the Eve of Universal Design," *Home* 34, no. 10 (1988): 104.

52. Patricia Leigh Brown, "Designs Take Heed of Human Frailty," *New York Times*, April 14, 1988, C1; Patricia Leigh Brown, "For the Aging and Disabled, Products They Can Use," *New York Times*, April 21, 1988, C1.

53. Yoshihiko Kawauchi, "Universal Design and Legal Advocacy for People with Disabilities in Japan," an oral history conducted by Mary Lou Breslin in 2002 and published in *Architectural Accessibility and Disability Rights in Berkeley and Japan* (Berkeley: Oral History Office, Bancroft Library, University of California, 2004), 23–24. The results were published in Kawauchi, *Universal Design*, the book that came out of this research.

54. Smith, "Advocate for Accessible Housing," 86; Kawauchi, "Universal Design and Legal Advocacy for People with Disabilities in Japan," 25.

55. Harding, *Whose Science? Whose Knowledge?*, 10. Social movement scholars studying the disability movement have often focused on the movement's relationship to policy. See Jerry Alan Winter, "The Development of the Disability Rights Movement as a Social Problem Solver," *Disability Studies Quarterly* 23, no. 1 (2003): 33–61.

56. Janet Reno, "Enforcing the ADA," Tenth Anniversary Status Report from the Department of Justice, Washington, D.C., 2000, http://www.ada.gov/pubs/10thrpt.htm.

57. Ed Pell, "Universal Design: One in Eight Americans Is over 65," *Kitchen and Bath Business*, September 1990, 40–41; Norman Remich, "Universal Design," *Appliance Manufacturer*, July 1992, 50–52.

58. AIA Colorado Field Report, "Caudill, Mace, and Church Selected as Barrier Free Design Awards Program Jurors," 1990, Ronald L. Mace Papers, MC 00260, Special Collections Research Center, North Carolina State University Libraries, Raleigh, N.C.

59. "1990 Colorado Universal Design Awards Program," Ronald L. Mace Papers, MC 00260, Special Collections Research Center, North Carolina State University Libraries, Raleigh, N.C.

60. D. W. Calmenson, "Accessible for All: Universal Design by Ron Mace," *Interiors and Sources* 8, no. 17 (1991): 28–31.

61. Mace, "Architectural Accessibility," 154.

62. See Chad Nilep, "'Code Switching' in Sociocultural Linguistics," *Colorado Research in Linguistics* 19, no. 1 (2006): 1–22.

63. Center for Accessible Housing, "Definitions: Accessible, Adaptable and Universal Design," fact sheet, North Carolina State University, Raleigh, 1991, from the private collection of Joy Weeber; Edie Lee Cohen, "Student Work: A Portfolio of Universal Design," *Interior Design* 63, no. 11 (1992): 98–101.

64. Ronald Mace, "Universal Design Leadership Initiatives Report," September 12–13, 1990, 7, Ronald L. Mace Papers, MC 00260, Special Collections Research Center, North Carolina State University Libraries, Raleigh, N.C.

65. Ibid., 4.

66. The CAH and Adaptive Environments Center continued developing resources for code compliance. Center for Accessible Housing, "Definitions"; Adaptive Environments Center, *Readily Achievable Checklist: A Survey for Accessibility*, ADA Access Facts Series (Boston: Adaptive Environments Center, 1991); Adaptive Environments Center, *Achieving Physical and Communication Accessibility*, ADA Access Facts Series (Boston: Adaptive Environments Center, 1995).

67. Ronald L. Mace, Graeme J. Hardie, and Jaine P. Place, "Accessible Environments: Toward Universal Design," in *Design Intervention: Toward a More Humane Architecture*, ed. Wolfgang F. E. Preiser (New York: Van Nostrand Reinhold, 1991), 155–76.

68. Story, Mueller, and Mace, *The Universal Design File*, 126.

69. Mace, "Universal Design Leadership Initiatives Report," 4.

70. Ibid., 8. See also Mace, "Architectural Accessibility," 55.

71. Barrier Free Environments, *UFAS Retrofit Manual* (Washington, D.C.: United States Architectural and Transportation Barriers Compliance Board, April 1991), 8; Lucy Harbor, letter to Catherine Shaw, 1991, Ronald L. Mace Papers, MC 00260, Special Collections Research Center, North Carolina State University Libraries, Raleigh, N.C.

72. U.S. Architectural and Transportation Barriers Compliance Board, *UFAS Retrofit Manual*, 8.

73. Ibid., 8.

74. Ibid., 3–4.

75. Ibid., 4.

76. Ibid., 27, 39, 136, 189, 2–3. Human factors and ergonomics data, no doubt through Steinfeld's influence, also appeared throughout.

77. J. S. Sandhu, "An Integrated Approach to Universal Design: Toward the Inclusion of All Ages, Cultures, and Diversity," in *Universal Design Handbook*, ed. Wolfgang F. E. Preiser and Elaine

Ostroff (New York: McGraw-Hill, 2001), 3.3–3.14; Jim Sandhu, "The Rhinoceros Syndrome: A Contrarian View of Universal Design," in *Universal Design Handbook*, 2nd ed., ed. Wolfgang F. E. Preiser and Korydon H. Smith (New York: McGraw-Hill, 2011), 44.3–44.12; European Institute for Design and Disability, "Stockholm Declaration," 2004, http://dfaeurope.eu/wp-content/uploads/2014/05/stockholm-declaration_english.pdf.

78. There was a long history of international barrier-free design, beginning with a 1961 conference in Stockholm. Goldsmith wrote Mace in 1993, as he was assembling his own history of the accessibility movements in Britain and the United States. He asked Mace what he thought of the idea that accessibility should be "for everyone" and how he should frame the history of this idea in his book. Goldsmith indicates that he also consulted with Tim Nugent, Edward Leonard, and Hugh Gallagher. Selwyn Goldsmith, letter to Ronald Mace, November 2, 1993, from the private collection of Joy Weeber. See also "Remove Architectural Barriers," ca. 1960, reprinted from the *Electrical Workers' Journal*, Official Publication of the International Brotherhood of Electrical Workers (AFL-CIO), 1–5, Elaine Ostroff Universal Design Papers, Archives Center, National Museum of American History, Smithsonian Institution; Kawauchi, "Universal Design and Legal Advocacy for People with Disabilities in Japan," 23–24. Kim Kullman studies Kawauchi's engagements with global accessibility ideas in "Universalizing and Particularizing Design with Professor Kawauchi," in *Mobilizing Design*, ed. Justin Spinney, Suzanne Reimer, and Philip Pinch (London: Routledge, forthcoming).

79. Selwyn Goldsmith, *Designing for the Disabled: The New Paradigm* (New York: Routledge Architectural Press, 1963); Kawauchi, *Universal Design.*

80. Steven Bodow, "Universal Design Conference in New York," *Architecture* 81, no. 7 (1992): 85; "Universal Design: Access to Daily Living," May 13–14, 1992, conference program, Ronald Mace Collection, National Museum of American History, Smithsonian Institution.

81. Barrier Free Environments, "Strategic Plan," 1991, Ronald L. Mace Papers, MC 00260, North Carolina State University Libraries, Raleigh, N.C.

82. Ronald Mace, Elaine Ostroff, James Mueller, John Salmen, Susan Goltsman, Cynthia Leibrock, and James DiLuigi, "The Differences between Accessibility and Universal Design," *Universal Design Newsletter* 1, no. 7 (1994): 2, 6; "Designs for the 21st Century," *Universal Design Newsletter* 2, no. 8 (1996): 1, 4.

83. "One Step Forward, No Steps Back," *Universal Design Newsletter* 2, no. 5 (1996): 1, 5; "Reach Out and Touch," *Universal Design Newsletter* 2, no. 5 (1996): 5; "New Products," *Universal Design Newsletter* 2, no. 5 (1996): 9.

84. "Accessing the Past," *Universal Design Newsletter* 1, no. 7 (1994): 1, 10; "Recreation Guidelines," *Universal Design Newsletter* 1, no. 7 (1994): 1, 4.

85. "ASAP Discusses Accessible Telecommunications," *Universal Design Newsletter* 2, no. 1 (1995): 7; "Design Tips," *Universal Design Newsletter* 2, no. 8 (1996): 8.

86. Bobrick Washroom Equipment, "Barrier-Free Washroom Guide," 1993, 10–11, Ronald L. Mace Papers, MC 00260, Special Collections Research Center, North Carolina State University Libraries, Raleigh, N.C.

87. Ashley Mog, "Threads of Commonality in Transgender and Disability Studies," *Disability Studies Quarterly* 28, no. 4 (2008), http://dsq-sds.org/article/view/152/152.

88. "Family Restrooms Make Mall Shopping Easier for Everyone," *Universal Design Newsletter* 2, no. 2 (1993): 5. Mace later explained such restrooms in terms of Universal Design. See Laura Herbst, "Nobody's Perfect," *Popular Science*, January 1997, 64–66.

89. "Unisex Toilets under Review," *Universal Design Newsletter* 2, no. 1 (1995): 5.

90. For a history and evaluation of UD education, see Polly Welch and Stanton Jones, "Advances in Universal Design Education," in *Universal Design Handbook,* ed. Wolfgang F. E. Preiser and Elaine Ostroff (New York: McGraw-Hill, 2001), 51.3–51.24.

91. "Educators Collaborate on Universal Design," *Universal Design Newsletter* 1, no. 2 (1993): 7.

92. Polly Welch, "What Is Universal Design?," in *Strategies for Teaching Universal Design,* ed. Polly Welch (Boston: Adaptive Environments Center and MIG Communications, 1995), 1–4.

93. Polly Welch and Stanton Jones, "Universal Design: An Opportunity for Critical Discourse in Design Education," in *Universal Design: 17 Ways of Thinking and Teaching,* ed. Jon Christopherson (Oslo: Husbanken, 2002), 205.

94. Charlotte Roberts and Brian Powell, "University of Southwestern Louisiana," in *Strategies for Teaching Universal Design,* ed. Polly Welch (Boston: Adaptive Environments Center and MIG Communications, 1995), 181. See also Welch and Jones, "Universal Design," 193; Brad C. Grant, Paul M. Wolff, and Michael Shannon, "California Polytechnic State University," in *Strategies for Teaching Universal Design,* ed. Polly Welch (Boston: Adaptive Environments Center and MIG Communications, 1995), 3.

95. "Educators Collaborate on Universal Design," *Universal Design Newsletter* 1, no. 2 (1993): 7; Welch and Jones, "Universal Design," 196.

96. Mark Chidister, Albert Rutledge, Arvid Osterberg, Robert Harvey, Fred Malven and Harlen Groe, "Iowa State University," in *Strategies for Teaching Universal Design,* ed. Polly Welch (Boston: Adaptive Environments Center and MIG Communications, 1995), 15.

97. Ibid., 13, 24.

98. John Salmen, "The Differences between Accessibility and Universal Design," *Universal Design Newsletter* 1, no. 7 (1994): 2.

99. Brent Porter, "Pratt Institute," in *Strategies for Teaching Universal Design,* ed. Polly Welch (Boston: Adaptive Environments Center and MIG Communications, 1995), 99.

100. Salmen, "The Differences between Accessibility and Universal Design," 2.

101. Welch and Jones, "Universal Design," 195–96; Ostroff, "Mining Our Natural Resources," 33–35. See also Lifchez, "Educator in Architectural Access," 89–90.

102. Michael Shannon, "California Polytechnic State University," in *Strategies for Teaching Universal Design,* ed. Polly Welch (Boston: Adaptive Environments Center and MIG Communications, 1995), 9.

103. Welch and Jones, "Universal Design," 212.

104. Edward Steinfeld, Jason Hagin, Gary Day, Theordore Lowne, Todd Marsh, Ole Mouritsen, and Abir Mullick, "SUNY Buffalo," in *Strategies for Teaching Universal Design,* ed. Polly Welch (Boston: Adaptive Environments Center and MIG Communications, 1995), 119.

105. Abir Mullick, "SUNY Buffalo," in *Strategies for Teaching Universal Design,* ed. Polly Welch (Boston: Adaptive Environments Center and MIG Communications, 1995), 133.

106. Edward Steinfeld, "SUNY Buffalo," in *Strategies for Teaching Universal Design,* ed. Polly Welch (Boston: Adaptive Environments Center and MIG Communications, 1995), 131.

107. Brad C. Grant, Paul M. Wolff, and Michael Shannon, "California Polytechnic State University," in *Strategies for Teaching Universal Design,* ed. Polly Welch (Boston: Adaptive Environments Center and MIG Communications, 1995), 4.

108. As disability theorist Tobin Siebers puts it, disability simulations reinforce an association of disability with pity or lack and work against an intersectional understanding of disability

because "the practice of peeling off minority identities from people to determine their place in the hierarchy of oppression is revealed to degrade all minority identities by giving a one-dimensional view of them. It also fails to understand the ways in which different identities constitute one another." Tobin Siebers, *Disability Theory* (Ann Arbor: University of Michigan Press, 2008), 28–29. See also Valerie Brew-Parish, "The Wrong Message," *Ragged Edge,* March/April 1997, http://www.raggededgemagazine.com/archive/aware.htm; Priya Lavlani and Alicia Broderick, "Institutionalized Ableism and the Misguided 'Disability Awareness Day': Transformative Pedagogies for Teacher Education," *Equity and Excellence in Education* 46, no. 4 (2013): 468–83; Michelle Nario-Redmond, Dobromir Gospodinov, and Angela Cobb, "Crip for a Day: The Unintended Negative Consequences of Disability Simulations," *Rehabilitation Psychology,* March 2017, 1–10.

109. Mace, "Universal Design Leadership Initiatives Report," 8–9.

110. Bernie Dahl, "Purdue University," in *Strategies for Teaching Universal Design,* ed. Polly Welch (Boston: Adaptive Environments Center and MIG Communications, 1995, 109.

111. Ostroff evaluated this approach favorably, comparing it to a simulation approach by saying that it encouraged interaction and empathy. Elaine Ostroff, letter to Brent Porter, May 5, 1994, Elaine Ostroff Universal Design Papers, Archives Center, National Museum of American History, Smithsonian Institution.

112. John Salmen, "Valuing People with Disabilities," *Universal Design Newsletter* 2, no. 7 (1996): 2.

113. Edward Steinfeld, Jason Hagin, Gary Day, Theodore Lownie, Todd Marsh, Ole Mouritsen, and Abir Mullick, "Studio Education through Universal Design," Department of Architecture, SUNY at Buffalo, Universal Design Education Project Report, May 17, 1994, 2, Elaine Ostroff Universal Design Papers, Archives Center, National Museum of American History, Smithsonian Institution.

114. Ibid.

115. "UDEP Update," *Universal Design Newsletter* 2, no. 1 (1995): 8.

116. "Designing the Future: Toward Universal Design," *Universal Design Newsletter* 1, no. 7 (1994): 6.

117. Brad Grant, quoted in transcript of symposium, "Designing the Future: Toward Universal Design," World Trade Center, Boston, November 17, 1994, 45, Elaine Ostroff Universal Design Papers, Archives Center, National Museum of American History, Smithsonian Institution.

118. John Salmen, quoted in transcript of symposium, "Designing the Future," 50.

119. Ronald Mace, quoted in transcript of symposium, "Designing the Future," 61.

120. Ibid., 62–63.

121. Ibid., 63.

122. The title of this section refers to Michelle Murphy, "The Girl: Mergers of Feminism and Finance in Neoliberal Times," *Scholar and Feminist Online* 11.1–11.2 (Fall 2012/Spring 2013), http://sfonline.barnard.edu/gender-justice-and-neoliberal-transformations/the-girl-mergers-of-feminism-and-finance-in-neoliberal-times/. Neoliberalism describes late capitalist ideologies, which rely upon the niche markets to address social problems, often by enfolding (rather than normalizing) difference.

123. My use of the terms "marketing" and "branding" here is quite literal. For a more conceptual exploration of disability as a product of "branding" (that is, as a construction of conceptual and material signification), see Elizabeth Depoy and Stephen Gilson, *Branding and Designing Disability: Reconceptualising Disability Studies* (London: Routledge, 2014). Depoy and Gilson use the

term "branding" much as I use "material-epistemic," that is, not simply as a semiotic practice but also as a corporeal and material one. Whereas Depoy and Gilson's projects of redesigning and rebranding disability focus on seamlessness and elegance as features of integrative design outcomes (242–51), my focus here is on parsing the histories and politics of disability marketing particularly in terms of the meaning these practices produce for Universal Design.

124. Pell, "Universal Design," 40.

125. Linda Broderson, "User-Friendly Design: The New Horizon," *Arthritis Today,* May–June 1989, 16–21.

126. Pell, "Universal Design," 41. See also Roberta Null and K. F. Cherry, *Universal Design: Creative Solutions for ADA Compliance* (Belmont, Calif.: Professional Publications, 1996); Steven Winter and Associates, *Accessible Housing by Design: Universal Design Principles in Practice* (New York: McGraw-Hill, 1997); Wilkoff, *Practicing Universal Design.*

127. Access Expo, press release, ca. 1991, Ronald L. Mace Papers, MC 00260, Special Collections Research Center, North Carolina State University Libraries, Raleigh, N.C.; Access Expo, "Access Expo Advisory Board Announced," press release, January 30, 1991, Ronald L. Mace Papers.

128. Access Expo, pamphlet, ca. 1991, 1, Ronald L. Mace Papers, MC 00260, Special Collections Research Center, North Carolina State University Libraries, Raleigh, N.C.

129. Ibid., 4.

130. DREDF, "Mainstreet—The 'Readily Achievable Project,'" documentary guide, 1991–92, 1–2, Ronald L. Mace Papers, MC 00260, Special Collections Research Center, North Carolina State University Libraries, Raleigh, N.C.

131. See Williamson, "Getting a Grip."

132. Remich, "Universal Design," 50.

133. Historians of neoliberalism locate the rise of the neoliberal state in the late 1970s. See David Harvey, *A Brief History of Neoliberalism* (Oxford: Oxford University Press, 2005), 9.

134. Center for Public Communication, *Whirlpool Home Life Issues Report: The American Home as Service Environment* (New York: Center for Public Communication, 1991), Ronald L. Mace Papers, MC 00260, Special Collections Research Center, North Carolina State University Libraries, Raleigh, N.C. The report cited issues such as household demographic diversity, affordability, and functionality as posing challenges and creating opportunities for more functional homes.

135. Ronald Mace, "Comments on Whirlpool Home Life Issues Report," April 8, 1991, Ronald L. Mace Papers, MC 00260, Special Collections Research Center, North Carolina State University Libraries, Raleigh, N.C.

136. On "human capital," see Murphy, "The Girl."

137. Mervyn Kaufman, "Universal Design in Focus," *Metropolis* magazine, November 1992, 39–53; "Access: Special Universal Design Report," *Metropolis* magazine, November 1992: 39–67; Calmenson, "Accessible for All"; Cohen, "Student Work."

138. Joyce Krisko, "Universal Design: Accessible to Everyone," *St. Louis Park Sun Sailor,* July 7, 1993; Jo Werne, "A Barrier-Free Design for Living," *Chicago Tribune,* May 12, 1992; Patricia Dane Rogers, "Getting a Handle on Good Design: Catalogues; New York's Museum of Modern Art Assembles a Collection of Tools that Make Life Easier for People with Disabilities," *Washington Post,* November 8, 1992.

139. Kate Rorbach, letter to Ronald Mace, February 12, 1991, Ronald L. Mace Papers, MC 00260, Special Collections Research Center, North Carolina State University Libraries, Raleigh,

N.C.; Center for Public Communication, *Whirlpool Home Life Issues Report;* Whirlpool, *The Less Challenging Home* (Benton Harbor, Mich.: Whirlpool Corp., ca. 1992); Jane Lehman, "Universal Design for Easier Living," *Washington Post,* December 30, 1995, E1; Cynthia Ingols and James Mueller, *Leviton Manufacturing Company, Inc.: Universal Design Marketing Strategy* (Boston: Design Management Institute Press, 1997).

140. James Mueller, "'Real' Consumers Just Aren't Normal," *Journal of Consumer Marketing* 7, no. 1 (1990): 51–53; James Mueller, "Toward Universal Design: An Ongoing Project on the Ergonomics of Disability," *American Rehabilitation* 16, no. 2 (1990): 15–33.

141. Mueller, "Toward Universal Design," 15–16.

142. Ibid., 17–18.

143. Mueller, "'Real' Consumers," 51; Mueller, "Toward Universal Design," 16.

144. James Mueller, "If You Can't Use It, It's Just Art: The Case for Universal Design," *Ageing International* 22, no. 1 (1995): 19–23.

145. Ingols and Mueller, *Leviton Manufacturing Company, Inc.,* 9.

146. The reasons for this transition are described in chapter 7.

147. Ibid., 4.

148. Ibid., 13.

149. Ibid., 11.

150. My framing of post-disability ideologies builds on critical race theory's challenges to "post racial" ideologies, which insist that racism is no longer a significant system of oppression because civil rights laws have ended material manifestations such as segregation. In the aftermath of the civil rights era, as Michelle Alexander has shown, race-neutral policies merely hide racial inequality within new institutions of mass incarceration. See Alexander, *The New Jim Crow.* For an earlier version of this argument, see Hamraie, "Universal Design and the Problem of 'Post-Disability' Ideology."

7. Entangled Principles

1. Denise Levine, *Universal Design New York* (Buffalo, N.Y.: Center for Inclusive Design and Environmental Access, 2013), 8.

2. Ibid. These ideas reflect arguments that Mace himself began to make in the late 1990s.

3. Josh Safdie, quoted in Szenasy, "Accessibility Watch."

4. Ibid.

5. Kafer, *Feminist, Queer, Crip,* 83.

6. John Salmen, "Defining the Universe," *Universal Design Newsletter* 4, no. 3 (1999): 2.

7. Center for Universal Design, "The Principles of Universal Design," Version 2.0.

8. These proliferations were, for the most part, post-1997 phenomena. On Universal Design in education, see Frank G. Bowe, *Universal Design in Education* (Westport, Conn.: Bergin and Gavey, 2000). In feminist theory and philosophy, see Ackerly, *Universal Human Rights in a World of Difference;* Laura Davy, "Philosophical Inclusive Design: Intellectual Disability and the Limits of Individual Autonomy in Moral and Political Theory," *Hypatia* 30, no. 1 (2015): 132. In queer theory, see Monika Myers and Jason Crockett, "Manifesto for Queer Universal Design," *SQS: Journal of Queer Studies in Finland* 6, nos. 1–2 (2012): 58–64. In disability studies, references to Universal Design and its underlying theories are frequent, particularly in reference to the social model of disability. See Susan Wendell, *The Rejected Body: Feminist Philosophical Reflections on Disability* (New York: Routledge, 1996), 55; Lennard Davis, *Bending over Backwards: Disability,*

Dismodernism, and Other Difficult Positions (New York: New York University Press, 2002), 31; Anita Silvers, "Formal Justice," in *Disability, Difference, and Discrimination,* ed. Anita Silvers, David Wasserman, and Mary Mahowald (Oxford: Rowman and Littlefield, 1998), 129; Michael Davidson, "Universal Design: The Work of Disability in an Age of Globalization," in *The Disability Studies Reader,* 2nd ed., ed. Lennard J. Davis (New York: Routledge, 2006), 117–18.

9. Barad, *Meeting the Universe Halfway,* 817.

10. Ibid., 30.

11. My narrative draws on several accounts of the process of writing the "Principles." Molly F. Story, one of the authors, offers a few accounts of the process. Molly F. Story, "Is It Universal? Seven Defining Criteria," *Innovation* (Spring 1997): 29–32; Molly Follette Story, "Maximizing Usability: The Principles of Universal Design," *Assistive Technology: The Official Journal of RESNA* 10, no. 1 (1998): 4–12; Story, Mueller, and Mace, *The Universal Design File,* 32–33; Molly F. Story, "Principles of Universal Design," in *Universal Design Handbook,* 2nd ed., ed. Wolfgang F. E. Preiser and Korydon H. Smith (New York: McGraw-Hill, 2011), 4.3; Molly F. Story, "Principles of Universal Design," in *Universal Design Handbook,* ed. Wolfgang F. E. Preiser and Elaine Ostroff (New York: McGraw-Hill, 2001), 10.4. I cross-referenced these accounts with interviews and correspondence with several of the authors. James Mueller, interview with author, October 10, 2011, Atlanta, Ga.; Abir Mullick, interview with author, October 21, 2011, Atlanta, Ga.; Edward Steinfeld, interview with author, October 4, 2011, Buffalo, N.Y.; Jon Sanford, interview with author, June 5, 2011, Atlanta, Ga.; Elaine Ostroff, interview with author, August 11, 2016, Westport, Conn.; Mike Jones, e-mail to author, September 14, 2011. I also cross-referenced these events to the extent available with print documents from the collections of Mace's work in his private home (from the personal collection of Joy Weeber), in collections of Mace's materials at the National Museum of American History (from the personal collection of Katherine Ott), and at the Special Collections of North Carolina State University. All characterizations of these events that are not my own appear in quotation marks.

12. For a detailed history of these cases, see Adam A. Milani, "'Oh Say Can I See—And Who Do I Sue if I Can't?': Wheelchair Users, Sightlines over Standing Spectators, and Architect Liability under the Americans with Disabilities Act," *Florida Law Review* 3 (2000): 523–99.

13. Sanjoy Mazumdar and Gilbert Geis, "Architects, the Law, and Accessibility: Architects' Approaches to the ADA in Arenas," *Journal of Architectural and Planning Research* 20, no. 3 (2003): 203.

14. Ibid.

15. Ibid., 205.

16. Department of Justice, "Memorandum of *Amicus Curiae* United States in Support of Plaintiffs' Application for a Preliminary Injunction and in Opposition to Defendants' Motion to Dismiss," United States District of Columbia Court, Civil Action No. 96-1354, 1996; Milani, "'Oh, Say, Can I See,'" 589. See also Elizabeth Savage, "Lobbyist for the Epilepsy Foundation: The Passage of the Americans with Disabilities Act," oral history conducted by Ann Lage in 2004 (Oral History Center, Bancroft Library, University of California, Berkeley, 2010).

17. Mazumdar and Geis, "Architects, the Law, and Accessibility," 206–7.

18. Center for Universal Design, "Introduction to Universal Design," *Universal Design Exemplars,* https://design.ncsu.edu/openjournal/index.php/redlab/article/view/127/72.

19. NIDRR is part of rehabilitation research funding that emerged after World War II to support civilians. Civilian rehabilitation research has been supported primarily through the Office of

Vocational Rehabilitation (OVR), established in 1954 under the Department of Health, Education, and Welfare. The OVR began funding research centers called Rehabilitation Research Training Centers (RRTC) in 1962 and Rehabilitation Engineering Research Centers (RERC) in 1972. Following the restructuring of federal agencies in 1979, the RRTC and RERC programs came to be funded by a new program, the NIDRR, under the Department of Education's Office of Special Education and Rehabilitation Services. In 2015 NIDRR was renamed the National Institute on Disability, Independent Living, and Rehabilitation Research (NIDILRR) and moved to the Department of Health and Human Services.

20. Edward Steinfeld, interview with author, October 4, 2011, Buffalo, N.Y.; Greg Vanderheiden, letter to Katherine Seelman, April 28, 1998; Trace Research & Development Center, "Some Notes on Universal Design," 1998. Prior to working at NIDRR, Seelman had worked with Mace, Ostroff, and others in the late 1980s and early 1990s to expand accessible housing practices to account for D/deaf and hard-of-hearing people. Katherine Seelman, letter to Ron Mace and Graeme Hardie, July 29, 1991; Katherine Seelman, "Final Report: Housing Accessibility for Deaf and Hard of Hearing People," unpublished report submitted to the Center for Accessible Housing, July 29, 1991. All documents cited in this note are from the personal collection of Joy Weeber unless otherwise noted.

21. Center for Affordable Housing. "CAH Meeting Minutes," 1995, from the personal collection of Joy Weeber; Center for Universal Design, "Draft copy of Mission Statement," from the personal collection of Joy Weeber.

22. Story, "Maximizing Usability," 7.

23. Many others were involved with the CUD during this time. Jan Reagan, a historian, archivist, and librarian, disseminated information and developed pamphlets for the organization.

24. The Trace Center moved to the University of Maryland in August 2016.

25. Story, "Principles of Universal Design," 10.5.

26. I use the qualifier "apparently" here to indicate that I am describing the optics of this group, not necessarily their private identifications.

27. Story, "Maximizing Usability," 7.

28. Story, "Principles of Universal Design," 10.5; Story, Mueller, and Mace, *The Universal Design File*, 32.

29. Ingols and Mueller, *Leviton Manufacturing Company, Inc.*, 9.

30. Story, "Principles of Universal Design," 10.5.

31. Ibid., 10.5–10.6.

32. Ibid.

33. Story, "Maximizing Usability," 7.

34. Center for Universal Design, "The Principles of Universal Design," Version 1.1 (12/7/95), from the personal collection of Joy Weeber.

35. John Salmen, "Evaluating Universal Design," *Universal Design Newsletter* 2, no. 5 (1996): 2.

36. Ibid.

37. Peter Orleans, "Comments on 'Principles of Universal Design,'" fax correspondence with Ronald Mace, March 28, 1996, from the personal collection of Joy Weeber.

38. Story, "Maximizing Usability," 10.

39. Story, "Principles of Universal Design," 10.6.

40. Dreyfuss, *The Measure of Man*, 4.

41. See chapter 6.

42. Americans with Disabilities Act (ADA), 42 U.S. Code § 12101(a)(7).

43. See Center for Universal Design, "The Principles of Universal Design," Figure I.5.

44. Simi Linton, *Claiming Disability: Knowledge and Identity* (New York: New York University Press, 1998), 14.

45. Siebers, *Disability Theory*, 8.

46. Story, "Maximizing Usability," 10.

47. David Harvey, *The Condition of Postmodernity: An Enquiry Into the Origins of Cultural Change* (Cambridge, Mass.: Blackwell, 1990), 145–47.

48. David Harvey, "The Right to the City," *New Left Review* 53 (September–October 2008): 31–32.

49. To benefit from the law, individual disabled people were to bring lawsuits on a case-by-case basis, but the law did not address systemic and institutional factors in inaccessibility, such as norms of the architecture profession or social inequality. See Satz, "Disability, Vulnerability, and the Limits of Anti-Discrimination"; Bagenstos, "The Future of Disability Law"; Andrew I. Batavia, "Ten Years Later: The ADA and the Future of Disability Policy," in *Americans with Disabilities,* ed. Leslie Francis and Anita Silvers (New York: Routledge, 2000), 283–92.

50. Story, "Maximizing Usability," 12.

51. Ibid., 8.

52. World Institute on Disability, "Universal Access Project Description," 1995, World Institute on Disability Records, BANC MSS 99/148 z, Bancroft Library, University of California, Berkeley. WID was a Berkeley-based organization founded by activists Ed Roberts, Judy Heumann, and Joan Leon in the early 1980s.

53. Greg Vanderheiden, "Curbcuts and Computers: Providing Access to Computers and Information Systems for Disabled Individuals" (keynote speech, "Computers for the Disabled," Trace Research & Development Center on Communication, Control, and Computer Access for Handicapped Individuals, Madison, Wisc., September 12, 1983), http://files.eric.ed.gov/fulltext/ED289314.pdf.

54. Steve Jacobs, "Section 255 of the Telecommunications Act of 1996: Fueling the Creation of New Electronic Curbcuts," Center for an Accessible Society, 1999, http://www.accessiblesociety.org/topics/technology/eleccurbcut.htm.

55. World Institute on Disability, "Universal Access Project Description."

56. Trace Research & Development Center, "Executive Summary: Revised Project Plan for Rehabilitation Engineering Research Center on Access to Computers and Information Systems," December 9, 1994, 44, World Institute on Disability Records, BANC MSS 99/148 z, Bancroft Library, University of California, Berkeley.

57. Universal Access Project Forum, "Principles of Universal Design Working Draft 9/7/95," World Institute on Disability Records, BANC MSS 99/148 z, Bancroft Library, University of California, Berkeley; Greg Vanderheiden and Maureen Kaine-Krolack, "Draft Access to the NII and Emerging Information Technologies by People With Disabilities, version 1.0," December 15, 1995, Universal Access Project Reports, World Institute on Disability Records.

58. Universal Access Project, "Draft for NTIA Advisory Meeting," January 1995, World Institute on Disability Records, BANC MSS 99/148 z, Bancroft Library, University of California, Berkeley.

59. Universal Access Project Forum, "Principles of Universal Design Working Draft 9/7/95"; Universal Access Project Advisory Committee, "Some Basic Principles of Universal Design,"

June 6, 1995, World Institute on Disability Records, BANC MSS 99/148 z, Bancroft Library, University of California, Berkeley.

60. Center for Universal Design, "The Principles of Universal Design," Version 2.0.

61. Mueller, interview with author, October 10, 2011.

62. Donald Norman, *The Design of Everyday Things* (1988; repr., New York: Basic Books, 2002), 188–89.

63. Ibid., 2–4.

64. Story, "Maximizing Usability," 6.

65. In this sense, Mace was adopting "flexibility" as resistance to or co-option of existing spaces, similar to strategies that Henri Lefebvre describes in *The Production of Space* (Oxford: Wiley-Blackwell, 1992), 388.

66. Norman, *The Design of Everyday Things*, 199.

67. I do not necessarily attribute these strategies and interventions to authorial intent. While I find patterns in the authors' strategies over time, it is possible that they were unaware of these patterns. Nevertheless, my close reading reveals these patterns as possible modes of knowing-making, with strategic outcomes for accessibility advocacy.

68. See chapter 1.

69. See chapters 1, 2, and 3.

70. Rob Imrie, "Universalism, Universal Design and Equitable Access to the Built Environment," 876.

71. Edward Steinfeld, *Hands-On Architecture*, vol. 3, part 1, *Executive Summary* (Buffalo: Department of Architecture, State University of New York, 1986), 20.

72. Edward Steinfeld, Victor Paquet, Clive D'Souza, Caroline Joseph, and Jordana Maisel, *Final Report: Anthropometry of Wheeled Mobility Project*, Report of the Center for Inclusive Design and Environmental Access for the U.S. Access Board (Buffalo, N.Y.: Center for Inclusive Design and Environmental Access, 2010). On the history of these refashioned practices, see Hamraie, "Universal Design Research as a New Materialist Practice." More recently, Steinfeld and his colleague Jordana Maisel have also proposed new Universal Design guidelines. Edward Steinfeld and Jordana Maisel, *Universal Design: Creating Inclusive Environments* (Hoboken, N.J.: John Wiley & Sons, 2012), 88.

73. Edward Steinfeld, Clive D'Souza, and Jonathan White, "Developing Evidence-Based Standards: A Case Study in Knowledge Translation," in *Universal Design 2014: Three Days of Creativity and Diversity* (Washington, D.C.: IOS Press, 2014), 89–98.

74. Steinfeld and Maisel, *Universal Design*, 97.

75. On Universal Design as a science, see Jordana Maisel, ed., *The State of the Science in Universal Design Research: Emerging Research and Developments* (Sharjah, UAE: Bentham Science, 2010).

76. On fat oppression, see Lori Don Levan, "Fat Bodies in Space: Controlling Fatness through Anthropometric Measurement, Corporeal Conformity, and Visual Representation," *Fat Studies* 3, no. 2 (2014): 119–29; Erin Pritchard, "Body Size and the Built Environment: Creating an Inclusive Built Environment Using Universal Design," *Geography Compass* 8, no. 1 (2014): 63–73. On design and size considerations related to dwarfism, see Amanda Cachia, "The Alterpodium: A Performative Design and Disability Intervention," *Design and Culture* 8, no. 3 (2016): 1–15. Deaf-Space architecture has sought to create spatial envelopes that support sign language communication and D/deaf culture. See Hansel Bauman, "DeafSpace: An Architecture toward a More Livable

and Sustainable World," in *Deaf Gain: Raising the Stakes for Human Diversity,* ed. H-Dirksen L. Bauman and Joseph J. Murray (Minneapolis: University of Minnesota Press, 2014), 377.

77. Ronald Mace, "Determinations of Exemplary Universal Designs," February 6, 1996, from the personal collection of Joy Weeber.

78. Japanese aging experts and designers began connecting with Universal Design experts in the United States in the early 1990s and offered useful critiques. See Ishi Masaaki Shiraishi, "Population Aging and Universal Design: An International Look," *Universal Design Newsletter* 2, no. 6 (1996): 2. The *Universal Design Newsletter* inaugurated an ongoing "World Update" column, written by Ostroff, in 1999. See Elaine Ostroff, "World Update," *Universal Design Newsletter* 4, no. 3 (1999): 7.

79. Story, "Principles of Universal Design," 10.8; Story, "Maximizing Usability," 6.

80. Edward Steinfeld and Beth Tauke, "Universal Designing," in *Universal Design: 17 Ways of Thinking and Teaching,* ed. Jon Christophersen (Oslo: Husbanken, 2002), 165.

81. Ibid., 167.

82. John Salmen, "U.S. Accessibility Codes and Standards: Challenges for Universal Design," in *Universal Design Handbook,* 2nd ed., ed. Wolfgang F. E. Preiser and Korydon H. Smith (New York: McGraw-Hill, 2011), 6.1.

83. Donald Norman, "Opening Remarks," Designing for the 21st Century conference, Hofstra University, New York, June 18, 1998, 8, Elaine Ostroff Universal Design Papers, Archives Center, National Museum of American History, Smithsonian Institution.

84. Ibid., 13.

85. In recognition of the large community of disabled users and experts in attendance, the conference provided print materials in multiple formats and required attendees to avoid the use of scented products in order to create access for people with chemical sensitivities. Designing for the 21st Century conference program, Hofstra University, New York, June 17–21, 1998, Ronald Mace Collection, National Museum of American History, Smithsonian Institution; Roberta Null, *Universal Design: Principles and Models* (Boca Raton: CRC Press, 2014), vii.

86. Null, *Universal Design,* vii; Jim Davis, "Design for the 21st Century Starts Now," *Ragged Edge Online,* November/December 1998, http://www.raggededgemagazine.com/1198/a1198ft1.htm; "Universal Design Conference, Part I," *Universal Design Newsletter* 3, no. 8 (1998): 4–5.

87. Elaine Ostroff, "Awards Ceremony," Designing for the 21st Century conference, Hofstra University, New York, June 19, 1998, 9–10, Elaine Ostroff Universal Design Papers, Archives Center, National Museum of American History, Smithsonian Institution.

88. Molly Story and James Mueller, "Measuring Usability: The Principles of Universal Design," in *Designing for the 21st Century: An International Conference on Universal Design of Information, Products, and Environments,* ed. J. Reagan and L. Trachtman (Raleigh, N.C.: Center for Universal Design, 1998), 126–29.

89. Edward Steinfeld, "Universal Design as Innovation," In *Designing for the 21st Century: An International Conference on Universal Design of Information, Products, and Environments,* ed. J. Reagan and L. Trachtman (Raleigh, N.C.: Center for Universal Design, 1998), 121.

90. Ruth Lusher, "Awards Ceremony," Designing for the 21st Century conference, Hofstra University, New York, June 19, 1998, 10–11, Elaine Ostroff Universal Design Papers, Archives Center, National Museum of American History, Smithsonian Institution.

91. Davis, "Design for the 21st Century Starts Now."

92. Simi Linton and Rosemarie Garland-Thomson, "Disability Studies: Theoretical Underpinnings of Universal Design," in *Designing for the 21st Century: An International Conference on*

Universal Design of Information, Products, and Environments, ed. J. Reagan and L. Trachtman (Raleigh, N.C.: Center for Universal Design, 1998), 50–51.

93. This book is an obvious exception. Other work addressing (or calling for further research on) the epistemological foundations of Universal Design includes Imrie, "Universalism, Universal Design and Equitable Access to the Built Environment." On retrofit as a critical disability concept, see Dolmage, "Mapping Composition."

94. Quotations in this paragraph are from Ronald Mace, "A Perspective on Universal Design," Designing for the 21st Century conference, Hofstra University, New York, June 19, 1998, Ronald Mace Collection, National Museum of American History, Smithsonian Institution.

95. Wolfgang Saxon, "Ronald L. Mace, 58, Designer of Buildings Accessible to All," *New York Times,* July 13, 1998.

96. John Salmen, "Saying Goodbye to Ron Mace," *Universal Design Newsletter* 3, no. 8 (1998): 2.

97. Institute for Human Centered Design, "Access to Design Professions," 1999, http://humancentereddesign.org/projects/access-to-design-professions. One outcome of this project was Ostroff, Limont, and Hunter, *Building a World Fit for People.*

98. Bruce Hannah and George Covington, "Unlimited By Design," exhibition brochure, Ronald Mace Collection, National Museum of American History, Smithsonian Institution; "Smithsonian Features Universal Design," *Universal Design Newsletter* 4, no. 1 (1999): 1, 10.

Conclusion

1. Ed Roberts Campus, https://www.edrobertscampus.org/design/.

2. William Leddy, quoted in Leddy Maytum Stacy, "Ed Roberts Campus—Building Community," YouTube, August 16, 2011, https://www.youtube.com/watch?v=7THtXFm_954.

3. Angela Hill, "Long-Awaited Ed Roberts Campus Opens in Berkeley," *Mercury News,* April 9, 2011.

4. Bay Area Rapid Transit, "A History of BART: The Concept Is Born," http://www.bart.gov/about/history.

5. Elaine-Maryse Solari, "The Making of an Archaeological Site and the Unmaking of a Community in West Oakland, California," in *Archaeology of Urban Landscapes: Explorations in Slumland,* ed. Alan Mayne and Tim Murray (Cambridge: Cambridge University Press, 2001), 22–38; John Landis and Robert Cervero, "Middle Age Sprawl: BART and Urban Development," *Access* 14 (Spring 1999): 2–15; Andrew Stelzer, "Will the Berkeley Flea Market Survive a Changing Neighborhood?," *KQED News,* March 17, 2016.

6. These trends of population emplacement and displacement are captured by the Anti-Eviction Mapping Project. See, for example, "Loss of Black Population, Bay Area, 1970–2010," http://www.antievictionmap.com/demographic-maps#/blackbay/; "Latin@ Population Change by Zip Code, Bay Area, 2011–2014," http://antievictionmappingproject.net/latina.html.

7. Tenants Together and the Anti-Eviction Mapping Project, "The Speculator Loophole: Ellis Act Evictions in San Francisco," April 2, 2014, http://antievictionmappingproject.net/speculatorloophole.html; Joe Fitzgerald Rodriguez, "Controversial Tech Shuttles on Road to Becoming Part of the City's Transit Ecosystem," *San Francisco Examiner,* September 30, 2016.

8. "$750K Grant May Bring Big Changes to South Berkeley," *Berkeleyside,* August 19, 2014; Emily Dugdale, "Friends of Adeline: 'Our Future Shall Be Determined by Us,'" *Berkeleyside,* April 5, 2015; Emilie Raguso, "Berkeley Neighbors Say Affordability Will Be Key to Proposed Adeline Street Project," *Berkeleyside,* July 24, 2015; Natalie Orenstein, "Neighbors Outline Demands for

Adeline Corridor Grant," *Berkeleyside,* May 11, 2015; "Berkeley: Apartments, Restaurant Slated for Former Funeral Home," *Mercury News,* May 3, 2016. On foreclosures and developments in this area, see Anti-Eviction Mapping Project, "Oakland, Development and Foreclosures," https:// ampitup.carto.com/viz/d009f934-03d6-11e5-9ba3-0e9d821ea90d/embed_map. Although the area containing data points ends just a few blocks from the Ashby station, it shows very clearly the rates of development and foreclosure along the Adeline Street corridor.

9. Joaquin Palomino, "How Many People Live on Our Streets?," *San Francisco Chronicle,* June 28, 2016. According to the U.S. Census Bureau, the Bay Area's population increased by over 90,000 between 2014 and 2015. Kimberly Veklerov, "Bay Area's Population Grows by More than 90,000 in a Year," *San Francisco Gate,* March 25, 2016. A 2012 study of occupants in single-room occupancy (SRO) hotels found that 75 percent were over fifty-five years of age and 62 percent were disabled. While housing conditions in SROs were poor, these housing units were also among the first to be replaced with condominiums and other developments, resulting in evictions. Sari Bilick, Joyce Lam, Jessica Lehman, and Josh Vining, "Seniors and Adults with Disabilities in SROs: Survey and Recommendations," report to San Francisco Board of Supervisors, June 2012, http://www.sfhsa .org/asset/ReportsDataResources/SeniorsAdultsDisabilitiesSROsJune2012.pdf.

10. "Breaking: Black Lives Matter Protesters Shut Down BART at West Oakland Station," *Daily Kos,* November 28, 2014, http://www.dailykos.com/story/2014/11/28/1348086/-Breaking -Black-Lives-Matter-Protesters-Shut-Down-BART-at-West-Oakland-Station.

11. David Perry and Lawrence Carter-Long, "Media Coverage of Law Enforcement Use of Force and Disability," Ruderman Foundation White Paper, March 2016, http://www.ruderman foundation.org/news-and-events/ruderman-white-paper.

12. "Many Boomers in Denial over Problems They Face Growing Old in Suburbs," *Miami Herald,* July 11, 2016.

13. Bay Area Rapid Transit, "Why New Cars," 2014, http://www.bart.gov/about/projects/ cars/why-new-cars.

14. Nate Berg, "How San Francisco Is Designing Its Metro Train of the Future," *CityLab,* September 16, 2014, http://www.citylab.com/commute/2014/09/how-san-francisco-is-designing-its -metro-train-of-the-future/380181/.

15. Ibid. See also John Wildermuth, "A Look inside BART's Ride of the Future," *San Francisco Gate,* April 17, 2014.

16. Berg, "How San Francisco Is Designing Its Metro Train of the Future."

17. Bay Area Rapid Transit, "BART, Disability Advocates Agree on Fleet of the Future Floor Plan," press release, February 27, 2015, http://www.masstransitmag.com/press_release/12049565/ bart-disability-advocates-agree-on-fleet-of-the-future-floor-plan; Erin Sherbert, "BART Passengers with Disabilities to Protest New BART Trains," *SF Weekly,* April 15, 2014. As activist and power chair user Corbett O'Toole put it, "my chair is only 24 inches wide and it takes up most of the space between the door and the center pole on the new Bart trains. My wheelchair is also about 36" long so you can see the problem of trying to get on or off the BART car." Corbett O'Toole, personal communication, July 31, 2014; see also Wildermuth, "A Look inside BART's Ride of the Future."

18. BART, "BART Board Votes to Change Fleet of Future Floor Plan," February 26, 2015, http://www.bart.gov/news/articles/2015/news20150226-0.

19. BART, "BART Board Votes to Change Fleet of Future Floor Plan."

20. Disability Organizing Network, "Disability Organizing Network Celebrates Victory over Barriers to Access on the BART's Fleet of the Future, Applauds Efforts of Advocates," press release, February 27, 2015, https://disabilityorganizing.net/news-topics/?id=586.

21. Wildermuth, "A Look inside BART's Ride of the Future."

22. Kafer, *Feminist, Queer, Crip,* 3.

23. Alice Wong, interview of Patty Berne, *Disability Visibility Project,* December 14, 2015, https://disabilityvisibilityproject.com/2015/12/14/dvp-interview-patty-berne-and-alice-wong/; Nomy Lamm, "This Is Disability Justice," *The Body Is Not An Apology,* https://thebodyisnotan apology.com/magazine/this-is-disability-justice; Mia Mingus, "Changing the Framework: Disability Justice," *Leaving Evidence* (blog), February 12, 2011, https://leavingevidence.wordpress. com/2011/02/12/changing-the-framework-disability-justice.

24. Patty Berne, "Disability Justice: A Working Draft," *Sins Invalid* (blog), June 10, 2015, http://sinsinvalid.org/blog/disability-justice-a-working-draft-by-patty-berne.

25. Silicon Valley Independent Living Center, "SVILC's Position Statement against Simulation Exercises," http://www.svilc.org/PDFs/SVILC%20Simulation%20Statement%20TXT.txt.

Index

Abel, Cora Beth, 172, 173
accessibility audits, 119–20
accessible products, 164, 211, 212, 213, 221
Accessibility Task Force, 259
access-knowledge: and activism, 115, 116, 119, 120; and anthropometry, 246; and the curb cut, 99; definitions of, 5, 6, 13, 30, 259, 260; and design, 34, 70, 173, 176, 204, 230; dissemination of, 198, 204, 207, 210, 253; history of, 9, 10, 12, 14–16, 33, 102, 131, 132, 134, 150, 155, 156, 172, 226; as an interdisciplinary field, 74, 80, 133, 185; and "Principles of Universal Design," 227–28, 231, 233, 234, 248–50; rehabilitative, 92, 93, 110, 111, 154; in relation to the user, 38, 42, 66, 113; and Ronald Mace, 181, 185. *See also* Mace, Ronald
accommodation, 13, 173, 195, 199, 242
ADA Accessibility Guidelines (ADAAG), 202, 205, 212
Adams, Andrew, 157
Adaptive Environments Center, 173, 206, 210
added value, 10, 75, 97, 214, 237, 242, 257
Adeline Street, 256, 257
aging, 11, 42, 66, 75–76, 90, 165, 172, 184, 257–58; and women, 77, 78, 80
Ahmed, Sara, 103
Alexander, Michelle, 65, 68, 82
"all," 65, 66, 69, 91, 92; and barrier-free design, 10, 97, 99, 151, 153, 164–65, 171; and disability, 74, 77, 127, 168, 169; and race, 68, 70, 72, 87, 93, 188, 257; and Universal Design, 173, 181, 182, 187, 240

American Association for Retired Persons (AARP), 187
American Institute of Architects (AIA), 91, 131, 133, 134, 137, 150, 151, 153, 156, 199, 229
American Sign Language (ASL), 12
Americans with Disabilities Act (ADA), 1, 6, 228–29, 238; post-ADA, 3, 5–8, 11, 220, 227, 230, 240; and Universal Design, 187, 198–99, 200–202, 205, 206, 211, 212, 214, 251–53, 257
Anderson, Tanisha, 257
ANSI A117.1, 12, 120, 143, 154, 157, 170, 247; 1961, 73–77, 86, 91, 110; 1980, 140, 158, 160, 168, 169, 171, 200
anthropometry, 21, 23, 44, 48, 50, 55, 73; and epistemic activism, 246, 247, 248; repurposing of anthropometric methods, 73, 109, 158, 160, 233
anticipatory access, 10, 201, 230
architect, 19, 85, 137, 202
Architectural and Transportation Compliance Board (Access Board), 150, 153, 154, 169, 170, 202, 203, 205
Architectural Barriers Act, 86, 91, 92, 143, 153, 256
Architectural Graphic Standards (Ramsey and Sleeper), 26–33, 38, 143, 188
architecture, 80, 132, 133; architectural history, 20–30, 33, 38, 43, 44, 136; architectural inhabitant, 21, 26, 27, 30, 38, 133, 136, 241; architectural standards, 15, 21, 26–27, 38, 120 (*see also* codes and standards); discourse of, 132, 137; universal, 26

325

A I M I   H A M R A I E is assistant professor of medicine, health, and society and American studies at Vanderbilt University.